Sociolinguistics and Social Theory

LANGUAGE IN SOCIAL LIFE SERIES

Series Editor: Professor Christopher N Candlin
Chair Professor of Applied Linguistics
Department of English
Centre for English Language Education & Communication Research
City University of Hong Kong, Hong Kong

For a complete list of books in this series see pages *v* and *vi*

Sociolinguistics and Social Theory

Edited by Nikolas Coupland
Srikant Sarangi
and
Christopher N. Candlin

An imprint of **Pearson Education**

Harlow, England · London · New York · Reading, Massachusetts · San Francisco
Toronto · Don Mills, Ontario · Sydney · Tokyo · Singapore · Hong Kong · Seoul
Taipei · Cape Town · Madrid · Mexico City · Amsterdam · Munich · Paris · Milan

Pearson Education Limited
Edinburgh Gate
Harlow
Essex CM20 2JE
England

and Associated Companies throughout the world

Visit us on the World Wide Web at:
www.pearsoneduc.com

First published 2001

ISBN 0-582-32783-0 PPR

British Library Cataloguing-in-Publication Data

A catalogue record for this book is available from the British Library

Library of Congress Cataloging-in-Publication Data

Sociolinguistics and social theory / edited by Nikolas Coupland, Srikant Sarangi, and Christopher N. Candlin.
    p. cm. — (Language in social life series)
    Papers presented at the 2nd Cardiff Roundtable in Language and Communication, held June 1997, Cardiff University.
    Includes bibliographical references and index.
    ISBN 0–582–32783–0 (pbk.)
    1. Sociolinguistics—Congresses.   2. Social sciences—Philosophy—Congresses.   I. Coupland, Nikolas, 1950–   II. Sarangi, Srikant, 1956–   III. Candlin, Christopher.   IV. Cardiff Roundtable in Language and Communication (2nd : 1997 : Cardiff University)   V. Series.
    P40.S579   2001
    306.44—dc21   00–067387

Set in 10/12pt Janson by 35

Printed in Malaysia, VVP

LANGUAGE IN SOCIAL LIFE SERIES

Series Editor: Professor Christopher N. Candlin
Chair Professor of Applied Linguistics
Department of English
Centre for English Language Education & Communication Research
City University of Hong Kong, Hong Kong

Small Talk
Justine Coupland (ed.)

Typography and Language in Everyday Life
Susan Walker

Sociolinguistics and Social Theory
Nikolas Coupland, Srikant Sarangi and Christopher N. Candlin (eds)

Contents

List of contributors

CHRISTOPHER N. CANDLIN is Chair Professor of Applied Linguistics at The City University of Hong Kong and Director of the Centre for English Language Education & Communication Research. He holds Honorary Professorships at Cardiff University, Lancaster University, Macquarie University, and the University of Technology, Sydney. His main research interests relevant to this volume are in discourse analysis and pragmatics, and their application to the analysis of workplace and professional-client communication, in the fields of law, dispute resolution, medicine and healthcare, and in disciplinary variation in academic discourse. Recent publications include: (with Ken Hyland) *Writing: Texts, Processes and Practices* (Longman, 1999), and (with Neil Mercer) *English Language Teaching in its Social Context* (Routledge). He edits and co-edits several major book series for international publishers: Pearson, Routledge and Continuum International.

NIKOLAS COUPLAND is Professor and Director of the Centre for Language and Communication Research at Cardiff University (Wales, UK). He is founding co-editor, with Professor Allan Bell, of the *Journal of Sociolinguistics* (Blackwell Publishers). His books include *Dialect in Use: Sociolinguistics Variation in Cardiff English* (University of Wales Press, 1988); *Language, Society and the Elderly* (Blackwell Publishers, 1991, with Justine Coupland and Howard Giles; *Sociolinguistics: A Reader and Coursebook* (Macmillan 1997, with Adam Jaworski); and *The Discourse Reader* (Routledge, 1991, also with Adam Jaworski).

DEREK EDWARDS is Professor of Psychology at Loughborough University. His main interests are in the analysis of discourse and conversation, and especially in discursive psychology, in which relations between psychological states and the external world are studied as common sense discourse categories and practices. He is author or co-author of various books including *Common Knowledge*, with Neil Mercer (Routledge, 1987), *Ideological Dilemmas*, with Michael Billig and others (Sage, 1988), *Discursive Psychology*, with Jonathan Potter (Sage, 1992), and *Discourse and Cognition* (Sage, 1997).

FREDERICK ERICKSON is George F. Kneller Professor of Anthropology of Education at the University of California, Los Angeles, where he also is a participant in that university's interdisciplinary Center for Language, Interaction, and Culture. A specialist in the use of video analysis in interactional sociolinguistics and microethnography, his work has focused especially on timing and rhythm in the social coordination of interaction, relationships of mutual influence between listening and speaking in interaction, and the signalling of multiple social identities in talk. His publications include (with Jeffrey J. Shultz) *The Counselor as Gatekeeper: Social Interaction in Interviews* (Academic Press, 1982). He has also written extensively on qualitative research methods in education.

MONICA HELLER is a Professor in the Department of Sociology and Equity Studies and the Centre de Recherche en Éducation Franco-Ontarienne, Ontario Institute for Studies in Education, University of Toronto, Canada. Her research focuses on political, economic and social dimensions of multilingualism, with a focus on francophone Canada. Her most recent book is *Linguistic Minorities and Modernity: a Sociolinguistic Ethnography* (Longman, 1999).

ADAM JAWORSKI is Senior Lecturer at the Centre for Language and Communication Research at Cardiff University. His book publications include *The Power of Silence* (Sage, 1993); *Silence: Interdisciplinary Perspectives* (Mouton de Gruyter, 1997); *Sociolinguistics: A Reader and Coursebook* (Macmillan, 1997), and *The Discourse Reader* (Routledge, 1999) (the last two with Nikolas Coupland).

PER LINELL is Professor of Communication Studies within the interdisciplinary graduate school at Linköping University, Sweden, since 1981. He has published widely within the field of discourse studies, particularly on professional–lay interaction. Another major interest of his is the history of the written language bias within the language sciences. His most recent book is *Approaching Dialogue: Talk, Interaction and Contexts in Dialogical Perspectives* (John Benjamins, 1998).

MIRIAM MEYERHOFF is Lecturer in Linguistics at the University of Edinburgh. She works on social and linguistic aspects of language variation and language change. Her particular interests are language and gender, and syntactic change and grammaticisation in creoles.

LESLEY MILROY currently holds the Hans Kurath Collegiate Chair of Linguistics at the University of Michigan and has taught at universities in Ireland, England and New Zealand. Her research interests include a range of topics in sociolinguistics, mainly variationist theory, bilingualism, conversation analysis and language ideology. Currently she is directing a research project on language diversity and language change in the city of Detroit. Among her publications are *Language and Social Networks, Observing and Analysing Natural Language, Linguistics and Aphasia* (with Ruth Lesser), *Authority in Language* (with James Milroy) *One Speaker, Two Languages* (edited with Pieter Muysken), *Real English* (edited with James Milroy).

JONATHAN POTTER is Professor of Discourse Analysis at Loughborough University. He has studied a range of social science topics and written widely on social philosophy, social psychological theory and qualitative methods. His most recent book (*Representing Reality*, Sage, 1996) attempted to provide a systematic overview, integration and critique of constructionist research.

BEN RAMPTON is a Reader in the School of Education at King's College London. His research concerns cover urban multilingualism, language education and interactional discourse. He is the author of *Crossing: Language and Ethnicity among Adolescents* (Longman, 1995) and a co-author of *Researching Language: Issues of Power and Method* (Routledge, 1992).

CELIA ROBERTS is a Senior Research Fellow in the School of Education at King's College London. Her publications in the fields of urban discourse, second language socialisation and intercultural communication include: *Language and Discrimination* (Longman 1992 with Davies and Jupp), *Achieving Understanding* (Longman 1996 with Bremer et al.), *Talk, Work and Institutional Order* (Mouton 1999 with Sarangi) and *Language Learners as Ethnographers* (Multilingual Matters 2000 with Byram et al.).

SRIKANT SARANGI is Reader in Language and Communication and Director of the Health Communication Research Centre at Cardiff University. His recent publications include *Language, Bureaucracy and Social Control* (1996, with S. Slembrouck), *Talk, Work and Institutional Order: Discourse in Medical, Mediation and Management Settings* (1999, with C. Roberts) and *Discourse and Social Life* (2000, with M. Coulthard). He is currently editor (with J. Wilson) of *TEXT: An Interdisciplinary Journal for the Study of Discourse*, and series editor (with C.N. Candlin) of *Advances in Applied Linguistics*, and *Communication in Public Life*.

RICHARD J. WATTS is Professor of English Linguistics at the University of Berne, Switzerland. One of his areas of research is the discourse of language issues in Switzerland. He is the editor of the international journal *Multilingua: Journal of Cross-Cultural and Interlanguage Communication*. Among his publications are *Power in Family Discourse, Politeness in Language: Studies in its History, Theory and Practice* (edited with Sachiko Ide and Konrad Ehlich) and *Standard English: The Widening Debate* (edited with Tony Bex). He is the co-editor of two book series, *Cross-Cultural Communication* for Peter Lang (with Ernest Hess-Lüttich) and *Language, Power and Social Process* for Mouton de Gruyter (with Monica Heller).

JOHN WILSON is Professor of Communication and Dean of Social and Health Sciences and Education at the University of Ulster, Jordanstown. His main areas of interest are sociolinguistics (including present research on the acquisition of dialect), discourse analysis, and pragmatics. He has published various papers on these subjects including major works such as *On the Boundaries of Conversation* (Pergamon, 1989) and *Politically Speaking* (Blackwell, 1990). Most recently he has been carrying out work on narrative constructions of European identity.

Editors' Preface and Acknowledgements

Sociolinguistics and Social Theory was, initially, the theme of a meeting of the Cardiff Roundtable in Language and Communication, held at Gregynog Hall (Newtown, Mid Wales) in July 1997, the second in the Roundtable series. The inaugural meeting, *Approaches to Media Discourse*, led to a book under that title edited by Allan Bell and Peter Garrett (1998). The Roundtable series is designed as a way of integrating and critically reassessing research themes which have particular contemporary salience in sociolinguistics, discourse or the study of human communication generally. Each Roundtable works by bringing together researchers who have distinctive personal or disciplinary perspectives on the designated theme and substantial research experience to draw on. Participants circulate position papers in advance of the meeting, which then becomes a forum for intensive discussion and interaction. Two subsequent meetings in the Roundtable series have been on the themes of *The Sociolinguistics of Metalanguage* and *Discourses of the Body*. Those of us who have been lucky enough to take part in more than one of these meetings appreciate the space — physical, social and intellectual — that they and the University of Wales conference centre at Gregynog Hall afford.

In the case of the *Sociolinguistics and Social Theory* Roundtable, we are especially appreciative of the financial support given by Longman/Pearson Education towards the costs of the meeting, alongside support given by the Centre for Language and Communication Research, Cardiff University. Also, in the case of Chris Candlin, we are very grateful for the support of the Centre for Language in Social Life, Macquarie University, Sydney.

This book, however, is not a proceedings volume. For one thing, not all of the original participants have been able to contribute. The ideas that do appear in the book certainly owe a great deal to the input of colleagues who are missing in print, but who contributed significantly to the success of the Roundtable meeting. Even so, we have not been able to capture the full richness of the dialogues and commentaries that followed the presentations.

Also, the chapters that follow are the result of significant reworking of original papers presented and a good deal of interchange between contributors since the Roundtable event. One contribution, the chapter by Lesley Milroy, has been added to the set emerging out of the original meeting. The time that has elapsed between the Roundtable meeting and this appearance in print has been longer than we originally hoped. As editors, we are grateful to our contributing colleagues for their patience and what we take as their faith in the project. But in some ways this delay has been productive, allowing us to give a better representation of the ideas that the meeting introduced, and a more integrated statement of the topic.

So why is 'sociolinguistics and social theory' a timely and important theme? First, because the enterprise of sociolinguistics is itself being reassessed. The boundaries of sociolinguistics have never been definitively established, and this is actually one of the discipline's salient characteristics. Sociolinguistics, which has always had a centrifugal tendency, has thrived on multi-disciplinary input — not only from linguistics but, most obviously, from sociology, social psychology, anthropology, linguistic philosophy and, more recently, cultural studies. There have always been different visions and versions of sociolinguistics, particularly because the in-putting disciplines are themselves internally diverse and changing. But the contemporary climate of sociolinguistics shows *radical* heterogeneity, along all the predictable fault-lines: qualitative versus quantitative methods, naturalism versus experimentalism, micro versus macro perspectives, descriptive versus critical orientations. All the foundational questions of sociolinguistics are therefore coming up for reconsideration, and not least: What is the 'proper', or at least the 'most productive', relationship to entertain between language and society? What dimensions of 'society' are most amenable to, or most in need of, analysis from a linguistic perspective? Indeed, what *is* society in sociolinguistics, and how has society been understood and theorised? What are the alternatives? Doesn't society need to be theorised differently in different places and at different epochs, and if so, what are the salient differences between 'society' now and when sociolinguists connected with it in the 1950s and 1960s? How should we orient to the language/society interface? What contributions can sociolinguistics make to general understandings of social practices? What are the methodological constraints and imperatives?

A second reason is apparent when we stand *outside* of sociolinguistics and look in. Language and discourse are not uniquely of interest to linguists and sociolinguists. Largely under the influence of European philosophical and critical thinking, most of the human and social sciences have come to invest, albeit in distinctive ways, in the explanatory potential of language and the analysis of social practice. Sociolinguistics is probably the discipline best placed to respond to this wave of enthusiasm for language, although it has only done so sporadically and tentatively up to now. Dealing as it does, with real-life language data, sociolinguistcs is better placed to reveal the diversity inherent in social practice. The field of social theory, diverse and diffuse as it is, shows much the same enthusiasm for language but it tends to remain an abstraction, excessively so for those concerned with the study of socially motivated language use. Attempts to update sociological and anthropological accounts of post-industrial capitalist societies have often pointed to the growing importance of language and communication — to new forms of literacy, new technological resources for communication and new ways for people to form communities and allegiances in a globalising world. Hence, one of our ambitions for the book is to show what can be achieved when sociolinguists explicitly turn their attention to the wider concerns of the social sciences. This shift to a more outward-looking sociolinguistics and to more genuine inter-disciplinarity must be the discipline's future.

Overall, there is a strong case that a sociolinguistics that does *not* concern itself directly with social theory will be impoverished in its designs and fragile in its social explanation. While it does not seem correct to argue, as many have done, that sociolinguistics has been 'atheoretical', it is true that sociolinguistics has been inexplicit about its theoretical assumptions, and especially about its sociological assumptions. A great deal of ground-breaking sociolinguistic research has, for all its strengths, operated with a bland and under-analysed social realism. Sociolinguists have made important contributions to research on social demography, but often without much enthusiasm for debating the theoretical complexities of social categorisation or the implications that follow from this. On the other hand, sociology, especially in the guise of ethnomethodology, has over-dosed on the theoretical critique of social categorisation, reaching a highly sceptical position about the viability of social categories as analytic tools and putting its trust in the constructionist power of language. A paradox lurks here, deserving further airing, and many chapters in this book orient to it in different ways.

A basic assumption made by contributors to this book is that sociolinguists need to be better listeners to the discourses of social theory, but not overly subservient to them. In fact they need to be front-line contributors to the theorising of social processes and social structure, rather than delegating this task wholesale to other social scientists. We return to many of these ideas in the Introduction (NC). In the book's concluding chapter, we take up the methodological tensions involved in aligning participant-oriented sociolinguistic analysis with broader social theoretical insights (SS and CNC). Essentially, then, we hope that this volume will serve as the beginning of a renewed dialogue about how 'the social order' and 'the linguistic order' should interconnect. This book is far from being the first opportunity to debate this question, which is a foundational one for sociolinguistics. But it may be the first time that such a diverse array of influential sociolinguists have jointly turned their heads towards this theme, in an intellectual climate that is, more than ever, open to theoretical interchange between linguistic and social research.

NC,
SS and CNC

References

Bell, Allan and Garrett, Peter (eds) (1998) *Approaches to Media Discourse*. Oxford: Blackwell.

Introduction: Sociolinguistic theory and social theory
Nikolas Coupland

1   Introduction

In this chapter I want to do three main things. The first is to assess the current standing and assumptions of sociolinguistics vis-à-vis 'theory'. What do sociolinguists mean by theory? Are there competing views? Does it matter, and if so how? Is sociolinguistics theoretically deficient, as has sometimes been claimed? I will make the case that sociolinguistics is not 'atheoretical' but that its discussion of theory has been muted and rather uncritical. I will argue that sociolinguistics doesn't need to aspire to developing one over-arching 'sociolinguistic theory', and that this is an unrealistic goal, but that a more reflexive and open approach to theory *is* now needed. As part of this, sociolinguistics needs to be aware of how its existing, generally tacit social theorising connects to broader theoretical traditions in sociology and in the other social sciences. (Some initial ideas about this appear in the Preface, and I elaborate on them below.)

Secondly, therefore, I present a schematic overview of some of the main social-theoretic traditions in sociology — which is certainly an ambitious task and involves much more generalisation than any individual perspective merits. On the other hand, taking a wide view makes it possible to argue, as Layder (1994) has done, that social theory has fallen into three generally distinct phases — although 'types' is a better and more neutral term, because there is no simple chronological relationship between them. Each of the three types shows radically different emphases and assumptions about what aspects of social life are important for social scientists to address. Each comes with its own set of favoured research methods, which introduces the important point that theory is not 'merely theory'; theory influences how research questions are formulated and carried through into description, analysis and application (see Roberts, Chapter 12). Against this three-part structure, we can then assess in more detail where sociolinguistics 'fits in' with the main currents of social theory, and how it might become more substantively engaged in social theory.

It becomes clear that the approach that came to dominate sociolinguistics in its early decades — the study of variation and change in language and dialect — is closely associated with one early-established, general type of social theory. It builds on the assumption that we confront social life as a structured set of social categories which, to some extent, control our social characteristics and opportunities. On the other hand, some important other strands of sociolinguistics, most of those using the terms 'discourse' or 'interaction' in identifying themselves, align rather more with a second type of social theory. This type assumes that social life and our entire experience of society is best seen as structured through local actions and practices (see Eckert 2000). This 'bottom-up' perspective is radically different from the first. In its more extreme forms we find approaches which reject the claim that social structures outside of local interactions have any reality. Sociolinguistics currently seems content to endorse both perspectives, with varying degrees of antagonism between them.

In the later part of the chapter I consider a third general type of social theory. We can call it an 'integrationist' perspective, where social theory actively tries to reconcile the distinctions between the first and second types and, especially, works to bridge the 'micro–macro divide'. A good deal of contemporary social theory can, in the very general terms being used here, be accommodated within this third type, although there are also very substantial differences between the agenda and emphases of different theorists and many gaps in current accounts. My main ambition for the chapter is to assess what integrationist social theorising, in all of its internal diversity, implies for sociolinguistics, and vice versa. I shall argue, in fact, that sociolinguistics can take on a major role in integrationist social theory, bridging between macro-social concerns and the analysis of local communicative practice, and between theory and application.

2 Sociolinguistics and 'theory'

Is sociolinguistics, as we generally know it, 'theoretical', and adequately so?[1] Sociolinguists have sometimes expressed their unease about theory and pressed the case for a better articulated or more unified sociolinguistic theory, or at least for sociolinguistics to be more reflexive in its theoretical dimension. It is in the spirit of contributing to this debate that this book has been designed. It does not seem right, however, to start with the assumption that there is a blatant or radical 'theoretical deficit' in sociolinguistics; even less that this volume will rectify some acknowledged theoretical shortcoming 'at a stroke'. Putting the contrary view, with a highly selective and partial list, we could point to sociolinguistics' considerable theoretical achievements to date: its theorising of language change (Labov 1994); of communicative competence and the social parameters of human interaction and ways of speaking (Hymes 1974); of the linguistic constitution of social context (Duranti and Goodwin 1992), and of interpersonal relations and adaptation (Giles and Powesland 1975); of sociolinguistic differentiation in speech communities, especially in respect of class, race and gender (Labov 1972); of social networks (Milroy 1987); of the role of inferencing in intercultural communication (Gumperz 1982); of language in cultural performance (Bauman 1977, 1992, 1996; Briggs 1993), and very many others. Sociolinguistics has worked at un-ravelling the theoretical significance of language variation generally, not only within or in criticism of asocial theories of language itself, but as a core dimen-sion of social policy and planning and in the analysis of social inequality.

Why, then, the unease? One recurring theme is that sociolinguistics has made its mark primarily as a *descriptivist* enterprise, most notable for its ability to generate facts about the distribution of linguistic forms in social environments. More than 20 years age Halliday (1978) made the rather acerbic point that sociolinguistics looked like a set of answers to questions that had yet to be specified. It is true that early sociolinguistic surveys of speech variation in urban communities were mainly descriptive and largely confirmed 'already known' generalisations about the co-variation of linguis-tic and social patterning — that degrees of 'standardness' in urban dialects could be predicted by social class positioning, or that women tended, in quantitative and frequency terms, to be 'more standard' speakers than men of equivalent social class. On the other hand, the 'merely descriptive' nature of urban surveys led to important insights. The sociolinguistic surveys conducted and inspired by Labov have resulted in a rich and comprehens-ive theoretical account of language change mechanisms, which would not have been possible from a thinner descriptive base. Survey-based findings provided basic data from which many broader theoretical initiatives, especially relating to social class, gender and intergroup contact, were launched.

No sociolinguist would deny that, as a minimal requirement, descriptive data about the social distribution of language forms need to be interpreted within a theoretical framework, but the question is how robust and how far-reaching the framework needs to be. Hudson (1996: 228) writes that 'we badly need a general [sociolinguistic] framework of ideas to integrate the facts into a whole that makes some kind of intellectual sense'. But if we take this definition of 'theory', it is difficult to see precisely what is lacking. There are many instances of sociolinguistic studies that are 'integrated' and that 'make intellectual sense'. The final chapter of Hudson's revised edition of the *Sociolinguistics* textbook is certainly a significant, new, integrative theoretical contribution in its own right. Other recent contributions include Figueroa's (1994) provocative critical review of three dominant sociolinguistic traditions and their theoretical bases — the traditions associated with Hymes, Gumperz and Labov, debated in her *Sociolinguistic Metatheory* — and Chambers's (1995) book entitled *Sociolinguistic Theory*. The existence of these treatments supports the view that there is no general or wholesale theoretical deficit in sociolinguistics.

But discontent persists. Romaine (1994), Coulmas (1997) and Williams (1992) have all commented on the status of sociolinguistic theory and argue that sociolinguistics needs more theoretical impetus. Romaine, like Hudson, suggests that sociolinguistics lacks a convincing theoretical model within which to situate and explain its findings and argues constructively (p. 226) for a model that would orient much more to social conflict and discrimination. Williams makes the same point, more trenchantly, although he urges sociolinguists to situate their work in relation to what is often called 'grand theory' — the major traditions of philosophical and sociological thought. Coulmas (1997: 3) sees sociolinguistics as isolated between social theory, which he says has 'gone its own system-theoretic way, maintaining at best a very esoteric interest in language and more commonly ignoring altogether the role of language in constructing society', and linguistic theory, which has resolutely turned its back on society and sociology. He is pessimistic about the likelihood of sociolinguistic theory coming to prominence under these circumstances. In these comments there are different understandings of what 'sociolinguistic theory' *is*, of how it is attainable, and presumably therefore different views of why it matters.

Two broadly different positions can be distinguished in sociolinguists' self-doubts about theory. The first position is a rather familiar one, echoing a long-running debate about the boundaries of sociolinguistics: **Position A: Sociolinguistic theory is 'proper' linguistic theory**. As Romaine (1994: 222) points out, one clearly-expressed position is that 'sociolinguistics proper' should be aimed at improving *linguistic* theory and at developing our understanding of the nature of language, and not at contributing to the enterprise of social science. The first use of the phrase 'sociolinguistics proper' seems to have been by Trudgill (in 1978), although it is closely reminiscent of Labov's personal stance in the often-quoted Preface to *Sociolinguistic Patterns* (1972; see also Coupland and Jaworski 1997). This position does not simply equate sociolinguistic theory with linguistic theory, because it holds that 'proper' linguistic theory would be *better* linguistic theory, and certainly different from current linguistic theory through being in some sense social. In his 1994 volume, Labov continues to make it explicit that his theoretical ambitions are contained within linguistics:

> The dominant approach to theory construction in our field is to build a model that corresponds point for point to each element of language structure, and to state the rules for relating parts of the model to each other and to the empirical facts. (Labov 1994: 4)

It is presumably according to the same argument that Hudson (1996: 252ff) finds it important to consider the implications that sociolinguistic data have for various theories of language structure. He argues along the lines that any theory of linguistic competence must represent what individuals know about language, and that their knowledge includes knowledge about the social distribution of forms and varieties. Chambers (1995: 30) also argues the 'different but compatible' line:

> It does not seem ... paradoxical for sociolinguistic theory to avoid specific proposals of theoretical linguistics while embracing its general conception ... Luckily, categorial theory [Chomskyan theory] and variation theory are separate enough that they need only share the general view of the language faculty. That shared view marks their common ground as linguistic theories. Beyond that, they have their own domains and ways of proceeding.

Trudgill's Preface to Chambers's *Sociolinguistic Theory* glosses Chambers's theme as 'linguistic variation theory' (p. xvi) and the author's own Preface locates that book's contribution specifically as overviewing correlational sociolinguistic (p. xvii), or urban dialectological (p. 1), research. It is obviously more feasible to define sociolinguistic theory as a contribution to linguistic theory if one defines ('proper') sociolinguistics as quantitative and variationist.

For that part of sociolinguistic research that deals with quantifying variation of linguistic forms across speakers or situations, there will always be the question of how and to what extent variable sociolinguistic data might be accounted for within competence grammars. There will also be, for some sociolinguists, a sense of responsibility to the 'parent discipline', which, at least in a simple morphological sense, linguistics seems to represent. On the other hand, the very concept of *socio*linguistic theory entails that there should be a degree of autonomy from the priorities of linguistics and from the assumption that sociolinguistics is what linguistics might have been, and certainly has *not* become. If, as Coulmas (1997: 4) suggests, 'linguistic theory is ... a theory about language without human beings', and if it remains this after almost 40 years of sociolinguistics, then the theoretical impact of sociolinguistics must be made elsewhere. Cameron's (1990) view is that a continuing allegiance to linguistic theory may be more a matter of reverence for the 'real science' of linguistics than a sense of responsibility. In a related way, Linell (in Chapter 4 of this volume) analyses ways in which sociolinguistics and discourse analysis have inherited emphases from theoretical linguistics.

All the contributors to this book share the view that, whatever we take 'theory' to mean in sociolinguistics, it is *not* delimited by, or subservient to, the priorities of linguistics itself. Interpreting sociolinguistics, in the name of the book series in which this volume appears, as the study of 'language in social life', sociolinguistic theory has to work explicitly at the language/ society interface and orient to both sides. Let us define 'a theory', for the moment, as a coherent set of linked observations, accounting for observable facts, with potential to generalise about them and explain them. By this definition, there are several well-articulated theories within sociolinguistics which relate to at least specific social dimensions or contexts of language and which have no direct links to linguistic theory in the Chomskyan sense.

This brings us to **Position B: Sociolinguistics is an accumulation of socially-relevant mini-theories**. Hudson's chapter (1996: 228) opens with a list of sociolinguistic 'subtheories', which he says are all well supported by evidence. His list is:

— the 'family-tree' and 'wave' theories of change
— variety-based and item-based models of language
— the 'classical' and 'prototype' theories of thought
— the Sapir–Whorf hypothesis about language and thought
— the 'face' theory of interaction
— the 'accommodation', 'network' and 'acts of identity' theories of linguistic choices.

Others would draw up very different lists. But many would support the view that sociolinguistics has produced, in Coulmas' (1997: 3) phrase, 'theories but no theory'. Hudson feels there is potential for integrating some 'subtheories', and he usefully considers some interrelationships among theories of facework, solidarity and accommodation, networks, acts of identity, and power.

Whether 'a greater integration of subtheories' is an appropriate future for sociolinguistic theory and is considered adequate will now depend on further debating of the nature of theory. According to the Popperian view (such as Popper 1968), science exists to falsify hypotheses articulated as cause–effect propositions. Perhaps this implies that we should scrutinise theories of facework (Brown and Levinson 1987) or interpersonal accommodation (Giles, Coupland and Coupland 1991) for their ability to meet the criteria of predictive modelling and falsifiability, and then of generalisability in the face of empirical data. It turns out, in fact, that facework/politeness and accommodation theories are rather untypical instances of sociolinguistic (sub)theories in that they *have* tried to meet Popperian criteria — at least in some of their guises, when they are stated propositionally, making testable predictions of linguistic 'outcomes' under specific circumstances. On the other hand, social scientists taking a more hermeneutic stance 'regard theory as primarily an interpretation of social reality which leads to understanding via adequate description . . . [They try to identify] the meaning of an action from the point of view of the social actor's own culture' (Turner 1996: 7). Ethnomethodology, conversation analysis and Gumperz's theory of conversational inferencing, all of which are debated in later chapters, are approaches which tend this way. These competing definitions of 'theory' also surface in many of the chapters that follow.

However, in neither of the two general 'positions' introduced above is there an imperative to find a single, over-arching sociolinguistic theory. The very fact that there are competing definitions of 'theory' itself implies that no unified theory is possible, or even desirable. We might say that the concept of a unified theory is ideologically alien to sociolinguistics, because it is premised on diversity and resistant to hegemony; and 'grand theory' often has a hegemonic flavour. What is more likely to be attainable is a series of programmatic principles[2] for the study of language in society which are sufficiently general to have some application in all or most communicative environments. It is in this sense that we could say that Hymes's (1974) arguments for a socially constituted linguistics, or conversation analysts' systematic uncovering of the interaction order (for example Drew and Heritage 1992), or the conversational inferencing approach of Gumperz (1982) are comprehensive sociolinguistic theories. They are comprehensive in having near-universal application, but they are not necessarily in competition with each other for accuracy or explanatory power. It is still surely a very desirable objective to continue to compare and contrast existing sets of programmatic principles, and to explore points of overlap or incompatibility.

3   Sociolinguistic theory as social theory

Position B, as sketched above, is a widely endorsed orientation to sociolinguistic theory at present, to the extent that there is any systematic and sustained discussion of theory 'mattering' in sociolinguistics. But when this is the stance adopted, there tends to be an *insularity* about theory, in the assumption that sociolinguistics should generate 'its own' theories — more or less comprehensive — to account for its data and their social implications. As we have seen, there have been sporadic appeals specifically for an independent sociolinguistic theory, which presumably means a theory that would be independent of both linguistic theory and social theory. In opposition to this line, I want to turn now to social theory itself and its relationships with sociolinguistics. We can consider the case that sociolinguistics should build its theory not only in relation to, but *as part of*, a wider theoretical enterprise. I shall summarise this as **Position C: Sociolinguistic theory is (or should be) social theory**.

Coulmas, quoted above, is surely wrong to suggest that social theory has only an 'esoteric' interest in language, as many contributors to this book point out (see particularly Sarangi, Chapter 1). Language–society relationships are not the exclusive concern of sociolinguists. In very different ways, but with a growing consensus of urgency, language has come to be seen as a key concern across the human and social sciences. Concerns with 'discourse', which are very prominent in this book, are almost as visible in sociology, history, geography, even business studies, and certainly in philosophy and literary and critical studies, as they are in linguistics. But this fact has not led to the active interdisciplinarity that might seem to follow naturally from it. Within sociolinguistics, there has been little awareness or interest in shared research agenda. Yet many of the following chapters demonstrate the high degree of fit between social theoretic and sociolinguistic priorities, once these are made explicit.

A quite different consideration is that sociolinguistics *already has* engaged substantially with social theory, but tacitly and non-reflexively, in the way it has established its questions and methods. For this reason, social theory is not optional in sociolinguistics, in the sense that any research design and any interpretation of data must make assumptions about social organisation and/ or social process. As Milroy and Milroy (1996) point out (and see Milroy, Chapter 9), Labovian variationism drew heavily on Talcott Parsons's (1942, 1952) stratificational concept of social class, when other social theories would have predisposed quite different models — such as Bourdieu's (1991) conception of linguistic markets, habitus and the symbolic and cultural power of language varieties (see Sarangi, Chapter 1; Jaworski, Chapter 5; Heller, Chapter 8; Erickson, Chapter 6). Similarly, the sociolinguistics of gender has followed very different empirical paths when gender has been theorised as, alternately, 'difference' or 'dominance' (Henley and Kramarae 1991; see also Meyerhoff, Chapter 2). Age has typically been seen from a neutral 'cohort' perspective in sociolinguistics when models of social alienation or disadvantage may, in some circumstances, be more appropriate (Coupland, Chapter 7). Sociolinguistic perspectives on interethnic or intercultural communication will differ greatly depending on whether we theorise intergroup relations in politically neutral terms or in the context of post-colonialism (Coupland 2000; Riggins 1997; Said 1978; cf. Rampton, Chapter 10; Watts, Chapter 11), and so on.

So what range of social-theoretic approaches do we need to consider, and how have they influenced sociolinguistics up to now? Figure 1 indicates some of the most clearly distinct theoretical traditions in the social sciences, and each of them has a *prima facie* relevance to language. The model is generally in agreement with Turner's helpful (1966) overview of social theory, and it corresponds to some of the main distinctions recognised in Layder (1994). For Layder, three key 'dualisms' or binary distinctions have provided the basic issues and tensions around which all social theorising has revolved: *macro–micro*, *structure–agency*, and *society–individual*. Chapters in the book return to these dimensions repeatedly. For present purposes, though, it is reasonable to follow Layder in distinguishing the three broad 'types' of social theory mentioned earlier, three different orientations to social explanation, defined by how they position themselves relative to these three dualisms.

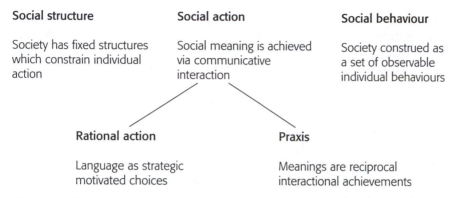

Social structure	Social action	Social behaviour
Society has fixed structures which constrain individual action	Social meaning is achieved via communicative interaction	Society construed as a set of observable individual behaviours

Rational action	Praxis
Language as strategic motivated choices	Meanings are reciprocal interactional achievements

Figure 1   Three social theoretic perspectives relevant to language

4   Type 1 social theory — socio-structural realism

The first type of social theory restricts itself very largely to the top-left part of Figure 1, and deals with the analysis of social structure and stratification. This emphasis is represented — in very different ways — by the sociology of Parsons and that of Marx. It gives clear priority to macro-level social organisation, where social structures are viewed as impinging on the lives and choices of individuals. In this first type, the theoretical challenge is to develop models of social structure, referring to large-scale social groups, social institutions and social changes, and to chart their effects. Individuals and their social lives at the micro-level, including their social actions and interactions, are of secondary or even peripheral concern, although individuals are expected to 'feel the effects of' social structures, as degrees of opportunity or constraint on their life choices, and, sociolinguistically, to express or index this structure in their speech. (See Carter and Sealey 2000 for a more differentiated account of realist social theory, and its relationship with sociolinguistics.)

As I have already suggested, Labov's variationist sociolinguistics is based in type 1 social theorising, and particularly in Parsonian assumptions. Despite its analytic interest in low-level (for example phonological and phonetic) speech phenomena, it is essentially macro-social in its design and ambition. It seeks to establish generalisations at the level of the social group, and especially to generalise about patterns of sociolinguistic differentiation within the speech community, which is therefore an important theoretical construct in Labov's work. In variationist research the urban community is a stratified social unit subsuming tiers or layers of social class and intersected by gender and age. It is a hierarchical ordering of demographic groups or cohorts, membership of which is both pre-assumed and then confirmed or refuted empirically with speech variation data, in a quantitative matrix. Individuals fill out the various matrices, but they are of importance only in contributing their data, in terms of their speech behaviour, to make up aggregated behavioural norms for sub-groups. In relation to the simple model in Figure 1, we might say that variationist sociolinguistics is designed in the top-left, but reaches over to the top-right when it inspects selected formal 'features' as aspects of 'language behaviour'.

Variationism is certainly not Behaviourist, in the fully experimentalist, 'stimulus–response' mode that this term implies. But variationist sociolinguistics does treat language (in fact, speech) as socially conditioned distributional patterning, rather than as locally motivated and, in that sense, 'functional' social action. For Labov, function is only relevant as a quality of the language *system* undergoing change (Labov 1994: 603–4). Systems — both social and linguistic — more than individuals have agency in this theoretical conception. Variationism, its proponents would argue, doesn't need to consider individual agency or social practice because its theoretical imperatives lie elsewhere — in the modelling of language and linguistic change.

5   Type 2 social theory – social action perspectives

The second type of social theory reverses the polarity of the first, and inflames the micro–macro debate by clearly prioritising social action and individual agency at the micro level. It occupies the top-middle and lower parts of Figure 1. Here we find sociology developing theories of social interaction itself as the primary, and indeed *the only*, locus of 'order'. For example, symbolic interactionism (Blumer 1969) 'emphasises the role of meanings, situations and experiences in social life' (Layder 1994: 8). But all phenomenological and ethnomethodological approaches, and social constructivist theory generally, feature in this area. The common thread is the assumption that 'higher-order' social structures and institutions have *no* meaningful existence outside of social interaction, and that the principal challenge is to establish how individuals make sense of social life in and through their local actions and interactions. Type 2 theories tend to cast type 1 theories as 'traditional' and even as suspect and naïve.

Both in sociolinguistics and in social theory generally, social action perspectives subsume two generally distinct versions (see the lower part of Figure 1). We can call them **rational action** and **praxis** perspectives, although these terms are not used consistently with these senses. In the sociolinguistic vision of rational action, linguistic codes and styles are assumed to be a matter of more-or-less conscious and strategic choice by rational social actors. 'Rationality' here means assuming that actors are aware of social norms for language and able to anticipate the consequences of their actions (which of course includes their actions in and through talk). Accommodation theory and politeness theory, as mentioned above, have generally accepted this premise. They have built predictive models in attempting to explain the relational motivations of speakers and the intended outcomes of their communication strategies. For example, accommodation theory (Giles, Coupland and Coupland 1991; see also Coupland, Coupland and Giles 1991) claims that speakers will reduce linguistic differences between themselves and other speakers if and when they actively want to communicate more efficiently with them, or to 'move closer' in relational terms. Politeness theory predicts that speakers will use more elaborate and more indirect forms of language (for example in making requests) when they want to reduce the level of threat that such actions impose on people's freedom of action (their 'negative face') or their good-standing (their 'positive face'). (Meyerhoff, Chapter 2, gives an integrated overview of social psychological research and its relevance to variationist sociolinguistics.)

These rationalist sociolinguistic 'mini-theories' generally reproduce the social theory of George Herbert Mead's (1932, 1934) *Mind, Self and Society*. In opposition to psychological Behaviourism and its belief that human and animal behaviour could be explained through concepts of stimulus and response, Mead argued that the individual's appreciation of social forces gave a fuller explanation of behaviour. He stressed people's understandings of the social implications of their behaviour in specific situations, and highlighted the agentive capacity of individuals, as social actors (again, see Layder 1994: 58–9). Indeed, Mead recognised the theoretical centrality of social interaction for understanding society in general, and the role of meaning-making in social actions, which in turn became the defining insight of symbolic interactionism. Rationalist theories of language use have been readily taken into sociolinguistics from social psychology and have had considerable impact on how sociolinguists routinely talk about talk. The assumption that meaning-making is done strategically, and against a background of speakers' specific social knowledge, and is negotiated progressively and interactively in social settings, is basic to the somewhat amorphous approach that we could call 'sociolinguistic discourse analysis'.

Quite otherwise, Conversation analysis (CA — see Atkinson and Heritage 1984; Boden and Zimmerman 1991; Drew and Heritage 1992) and its new, close partner, discursive psychology (see Antaki and Widdicombe 1998; Edwards and Potter 1992; Potter and Wetherell 1987; Potter and Edwards, Chapter 3) respect and carry forward the priorities of praxis theories (see the right side of the lower portion of Figure 1). Garfinkel's ethnomethodology (Garfinkel 1967) has been the most influential theory of praxis, famously developed and grounded conversationally in the work of Sacks (for instance Sacks 1992). In praxis theory, analysts do not assume that speakers are fully rational, in the sense introduced above. They hold that the outcomes of talk are largely unforeseeable, that talk or conversation develops its own momentum, and that meanings are therefore *contingent* (they depend on other meanings around them) and *emergent* (they surface progressively and incrementally from the flow of talk). Agency tends to be construed as shared between participants, so meanings and talk itself are said to be *co-constructed*, or else, more radically, agency is attributed to the process of social interaction itself. This is to take a similar line to symbolic interactionism, but to emphasise even more strongly the contingency and mutuality of meaning-making in discursive interaction. Here we see the role of the individual waning once again, whereas for Mead the individual was the focus of the theoretical model.

CA and ethnomethodology are alive and well within modern sociolinguistics, but it is important to recognise that they were, first and foremost, developments within the non-linguistic social sciences and found their shape in opposition to other tendencies there. Discursive psychology, for example (again see Potter and Edwards, Chapter 3), is principally a reaction against socio-structural determinism in social psychology, and against the dominant quantitative and experimental traditions of psychology as a whole. Many of its authors (for example Antaki and Widdicombe 1998) write polemically against structural–functionalist social psychologists who, rather like variationist sociolinguists, have often reified social class, age, gender and ethnic identities as socially and psychologically real and 'natural' entities.

6   Sociolinguistic agnosticism?

My main argument so far has been that some specific sociolinguistic traditions possess rather well-established forebears in theoretical social science. Sociolinguistics *has* been promulgating and contributing to 'social theory', although these connections have rarely been debated. For three or four decades, variationist research, which I have construed as a type 1 theoretical approach, has been in the ascendancy. Even when the research questions addressed are not the Labovian ones about systematic language change through time and space, a good deal of sociolinguistic research continues to be survey-based studies of social differentiation in language, following type 1 principles.

But it would be wrong to claim that sociolinguistics has been dogmatically committed to this mode of inquiry. What is most striking about contemporary sociolinguistics — as represented in the spread of articles published in major journals, for example — is its eclecticism, and how type 1 *and* type 2 theories, and methodologies associated with both, exist *in parallel*. It is certainly not the case, in line with strong versions of type 2 theory, that predetermined socio-structural categories are outlawed in sociolinguistics. Studies continue to report research organised around gender, ethnic, social class and age categories where these groupings are treated, more or less explicitly, as independent variables. On the other hand, micro-analytic studies and studies orienting to social practice are strongly evident, usually under the generalised title of discourse analysis (see Jaworski, Chapter 5; Erickson, Chapter 6). These studies, taken as a group, often do not meet the full criteria for type 2 membership, however, because they offer a mitigated social action approach. They show awareness of the limits of social explanation on the basis of analysing textual (including conversational) instances, and link these instances to wider matters of social structure or social conflict. That is, many discourse-based sociolinguistic studies see conversational data as *illustrative of* social processes and effects, rather than actually as constitutive of social order. Studies in conversation analysis and discursive psychology are more reflexively and critically bound to the constructivist model, and more resolutely of type 2. It is only in these cases that we see a systematic effort to keep theory in its pure typological form.

Does this general agnosticism matter? It seems to me that in some ways it doesn't, and even that there are positive advantages for sociolinguistics in refusing to commit wholeheartedly to a major social theoretic 'type'. In other ways it most certainly does matter. Let us consider the potential benefits of a relatively agnostic stance first.

To organise social and sociolinguistic theories into types is not to credentialise them. What we are implying to be 'theoretical purity' (and the terms 'coherence' and 'consistency' could feature here too) can often be experienced as dogma, and even as systematic, wilful myopia. What is gained in terms of coherence can be lost in terms of insight or applicability. Labovian variationism, for example, risks consolidating notions of class, race, age and gender and assuming that these are sociological constants. On the contrary, as several chapters in this book suggest, social formations acquire salience at particular historical moments, and their constitution can change radically from one era to another. Social class in contemporary UK society, for example, has not only different qualitative characteristics but also different social relevance from 50 years ago. People are much less firmly 'classed' by their place in the system of production and by their family ties, and, while deprivation persists, social class is less easy to index economically. Type 1 theorising is not well attuned to the experiencing of social group membership, which can often be variable and locally contextualised.

Similar problems can be identified with type 2 theorising. CA, for example, has thrived by setting its field and terms of operation very rigidly indeed, and policing its principles. It looks for understandings and demonstrations of conversational order in relation to sequence. It studiously avoids (or tries to avoid) interpretations in terms of human motivations or social norms. It limits its own access to what in other traditions would be considered obvious social-group-based explanations. It insists that its insights must be insiders' insights — what makes talk orderly and understandable *for them, at that moment*. In consequence, CA has needed to develop certain principles to determine its own interpretive activities — a CA charter for interpretation. One key instance is the principle of 'procedural consequentiality' (Schegloff 1992) which stipulates that aspects of social context (such as a speaker's gender or age) should only be implicated in an interpretation of talk if that social category is shown to be relevant for speakers at any given moment.

This is an extremely demanding, and in fact a debilitating, condition, at least by the standards of most non-CA and non-praxis-oriented theory (see Coupland in press a, and Antaki and Widdicombe 1998, as well as Potter and Edwards, Chapter 3, for different sides of this debate).

By comparison, most sociolinguists doing their work through discourse would hold to a weaker version of the consequentiality condition. The CA objection that social-contextual attributions are often bandied around too freely in sociolinguistics, leading to unwarranted explanations that are said to be 'self-evident', is powerful and certainly correct. For example, it is too easy to rush into the explanation that one speaker interrupted another 'because he was a male' or 'because her institutional role warranted that action', or 'to be assertive'. CA has focused attention on a major problem in qualitative research — how to warrant interpretations of local practices, and how to be sure that a social categorisation is relevant to a specific instance of practice. But it does not follow that CA's own response is a necessary or a useful or a practical one. CA's own criteria for warrantability are too restrictive and, in fact, unworkable. If we wait to find evidence at the surface of talk that speakers are 'really' orienting to some social categor-isation, such as in the gross case (which is itself not unproblematic) of speakers mentioning that social category in their talk, we may well not find it. Thereby we may 'decategorialise' interpretations, which is as pernici-ous a way to skew readings of data as is 'overcategorialising'. Billig (1999) has made the case that CA does not in fact live up to its own charter for interpretation — that it imposes its own assumptions about the orderliness of conversation onto its data, and uncritically accepts some sorts of categor-isations of speakers, for example as 'members' of culturally specific groups. (Schegloff's response to this critique is published as Schegloff 1999, and a further exchange between the authors follows it.)

As I suggested earlier, sociolinguistics has a propensity for non-dogmatic theory because of the diversity of its origins (see Samarin's and Hymes's recent retrospective comments on the origins of sociolinguistics — Samarin 2000, Hymes 2000). 'Openness to variation' is a disciplinary ideology that applies as much to sociolinguistic metatheory as to sociolinguistic data. Type 2 praxis theories in their 'purest' forms, having been born within oppositional sociological and psychological environments, have not needed to accommod-ate the theoretical influences of linguistic philosophy (such as from Austin and Grice) and the communication pragmatics perspective (Watzlawick *et al.* 1967) that emanated from it. One of the key insights of linguistic pragmatics is that the meanings of language texts reside in the complex interplay be-tween textual form and social and socio-psychological contexts. Radical type 2 theories can easily appear overly text-bound and technicist by comparison with the richly contextual approaches of discourse analysis and ethnography.

Sociolinguistics' relative agnosticism about theory is therefore to be ex-plained historically. Sociolinguistics lies at the intersection of several different theoretical traditions and finds it impossible, and probably undesirable, to commit to a single dogmatic theoretical type. Once again, this is not an argument against theory *per se*, or against critical reassessment of theory. Figueroa (1994) and Markova (1982) maintain that 'metaworries' do matter, and this is also surely correct. Their reasons include that it becomes imposs-ible to consider alternatives to adopted ways of thinking and researching; also that we lose perspective on the social significance of data. There is always a risk of an uncritical orthodoxy developing (Figueroa 1994: 18), and this volume is partly a response to that risk.

7 Type 3 social theory – integrationism

We can now return to Layder's overview of social theory and consider his third general type. In sociological theories of type 3, Layder groups those that, in one way or another, *reject* and try to *transcend* the dualisms that define the first two types. Layder primarily lists the work of Foucault, Elias and Giddens as belonging to this third type, although we can certainly add Bourdieu, Habermas and Bakhtin to them, and doubtless others. Evidently this is another broad and internally differentiated category, and broader than the first two types. Authors of the chapters that follow in this volume con-nect in diverse ways with many of these 'integrationist' social theories (Sarangi's overview and comparison of Foucault, Bourdieu and Habermas in Chapter 1 sets the scene well), and I make no attempt to review them individually here. But the future theoretical shape of sociolinguistics will be determined by how sociolinguists orient to integrationist social theories, and it may be useful to highlight some key themes that have arisen and how they challenge sociolinguistic orthodoxies.

7.1 Sociolinguistics and the limits of contextualisation

Sociolinguistics has pioneered the analysis of language–context relationships — most obviously, as mentioned earlier, in Hymes's taxonomic account of 'factors' or 'dimensions' that impinge on speech events (see for example Hymes 1974). The classical Hymesean dimensions of social context attend most directly to event-internal states and processes, such as 'participants', 'instrumentalities' and communicative 'keyings' in talk. But they also point, less directly, to macro-social realities, assuming that the concept of 'particip-ants', for example, subsumes socially endorsed and known identities, or that the concept of 'norms of interpretation' refers to the cultural familiarity of speech events. As noted earlier, the hallmark of integrationist social theorising is to situate macro and micro social orders within the same frame of analysis. Hymes's ethnography of speaking already seems to have taken us some way towards integrationism. Pressing a little harder, as Heller does in Chapter 8, we can see that the content and sequencing of communicative practice — classroom talk in Heller's case — not only reflects wider, ideological norms in the community but realises or activates them. Language texts and utterances, that is, witness and embody cultural discourses, in Foucault's (1980) sense of this term. In the more material sense of the term 'discourse', discourse and society shape each other (Fairclough 1992: 9).

The strong tradition of critical discourse analysis (CDA) in sociolinguistics invites us to consider the socio-political contexts of discourse and the perspectives from which utterances are made (see for instance Fairclough and Wodak 1997; Wodak 1996). The approach assumes that linguistic analyses of material texts (conversational, written, etc.) can identify different discourses, often associated (in Bourdieu's terms) with specific fields of practice and organised as communicative genres. The meanings of these discourses, partially realised in specific texts or textual fragments, are determined by higher-order knowledge systems or ideologies ('discourses', again, in the Foucauldian sense). Hence it becomes possible to analyse racism, for example, at the same time as an ideological formation linked to specific historical movements and conflicts, and also as a quality of the individual utterance in context. Specifically, the utterance qualifies as 'racist' only when it can be shown to be linked through to a socio-historical discourse of racism, which its deployment in a particular social context makes relevant.

Giddens's notion of 'structuration' (for example 1987: 60ff.) similarly proposes that social structure, and even 'the structural properties of institutions', need to be viewed as 'the patterns of relationships observable in a diversity of social contexts'. This implies an analytic focus on local practices, of which talk is probably the most salient and the most accessible. Giddens does not himself undertake the observation and analysis of 'institutional discourse', and the theoretical account of structuration is to that extent incomplete without sociolinguistics. Furthermore, sociolinguistics is able, drawing on its own analytic resources, to develop much more differentiated and hence, arguably, *better social theoretic* accounts of structure and agency, through its analysis of local practices of talk.

To take one example, sociolinguistics has developed Goffman's (1974, 1981) insights into the 'framing' of discourse by showing (for example as Tannen and Wallat [1987/2000] have done; see also Coupland, Robinson and Coupland 1994, J. Coupland 2000) how speakers, in those settings we usually consider to be 'institutional', move between 'institutional' and 'personal' framings of talk. It is not so much that talk in, for example, a geriatric medical consultation, uniformly and absolutely realises the institution of geriatrics. Rather, we can show that participants orient, variably and creatively, to the normative constraints of the institution. At some moments they acquiesce to the roles and expectations of 'a geriatric medical consultation', which *de facto* reproduces this institutional order, while at other times they deviate from and play with that predictable framing of their interaction. This suggests that people do in fact work with a pre-discursive concept of social order, as well as being active agents in their reproduction (or modification) of it.

For this reason if for no other, sociolinguistic analyses of discourse, 'critical' or other, do not make more traditional sociological analyses redundant, and the crucial issue here is *how much* we feel we can genuinely know about social structure through the analysis of local practice, We still arguably need to appeal to the historical and political architecture of, say, geriatrics, because it impinges on (motivates, complicates, normalises, etc.) particular moments of practice. In interpretation, there needs to be a movement from structure to practice as well as from practice to structure. The local analysis of practice is important not only when it confirms generalisations about social order, which may have been reached independently of sociolinguistic investigation. It is important particularly when it *qualifies* or conflicts with normative generalisations. As Erickson cautions (Chapter 6), we should not give up too soon on analysing our language data, however tempting the appeal of pre-existing, 'explanatory' social theories. Close sociolinguistic attention to language data may undermine as well as endorse the generalisations of 'pure theory'. As Wilson (Chapter 13) notes, Bourdieu is open to criticism for the apparent determinism of his notion of habitus, as a way of explaining class-related communicative predispositions in speech and other forms of practice.

7.2   Sociolinguistics and globalising modernity

Two of the most insistent themes of modern social theory are globalisation (see for example Z. Bauman 1998) and the transition out of 'high' modernity into late-modernity (for example Giddens 1990, 1991, 1994). Both themes have direct implications for the social investigation of language and discourse, and again *vice versa*. Economic and cultural globalisation are, for example, as Watts shows in Chapter 11, partly evidenced in pressures towards language shift and forces resisting shift. Language, and in many cases the English language, is the medium of cultural globalisation. Sociolinguistics has already produced important analyses of linguistic attrition in the wake of colonial expansion (such as Skutnabb-Kangas and Phillipson 1994), although the full implications of globalisation for sociolinguistic theory have yet to be worked out.

One strand has to do with reflexivity, if, as Giddens and others have argued, a key quality of late-modern societies is how their practices are mirrored back to social actors themselves. The obvious social correlate of reflexivity is the upsurge in mass media communications and the development of new communication technologies. It would be surprising if the multiplication of opportunities to communicate, and to witness and replay our own communicative acts, did not impact on the nature of language use rather fundamentally. Styles of language, used 'knowingly', take on the quality of stylisation (Rampton 1995; Coupland in press b, in press c). Cultural forms, even the use of local languages and varieties, are loosened from their authenticating contexts and become more performance-like. As Giddens points out, late-modernity is generally hostile to tradition, and can be seen as a process of detraditionalisation. But at the same time, the frightening openness of late-modernity presses people to rediscover a sense of rootedness, which he calls 'retraditionalisation'. Sociolinguistics has not considered these possibilities in any detail, and has been unquestioning of the social and cultural 'authenticity' of its data.

7.3   Language, social groups and social identities

Social identity is, more than any other aspect of social theory, sociolinguistics' home ground. We have become accustomed to interpreting language variation in relation to the symbolic potential of language — how languages can, in Fishman's dictum, be rallying points for ethnic cohesion and how accents and dialects can mark class and regional affiliations. Wider theorising of social identity, especially under the influence of cultural studies, has been valuable for sociolinguistics in challenging the orthodoxy of these assumptions. Theorists such as Said (1978) and Bhabha (1994) have objected to *essentialist* assumptions about social identity which link people to group designations on the basis of simple and apparently unvarying attributes (place of birth, race and associated ethnic memberships). Said famously argues that 'orientalism', for example, is a political construction of westerners, designed to perpetuate power imbalances. Bhabha introduces the notion that social identities actually show *hybridity* rather than stability. Sociolinguistics' tolerance of independent variables such as sex, class or age readily essentialises people into these groupings, making the assumption that aggregated patterns of language variation are adequately explained by individuals' sex, class or age 'identities'.

This is a clear instance where emphases in non-sociolinguistic theory have been emancipating for sociolinguistics, best embodied in Rampton's perspective on language *crossing* — the use of non-ingroup varieties and styles for local effect (see again Rampton 1995; also 1999, and Chapter 10). Sociolinguistics is now more open to the constructivist power of language to effect social identities in context (Coupland, Chapter 7), and to the socio-political implications of identity ascriptions and impositions (Heller, Chapter 8; Milroy, Chapter 9; Watts, Chapter 11). However, in the sociolinguistic theorising of identity, we should resist both essentialising *and de-essentialising* tendencies in their extreme forms. Social group membership is by no means static and 'given' by social attributes, or of course by language and speech characteristics themselves. But neither are social identities written sociolinguistically on a *tabula rasa* in a socio-historical vacuum. Empirical studies can be designed to assess which facets of social identity, in and through language, are marked as essential and which as contingent. Sociolinguistics, as I argued earlier, can feed back the results of its analyses of discourse into more subtle and contextually specific theories of social identification. Once again, sociolinguistic theory can aspire to being *better social theory* in this domain.

7.4   The theory–application link

As many of the following chapters show, sociolinguistics can therefore contribute more than 'good descriptions' and 'social facts'. For some sociolinguists, this will not actually be a new challenge, even though it may need a restructuring of how we represent the discipline to ourselves and others. Sociolinguistic theory could be our best systematic and explanatory accounts of how people position themselves and their social worlds through language — of how, in Hasan's words, 'language is used for the living of life, how it acts in the creation, maintenance, and alteration of human relations, which range from consensus to conflict, from cooperation to exploitation, and from accommodation to submission' (Hasan 1993: 79).

But sociolinguists may have the reservation that, in aspiring to richer, wider or more comprehensive theoretical accounts, they are turning their back on real-world applications of their research. Sociolinguistics has always had an active socio-political dimension, and many would see a concern for social justice in language issues as its main rationale. We think of Labov's early invective against what he saw as repressive determinism in early versions of Bernstein's codes hypothesis, and his involvement in the Ann Arbor 'Black English' trial. Rickford's more recent involvement in the Oakland 'Ebonics' controversy (see Rickford 1999) continues this tradition. Hymes has been vociferous in support of Native American language rights for many decades. Fishman's theoretical work has centred on principles of linguistic self-determination and minority language rights, and so on. Here again we potentially confront the concern that 'developing theory' is an intellectually elitist activity, incompatible with applied and especially interventionist initiatives.

I think this is to under-represent the scope of 'theory', which must include the discipline reflexively theorising its own relationship with society and social affairs, and its own place in influencing the moral and even the political order. Language is arguably the dimension of social life that is least well understood by its practitioners ('everyday speakers') and by those who lobby for or against its forms of use (Cameron 1995; Lippi-Green 1997). Notwithstanding the instances of direct intervention that I mentioned above, sociolinguistics has had relatively little impact on public appreciation of the nature of language, and of its social functions. We can explain some of this failure, I think, by reference to the inexplicitness of sociolinguistic theory to date and its general lack of critical engagement with socio-political issues. Critical linguistics and critical discourse analysis have been the notable exceptions, and they are increasingly impacting on the mainstream of sociolinguistic research. A 'critical' approach implies evaluation of social norms and working for social change. As Giddens notes, 'the best and most original ideas in the social sciences, if they have any purchase on the reality it is their business to capture, tend to become appropriated and utilized by social actors themselves' (Giddens 1987: 19). Similarly, there is a permeable membrane between academic and theoretical sociolinguistics and social action itself. Theory may be 'good for sociolinguists to think with' (Roberts, Chapter 12) but it should also be the distillation of sociolinguistic knowledge and values as it approaches the interface with social policy and social practice. After all, academic theorising is, from one point of view, just another index of the increasing reflexivity of society.

8   The structure of the volume

The rest of the book is divided into four Parts. In Part One Sarangi overviews how three highly influential social theorists, Bourdieu, Foucault and Habermas, have oriented to language in their work. Bourdieu and Giddens in particular attract the attention of later contributors. Sarangi's review helps us appreciate not only how but why specific social theories came to focus on language. I have been more concerned, in this Introduction, to consider why sociolinguistics should turn its face to social theory. But it becomes clear in Sarangi's account that social theory has already been explicit about its need for a sociolinguistic component, even if language is understood differently by the three theorists he considers.

Meyerhoff similarly starts outside of sociolinguistics, with an overview and an attempted integration of several of the principal theoretical traditions of social psychology. The chapter shows that sociolinguistics has been rather selective in its use of social psychological theorising to date and opens new ground for more integrated explanations. These are well illustrated in a following analysis of sociolinguistic variation in conversational Bislama (Vanuatu creole). Then, from another, wholly different, psychological tradition, Potter and Edwards critique standard sociolinguistic treatments of cognitive processes as an explanatory resource. Their stance is closely allied to ethnomethodology and CA and they emphasise the discursive construction and organisation of 'cognitive objects', in preference to *a priori* acceptance of the validity and relevance of cognitive operations (motives, influences, stereotypes, and so on).

Part Two explains and illustrates sociolinguistic orientations to 'discourse', firstly, in Linell's chapter, from a historical point of view. Linell argues that, despite widespread acceptance of the need to articulate a dynamic and context-sensitive account of language, dynamic processes are inherently difficult to capture analytically. He then traces the residues of 'static' analysis in sociolinguistics, including a 'written language bias'. Therefore, although much social theory stresses the role of social action in the structuring of society, it proves difficult to overcome the propensity to analyse language as a set of forms. Linell's point is therefore pertinent for integrationist social theory generally, if we assume that some forms of sociolinguistic analysis are essential to bridging the micro–macro divide.

Jaworski assesses the utility of Bourdieu's metalinguistic apparatus for analysing power discourses in one specific domain — that of art criticism. There is a particular salience to invoking Bourdieu's theory in this domain, because he himself writes specifically about the role of artistic 'taste' as a form of symbolic capital. But Jaworski completes the cycle of integrationist social theory by supplying the detailed analysis of textual instances. He shows how artistic criticism and judgement involve status and power moves, within a specific field of discourse and among initiated practitioners.

If Jaworski's chapter, like others, shows the utility for sociolinguistics of engaging with pre-existing social theory, Erickson cautions against over-eager and uncritical borrowing from such sources. With reference to several instances from his data on intercultural gatekeeping selection interviews, he shows that Bourdieu-type theorising of the sociolinguistic reproduction of social class may overgeneralise, relative to the facts of local instances. Hence his notion of 'wiggle room' — the space that sociolinguistics needs to maintain between its own bottom-up interpretations of data and social theory-driven generalisations. This cautionary argument does not, I think, militate against integrationism. On the contrary, it implies that the sociolinguistic wing of social theory needs to be taken seriously, especially when analyses of local instances refute data-free oversimplifications. The issue is of political significance, since attested exceptions (to the theorised norm of social class reproduction, for example) are where social change becomes possible.

In Part Three five chapters take up different aspects of social classification in sociolinguistics, and all the 'traditional' dimensions — class, race/ethnicity, age, gender — are addressed. My own chapter reviews the rather narrow ways in which age has been theorised in sociolinguistics, mainly in subservience to the apparent time method of studying linguistic change. In contrast, I show that contemporary social theorising of the lifespan is far less deterministic — less bound to chronological age as a criterion and more open to appreciating self-definitional possibilities in later life in late modernity. Heller's more empirical approach shows how the sociolinguistic analysis of classroom talk, in ethnographic data from Franco-Ontarian schools, reveals the interpenetration of socio-historical and socio-political ideologies. Institutionalised (French) monolingualism is not only a matter of explicit educational policy. Its ideological force is felt at the level of the individual utterance, as when teachers monitor and seek to sanitise students' lexical usage into 'purer' forms of French.

Milroy's chapter is a meta-analysis of how certain social dimensions come to be taken up by sociolinguists, non-randomly in certain communities. This important perspective challenges the orthodox view that social categories, such as race and class, are 'natural' and 'independent' social realities which sociolinguists can and should address, as equivalents. Public conceptions of 'standard English', Milroy shows, differ quite radically in the USA and in the UK. In the UK, 'standard English' is historically associated with high-prestige speakers and especially in social class-linked status. In the USA, 'standardness' had more obviously racial connotations, even from the early years of settlement. This distinction is visible not only in academic socio-linguistics but in popular cultural texts, such as letters complaining about linguistic usage, published in newspapers.

Rampton's chapter gives a rich account of the theoretical foundations of his approach to sociolinguistic crossing, its linkage to Gumperz's interactional sociolinguistics as well as to recent developments in cultural studies and linguistic anthropology. Rampton's theoretical but also empirical concern in the chapter is with ethnic identification, and crossing in the talk of Asian, Black and Anglo British school students. But it would be useful to consider how easily, or otherwise, this general anti-essentialist orientation to 'groupness', which Rampton has pioneered in sociolinguistics, transfers to other social categorisations. The research has not been done, but contexts and contents of identity stylisation are undoubtedly hugely widespread, even though the social functioning of non-ingroup styling is likely to be diverse. Following from my earlier remarks in this chapter, it will be necessary to establish how crossing and stylisation achieve cultural continuity as well as fragmentation, and to try to assess longer-term as well as shorter-term implications.

Finally in this Part of the book, Watts brings the concepts of language ideology and competing discourses to bear, through a critical analysis, on a classical arena of 'macro-sociolinguistics' (or 'the sociology of language') — language planning policy documents on the status of national languages in a multilingual community, Switzerland. The analysis implicitly shows how *un*critically sociolinguistics has tended to be in its avowedly 'macro' dimen-sion, where the sorts of insight developed in relation to talk and text have been overlooked in rather 'straight' readings of social policy pronounce-ments, declarations of rights, and so on. Discourses about language policy are nonetheless discourses, and Watts shows they are far from immune to the processes of selective representation, omission and perspectivisation that are endemic in all rhetorical arguments. Watts also demonstrates how socio-linguistic insights are channelled and shaped in the service of particular interest groups, and the relationship between theory and intervention is in the air throughout.

The two Retrospective Commentators, in Part Four, of course speak for themselves. In their selective reviewing of earlier chapters and constructively antagonistic texts, Roberts and Wilson both invite us to reflect on the state of sociolinguistics, both with and without social theory. Their main question is: 'So what?', and readers will of course reach their own conclusions. The book concludes with the chapter by Sarangi and Candlin where they revisit many of the foundational links between social theoretical and sociolinguistic practice at the methodological level. My own view is that viewing social theory from inside sociolinguistics is not unlike the first experience of international travel (at least as it is mythically interpreted). A panoply of intriguing new possibilities opens up, and the effect is both seductive and disorienting. Attempts to learn a new language will be of variable success, and some travellers will acculturate fully while others retrench. Travel is no guarantee of intercultural convergence, and in some cases the whole experience may only serve to make us value home territory all the more. But our explorations will probably make the world appear smaller, and we may well meet others travelling in our direction. At the least, we will come to see the familiar through different eyes.

Notes

1   This section of this Introduction is a revised and extended version of Coupland (1998). I gratefully acknowledge Allan Bell's and Adam Jaworski's constructive input into that earlier text.
2   Theory building, rather than theory alone, is often held to be a desired outcome of scientific research. Research which follows programmatic principles will necessarily be theoretical, in one sense of 'theory', compatible with Popper's claim that there is no 'theory-free' observation or description. Again then we can argue that all sociolinguistic research which follows programmatic principles (and that is pretty well all sociolinguistic research) is inherently theoretical (Jaworski, personal communication).

References

Antaki, Charles and Widdicombe, Sue (eds) (1998) *Identities in Talk*. London: Sage.
Atkinson, J. Maxwell and Heritage, John (eds) (1984) *Structures of Social Action: Studies in Conversation Analysis*. Cambridge: Cambridge University Press.
Bauman, Richard (1977) *Verbal Art as Performance*. Prospect Heights, IL: Waveland Press.
Bauman, Richard (1992) Performance. In R. Bauman (ed.) *Folklore, Cultural Performances, and Popular Entertainments*. New York and Oxford: Oxford University Press, 41–49.
Bauman, Richard (1996) Transformations of the word in the production of Mexican festival drama. In Michael Silverstein and Greg Urban (eds) *Natural Histories of Discourse*. Chicago and London: University of Chicago Press, 301–327.

Bauman, Zygmunt (1998) *Globalization: The Human Consequences*. Cambridge: Polity Press.

Bhabha, Homi (1994) *The Location of Culture*. London: Routledge.

Billig, Michael (1999) Whose terms? Whose ordinariness? Rhetoric and ideology in Conversation Analysis. *Discourse and Society* 10, 4: 543–558.

Blumer, Herbert (1969) *Symbolic Interactionism: Perspectives and Methods*. New Jersey: Prentice Hall.

Boden, Deidre and Zimmerman, Don (eds) (1991) *Talk and Social Structure: Studies in Ethnomethodology and Conversation Analysis*. Oxford: Polity Press.

Bourdieu, Pierre (1991) *Language and Symbolic Power*. London: Polity Press.

Briggs, Charles (1993) Generic versus metapragmatic dimensions of Warao narratives: Who regiments performance? In John A. Lucy (ed.) *Reflexive Language: Reported Speech and Metapragmatics*. Cambridge: Cambridge University Press, 179–212.

Brown, Penelope and Levinson, Stephen (1987) *Politeness*, 2nd edn. Cambridge: Cambridge University Press.

Cameron, Deborah (1990) Demythologizing sociolinguistics: Why language does not reflect society. In J.E. Joseph and T.J. Taylor (eds) *Ideologies of Language*. London: Routledge, 79–93.

Cameron, Deborah (1995) *Verbal Hygiene*. London: Routledge.

Carter, Bob and Sealey, Alison (2000) Language, structure and agency: What can realist social theory offer to sociolinguistics? *Journal of Sociolinguistics* 4, 1: 3–20.

Chambers, J.K. (1995) *Sociolinguistic Theory: Linguistic Variation and its Social Significance*. Oxford: Blackwell.

Coulmas, Florian (1996) Introduction. In Florian Coulmas (ed.) *The Handbook of Sociolinguistics*. Oxford: Blackwell, 1–11.

Coupland, Justine (ed.) (2000) *Small Talk*. London: Pearson Education.

Coupland, Justine, Robinson, Jeff and Coupland, Nikolas (1994) Frame negotiation in doctor–elderly patient consultations. *Discourse and Society* 5, 1: 89–124.

Coupland, Nikolas (2000) 'Other' representation. In Jef Verschueren, Jan-Ola Ostman, Jan Blommaert and Chris Bulcaen (1999) *Handbook of Pragmatics Installment 2000*. Amsterdam and Philadelphia: John Benjamins.

Coupland, Nikolas (in press a) Review of Charles Antaki and Sue Widdicombe (eds) *Identities in Talk*. London: Sage. *Journal of Sociolinguistics*.

Coupland, Nikolas (in press b) Language, context and the relational self: Retheorising dialect style in sociolinguistics. In John Rickford and Penelope Eckert (eds) *Style in Sociolinguistics*. Cambridge: Cambridge University Press.

Coupland, Nikolas (in press c) Dialect stylisation. *Language in Society* 30, 3.

Coupland, Nikolas and Jaworski, Adam (eds) (1997) *Sociolinguistics: A Reader and Coursebook*. London: Macmillan.

Coupland, Nikolas, Coupland, Justine and Giles, Howard (1991) *Language, Society and the Elderly*. Oxford and Cambridge, MA: Blackwell.

Drew, Paul and Heritage, John (eds) (1992) *Talk at Work: Interaction in Institutional Settings*. Cambridge: Cambridge University Press.

Duranti, Alessandro and Goodwin, Charles (eds) (1992) *Rethinking Context: Language as an Interactive Phenomenon*. Cambridge: Cambridge University Press.

Eckert, Penelope (2000) *Linguistic Variation as Social Practice*. Maldon, MA and Oxford: Blackwell.

Edwards, Derek and Potter, Jonathan (1992) *Discursive Psychology*. London: Sage.

Fairclough, Norman (1992) Introduction. In Norman Fairclough (ed.) *Critical Language Awareness*. London and New York: Longman.

Fairclough, Norman and Wodak, Ruth (1997) Critical discourse analysis. In Teun van Dijk (ed.) *Introduction to Discourse Analysis*. London: Sage, 258–284.

Figueroa, Esther (1994) *Sociolinguistic Metatheory*. Oxford: Pergamon.

Foucault, Michel (ed. C. Gordon) (1980) *Power/Knowledge: Selected Interviews and Other Writings 1972–1977*. Brighton: Harvester.

Garfinkel, Harold (1967) *Studies in Ethnomethodology*. Englewood Cliffs, NJ: Prentice-Hall.

Giddens, A. (1987) *Social Theory and Modern Sociology*. Cambridge: Polity Press.

Giddens, A. (1990) *The Consequences of Modernity*. Cambridge: Polity Press (in association with Basil Blackwell).

Giddens, A. (1991) *Modernity and Self-Identity: Self and Society in the Late Modern Age*. Cambridge: Polity Press (in association with Basil Blackwell).

Giddens, A. (1994) Living in a post-traditional society. In U. Beck, A. Giddens and S. Lash, *Reflexive Modernization: Politics, Tradition and Aesthetics in the Modern Social Order*. Cambridge: Polity Press, 56–109.

Giles, Howard and Powesland, Peter (1975) *Speech Style and Social Evaluation*. London: Academic Press.

Giles, Howard, Coupland, Nikolas and Coupland, Justine (eds) (1991) *Contexts of Accommodation: Developments in Applied Sociolinguistics*. Cambridge: Cambridge University Press.

Goffman, Erving (1974) *Frame Analysis: An Essay on the Organization of Experience*. New York: Harper & Row.

Goffman, Erving (1981) *Forms of Talk*. Oxford: Blackwell.

Gumperz, John J. (1982) *Discourse Strategies*. Cambridge: Cambridge University Press.

Halliday, M.A.K. (1978) *Language as Social Semiotic*. London: Edward Arnold.

Hasan, Ruqaiya (1993) Contexts for meaning. In James E. Alatis (ed.) *Language, Communication and Social Meaning*, Georgetown University Round Table on Languages and Linguistics 1992, Washington DC: Georgetown University Press, 79–104.

Henley, Nancy M. and Kramarae, Cheris (1991) Gender, power and miscommunication. In Nikolas Coupland, Howard Giles and John Wiemann (eds) *Handbook of 'Miscommunication' and Problematic Talk*. Newbury Park: Sage, 18–43.

Hudson, R.A. (1996) *Sociolinguistics* (2nd edn). Cambridge: Cambridge University Press.

Hymes, Dell (1974) *Foundations in Sociolinguistics: An Ethnographic Approach*. Philadelphia: University of Pennsylvania Press.

Hymes, Dell (2000) The emergence of sociolinguistics: A response to Samarin. *Journal of Sociolinguistics* 4, 2: 312–315.

Labov, William (1972) *Sociolinguistic Patterns*. Philadelphia: University of Pennsylvania Press.

Labov, William (1994) *Principles of Linguistic Change, Volume 1: Internal Factors*. Cambridge, MA and Oxford: Blackwell.

Layder, Derek (1994) *Understanding Social Theory*. London: Sage.

Lippi-Green, Rosina (1997) *English with an Accent: Language, Ideology and Discrimination in the United States*. London: Routledge.

Markova, I. (1982) *Paradigms, Thought and Language*. London: John Wiley.

Mead, George Herbert (1932) *Philosophy of the Present.* LaSalle, IL: Open Court.

Mead, George Herbert (1934) Mind, self and society. In C.W. Morris (ed.) *Mind, Self and Society.* Chicago: Chicago University Press.

Milroy, James and Milroy, Lesley (1996) Varieties and variation. In Florian Coulmas (ed.) *The Handbook of Sociolinguistics.* Oxford: Blackwell, 47–64.

Milroy, Lesley (1987) *Language and Social Networks,* 2nd edn. Oxford: Blackwell.

Parsons, J. Talcott (1942) Age and sex in the social structure of the United States. *American Sociological Review* 7: 604–616.

Parsons, J. Talcott (1952) *The Social System.* London: Tavistock Press.

Popper, Karl (1968) *Conjectures and Refutations: The Growth of Scientific Knowledge.* New York: Harper & Row.

Potter, Jonathan and Wetherell, Margaret (1987) *Discourse and Social Psychology.* London: Sage.

Rampton, Ben (1995) *Crossing: Language and Ethnicity Among Adolescents.* London: Longman.

Rampton, Ben (ed.) (1999) *Styling the Other.* Thematic issue of *Journal of Sociolinguistics* 3, 4.

Rickford, John (1999) The Ebonics controversy in my back yard: A sociolinguist's experiences and reflections. *Journal of Sociolinguistics* 3, 2: 267–275.

Riggins, Stephen Harold (ed.) (1997) *The Language and Politics of Exclusion: Others in Discourse.* Thousand Oaks, CA: Sage.

Romaine, Suzanne (1994) *Language in Society: An Introduction to Sociolinguistics.* Oxford: Oxford University Press.

Sacks, Harvey (1992) *Lectures on Conversation.* (Ed. Gail Jefferson, 2 vols.) Oxford and Cambridge, MA: Blackwell.

Said, Edward (1978) *Orientalism.* London: Routledge & Kegan Paul.

Samarin, William J. (2000) Sociolinguistics as I see it. *Journal of Sociolinguistics* 4, 2: 303–311.

Schegloff, Emmanuel A. (1992) In another context. In A. Duranti and C. Goodwin (eds) *Rethinking Context: Language as an Interactive Phenomenon.* Cambridge: Cambridge University Press, 191–228.

Schegloff, Emmanuel A. (1999) 'Schegloff's texts' as 'Billig's data': A critical reply. *Discourse and Society* 10, 4: 558–572.

Skutnabb-Kangas, Tove and Phillipson, Robert (eds) (1994) *Linguistic Genocide in Education.* London: Lawrence Erlbaum.

Tannen, Deborah and Wallat, Cynthia (1987) Interactive frames and knowledge schemas in interaction: Examples from a medical examination/interview. *Social Psychology Quarterly* 50, 2: 205–216. Reprinted in Adam Jaworski and Nikolas Coupland (eds) (2000) *The Discourse Reader,* 2nd edn. London: Routledge, 346–366.

Trudgill, Peter (ed.) (1978) *Sociolinguistic Patterns in British English.* London: Edward Arnold.

Turner, Bryan, S. (1996) *The Blackwell Companion to Social Theory.* Oxford: Blackwell.

Watzlawick, P., Beavin-Bavelas, J. and Jackson, D. (1967) *The Pragmatics of Human Communication.* New York: Norton.

Williams, Glyn (1992) *Sociolinguistics: A Sociological Critique.* London: Routledge.

Wodak, Ruth (1996) *Disorders of Discourse.* London: Longman.

Part

I

Language, theory and the social

1

A comparative perspective on social theoretical accounts of the language–action interrelationship
Srikant Sarangi

1   Introduction

In this chapter, my aim is to examine in a comparative mode some of the prevalent social theoretical accounts of language-as-action, and to do so against the backdrop of the social/discursive turn in linguistics. My focus is not so much on how social theorists deal with constructs such as power, knowledge, domination, deviance, etc., but rather on how they conceptualise the role of language vis-à-vis these social phenomena in their theorisation of society. I limit my discussion to three social theorists — Habermas, Foucault and Bourdieu — and their language-oriented writings. My choice of these three social theorists may appear arbitrary; it may even be controversial to label them as social theorists. Foucault is very much regarded as a historian: far from offering a new theory of social order, he focusses on deconstructing such theories. Bourdieu categorically denounces any specific intellectual labelling of himself: he calls himself a critical writer interested in social change, and offers a defence of his work against 'theoricist' readings (Calhoun *et al.* 1993). Habermas is more close to the tradition of critical theory as developed in the Frankfurt School, with his emphasis on language-based communicative interaction as foundational to the evolution of social life.

   My motivation for this choice, apart from being constrained by the scope of this chapter, is that these three social theorists explicitly engage with linguistic paradigms of Saussure, Chomsky, Austin, etc., and in their work address central (socio)linguistic concepts such as communicative competence, ideal speech situation, symbolic and indexical dimensions of language. Also, they are frequently invoked as explanatory resources in the sociolinguistic and discourse analytic literature. Foucault has been enshrined in the work of critical discourse analysis (see in particular Fairclough 1989, 1992) and so is

Bourdieu, perhaps more in the field of sociolinguistics of education and identity politics (see Erickson, Heller, Watts this volume). Habermas has contributed significantly to the discussion of universalist pragmatics, with its focus on action as linguistic activity.

Although Habermas, Foucault and Bourdieu draw upon language in their theorisation of social structure and agency, they do not actually analyse language data to show the interrelationship between micro- and macro-contexts. For instance, they do not undertake to illustrate what might constitute a competent display of communicative action sequences in real-life situations. I therefore draw upon a data setting — the psychotherapeutic clinic — in order to assess the extent to which these social-theoretical models of language-as-action can illuminate our understanding of social life (in this case, talk-in-interaction in the clinic). It also remains to be seen whether any of the social-theoretical assumptions about the role of language in social interaction can be challenged on the basis of a detailed analysis of socio-linguistic data.

In what follows I begin with a brief overview of the social/discursive turn in linguistics. This provides a backdrop against which I compare the social-theoretical accounts of language–action interrelationship. Next, I offer a detailed discussion of the three individual social-theoretical frameworks, accompanied by data extracts from a psychotherapeutic clinic. I adopt a further comparative stance in order to see which social-theoretical framework is more suited to our analysis of psychotherapeutic talk, and whether there are identifiable overlaps and contradictions when different analytic frameworks are brought to bear on a given data site.

2   The social/discursive turn in linguistics

In general terms, language stands at the intersection between social sciences (language as social activity — to include action and interaction) and natural science (language as a scientific system and therefore a separate entity out there). Historically speaking, the study of language has always been an inter-disciplinary project, and not confined to linguistics. Scholars from a range of disciplines (e.g., Bakhtin, Benveniste, Derrida, Lacan, Lévi-Strauss, Nietzsche, Volosinov, Vygotsky, Wittgenstein) have foregrounded a view of language in the development of their distinct approaches to the study of human thought and action vis-à-vis social and cultural factors. For instance, both Lévi-Strauss (1963) and Lacan (1968) share the view that 'the deep structures of human consciousness' can only be grasped by paying attention to their lin-guistic realisations. Lévi-Strauss argues in favour of how invariant linguistic rules can contribute to our understanding of 'structural relations' in the anthropological sense (for example, kinship structure). In the psychoanalytic setting, Lacan insists that the language in which dreams are reported, not the dreams themselves, should become the prime object of analysis.

Within linguistics, language has been objectified as a system (Saussure, Jakobson, Chomsky, etc.). Saussure (1966 [1916]) proposed a set of binary oppositions or dualities in the study of language (for instance, duality of individual and society; duality of langue and parole; duality of concrete and abstract; duality of identity and opposition). Contrary to what many scholars believe, Merleau-Ponty (1974) argues that Saussure was primarily concerned with the speaking subject and the inseparability of synchrony and diachrony. Craib (1998: 39) summarises Merleau-Ponty's reading of Saussure as follows:

> [Saussure's] system of differentiation is the means of generating meaning within the 'life-world' of a society and to learn a language is to learn the rules of differentiation around which structure is built. In this sense language pre-exists what can be said with it; but at this level the structure of a language only makes meaning possible — it is actualised in use, and here we are referred back to the speaking subject.

It is worth noting Saussure's views about how meaning is realisable through, and also constrained by, language structure. This relationship between pre-existent language structure and situated meaning can easily be mapped on to the relationship between social structure and social action (see section 3 below). At the interactional level, as we will see later in our illustrative data taken from a psychotherapeutic setting, everyday formulation of unfamiliar experience does impinge upon the relationship between language structure, human experience and agency. There are several overtones here which suggest why Foucault drew upon Saussure's view of the sign in his project on de-centring the human subject in favour of discourse formations (see section 4.2 below).

Much of mainstream linguistic theory has, however, flourished without a view of language as action, that is, without taking on board the mediating role of language in the shaping of individual–society relations. The development of linguistics as a descriptive science in the Chomskyan tradition is the farthest one can get in keeping language and social action apart. It also marks a disjuncture in the sense that Chomsky does not adequately acknowledge what other disciplinary studies have contributed to the study of language in its social, cultural context.[1] Although Chomsky's (1957, 1965) theorisation of language is devoid of any social praxis, we notice a paradox when he swaps his scholarly 'linguistic' hat in favour of political activism in order to analyse the ideological underpinnings of contemporary political discourse. If we were to undertake a comparative analysis of Chomsky's political writings and linguistic writings, we would probably notice striking differences at the textual level. This would support the Foucauldian thesis that language (in the sense of discourse) shapes our positions as speaking subjects. At another level, it is arguable that Chomsky's radical views in the political domain receive the currency they do because of his status as a pioneering linguist. In Bourdieu's terms, Chomsky is able to transform one form of capital into another even when the two stances and their discoursal realisations do not share a common basis. Perhaps Habermas would see such an explicit or implicit invoking of the linguist identity as undermining Chomsky's participation in the public sphere. But, as we will see, it is Chomsky's views about language structure and linguistic competence, rather than his radical political views, which attract the attention of social theorists such as Habermas and Bourdieu.

As an antithesis to Chomsky's sole focus on 'language structure', Halliday (1973, 1985) makes 'language use' his topic of study and this leads him to analyse linguistic action at the ideational, textual and interpersonal levels. While Chomsky the linguist has nothing to do with language-as-social action, Halliday insists that language cannot be studied in the social void. Against this bipolarity, we can see the pragmatic linguistic tradition, with its origin in philosophy, building a bridge across the formalist and functionalist views of language, but with little reference to social structure. Although linguistic philosophers such as Austin (1962) and Searle (1969) view language as action, the social context which mediates meaning-making is taken as unproblematic. This is in addition to the difficulty associated with taxonomising all potential speech acts in a given language (Turner 1974). As Bourdieu (1991) rightly points out, the meaning of what is said depends crucially upon the status and role the speaker of the utterance occupies in a given social milieu. It is this social milieu which remains undertheorised in the speech act model of performative action.

In the 1970s, the dominant paradigms of sociolinguistics (e.g., Labov 1972a, 1972b; Gumperz and Hymes 1972) addressed the 'social' dimension in different ways (variational distribution of linguistic parameters, competence- and rule-based ethnography of speaking, contextualisation cues and indexicality, etc. — see Coupland's introduction to this volume). In their early works, both Labov and Hymes focused on the variable relationship between society and language use, but the model of society itself does not receive critical scrutiny. In critiquing Bernstein's (1971) stratified model of elaborate codes and restricted codes, Labov (1972b), for instance, goes on to illustrate in empirical terms the logical and variable structure of Black Vernacular English. What we have here is a detailed linguistic description of an individual style rather than a social explanation of linguistic action. And this can be seen as an antithesis to the social theoretical position on the explanatory power of the deficit/deprivation hypothesis which does not consider actual instances of language use as a basis for such theorisation.

If we turn our attention to the critical linguistic tradition, and more recently its offshoot, critical discourse analysis (CDA), we notice stronger explanatory links between social practice and language use. This tradition draws heavily on social theorists such as Foucault, Bourdieu and Habermas (the last, to a much lesser extent). The social analysis (or 'structural' analysis in the Foucauldian sense) is often complemented by systematic textual analysis as a way of establishing the dynamics of discourse practice and social practice. More recently the tradition of critical discourse analysis has come under criticism of three different sorts and it may it useful to list them here:

1. Widdowson (1995, 1998, 2000), in rather strong terms, characterises this tradition as 'an exercise in interpretation' and therefore 'invalid in analysis'. According to him, 'interpretation in support of belief takes precedence over analysis in support of theory', and this begs the question as to what 'critical' is supposed to mean in 'critical discourse analysis'. Moreover, interpretation in this tradition is ideologically committed. It privileges particular meanings, and undermines alternative readings: indeed all texts get read in the same way without taking into account what intentions individual text producers might have had in their minds and how ordinary people actually read texts. Fairclough (1996) sees Widdowson's position as a reduction of discourse analysis to linguistic pragmatics and warns against 'a prediscoursal theory of the subject and of context' which assumes that subjects and contexts are constituted prior to and outside of discourse.

2. Hammersley (1996) deals extensively with the philosophical foundations underlying the notion 'critical', as it becomes increasingly fashionable for many disciplines to define their research practices in terms of 'being critical'. On the one hand, Hammersley finds CDA adopting uncritical, crude positions on key social theoretical issues — often reducing everything to a relation of domination between the oppressor and the oppressed. On the other hand, CDA appears to be too ambitious in aiming for social change, as if social change in itself is always desirable. But this ambition, according to Hammersley, leads to over-interpretation of data, that is, ideological evaluation becomes inseparable from textual analysis. This last point reinforces Widdowson's claim that CDA is ideologically committed to a specific form of interpretive practice.

3. Stubbs (1994, 1997) voices a further critique as he challenges CDA's theoretical and methodological assumptions. At a theoretical level, he invokes Frawley's (1987: 361) allegation that discourse analysts, by blowing the 'neo-empiricist, contextual trumpet', undermine the achievements of formal linguistics. This seems to be the orientation despite Halliday's (1985: 345) caution that 'the study of discourse . . . cannot properly be separated from the study of grammar that lies behind it'. We can see here the echoing of the tension Widdowson alludes to between interpretation and analysis. Context becomes equated with interpretation and text organisation as analysis. Stubbs turns this tension into a methodological issue. According to him, although critical discourse analysts

make plausible observations about text organisation, their linguistic basis is inadequate. In other words, they leap to making generalisations about social representation and change without sufficient (socio)linguistic evidence. The stronger version of this position would read: the social must be analysed linguistically.

What emerges from this critique is that the role of language in mediating social life is not at dispute. The method of linguistic analysis and the nature of claims made on the basis of such analysis remain contentious, as would be the case for other analytic frameworks (Sarangi and Roberts 1999). Also at issue is the lack of questioning of language theorisation across the social theoretical domain, even though many discourse analysts draw upon a selective set of social theorists in order to achieve explanatory credibility. This is not to say that corpus-based linguistic evidence, despite its representativeness in terms of distributional patterns, is an adequate basis for making claims about the interrelationship between social action and social structure. Against this backdrop, let me turn to the social theoretical site.

3   Interface of social structure and action from the social-theoretical perspective

Many of the long-standing debates in social theory are constituted in binary oppositions such as macro vs micro, objectivism vs subjectivism, agency vs determinism, etc. (see Coupland's introduction and Sarangi and Candlin's concluding chapter, this volume). Indeed all such oppositions can be mapped on to the overall dualism of social structure and social action. The development of social theory as a scholarly discipline over the last three centuries can be seen as a reconfiguration of the structure–action interrelationship. In more recent years, there is a noticeable shift from the primacy of social structure to that of social action, and the resultant move away from a positivistic theory of action towards a voluntaristic theory of action (Parsons 1949). For instance, while Marx's theory of Capitalism was primarily about social structure, it did allow room for social action by projecting the proletariat to revolt, only as a collective consciousness. Durkheim, among others, also viewed social structure as determining social action, as illustrated in his classic studies *On the Division of Labour in Society* (1933) and *Le Suicide* (1930). In his attempt to explain suicide rates, Durkheim summarily dismisses explanations based on individual motives, and favours the social milieu explanation.[2] His adage that 'the social must be explained socially' brings to the fore the significance of the social factor (that is, society is a reality *sui generis*) as opposed to 'individualistic positivism'. For him, the social — defined as a matter of things beyond the individual power of control — is a residual category which stands in opposition not only to the individual, but also to the biological.

The term 'social', however, takes a different meaning as far as Wright Mills (1970 [1959]) is concerned. He regards Parsons' (1951) model of society as a prototypical example of 'grand theory' which is too systematic, abstract and normative to deal with social change.[3] In claiming (1970: 9) that '[N]either the life of an individual nor the history of a society can be understood without understanding both', Wright Mills stresses that changes at the personal level are intricately linked with institutional and structural changes. It is this linkage which forms the basis of what he calls 'sociological imagination' that 'enables us to grasp history and biography and the relations between the two within society' (1970: 12). As he puts it (1970: 14): 'Perhaps the most fruitful distinction with which the sociological imagination works is between "the personal troubles of milieu" and "the public issues of social structure"'.

There are two main points in Wright Mills's formulation: (i) the social and the personal are interwoven into each other, and (ii) social changes need to be accounted for in any sociological undertaking. To an extent, Giddens (1979), as a second generation theorist, blurs the distinction between social structure and individual action as he proposes a way out of such dualisms — hence his emphasis on concepts such as 'duality' and 'structuration'. These are apt linguistic coinages to contain the dynamism between structure and action, and not a denial of such categorisation. However, as Craib (1998) points out, one problem with such integration is that we may lose sight of what each component element is.

The counterpoint to deterministic grand social theory comes from the tradition of phenomenology, and later ethnomethodology, of social action and practical reasoning (Garfinkel 1967; Goffman 1967; Schutz 1971a, 1971b). The focus here is not so much on social structure and change, but on the social order and its situated accomplishment in interactional settings, typified in Goffman's call for the study of the interaction order on its own merit. Schutz talks (1971b: 29) about our 'lived experiences' in the 'Here and Now of a concrete We-relation' as he calls (1971a: 207) for the recognition of multiple 'orders of realities, each with its own special and separate style of existence'. The 'natural attitude' of the participants (that is, members' method) is thus preferred to the 'theoretical attitude' in the study of human action in the social world.

4   The language dimension in/of social theory: Habermas, Foucault and Bourdieu

One aspect of social theory, or any theory for that matter, is its reliance on language and metalanguage. Often the metalanguage stands for the theoretical insights, although this might amount to using rough conceptual means for capturing the complex social reality. In a sense, the Sapir–Whorf hypothesis that language shapes thought also applies to social theorists dealing with the social order. In following the Foucauldian footsteps, one could argue that the language of social analysis could potentially impose a social order. Indeed what marks Foucault as a post-structuralist is that he shows how the human sciences are constituted in the figurative modes of language. In this respect, the language of one social theory vs another may be a candidate for socio-linguistic and discourse analytic investigation — a topic which falls outside the remit of my discussion here. Instead, in what follows I make an attempt to reassess two interrelated questions concerning the similarities and differences between three social theorists — Foucault, Bourdieu and Habermas — in relation to:

(i)   how language is conceptualised in their work (as a system of signs, as communicative and strategic action, as an instrument of power, etc.) and what models are borrowed from linguistics (for example, Foucault's reliance on Saussure).

(ii)   how language is positioned vis-à-vis other 'social' entities such as knowledge, truth, the human subject, social processes and strategies of domination; and how language is seen as the link between social structure and social action/identity.

It is important to recognise that a search for a unified theory of language in the work of each social theorist is as problematic as an attempt to juxtapose one theorist against another. On the other hand, only a comparative analysis of their accounts of language-as-action (broadly taken to include discourse) can enable us to assess their applicability to interactional sociolinguistics. In my attempt to tease out social structure from social action (in the social-theoretical sense), I select the data site of a psychotherapeutic clinic, with an analytic focus on presentation of self and personal experience. It is worth noting that the psychoanalytic/psychotherapeutic setting cuts across the social theoretical and sociolinguistic divide. As a site it has received due attention from Habermas (1972) and from Labov and Fanshel (1977). For Habermas, both psychoanalysts and social theorists are involved in a form of hermeneutic interpretation of meaning in social interaction and use such an interpretive stance as a means for bringing about social change. As Giddens (1985: 126) puts it: 'Psychoanalytic therapy aims to change behaviour, by the very process of transmuting what happens to the individual into what the individual makes happen'. Habermas argues for social theory to occupy a similar position for accomplishing social change. With regard to Labov and Fanshel, the psychotherapeutic clinic is an inference-rich setting, as it requires the therapist to use discourse expansion rules while looking for coherence in patients' narratives. They (1977: 138) go on to claim that the psychotherapist must have the ability 'to act as an arbiter of social norms — as an informal sociologist' in order to evaluate patients' feelings and experiences.

4.1   Habermas: language as communicative action

Habermas is primarily concerned with the theorisation of the language–action relationship, and the extent to which communication (as symbolic interaction) is central to the evolution of society. Habermas's initial preoccupation has been with the theory of knowledge in the tradition of the Frankfurt School, but the publication of *Theory of Communicative Action* in two volumes (1987, parts of which were first published in *Inquiry* (1970a and 1970b)) marks his linguistic turn. This is a shift from a theory of knowledge to a theory of language as the basis for critical social theory. Here he proposes a theory of communicative action as a form of coordinated social interaction oriented toward understanding (*Verständigung*) and consensus (*Einveständnis*).

Habermas builds on Weber's (1947 [1922]) model of action which emphasises the notion of the 'acting individual' and 'explanatory understanding' in order to account for economic rationality and rule-oriented rationality (to include social action as rule-following in both constitutive and regulative terms). By 'social action', Weber means action which takes account of the behaviour of others and is thereby oriented in its course.[4] The notion of a rational actor/agent is thus central to Weber's thinking: social action involves subjective meaning (what the actor meant by it) and intersubjective meaning (what the action meant). Weber proposes four 'ideal' types of action, with the proviso that most everyday actions are of mixed type:

a)   instrumental rational action (*zweckrational*; economic type of rationality, caught up in calculations and exchange values)
b)   value-rational action (*wertrational*; cost/benefit analysis is sacrificed when the goal being pursued is seen as all important)
c)   traditional action (norm-bound . . . 'simply a dull reaction to accustomed stimuli')
d)   affective action (prompted by unreflective desire).

Habermas's framework idealises the dimensions of rationality and intentionality as forms of human action. In other words, he not only differentiates between action types, but also between action and communication in relation to understanding. He sees language as communication (to include distorted communication) and strategic rationality as parasitic on communicative rationality. For him, communicative action (as distinct from strategic and instrumental action) is paramount to the 'lifeworld' and its reproduction.[5]

In more specific terms, Habermas is critical of Chomsky's (1955, 1965) theory of linguistic competence. According to him, Chomskyan theory of language is inadequate to account for communication and understanding as it is based on three implicit assumptions: monologism, a priorism, and elementarism (1970b: 360). By comparison, he suggests (1970a: 205) that the requirements of a theory of communicative competence are to be found in 'an analysis not of the linguistic competence of a native speaker, but of systematic distortion of communication of the kind postulated by psycho-analytic theory'. Communicative competence, according to Habermas, must account for distorted communication such as psychoanalysis where language expressions deviate from normal linguistic rules, and are marked with repetitions and discrepancies between the various levels of performance. Systematically distorted communication between a psychoanalyst and a patient is premised on the view that apparently incoherent stretches of talk by the patient can be understood as meaningful in terms 'scenic understanding': '"Scenic understanding' is therefore based on the discovery that the patient behaves in the same way in his symptomatic scenes as he does in certain transference situations: such understanding aims at the reconstruction, confirmed by the patient in an act of self-reflection, of the original scene' (1970a: 208). Habermas (1970a: 217) sums up his position as follows:

> The common semantic analysis of incomprehensible utterances, which leads to hermeneutic understanding, makes use of the non-analysed communicative competence of a native speaker. On the other hand, the special type of semantic analysis which deals with manifestations of a systematically distorted communication and affords an explanatory understanding, presupposes a theory of communicative competence.

Whereas for Chomsky the ideal native speaker is central to his theory of linguistic competence, for Habermas, 'communicative competence means the mastery of an ideal speech situation' (1970b: 367) involving the validity-claims of meaningfulness, truth, justification and sincerity. This is recast by McCarthy (1973: xiii) as 'the relation between communicative action or interaction and discourse, the consensus theory of truth, and the supposition of the ideal speech situation'. The ideal native speaker thus gives way to the ideal speech situation.

It is worth pointing out the different ways in which Habermas and Hymes conceive of the notion of 'communicative competence'. According to Habermas (1970b: 374):

> Communicative competence should be related to a system of rules generating an ideal speech situation, not regarding linguistic codes which link language and universal pragmatics with actual role systems. Dell Hymes, among others, makes use of the term 'communicative competence' in a socio-linguistically limited sense.

The 'limited sense' in Habermas's formulation alludes to Hymes's (1964) model of ethnography of speaking, which deals with actual speech events rather than an ideal speech situation and truth/validity claims. On a closer look, we know that Hymes's model is far from being limited: Hymes does take into account various 'components of communicative events', which include role-relations. Both Hymes and Habermas regard communicative competence to be more than an extension of linguistic competence to social situations, but they differ at the level of abstraction and theorising. Habermas's universal pragmatics builds on speech act pragmatics developed by Austin (1962): the notion of performatives as verbal predicates that bring about social action through utterances. In this tradition language is conceived of as action, and by implication the speech act is the unit of linguistic analysis. For Habermas, the notion of 'performative utterance' remains a basic unit for analysing communicative action, although there are insuperable problems with such atomistic analysis especially in interactional contexts. This is where one can easily see the utility of Hymes's model of ethnography of speaking which is not bounded by codes alone. It is however interesting to note that Habermas is able to apply the notion of communicative competence to the domain of 'systematically distorted communication'.

Let us now consider Habermas's notion of communicative competence in order to account for the interactional dynamics in a psychotherapeutic clinic. A crucial marker which makes such a clinic a unique communication setting is the occurrence of 'self-reflection' by the patient as s/he attempts to communicate as well as understand his/her experiences — a form of 'explanatory understanding' in the Weberian and Habermassian sense. 'Self-reflection' as I am using the term here is different from Goffman's (1981) notion of 'self talk'. For Goffman, self-talk is a form of situational impropriety, especially in the public domain. It is 'situational in character, not merely situated' (1981: 85): 'To talk to oneself is to generate a full complement of two communication roles — speaker and hearer — without a full complement of role-performers, and which of the two roles — speaker or hearer — is the one without its own real performer is not the first issue' (1981: 80). Habermas draws on Freudian and Nietzschean doctrines of psychoanalysis where 'self reflection is no longer the act of an absolute ego but takes place under the conditions of communication between physician and patient forced into being by pathology...the physician's Socratic questioning can aid a sick person's self-reflection only under pathological compulsion and the corresponding interest in abolishing this compulsion' (Habermas 1972: 287). Self-reflection, in this sense, is a context-specific, goal-driven speech activity.

In the psychotherapeutic setting that I am concerned with here, language, in its self-reflective mode, is not only the resource for (inter)action; it is also the topic of conversation. It involves the patient and the doctor formulating through words the experience of pain, while at the same time being reflective about the limits of everyday language and social interaction in the normative sense. It is not a simple matter of giving pain a verbal outlet; it is through the use of words that pain becomes realisable and thus understandable. As we will see, language has an externalising function in therapeutic settings. For a diagnosis to be made, verbal expressions have to be taken on board. It would lead us to see where social theoretical accounts of language as action may be lacking, and the extent to which the Habermassian project on communication and understanding (including self-understanding through self-reflective talk) may be a useful starting point.

The patient (male, in his early thirties), a media professional, has been diagnosed as having a genetic disorder which results in blurred vision, and as with many genetic conditions, there is no cure for this.[6] It becomes a case of coping — or what the doctor refers to as the patient having to make 'emotional adjustments'. My first point of analysis is how this therapeutic activity is constituted in a view of language as (inter)action. The following extract is taken from the very beginning of the encounter:[7]

Example 1

01   P: [yeah I didn't know] to to be honest ((under slight laughter)) I wasn't sure really sure why (.5) I was seen today anyway to be [perfectly] honest

02   D: [no] right (.5) I thought (.) there'd be some idea that you might want to talk to someone (.) a bit more open really

03   P: =well I suppose in a sense (.) I did when I first requested but I think the ehm (1.5) initially I wanted to speak to somebody I didn't know

04   D: yeah (.)

05   P: because (.) ehm it's very difficult to (.5) express your feelings with people you know because you know you gonna hurt them

06   D: you mean your family or [someone]

07   P: [oh fa]mily or friends whatever [you know]

08   D: [yes] indeed (.)

09   P: so you tend to bottle things up (.) you know I [think] that you- it's very

10   D: [yeah]

11   P: I don't know (.) people keep and the other thing people you talk to seem to gh- (.5) seem to ask you the same- you know are you angry and I go no:::: (.) I'm frustrated that's a form of anger but I'm not (.5) I'm not blaming anyone I'm not saying why me why not somebody else I'd rather it was (.5) I mean if that is it's a genetic thing I'd rather it'd happen to me than to either of my brothers but

As we can see, both D and P are jointly framing the situation they are in, and they do so by bracketing off other everyday conversational activities. As far as P is concerned, the act of 'expressing feelings with people you know' is a dispreferred option because 'you gonna hurt them' (turn 5). This consideration then results in a situation where 'you tend to bottle things up' (turn 9) in order to avoid frustrations and blame attributions. The only alternative now is to ask for counselling which does not involve 'giving off' impressions. The addressee needs to be 'someone you don't know' for the bottled up feelings to be worded (turns 3 and 5). This is the premise on which therapeutic conversation is going be based, and already we can see how this positioning of the participants early on in the interaction deviates from what is regarded (by analysts and participants) as archetypes of conversation between friends and equals with shared communicative practices. In turn 11, P dramatises what an everyday episode typically looks like, where friends and relatives might prematurely offer advice and show pity, and thus foil the therapeutic activity (Turner 1972; Jefferson and Lee 1981).

Against the idealised situation of everyday conversational talk, then, therapeutic talk-in-interaction becomes recognisable as 'distorted', as talk between strangers, but this is a mutually agreed scenario as far as the participants are concerned. Such an explicit framing of the speech event, with a distinctive distribution of role-relationship and participation-structure, becomes a necessary means to achieve 'explanatory understanding' and emotional intersubjectivity. The interaction develops as follows:

Example 2

01 P: I think I think that ehm (.5) eh wha- why I did ask ask for well why I did ask for counselling or- originally was because I thought well (.5) .hhhh if I could talk to somebody who is paid to listen to me for half an [hour just rabbiting on basically ((slight laugh)) you know]

02 D: [((laughing)) he he he he he he he he]

03 P: maybe it will ehm (.)

04 D: .hhh okay

05 P: =maybe it will help will help clear (.) you know (.) [make] things a bit more

06 D: [yeah]

07 P: clear to myself sort of thing (.) that was why I was- that was my original [thinking]

08 D: [so instead] of someone just being there because I don't know (.) they're a friend or something if someone (.) I don't know if someone paid to listen [to you]

09 P: [well I don't mean] paid as something that you know I was- you know what I was trying to say was you know that (.) I can just rabit on to somebody

10 D: yea:::h

11 P: ehm(.)

12 D: there have been [^^^^^^^^^ ((laughing)) he he] heh he he he [he he]

13 P: [about about myself basically yes] [you know] (.5) although (.) 'cause one- the worst thing is I I- I- don't know whether I'm just going through what other people go through as well is that you don't (.5) you don't want to turn to talk feeling this (.) get (.) so people think you're feeling sorry for yourself you know

14 D: =okay so it's (.) it's how much of the stage can you take in any (.) conversation with a friend and [always steal] the show

15 P: [that's right]

As far as P is concerned, the therapeutic interaction creates the space for him to produce self-reflection, which is characterised as 'rabbiting', as talking to 'somebody who is paid to listen'. The expression 'paid to listen' is interesting in this context, apart from the fact that this is an allusion to the consumerist model of health and social care. By positioning the co-participant as one who is 'paid to listen', P legitimises the activity as one of self-reflection, and so therapeutic in itself. In other words, self-reflection will help clear things, leading to self-understanding and as a means to achieving emotional adjustment (turn 7). The act of self-reflection, however, is premised upon the presence of an addressee, who is 'paid to listen'. It has to be a ratified listener, whose co-presence is professionally legitimated. The professional listener is seen as someone who is capable of not only making sense of P's private experience, but she is one who may be able to find a pattern in P's condition that aligns with other people's experience in similar situations (turn 13). Note also D's formulation in turn 14 which juxtaposes everyday conversation with therapeutic conversation in terms of 'how much of the stage can you take in any conversation'. D draws specific attention to the dramaturgy metaphor: the extent to which the patient can take centre stage and 'steal the show' instead of becoming an object of pity or target of questions (see example 1, turn 11). Thus, self-reflective talk goes beyond front-stage impression management, and can lead to 'explanatory understanding'. In allowing for self-reflection, the therapeutic setting puts P at the centre of the stage: he is the speaking subject, with D occupying the role of an involved listener. By contrast, in the conversational setting, friends and family members, unlike the professional doctor, are unable to occupy differentiated receiver roles, thus preventing the outlet for self-reflection.

Here we may invoke Habermas's notions of 'ideal speech situation' and 'communicative competence'. In both examples 1 and 2, P displays his communicative competence in differentiating between this situation of self-reflection and that of the everyday conversational setting involving friends and relatives where 'explanatory understanding' is not prioritised. P, unlike his friends and relatives, can be seen as displaying communicative competence in this therapeutic setting only if we apply a different set of criteria with regard to what constitutes the goal of therapy. The notion of an ideal speech situation is implicit here, as is a distinction between communicative and strategic aspects of language use. The therapeutic setting is not only distinct from everyday conversations, but it is also different from other mainstream medical encounters (Sarangi 2000). Unlike most medical encounters, the occurrence of self-reflection, which comprises self-assessment by the patient in a diagnostic mode, is a characteristic feature of the therapeutic talk. A successful therapeutic outcome is reliant upon what a patient chooses to include in self-reflection. We can see this in the next extract:

Example 3

```
01 P:  as it happens today you called [you called me up on quite] quite a good day
02 D:  [^^^^^^ ^^^^^^ ^^^^^^]
03 P:  and I'm not feeling too bad to be ((laughing)) perfectly [honest with]
04 D:  [oh:::::] well that's not so good as far as I'm concerned
05 P:  =I know it [probably isn't I was just thinking myself] and I said it
```

06 D: [and I'm I will](.) maybe:::::::::: you know (.) you're eager to (1.0) to be clear about the
        bit of you that is coping you know maybe that's an important (.) part of today [to tell me]
        and therefore as you say (.) in verbalising it to me::: (.)
07 P: [possibly yeah]
08 D: clarifying it for yourself
09 P: I think so
10 D: =that you've come quite a long way
11 P: I think so in a sense (.) for me it's just a sort of (1.5) >>it's like an ego boost for me to tell
        you what I have done and haven't done
12 D: =yeah (.5)
13 P: in a sense it's not an ego boost as such but at least by m- by me (.) talking about it
14 D: yeah
15 P: =it sort of brings it back on myself
16 D: =yeah
17 P: =what I've had to go through and what I h- have coped with and
18 D: =yeah and that's good for you
19 P: =you know it's [all sorts of things]
20 D: [what are the days] then from what you said where either you get very depressed or
        very anxious

Against the criteria of successful counselling/therapy activity, what may
be a 'good day' for the patient can potentially be a 'bad day' for the doctor.
The patient needs to talk out when s/he is most depressed, and that would
position the doctor to bring things back on the patient. Self-reflection can
thus be optimised for the benefit of the patient. Language in the therapeutic
context then becomes a means for communication, with diagnostic possibilities, as well as a prompt for self-understanding. Rather than communication
and understanding remaining separate, we see here a convergence of perspectives. The patient has to communicate his feelings and emotions to the
therapist, who might then be able to offer assistance, and this in turn might
help the patient to articulate his feelings more accurately, leading to explanatory understanding. In other words, self-reflection has to be elicited and be
heard as other-directed, unlike Goffman's (1981) notion of self-talk as discussed earlier. As we can see, in turn 6, D reformulates P's concerns in more
specific terms: 'to be clear about that bit of you that is coping'. Notice also
D's choice of terms: 'verbalising', which may mean that P's experience needs
to be worded and thus made meaningful. Verbalisation is a more active
process in the constitution of the very experience with the aim of 'clarifying
it for yourself' (turn 8). For P, it can serve as an 'ego boost' by concentrating
on positive achievements in a reflective mode.

In my analysis so far I have implicitly drawn upon Goffman's (1981)
participant framework in relation to how the therapist and patient define the
frames of interaction and manage footing shifts. We notice that much of the
frame negotiation and footing shift is accomplished at an explicit level, thus
alerting us to the role of language-as-action in relation to understanding. An
appeal to Habermas — especially the idea that explanatory understanding is

central to communicative competence — allows for analysing further the institutional nature of therapeutic interaction. It is difficult to tease out the various levels of action that Habermas talks about, including the distinction between communicative action and strategic action and the primacy of the communicative function of language over the strategic use of language.[8] For our purposes, the therapist and the patient here are engaged in both communicative and strategic interaction. Rather than Habermas's concepts explaining sociolinguistic interaction, it seems that sociolinguistic data analysis makes it possible to point out what Habermas might be getting at through his theorisation of language-as-action vis-à-vis ideal/distorted communication.

Let me now briefly turn to the two other social theoretical positions — of Foucault and Bourdieu — on the role of language in communication and social action, once again in relation to psychotherapeutic talk.

4.2   Foucault: the 'being of language'

My discussion here will be limited to two of Foucault's early publications — *The Order of Things* (1970) and *The Archaeology of Knowledge* (1972), both of which deal explicitly with his concerns about language. Foucault's interest in language is a consequence of his discontent with the philosophical preoccupation with the centrality of 'the subject' in relation to truth and knowledge claims. In his project, following the lead from Nietzsche's 'prisonhouse of language' which removed the human agent from the centre of thought, 'the subject' is displaced in preference to what he (1970: 42) called the 'being of language' in Renaissance thought. This marks the transformation of language from its representative function to meaning and signification.

Foucault's perspective on language is historical, or in his words, genealogical, as he charts the different conceptualisations of language since the classical period. According to him, language 'thickened' and took on a 'peculiar heaviness' in the Renaissance period — away from the transparency of representation which characterised the classical age. In sum, language becomes a constraint as well as an object in Foucauldian analysis. In *The Order of Things*, he raises the following questions (1970: 306):

> What is language? What is a sign? What is unspoken in the world, in our gestures, in the whole enigmatic heraldry of our behaviour, our dreams, our sicknesses — does all that speak, and if so in what language and in obedience to what grammar? Is everything significant, and, if not, what is, and for whom, and in accordance with what rules? What relation is there between language and being, and is it really to being that language is always addressed — at least, language that speaks truly?

Foucault takes a broad view of language, which includes signs, gestures, etc., and he keeps language separate from speaking (see, for example, his formulation 'language that speaks'). His view of language-as-action is perhaps best summed up in what he calls the 'theory of the verb' (1970: 92–93):

> The proposition is to language what representation is to thought, at once its most general and most elementary form . . . In the proposition, all the functions of language are led back to the three elements that alone are indispensable to the formation of a proposition: the subject, the predicate, and the link between them . . . The verb is the indispensable condition for all discourse; and wherever it does not exist, at least by implication, it is not possible to say that there is language . . . The verb must therefore be treated as a composite entity, at the same time a word among other words, subjected to the same rules of case and agreement as other words, and yet set apart from all other words, in a region which is not that of the spoken, but rather that from which one speaks. It is on the fringe of discourse, at the connection between what is said and what is saying itself, exactly at that point where signs are in the process of becoming language.

> The entire species of the verb may be reduced to the single verb that signifies *to be* . . . The entire essence of language is concentrated in that singular word . . . Language is, wholly and entirely, *discourse*; and it is so by virtue of this singular power of a word to leap across the system of signs towards the being of that which is signified. (1970: 94)

For Foucault, the essential function of the verb — *to be* — is that it affirms. He gives the example of someone yelling or making a noise in the wilderness. As he puts it (1970: 92), 'it is in fact the proposition that detaches the vocal sign from its immediate expressive values and establishes its supreme linguistic possibility'.[9] Discourse, not expression, becomes the essence of language.

Let us now return to our data site to see how Foucault's notion of 'being of language' and the displacement of the knowing subject can be extended to what the doctor and the patient do in psychotherapeutic interaction.

Example 4

01 D: =I think to to a certain extent yo- you can (.) you ehm (.) you can get to a stage where (.5) you can (.5) you find it easier to (.) articulate your own feelings
02 P: yeah (.)
03 D: at the same time you're you're only beginning to understand those feelings
04 P: =yes I hear what you're saying
05 D: =if you see that does that make sense
06 P: =yeah it does indeed (.) you do find that as you put words to them (.) that the words in themselves clarify the emotions and clarify the meanings and you go on to refine it further is that
07 D: =I think so to a certain extent (.)

As we have already seen in the previous examples, self-reflection creates the interactional space for formulating unfamiliar feelings and emotions. Here our attention is drawn to the role of language in one's articulation of feelings and in one's understanding of the meanings of such feelings. Words are stripped of their representational function; they constitute the feelings and emotions, and clarify their meanings. A shared understanding of the language of feeling, it seems, is central to the therapeutic relationship and outcome. Language here is not only the means of expression; it can potentially become the experience itself. As Schutz (1974: 69–70) points out: 'It is misleading to say that experiences have meaning . . . Rather, those experiences are meaningful which are grasped reflectively. The meaning is the way in which Ego regards experience'.

Categorisation of experience is also a professional concern, as can be seen in the next extract. Professionals often impose categories and so define the pathological status of the patient needing intervention. What we have seen as 'explanatory understanding', in the Habermassian sense, can give way to the professional knowledge/power dynamics in Foucault's terms.

Example 5

01 D: but you and I are talking about pain too aren't we (.) [we're] talking about a different (.) [pain]
02 P: [a-] [a diff]erent type of pain not physical pain but mental pain
03 D: yeah an- and emotional pain that's in your heart [as] well as in your head
04 P: [yeah] =oh yeah [definitely]
05 D: [it's in] it's the whole of you (.) [it's you you your] ache
06 P: [oh I think so yeah] =yeah basically yeah
07 D: =you know your body cried
08 P: yeah definite (.) oh yeah I think very much so (.) I think it's
09 D: =you know you might not have wept tears but your body has ached [^^ ^^^^ ^^^^^^]
10 P: [oh yes yeah] and you get eh (.) obvious thing- an obvious (.) sort of (.) feelings of stress
11 D: =yeah and you need to let that sort of thing come out a little bit of course I mean I (.) I've resisted making any sort of ((slight laugh)) prescriptions [today but]
12 P: [((laughing))] (.5)
13 D: y::: you know you need to adapt (1.0) and let it out a bit you you (cope) (.) intellectually and socially and you're getting your mind round this which is in (.) which in my language is a very big thing to be able to get [your mind] round it
14 P: [yeah]
15 D: and be able to think about it (.5)
16 P: .hhhh I think (it mostly) is different matter that [that could not]
17 D: [I think] it is actually it is (.)
18 P: I think (.) intellectually I think I've I've (1.0) coped (.) quite well (.5) but ehm (.)
19 D: there's a bit of a lag maybe [in that]
20 P: [possibly] yeah (.) I think emotionally I'm [still not] (.) not quite
21 D: =no it will catch up [(.) it will catch up]
22 P: [there (.) but eh]
23 D: so just a bit of a lag

24 P: I think so
25 D: as you're processing it because (.) if you got words then you are processing it and (.5) you know the very fact that you and I can
26 P: [as I said to you before the fact that I] can talk about it
27 D: [acknowledge that it's pain] =yeah
28 P: =say well (.) I am in pain (.) [constant] pain you know
29 D: [yeah] =yes are
30 P: eh (.5) well it's something you just don't say (.) ((laughing))

Here we have an example of how one needs to draw upon the existing language resources in one's attempt to articulate pain. P needs to be creative in bringing this pain to the surface level, both for him to understand it and also to communicate it to D. Together they are able to draw distinctions between physical pain and mental pain (turns 1 and 2; turns 25–27). Expressions such as 'your body cried' (turn 7), 'getting your mind round this' (turn 13), etc., may seen psychoanalytic jargon, but it seems as if P is quite comfortable with such metaphorical formulations, especially when everyday language is found lacking to express such emotions. We notice that P draws a sharp distinction between 'intellectual coping' and 'emotional coping' (turns 18 and 20), and to a certain extent the interaction is now turning into a language game, as both participants foreground a notion of 'being of language'. The interaction continues as follows.

Example 6

01 P: yeah it was good I kept sort of thinking (if I am aren't going off) to be honest ((laughing)) he he he
02 D: =yeah okay
03 P: =yeah because I mean as I say you don't (.) you don't (.5) it's (1.0) [^^^] you're gonna have things going through you through your mind think things through (.5) sometimes it's only when you when you speak (.5)
04 D: yeah
05 P: =that they come back home to you
06 D: exactly and maybe we used some slightly different words and some different concepts today that have given it a different shape
07 P: =well the other thing is I've I probably used words to you that I wouldn't use to (.5) other people anyway
08 D: yeah (.)
09 P: you know [but] (.) so no it's been useful

In turns 3–5, P draws our attention to how the spoken word makes it possible to understand inner feelings — to think things through (see Schutz above on making experience meaningful through reflection). Both D and P collude in the specialist use of vocabulary as a means of achieving this understanding. It is this self-reflective, specialist talk, according to P, which makes the therapeutic encounter stand out from talking to other people (see our earlier discussion of examples 1 and 2). It suggests that words become more context-dependent, and in this respect, the centrality of speaking (speech as both communication and understanding) in therapeutic interaction becomes quite evident.

In some ways, Foucault's interest is in the language–thought (or language–cognition) relationship. In *The Order of Things*, Foucault discusses the problematic relationship between words and things. According to him, 'we are already, before the very least of our words, governed and paralysed by language'. (1970: 298) This is often referred to as 'the linguistic paralysis of thought'. Echoing the Sapir–Whorf hypothesis, Foucault goes on to claim that language constitutes our categories of thought (as in categorisation of different kinds of pain above), and therefore to question language can amount to questioning thought itself. This position is what he later designates as 'episteme' or the 'archaeological' level of discourse.

We can summarise this section by identifying three different, but inter-related, stages in Foucault's linguistic awareness. The first phase draws on the Saussurean tradition of semiological structuralism based on the notion of 'sign' as an abstract and indiscrete entity. This allows Foucault to shift focus away from the human agent as the bearer of action-events to human subjects as an object of linguistic events. The speech acts performed by individuals are dependent on what is allowable within a given semiotic structure of language.[10] This amounts to prioritising the system of signs over the meaningful acts of the subject. As Honneth (1991: 124) points out, the 'linguistic order is not, however, the product of the meaning-bestowing acts of subjects; rather, it is the product of an arbitrary arrangement of linguistic elements'.

At the second stage, Foucault seems to be moving further away from this view with his notion of 'statement' as central to his conceptualisation of language as a system (see *The Archaeology of Knowledge*). Minimally, he defines statements as an 'existence function of signs' — almost moving from the realm of langue to parole. According to Foucault (1972: 82), 'a graph, a growth curve, an age pyramid, a distribution cloud are all statements'. The priority of the system of signs over the meaningful acts of the subject (and intentionality) is now reconfigured:

> If a proposition, a sentence, a group of signs can be called 'statement', it is not therefore because, one day, someone happened to speak them or put them into some concrete form of writing; it is because the position of the subject can be assigned. To describe a formulation qua statement does not consist in analysing the relations between the author and what he says . . . but in determining what position can and must be occupied by any individual if he is to be the subject of it. (1972: 95–96)

Foucault is drawing our attention here to how social rules permit certain statements to be made, and to be identified as true/false. As he sees it, statements are not produced by speakers; in fact statements determine the role that a speaker must assume in making use of a statement.

The final phase has to do with the notion of discourse which goes beyond the cumulative effect of statements, as constituted in discursive formations. Foucault defines *discourse* as 'the group of statements that belong to a single system of formation' alongside the notion of *discursive formation*, which is 'the principle of dispersion and redistribution, not of formulations, not of sentences, not of propositions, but of statements' (1972: 107–8). He adds:

> Of course discourses are composed of signs; but what they do is more than use these signs to designate things. It is this *more* that renders them irreducible to the language (langue) and to speech. It is this 'more' that we must reveal and describe. (1972: 49)

Foucault however acknowledges that he has used the term discourse to mean different things:

> [I]n the most general, and vaguest way, it denoted a group of verbal performances; and by discourse, then, I meant that which was produced (perhaps all that was produced) by the groups of signs. But I also meant a group of acts of formulation, a series of sentences or propositions. Lastly — and it is this meaning that was finally used (together with the first, which served in a provisional capacity) — discourse is constituted by a group of sequences of signs, in so far as they are statements, that is, in so far as they can be assigned particular modalities of existence. (1972: 107)

It is in the last sense that we can talk about clinical discourse, psychiatric discourse, educational discourse, economic discourse, etc. Foucault's interest in the interrelationship between language, knowledge and power leads him to characterise discourse not so much in its representative or communicative functions, but in its function as a means for controlling others', and inevitably one's own, actions. This is linked to his views about how various disciplines (such as medicine, psychiatry, criminology) develop mechanisms of social control through their use of categorisation and classification systems primarily in the medium of language. According to Foucault (1972: 32), 'mental illness was constituted by all that was said in all the statements that named it, divided it up, described it, explained it, traced its developments, indicated its various correlations, judged it, and possibly gave it speech by articulating, in its name, discourses that were taken as its own'. In doctor–patient encounters, for instance, this would mean that doctors will tend to categorise patients' experiences by drawing upon their expertise on how to see 'things' while patients struggle to give expression to their feelings and experiences through the vehicle of 'words'. In the psychotherapeutic setting, however, the patient takes on an active role in the categorisation of feelings and experiences.

4.3   Bourdieu: the economics of linguistic exchange

In moving from Foucault to Bourdieu, a connection can be made with regard to the notion of discourse as discussed above and by linking it to the politics of authority and identity in institutional/professional settings. For Bourdieu, as with Foucault, discourse is endowed with symbolic power, and over time becomes a means of legitimation and domination. The current shift in the field of education from teacher-led learning towards self-learning may serve as an example. Such a shift no doubt brings about a reconfiguration of teacher–learner role-relations, but it still allows for a sustenance of the existing power asymmetry, although now manifest differently at the discoursal level. What is interesting though is the fact that the educational discourse couched in self-learning is gradually colonising other professional domains, including the field of medicine, and for our purposes, the psychotherapeutic clinic.

From early on, Bourdieu (1976: 645) has taken a well-defined stance on linguistics as a discipline:

> It may be wondered what business a sociologist has to be meddling nowadays with language and linguistics. The fact is that sociology cannot free itself from all the more or less subtle forms of domination which linguistics and its concepts still exert over the social sciences, except by taking linguistics as the object of a sort of genealogy, both internal and external.

The development of a genealogy of language study, according to Bourdieu, is essential if we are to account for 'the social conditions of possibility': 'the expressive intent, the way of actualising it, and the conditions of its actualisation are indissociable' (1976: 647). He goes on to add, 'What speaks is not the utterance, the language, but the whole person (this is what those who look for the "illocutionary force" of language in language forget' (1976: 653). Although Bourdieu endorses the Austin/Searle model of performative action, he stresses that his interest is not just in understanding utterances but in the social conditions of production (and implicitly, reception) of utterances.

It is not surprising that Bourdieu is critical of Chomsky's focus on linguistic competence as well as the early work on communicative competence, Habermas included, which fails to take on board 'the social space of production of discourse'. He hurls a similar attack at interactionist models: 'To forestall any "interactionist" reduction, it must be emphasised that speakers bring all their properties into an interaction, and that their position in the social structure (or in a specialised field) is what defines their position in the interaction' (1976: 664). This provides a transition to Bourdieu's economic theory of language (and hence the economic analogies such as capital, field, market, interest, profit, etc.).

In *Language and Symbolic Power* (1991), Bourdieu develops a model of praxis whereby language is conceptualised, not as an object of analysis or 'logos' as in the structural linguistic tradition, but as an instrument of power and of action. Linguistic utterances seem to have values in a specified market, and hence linguistic exchange can be conceptualised in parallel with economic exchange systems — cf. the economism of Weber (1947 [1922]). For Bourdieu, utterances (and for that matter, words, languages, discourses) do not have intrinsic status of their own; they derive power from the legitimation and authority with which they are backed. He sees every linguistic exchange as having the potentiality of an act of power: linguistic relations, by definition, are always relations of symbolic power (cf. Foucault's mapping of power on to the relational plane). According to Bourdieu, 'authority comes to language from the outside' (Bourdieu and Wacquant 1992: 147). This makes it difficult to accept the illusion of 'linguistic communism', with everyone having equal access to communicative competence in the Habermassian sense. Bourdieu's economic model thus goes beyond the communicational models in accounting for socio-cultural effects of linguistic action.

Bourdieu also makes a connection between social structure and action. In his terms, social structure and social action can be mapped on to 'field' and 'habitus'. Habitus has a linguistic manifestation, and its meaning potential is tied up to a given field of practice. His view of social agents as products of history allows him to overcome the shortcomings of the 'detemporalised conception of action that informs both structural and rational-choice views of action'. In other words, action is constituted in practice, rather than just being a product of history. As Bourdieu puts it, 'structures produce habitus, which determines practices, which reproduce structures' (Bourdieu and Wacquant 1992: 135). By extension, interactional and structural analysis must go hand-in-hand in order to avoid what he calls 'the occasionalist fallacy' (Bourdieu and Wacquant 1992: 144).

Although Bourdieu's theory of language is predominantly about class relations and the role of education in sustaining social stratification, his notions of habitus, capital and symbolic power — as constituted in language — are pertinent to the psychotherapeutic setting. Self-reflection, as we have been discussing so far, can be seen as having a specific value in the field of psychotherapy. This focus on self-reflection also positions participants in a specific interactional configuration, very similar to educational discourse (see below). The inequal power-relations are implicit in this clinical site to the extent that it is the patient, not the therapist, who is expected to do the self-reflection. Returning to our data site, let us consider how the therapeutic relationship, with its primacy on self-reflection, takes the form of an educational encounter. The psychotherapist (D) uses the instructional frame and within it, metaphors of learning, as a way of defining the encounter as symbolically salient and being constituted in an asymmetrical role-relationship. D is no longer someone who is simply 'paid to listen' (see examples 1 and 2), but she has to adopt a teacher's role in order to evaluate the patient's ability to cope under the present circumstances.

Example 7

01 D: so you're going into a world (.) where (.5) you are at the beginning of learning in a sense
02 P: effectively I think so yeah
03 D: =you know you (.) eh eh- to stay with your sort of profession which is one of wor:::ds
        the written word
04 P: =mmmh
05 D: =you're at the stage (.) of (.) it seems you've passed learning the alphabet (.) you've done
        that bit it seems you've done a lot of ground work (.) you're putting words together and
        you're putting sentences together and you're not quite sure yet (.) whether you've got
        them in the most sort of musical way
06 P: =know what the meaning is as well
07 D: =or [exactly exactly so there's] (.) so there's some sort of nuances that are (.)
08 P: [((laughing)) yeah]
09 D: still being [worked through]
10 P: [I think so] yeah
11 D: =but (.) it seems you've done a lot of the ground work
12 P: all these other little things (.) (they sort of fester your mind in it) before you actually
        (get anything) oh she- she was quite nice actually you know blah blah and that's the end
        of it (.5) but (.) the build-up to it
13 D: yeah so [written in-] written into our agenda today then is what (1.0) what
14 P: [sometimes]
15 D: wasn't initially spoken but you're talking about (.) you mentioned the meaning of things
        (.5) symbolically in coming to a hospital that raises expectations of as you say cure
16 P: it does to a certain extent ehm (.5)

The activity is framed as progressive learning, and language-based metaphors occupy a central place in characterising this process. D legitimises her facilitator role as someone who is there to provide the scaffolding for self-reflective talk, which may then lead to action (here, understanding). This scaffolding scenario is discursively realised with the help of metaphors, especially drawn from the domain of self-learning and from the domain of the written word — the latter coinciding with the patient's professional background as a media professional. These metaphors not only create an opportunity for the patient to relate ecologically to his professional environment, they also enable D to establish rapport with P's world of feelings. In turn 5, D uses the metaphor of learning alphabets, words and sentences in a cumulative way so as to capture the patient's current state. As we can see, in turns 6ff, P colludes with such a characterisation, while accepting that there are still nuances to be worked through. What seems relevant at this stage is to confirm the starting point of the learning curve — where you are now. The interaction reminds us of an appraisal interview as D not only checks P's progress against a continuum of coping abilities, but she also offers positive feedback for what has been achieved so far (turn 11). In turns 13 and 15, D explicitly returns to the institutional agenda as well as the unspoken aspects of the interaction. Note also D's emphasis on the symbolic potential of a hospital visit, which may contribute towards outcome expectations. The institution of the hospital makes it possible for the psychotherapist to take the role of a facilitative teacher (cf. the 'paid to listen' characterisation of D in examples 1 and 2), who seems to be in charge of a learner devoted to self-learning.

The self-learning metaphors continue to characterise the therapist–patient role-relationship, and the positioning of the learner becomes even more complex as the interaction develops. Self-reflection on the part of the patient now gives way to the authoritative voice (formulated in figurative language) of the psychotherapist.

Example 8

01 D: =then (.) you know I would hope that w- you know maybe we could have another conversation
02 P: =okay lovely
03 D: =I know uh (.) really to see where you are in (.) you know
04 P: yeah
05 D: some time in the future really
06 P: okay great
07 D: okay well I mean I've learned quite a bit from
08 P: = ((laughing))
09 D: someone (.) finding their way in the world again
10 P: =oh that's why it's like being being a child again to be honest just learning different ehm
11 D: well it is and it isn't in that now you have the skills of an eh well experienced adult
12 P: =yeah
13 D: =you relearn things rather than being a totally helpless infant [(.) and] that may be one of the biggest things that you've had to do
14 P: [that's true yeah]
15 D: whereas it might have triggered a sort of infantile fears in you of total dependency
16 P: =yeah
17 D: =you've learned (.) in the subsequent weeks since you were given the diagnosis that in fact you're not entirely an infant but that you are an adult (.) who has had to start as if he was beginning in the world again
18 P: that's right yeah
19 D: =but the advantage this time is
20 P: =yes
21 D: that you know
22 P: =I've got the previous experience
23 D: you've got the previous experience
24 P: yeah
25 D: and you're obviously a resourceful character

Here the child–adult dualism helps to foreground the fact that learning is simulation *par excellence*. The ability to cope with one's present condition by drawing upon previous experience as a learning resource is presented as a way forward. P's formulation in turn 10, 'it's like being a child again', calls for an expert assessment. D reformulates P's task as one of 'relearning things rather than being totally helpless' (turn 13). The notion of self-learning is reinforced by D as she discounts the 'sort of infantile fears in you of total dependency' (turn 15). D uses the medical vocabulary 'diagnosis' (turn 17), not in the medical sense of diagnosing the condition of illness, but as a way of foregrounding the patient's current learning state. P is thus characterised not as an infant trying to learn, but as someone who has the skills of a well experienced adult (turn 11), and 'who has had to start as if he was beginning in the world again' (turn 17). The economics of learning becomes evident: as a well experienced adult, with the necessary skills acquired from previous experience, P does not need to struggle as a child might under these circumstances. In Bourdieu's terms, previous experience is part of one's habitus; it is also a form of symbolic capital whose exchange value needs to be recognised in the field of psychotherapy. This contrastive differentiation between a child-learner and an adult-learner learning like a child is a display of D's professional expertise in ascertaining P's predisposition towards learning to cope. At a symbolic level, it reframes the encounter in institutional terms, with D having the expertise/authority to carry out this diagnostic task. Although this might suggest an asymmetrical role-relationship between D and P, it is worth noting that D casts herself as a learner to start with (in turns 7 and 9) by treating this conversation as a learning opportunity for her as well.

It seems that psychotherapeutic talk is more amenable to a Habermassian or Foucauldian analysis, than it is to a Bourdieuan analysis. This is not surprising, given that both Habermas and Foucault deal extensively with the psychoanalytic setting and the hermeneutic dimensions of interpretation in their theorisation of the language–action interrelationship. However, Bourdieu's economic model offers an explanatory platform, in the sense that the discourse of self-learning (as habitus forming) may be seen as acquiring symbolic significance in the field of psychotherapy. By looking at psychotherapeutic talk alongside learner-centred educational discourse, it is possible to forge an analytic link between social structure and situated action, and perhaps overcome Bourdieu's 'occasionalist fallacy'.

5   Conclusion

The current major debate within social theory is not about the role of language, but about micro- and macro-explanations of social phenomena. What emerges from the above cursory account is that the micro–macro debate in social theory finds a useful outlet in language as a mediating force. As we have seen, Habermas, Foucault and Bourdieu, in their own ways, have all taken language to fill out the micro–macro divide/link. My starting point in this chapter has been that the role language plays in bridging or separating structure and action is very much assumed in many social theoretical accounts, and is especially drawn upon to explain changes in social practice and social order. What receives less attention, especially with regard to recent social-theoretical debates, is the conceptualisation of language in the theorising of society. This poses an essential question as to how linguists, broadly defined to include sociolinguists and discourse analysts, should respond to the call for a language-based approach to social life (that is, beyond seeing language as one of the many social variables to explain linguistic behaviour). In asking these questions, I believe, we go beyond the issue of whether or not there are necessary and sufficient conditions for one discipline (mainly sociolinguistics) to borrow insights from another (social theory). Since both social theorists and sociolinguists are united in their shared interest in the study of social reality, a case can easily be made for social theorists to begin to take on board sociolinguistic insights in their theorising about society.

It is already evident from my discussion that a definitive categorisation and comparison of different social theorists' accounts of the language–action interrelationship is an onerous task. Given their intellectual origins and orientations, there are bound to be differences at all levels, not to mention their individual styles of writing (sometimes bordering on incomprehensibility) and the difficulties associated with the translations of the original works — in itself a linguistic project! In terms of orientations, Habermas remains a philosophically minded critical theorist; Foucault is very much a historically minded social theorist; and Bourdieu continues as a practice-based cultural critic. Despite their different orientations, they share a view of language as social action. This is borne out by the fact that their theoretical insights can be mapped on to the interactional plane, in different but cumulative ways. There should be a word of caution in that the mappings I have attempted do not necessarily count as proof of the individual theoretical positions. In any case a data site such as the psychotherapeutic clinic should not simply be regarded as a testbed for social theory.

It is, however, important to point out that the central notions such as 'communicative competence', 'ideal/distorted speech', 'explanatory understanding', 'being of language', 'self-reflection', etc., go beyond their usefulness as analytic categories. These happen to be participant categories to the extent that participants draw upon such categories, implicitly and explicitly, in their competent accomplishment of the situated encounter. In particular, the Habermassian notions of communicative competence and idealised speech situation allow us to see the very purpose language serves in ensuring 'explanatory understanding'. If we were to use 'normative' conversational systems, psychotherapeutic interaction could look asymmetrical, with the therapist using jargon, controlling interaction, adopting an expert stance, etc. But such a normative analysis is likely not to take the goals and perspectives of the participants, who may willingly suspend their belief in communicative action from time to time and act strategically to achieve a specific outcome. The difficulty remains, however, as to how to unpack at the interactional level the different types of actions Habermas talks about. But it is relevant to note that psychotherapeutic interaction affords a mix of communicative and strategic action types, as patients orient themselves towards making sense of their experience through self-reflection. We have also seen the extent to which a Foucauldian account is capable of showing how the 'decentering of the subject' coincides with the 'being of language'. On this basis one may speculate as to how certain discourses (for example, therapeutic talk as a hybrid form of self-reflection and self-learning) evolve and become legitim-ised over time. The Bourdieuan perspective has drawn our attention to the symbolic potential of therapeutic talk when it is cast in an instructional mode. A major conclusion then is that in the psychotherapeutic setting, self-reflection by the patient takes precedence over other matters and that such self-reflection is facilitated through a mode of self-learning — both contrib-uting to the Foucauldian notion of 'being of language'.

Finally, it seems that the structure/agency dialectic, which is at the heart of much social theoretical debate, can be understood better with socio-linguistic analyses of participant structure in talk-in-interaction. Social structure needs to be reconceptualised as the domain of actions — a domain which exists on the ground and is therefore available for micro-level analysis. The issue of affordance is central here. Even Giddens's notion of structuration needs to have a discoursal basis which affords sociolinguistic inquiry. The core question to ask is: how can sociolinguistic analyses of talk relate to social theory — even theories which invoke language in some explicit sense? A weaker claim here is that close analyses of text can sharpen social theorists' assumptions and claims about social reality. A somewhat stronger position would be to see if our understanding of social action is helped by such an application. If we were to return to Durkheim's adage — the social must be explained socially, which has a kind of circularity built into it — there is much to be gained if we reframe it to say 'the social must be explained sociolinguistically'.

Notes

1. See Rorty (1967) for a discussion of the linguistic turn in philosophy and Silverman and Torode (1980) for a comprehensive overview of the the-ories of language across a range of disciplines, e.g., sociology, linguistics, philosophy, literary criticism. For a detailed discussion of 'discourse as topic' and 'discourse as resource' in linguistics and other social science disciplines, see Sarangi and Coulthard (2000).
2. Parsons (1949) traces how Durkheim's account of division of labour is non-social as it is based on the principle of population. In *Le Suicide*, however, Durkheim comes across as a social realist.

3. Wright Mills (1970: 42) borrows the notions of syntax and semantics to characterise the pitfalls of grand theory: 'Grand theory is drunk on syntax, blind to semantics'.

4. For a critique of Weber's view of action, see Schutz (1974): 'Weber makes no distinction between the *action*, considered as something in progress, and the completed *act*'.

5. Habermas's theory of communicative action is intermeshed with his theory of the public sphere which includes the lifeworld (e.g., individual, family, peer group) and the systems (e.g., state, market).

6. I am grateful to the participants for allowing me to record the conversation for analysis, as part of my ongoing study of 'Risk Communication in Genetic Counselling', funded by The Leverhulme Trust (RF&G/2/9800687).

7. I will use the following (simplified) transcription conventions: dots or numericals between round brackets denote pause; texts within double round brackets are glosses; square brackets signal overlaps; equal sign (=) means latching; extended colons stand for lengthened sound and untranscribable segments are signalled by [^^^^^].

8. See Cooke (1994) for a critique of Habermas's claim about the functional primacy of communicative action.

9. One can draw parallels here to Sacks's (1992) analysis of '[The baby cried. The mommy picked it up]' along the lines of 'membership categorisation device'. Although no explicit genitive is used, we recognise the mommy to be the baby's mommy by applying what Sacks calls 'the consistency rule', i.e., the categories 'baby' and 'mommy' belong to the same collection, family.

10. Foucault draws a distinction between the grammatical unit of the sentence, the logical unit of the proposition and the pragmatic unit of the speech act.

References

Austin, J. (1962) *How to Do Things with Words*. Cambridge, MA: Harvard University Press.

Bernstein, B. (1971) *Class, Codes and Control, vol. 1: Theoretical Studies Towards a Sociology of Language*. London: Routledge & Kegan Paul.

Bourdieu, P. (1976) The economics of linguistic exchanges. *Social Science Information* 16, 6: 645–668.

Bourdieu, P. (1991) *Language and Symbolic Power*. Ed. J.B. Thompson, translated G. Raymond and M. Adamson. Cambridge, MA: Polity Press.

Bourdieu, P. and Wacquant, L.J.D. (1992) *An Introduction to Reflexive Sociology*. Cambridge: Polity Press.

Calhoun, C., LiPuma, E. and Postone, M. (eds) (1993) *Bourdieu: Critical Perspectives*. Cambridge: Polity Press.

Chomsky, N. (1957) *Syntactic Structures*. The Hague: Mouton.

Chomsky, N. (1965) *Aspects of the Theory of Syntax*. Cambridge, MA: MIT Press.

Cooke, M. (1994) *Language and Reason: A Study of Habermas's Pragmatics*. Cambridge, MA: MIT Press.

Craib, I. (1998) *Experiencing Identity*. London: Sage.

Durkheim, E. (1930) *Le suicide* (new edition). Paris: F. Alcan.

Durkheim, E. (1933) *On the Division of Labour in Society*. Translated George Simpson. New York: Macmillan.

Fairclough, N. (1989) *Language and Power*. London: Longman.

Fairclough, N. (1992) *Discourse and Social Change*. Cambridge: Polity Press.

Fairclough, N. (1996) A reply to Henry Widdowson's 'Discourse analysis: a critical view'. *Language and Literature* 5, 1: 49–56.

Foucault, M. (1970) *The Order of Things: An Archaeology of the Human Sciences*. London: Tavistock.

Foucault, M. (1972) *The Archaeology of Knowledge*. London: Tavistock.

Frawley, W. (1987) Review article: T.A. van Dijk (ed.) *Handbook of Discourse Analysis*. *Language* 63, 2: 361–397.

Garfinkel, H. (1967) *Studies in Ethnomethodology*. Englewood Cliffs, NJ: Prentice-Hall.

Giddens, A. (1979) *Central Problems in Social Theory*. London: Macmillan.

Giddens, A. (1985) Jurgen Habermas. In Q. Skinner (ed.) *The Return of Grand Theory in the Human Sciences*. Cambridge: Cambridge University Press, 121–139.

Goffman, E. (1967) *Interaction Ritual: Essays on Face-to-Face Behaviour*. New York: Doubleday Anchor.

Goffman, E. (1981) *Forms of Talk*. Oxford: Blackwell.

Gumperz, J.J. and Hymes, D. (eds) (1972) *Directions in Sociolinguistics: The Ethnography of Communication*. New York: Holt, Rinehart & Winston.

Habermas, J. (1970a) On systematically distorted communication. *Inquiry* 13: 205–218.

Habermas, J. (1970b) Towards a theory of communicative competence. *Inquiry* 13: 360–375.

Habermas, J. (1972) *Knowledge and Human Interests*. Translated J. Shapiro. London: Heinemann.

Habermas, J. (1987) *The Theory of Communicative Action, Vols 1 and 2*. Translated T. McCarthy. Boston: Beacon Press.

Halliday, M.A.K. (1973) *Explorations in the Functions of Language*. London: Longman.

Halliday, M.A.K. (1985) *An Introduction to Functional Grammar*. London: Arnold.

Hammersley, M. (1996) On the foundations of critical discourse analysis. *Language and Communication* 17, 3: 237–248.

Honneth, A. (1991) *The Critique of Power: Reflective Stages in a Critical Social Theory*. Translated K. Baynes. Cambridge, MA: MIT Press.

Hymes, D. (1964) Introduction: toward ethnographies of communication. *American Anthropologist* 66, 6: 12–25.

Jefferson, G. and Lee, J. (1981) The rejection of advice: managing the problematic convergence of a 'troubles-telling' and a service encounter. *Journal of Pragmatics* 5: 399–422.

Labov, W. (1972a) *Sociolinguistic Patterns*. Philadelphia: University of Pennsylvania Press.

Labov, W. (1972b) *Language in the Inner City: Studies in the Black English Vernacular*. Philadelphia: University of Pennsylvania Press.

Labov, W. and Fanshel, D. (1977) *Therapeutic Discourse: Psychotherapy as Conversation*. New York: Academic Press.

Lacan, J. (1968) *Speech and Language in Psychoanalysis*. Translated A. Wilden. Baltimore: Johns Hopkins University Press.

Lévi-Strauss, C. (1963) *Structural Anthropology*. Translated C. Jacobson and B. Schoef. New York: Basic Books.

McCarthy, T. (1973) A theory of communicative competence. *Philosophy of the Social Sciences* 3: 135–156.

Merleau-Ponty, M. (1974) *The Prose of the World*. London: Heinemann.

Parsons, T. (1949) *The Structure of Social Action, Vols I and II*. New York: Free Press.

Parsons, T. (1951) *The Social System*. Glencoe, IL: Free Press.

Rorty, R. (ed.) (1967) *The Linguistic Turn: Recent Essays in Philosophical Method*. Chicago: University of Chicago Press.

Sacks, H. (1992) *Lectures on Conversation*. Oxford: Blackwell.

Sarangi, S. (2000) Activity types, discourse types and interactional hybridity: the case of genetic counselling. In S. Sarangi and M. Coulthard (eds), *Discourse and Social Life*. London: Longman, 1–27.

Sarangi, S. and Coulthard, M. (2000) Discourse as topic, resource and social practice: an introduction. In S. Sarangi and M. Coulthard (eds), *Discourse and Social Life*. London: Longman, xv–xli.

Sarangi, S. and Coulthard, M. (eds) (2000) *Discourse and Social Life*. London: Longman.

Sarangi, S. and Roberts, C. (1999) The dynamics of interactional and institutional orders in work-related settings. In S. Sarangi and C. Roberts (eds) *Talk, Work and Institutional Order: Discourse in Medical, Mediation and Management Settings*. Berlin: Mouton de Gruyter, 1–57.

Saussure, Ferdinand de (1966 [1916]) *Course in General Linguistics*. Translated W. Baskin. New York: McGraw-Hill.

Schutz, A. (1971a) *Collected Papers I*. The Hague: Martinus Nijhoff.

Schutz, A. (1971b) *Collected Papers II*. The Hague: Martinus Nijhoff.

Schutz, A. (1974) *The Phenomenology of the Social World*. London: Heinemann.

Searle, J. (1969) *Speech Acts*. Cambridge: Cambridge University Press.

Silverman, D. and Torode, B. (1980) *The Material Word*. London: Routledge & Kegan Paul.

Stubbs, M. (1994) Grammar, text and ideology: Computer-assisted methods in the linguistics of representation. *Applied Linguistics* 15, 2: 201–223.

Stubbs, M. (1997) Whorf's children: critical comments on critical discourse analysis (CDA). In A. Ryan and A. Wray (eds) *Evolving Models of Language*. Clevedon: BAAL/Multilingual Matters.

Turner, R. (1972) Some formal properties of therapy talk. In D. Sudnow (ed.) *Studies in Social Interaction*. New York: Free Press, 367–396.

Turner, R. (1974) Words, utterances and activities. In R. Turner (ed.) *Ethnomethodology*. Harmondsworth: Penguin, 197–215.

Weber, M. (1947 [1922]) *The Theory of Economic and Social Organisation*. New York: Oxford University Press.

Widdowson, H. (1995) Discourse analysis: a critical view. *Language and Literature* 4, 3: 157–172.

Widdowson, H. (1998) Review article: The theory and practice of critical discourse analysis. *Applied Linguistics* 19, 1: 136–151.

Widdowson, H. (2000) Critical practices: on representation and the interpretation of text. In S. Sarangi and M. Coulthard (eds), *Discourse and Social Life*. London: Longman, 155–169.

Wright Mills, C. (1970 [1959]) *The Sociological Imagination*. Harmondsworth: Penguin.

2

Dynamics of differentiation: On social psychology and cases of language variation
Miriam Meyerhoff

1 Introduction

Communication between individuals necessarily requires a foundation of shared norms.[1] This makes interindividual and intergroup variation an intriguing and inviting locus for research. Speakers should find variation counter-functional and avoid it, yet as we know it is an integral part of the dynamics of all communication. In modelling language use and language variation, the goal is to create a model which accurately represents the fact that different linguistic variants may differ in significance in different places, at different times, and for different speakers. If we succeed in this goal, language variation emerges as simply a function of meaningful social patterns. Each chapter in this volume is concerned with the intersection between social theory and language variation, largely leaving aside the role that language-internal factors play in constraining variation. The brief of this particular chapter is to consider how principles and theories from social psychology inform the study of language variation, and to what extent naturally-occurring data on language variation might fruitfully inform theories of social psychological behaviour.

As case studies, this chapter will examine three variables in Bislama (the creole spoken in Vanuatu, an archipelago in the SW Pacific). One principle and one strategy from social psychology will be explored in the light of these variables. The principle, that mutual (un)certainty affects interactants' behaviour (uncertainty management, Gudykunst 1995), and the strategy, communication accommodation (CAT), (Giles and Coupland 1991), both derive from intergroup theory, which holds that individuals possess and construct a range of interindividual and intergroup identities through their actions.

Let me address from the outset something that I believe is a common misperception about the spirit of intergroup theory, and which needs to be understood before the usefulness of principles like CAT and uncertainty management can be evaluated. Intergroup theory neither requires nor assumes that group membership is static or unproblematic. Since its inception, the literature has talked consistently of *processes* (for example, Tajfel and Turner 1986) — group membership and individual identity are constantly contested, constructed or reinforced through interaction. Emergent experiences of the self and others are absolutely central principles of the theory. The fact that intergroup theory has always been about the contingent and co-constructed nature of identity makes it particularly relevant given the current preoccupations of sociolinguistics and social theory.

The remainder of this chapter consists of three parts. The first section explores the ways in which different levels of situational (in)determinacy or (un)certainty between interlocutors might be seen as motivating different linguistic strategies. I will use **(un)certainty** to refer conventionally to an individual's epistemological state, and also somewhat unconventionally to refer to the degree of situational stability or determinacy. It is hoped that the decision to deal with both phenomena under the one term will emerge as a useful discursive gambit in the discussion that follows. There is frequently (though not necessarily) a link between unstable or indeterminate situations and an increase in participants' uncertainty about what is going on. By including situational indeterminacy under the umbrella of uncertainty, different social and psychological functions for variation exhibit more coherent patterns than they might otherwise.

In exploring the relationship between language and certitude, we follow earlier work — for example, Duranti (1997, ch.2), Giles and Coupland (1991, ch.2) and Hogg (1996). Because certainty can be seen as a gradient property, and because linguistic variation often appears as a graded phenomenon within and across recognisable groups of speakers, this parallelism seems to be worth pursuing. It will be seen that many motivations for language variation are already obliquely cast in terms of factors related to certainty about self and others.

Section 3 sketches three variables found at different levels of linguistic structure in one speech community. In order to account fully for the variation observed, it will be seen that speakers' perceptions of the interaction, including their identifications of self and others, and situational changes in these identifications (even within an interaction) need to be considered. It will be seen that the linguistic variation observed is consistent with analyses based on the need to manage interactional uncertainty, and that accommodation is implicated as a strategy for effecting uncertainty reduction.

In the final section, these variables will be reviewed in relation to the motivational paradigm in section 2.

2   Motivating language variation

It is not enough, of course, to simply establish a systematic relationship between linguistic and non-linguistic variables. An analysis is strengthened greatly if some motivation for the co-occurrence can be established. To date, the motivations for interlocutors that have been proposed in sociolinguistics might be summarised in four ways: Accrue social capital; Avoid or minimise risk; Maximise fit with others; Maintain individual distinctiveness. Although the labels that will be used are new, the concepts are familiar from socio-linguistics. In this section the evidence that has been adduced for each of these is reviewed, and attention is drawn to another impulse that may be im-plicated in variation — Test hypotheses about others.

2.1   Accentuate the positive — A: Accruing social capital

One of the triumphs of sociolinguistics has been to demonstrate that the distribution of linguistic variants is often significantly associated with speakers of different social groups, and it is clear that some of these groups have greater access to social or economic capital than others.[2] It has been proposed, therefore, that these variables either are a material accessory of these groups' access to social or economic capital, or are metaphorically asso-ciated with other material trappings of this access to capital. Whether these variables are actual or virtual trappings of power makes no difference to us here, as Deleuze and Guattari rightly point out that in language the actual and the virtual are understood only in terms of each other (1987: 99, a point we will return to in section 3.2).

Analyses of variation that treat language as a coin in the wider cultural marketplace generally go on to interpret the frequent use of a particular variant as an indication of the speaker's conscious or unconscious desire to access the privileges and social capital associated with the prototypical users of that variant (see for example Kroch 1978, Sankoff and Laberge 1978). Macro-level variation between social classes is a manifestation of differences in access to and control over social capital. By extension, micro-level or styl-istic variation is treated as a linguistic metaphor of social climbing.

Labov (1972) used this reasoning to account for the cross-over effect documented for the lower middle class; Trudgill (1972) used it to account for discrepancies between performance and self-report data; and it has been invoked to account for the finding that women's speech may approximate the variants with highest prestige more than men's does (this last point is by no means always true; see Haeri 1996, James 1996). Subgroups of speakers with comparatively little economic capital or social status are hypothesised to implicate or appropriate social capital by emulating the speech that is prob-abilistically associated with people who possess comparatively more social capital. This line of reasoning has been extremely influential in sociolinguistics and undoubtedly there is truth to it; however, it is by no means the only motivation that explains patterns of inter- and intraspeaker variation.

2.2   Eliminate the negative – B: Avoiding or minimising risk

Human behaviour is not only motivated by positive aspirations. A desire to avoid possible negative outcomes is also a strong factor. Although this motive has received little attention in sociolinguistics, it features prominently in other fields; for example, it heads Robinson's (1985) typology of language functions. Goffman noted (1959: 36) that social mobility involves not just upward mobility, but also a desire to find 'a place close to the sacred centre of the common values'. Establishing such a place often requires distancing yourself from behaviours and groups of people associated with the peripheries. Avoidance, he points out, can maximise instrumental and affective gain.

He gives the example of a tenant who might choose not to spend money even if it would be beneficial to him/her, if the tenant is worried that a display of wealth might suggest to the landlord that the tenant could afford a higher rent. Goffman also noted a paradox of avoidance: 'negative idealisation' (Goffman 1959: 40) strategies may actually attract someone else, as when a person feigns helplessness or a lack of skills in order to arouse protectiveness or assistance from others. According to Goffman, acts of self-abnegation show that avoidance may be constructed in two quite different ways: positively, when the actor seeks to avoid deleterious group associations; negatively, when (in the interests of interpersonal factors) the actor adopts a stance that is poorly esteemed in the wider community.

Gordon (1997) argues that risk avoidance is a factor contributing to some women's use of variants more closely associated with higher socio-economic groups. Her data suggest that lower class accented varieties of New Zealand English trigger negative attitudes about a woman's morality and likely social success. This hypothesis needs to be more fully tested (perhaps by isolating some of the social variables collapsed in her study), but her results suggest that if women do use more prestige forms than men, it may not be to claim social benefits (or status). They may be avoiding social costs.

Similarly, Bucholtz (1999) shows that the linguistic behaviour of a small group of adolescent girls is tied to their broader patterns of resistance to ideals about feminine behaviour. Compared to classmates who are more actively constructing prototypical feminine identities, the nerd girls lag noticeably in the ongoing California vowel shift (fronting of /u/ and /o/). These girls avoid both the social and the linguistic activities that are associated with identities they reject. In ongoing work on language variation in Morocco, Atiqa Hachimi points out that ethnic or religious identifications prompt some speakers to avoid French or regional varieties of Moroccan Arabic (Hachimi, in press).

It might seem that balancing the motivations *Accrue social capital* and *Minimise risk* would sometimes result in a cognitive dissonance since in some cases they are diametrically opposed. In fact, it seems that evaluating positive and negative outcomes involves quite different processes. Kahneman and Tversky (1979) showed that people do not evaluate likely losses the same way they evaluate likely gains. When subjects in their study were asked to choose between a small, but certain, gain (a 100% chance of getting $3000) and a large, probable gain (an 80% chance of getting $4000), they choose the smaller, yet certain option. But when the same people were asked to choose between two loss options — a small, but certain loss (100% chance of losing $3000) and a greater probable loss (80% chance of losing $4000), they preferred to take their chances with the latter. In other words, people evaluate probabilities differently depending on the perceived outcome. If they possibly can, they try to avoid a loss (even if this exposes them to greater overall risk).

What might this mean for linguistic behaviour? It means that variants associated with negative or undesirable outcomes should show more robust avoidance effects. If, for example, New Zealand women (as opposed to men) see the identity constructed in use of working-class variants to be a cost, then there should be evidence that women avoid the use of these variants more than men, even if it exposes them to other risks such as being seen as social climbers.

2.3   The Balancing Act — C: Maximising fit; D: Maintaining individual distinctiveness

Freud noted a tendency for antagonism between groups to be underpinned by a perception of increased coherence within groups, and summed this up with the now-famous aphorism 'the narcissism of minor differences' (Freud 1961 [1930]: 68). His insight was that group distinctions may be harnessed in the service of improving a sense of self-worth. In this section, the manner in which this insight has developed in the social psychology of language and in sociolinguistics will be considered. It will be seen that the interrelatedness of processes of ingroup and outgroup contrast continues to be an important factor in accounting for linguistic variation. It will be suggested that acting on the basis of these contrasts presupposes a relatively high degree of certainty, even if (as will be discussed) this certainty is misplaced.

Billig and Tajfel's (1973) studies of the minimal group effect showed empirically the profound influence that quite arbitrary distinctions between groups can have on the strength of individuals' identifications with other members of their ingroup. In a series of experiments, they showed that ingroup favouritism emerged even when quite arbitrary intergroup demarcations were drawn. Individuals' pervasive use of stereotypes to maximise distinctions between groups can be seen as highly functional. If such discriminations increase the perceived coherence of ingroup characteristics, then the process increases an individual's self-knowledge. Freud's characterisation of the process as narcissism captures this aspect of the functionality. Categorisation, therefore, can be seen as fundamentally about reducing uncertainty concerning the self.

In other work, the functionality of categorisation as a means of reducing uncertainty about *others* has been emphasised. Rosch (1975) showed that in various perceptual domains, colours, numbers and planes, people rely heavily on reference points, or prototypes, that they have constructed for that domain when they evaluate new input. Earlier experiments by Kahneman and Tversky (1973) indicated that in a highly subjective perceptual domain people rely on prototypes, too. People were asked to predict a student's future grades on the basis of the student's performance in several other tasks. One measured the student's sense of humour; another measured the student's results in a 'concentration' test. Even though people were told that both of these tests were very bad predictors of future performance, they consistently used the concentration results to predict future performance. In other words, because people's prototype of a successful student includes the ability to concentrate, this characteristic is used as a reference point for further categorisation; because their prototype of a successful student does not include sense of humour, this was ignored.

Recent work by Oakes (1996, Oakes *et al.* 1998) argues that categorisations of self and other are more than complementary, they are inextricably linked. The *meta-contrast principle* predicts that a group of individuals will be classified (and treated) as members of an outgroup, when the differences between all of them and all the members of another group is greater than the differences between themselves. Take a very simple example. Imagine you are being introduced to your partner's family for the first time on her/his birthday. Now suppose that in your own family birthdays are always celebrated with great festiveness and with much the same routines, and suppose that there is a radical difference between your family's typical celebrations and the low-key way your partner's family celebrates. The meta-contrast principle holds that under these circumstances you are more likely to perceive your partner's family members as an outgroup. On the other hand, suppose some people in your family have always made a huge occasion out of birthdays and others prefer to ignore them. Because there is great variance within your own group, the meta-contrast principle holds that the modest celebration your partner's family holds may not trigger the same kind of outgroup categorisation.

By presenting intra- and intergroup processes as a dynamic system, the meta-contrast principle shares the spirit of much recent work in sociolinguistics. That work has focussed on the fact that speakers may pay more or less attention to their various personal and group identifications in different situations or contexts. The meta-contrast principle locates changes in the salience of identities in a change to the way the ratio of ingroup-outgroup differences is appraised, while the tendency in sociolinguistics seems to be to cast changes in speakers' attentional state as the determining factor (that is, attention to some contrasts vitiates attention to others).[3]

Let us proceed, in line with the bulk of the social psychology literature, to assume that generally people attend quite closely to within-group and between-group relationships, and that they tend to focus on similarities within groups and differences between groups, mindful of the restrictions to this generalisation that we have noted. The similarities and differences that are attended to must be evaluated in terms of various behaviours. Since ingroup similarities and outgroup distinctions may be indexed linguistically, communication accommodation may be a useful tool to this end.

Giles's principles of accommodation (Giles and Smith 1979, Giles and Coupland 1991, Gallois *et al.* 1995) were an attempt to state with greater clarity the relationship between speaker attitudes and linguistic variables. At the time accommodation emerged in the 1970s, the dominant focus in sociolinguistics was on quantitative studies of variation at the level of the speech community. CAT reminded the field that even if group distinctions are marked, when all is said and done it is individuals, full of likes, prejudices and expectations, who interact with each other. This was a period in which sociolinguistics was increasingly focussed on what the implications of within-group similarities were for theories of language change, and CAT also served as a reminder that different intergroup motivations might result in the same outcome (a perspective adopted and elaborated in Trudgill 1986). So, convergence with ingroup members and divergence from outgroups may be signalled or effected by the same variants (such as comparatively backed variants of /u/ and /o/ in Bucholtz's study). The complicated picture of a single variable indexing many non-linguistic factors emerges because of the possible overlap between convergence and divergence.

Principles of accommodation have played a fundamental role in formulating some of the better-articulated models of language variation and change. The gravity model (Trudgill 1974, Callary 1975) was based on the observation that social and linguistic innovations disperse from urban centre to urban centre, generally skipping rural regions in between. The insight of this model is that people in urban centres (even when they are great distances apart) are more attuned to each other than they are to people who may be physically closer, but are evaluatively quite distinct.

However, it is also crucial to note that communicative accommodation is a strategy and not a motivation. Although accommodation may conventionally be used to satisfy intergroup differentiation, the discussion of inclusive pronouns will show that it may also be used as a strategy to satisfy other motives, that is, to test hypotheses (see below). Britain's (1997) analysis of sound change in the Fens also suggests that practices of accommodation may superficially reflect the testing of hypotheses.

At the start of this section, it was claimed that in order for speakers to accentuate ingroup similarities and outgroup distinctions, a good deal of situational certainty is required. The suggestion is that the attunement required in order to *maximise fit* and *maintain distinctiveness* can only take place when at least one of the participants has a clear notion about the salient identifications for self, for other or for the interaction as a whole. Such certainty about intergroup boundaries and/or interpersonal allegiances may not, of course, be correct. As interlocutors, we often identify others in ways that are at odds with the ways they self-identify (Gudykunst 1995: 32) and such misattributions may generate instability and participants may use accommodative strategies to reduce this (see below, and 2.1). Nevertheless, some clear (even if mistaken) idea of these things is required for accommodative or intergroup processes to unfold. In this, I take issue directly with Dittmar and Schlobinski's characterisation of accommodation, specifically convergence. They suggest (1988: 158) that cognitive uncertainty is a precondition for convergence. I argue here that when linguistic variation is motivated by the intergroup principles discussed in this section, it is intended to position speaker and hearer in quite specific ways, and seldom challenges existing group boundaries and memberships.

If this is correct, it establishes an interesting contrast with the first two motivations discussed above. Motivations A and B have built into them a notion of some situational instability or situational uncertainty that speakers exploit. In order for use of a variant to be seen as a means of *accruing capital* or *avoiding risk*, interactants must mutually recognise the social salience and the social significance of intergroup (or interindividual) factors, and they must mutually recognise which variants index the salient groups. Yet a degree of uncertainty, or the potential for uncertainty, must also exist. They must recognise that the process by which linguistic and non-linguistic variables index each other is not fixed. Unless there is some indeterminacy over the extent to which the mapping between social and linguistic variables is natural or immutable, variants could not be manipulated as tools, for example in formal situations.

Although these four factors are most frequently invoked as motivating linguistic variation, once they are evaluated in terms of degrees of certainty it becomes apparent that part of the picture is missing. I turn now to consider how a state of great uncertainty, when much about the intergroup and interpersonal context is new or unknown, affects linguistic variation.

2.4   It's a jungle out there — E: Test your hypotheses about others

A considerable amount of theorising and experimental work in social psychology has been based on the proposition that the formulation and testing of hypotheses is a cornerstone of interaction. However, because sociolinguistic models have treated shared evaluation and familiarity of speech norms as a benchmark, individuals' uncertainty about others has seldom been part of the theory.

Berger and Calabrese (1975) and Sunnafrank (1983) showed the importance of hypothesis testing in interpersonal behaviour. In these studies, when a person's hypotheses about a new, or strange, interlocutor were supported by the other person's behaviour, subjects reported that they felt increased attraction to the other. But when the other person behaved in ways that were inconsistent with a subject's hypotheses, that is, in cases where uncertainty persisted, subjects report lessened attraction.

Strongly influenced by Simmel's 1971 [1908] essentially interpersonal account of interactions between strangers, Gudykunst asks what it means to be a stranger more generally. He proposes (1995: 10) employing stranger effects in the analysis of a wider range of interactions, arguing 'Strangers . . . are people who are different because they are members of other groups . . . everyone we meet is a potential stranger'. Articulating this theoretical position with the empirical framework of Berger's work, Gudykunst formulates an array of hypotheses pertaining to uncertainty management in encounters. He suggests that an important initial step is to formulate and then proceed to test the hypotheses we have about our interlocutors' group membership. These hypotheses, he suggests, will be shaped in large part by the similarities they are perceived to have with other members of groups we are familiar with. When someone's behaviour is consonant with or confirms our group stereotypes, uncertainty about the stranger is reduced, and this is seen as desirable. Note that this, again, depends on an analysis of stereotypes as highly functional, since they provide a framework in which to interpret others' behaviour and allow us to conceive of how others interpret our behaviour. It is worth noting, too, that people attend to behaviour or impressions that match expectations a good deal more than they attend to those that do not. To the extent that we see someone's behaviour as confirming our hypotheses about how they should or will interact next, we adapt our own behaviour and construct further hypotheses about the other person (this cyclic perspective is also found in Cronen et al.'s 1988 coordinated management of meaning).

The effects of this ongoing process of hypothesis testing are evident in speech. Rampton (this volume) illustrates what happens when there is a disruption to speakers' expectations. His data show that when there is a dissonance between interactants' perceived social roles and their behaviour, the speakers fall back on ingroup routines, which reaffirm and strengthen problematised identifications. Since accommodative gambits may be used towards similar ends, CAT is again relevant. This will be seen in 3.1 below, where it is suggested that similar intraspeaker variation (between inclusive and exclusive pronouns) reflects and communicates hypothesis testing about salient group identifications.

In some cases, hypothesis testing may be accompanied by other markers of increased wariness on the part of a participant. Hypotheses may be novel,

Table 2.1   Mapping of social psychological motivations for language variation in relation to degrees of (internal and external) certainty

Situational certainty ───	Situational instability	Epistemological uncertainty
Maximise fit; be distinct	*Accrue capital; avoid risk*	*Test your hypotheses*

appropriate to a first encounter, or based on a history of interactions. Wariness is *a priori* more likely to be associated with new encounters, and with cases where pre-existing hypotheses are radically challenged by someone's behaviour. Thus, wariness asymmetrically entails hypothesis formulation and testing.

The principle of interactants testing hypotheses about the situation and each other is fairly well integrated into social psychology, but to the best of my knowledge, it has not been seriously integrated into accounts of socio-linguistic variation. It seems to merit our consideration, since because of the very high degree of epistemological uncertainty involved, it counter-balances a scale of certainty which appears to be emerging from this larger discussion — a scale that may be a useful heuristic.

Certainty about the social situation (which, obviously, is taken to include both interpersonal and intergroup certainty) can be represented as in Table 2.1. Let me stress that the purpose of this chapter is not to claim or even suggest that speaker certainty is a monistic concept accounting for all linguistic variation. Part of the purpose in laying these motivations out in the form of Table 2.1 is to give them all equal salience as we proceed to the linguistic analysis in the next section. There, it will be shown that in different sociolinguistic contexts, their explanatory power differs. In other words, the scale in Table 2.1 is simply a way of schematising one socio-psychological factor necessary for a complete picture of sociolinguistic variation. In the schema, there is an intermediate point between certainty and uncertainty. For the purposes of this discussion, this point has been characterised as being those situations in which speakers think they know something about the social and personal identities that are salient in the interaction, but their fixity is uncertain and therefore contestable.

There is one further caveat for reading Table 2.1. The layout is not intended to assert that these motivations are independent of each other. In fact, it is unlikely that any single one will account for all facets of the intergroup and interindividual variation observed in a speech community (as will be discussed in 3.3).

Ascribing social or psychological motivations to naturally-occurring data (as opposed to data gathered in controlled experiments) is always a subjective business, but subjective need not mean that the analysis is blindly biased towards one perspective. In order to evaluate the most appropriate motivation(s) for a given example of variation, we expect the analyst to adduce additional social or affective information. This information about the speakers or the context needs to be just as robust as the data on the distribution of variants. Of course, for social and affective data to be considered 'robust' may require that analysts employ different measures from the measures used to examine the distribution of linguistic variants. This kind of data may not be equally amenable to tests of statistical significance; robustness in this case may instead mean that it represents systematic observations about the individuals or groups involved. In the next section, three linguistic variables are introduced. For each of them, a case can be made that a full account of the variation requires that speakers' motivations and attitude towards the interlocutor(s) be taken into account. In each case, the role speaker motivations have to play in shaping the variation observed will be supported by observations of the social and interactional norms in the wider speech community.

3 An analysis of variables

Three linguistic variables found in conversational Bislama (a pidgin/creole spoken by about 180,000 people in Vanuatu) are discussed in this section:

1. the distribution and function of semantically **inclusive pronouns**
2. the distribution and use of **apologies**, and
3. the distribution of phonetically **null subjects**.

The section concludes with observations about differences in the nature of linguistic variables and some methodological implications of these differences.
   All three variables occur at the level of clausal or interclausal structure. None is subject to stereotyping in Bislama; in other words, the variation occurs below the level of speakers' consciousness. The data is drawn from tape-recordings of conversations made in urban and village settings in northern Vanuatu between 1994 and 1995.[4] Reflecting the chief concerns of this volume, this paper will not examine the linguistic factors constraining the variation (though there are in fact significant morphosyntactic constraints on the use of null subjects in Bislama), focussing rather on what these three variables suggest about the relationship between language and social psychological theory.

3.1 Literal and metaphorical inclusiveness

Bislama makes a grammatical distinction between first person plural (1p) references that are *inclusive* of the addressee and 1p references that are *exclusive* of the addressee. These are shown in examples (1) and (2) respectively. The two forms, *yumi* (/yumi/ 'we, inclusive') and *mifala* (/mifəla/ 'we, exclusive') are compositionally derived from English (*yumi* from 'you' and 'me'; *mifala* from 'me' and 'fellow'), but the grammatical distinction itself is a likely substrate influence (the vernacular languages spoken in Vanuatu also grammaticise this person and number distinction).[5]

Example 1

Sapos   hem i   no ripotem mifala ating   bambae mifala i   givim moa yet.
suppose 3s   AGR no report 1p.excl probably IRR   1p.excl AGR give   more yet
'If he hadn't reported us (exclusive) we (exclusive) probably would have given him even more.'

Example 2

Hemia   se yumi   stap ya,   i   no gat fulap   man.
that.one say 1p.incl stay SPEC, AGR no get full.up man
'Before that, when we (inclusive) were there there weren't many people.'

Bislama speakers generally select *yumi* or *mifala* to reflect whether or not the speaker and the addressee(s) were literally co-agents or co-experiencers of an event; out of 61 tokens of *yumi* in the transcribed corpus, 47 denote literal inclusion of the addressee(s). However, for the remaining 14 tokens (23% of the total) it could not have been literally true that both the speaker and addressee experienced or engaged in an activity, and among these uses (which I will call metaphorical), some interesting patterns emerge.

Yumi was used as a way of expressing metaphorical, or non-literal, inclusion in both the town and village communities, and an examination of the social contexts in which *yumi* was used metaphorically suggests that its function is to downplay the salience of an agentive identity and to highlight the salience of some other socially shared characteristic. In this way, its use implicates a desire that the speaker and addressee be seen to share some form of group membership.

Two facts support the analysis of *yumi* as foregrounding a perceived shared identity. First, the semantics of inclusive and exclusive pronouns are inherently tied up with the formation of ingroup vs outgroup ties. Second, fieldwork in 1995 and 1998 found that when speakers of different ages and backgrounds were quizzed directly about this use of *yumi*, they explained it as a politeness strategy, and sometimes even in terms of 'not wanting to leave someone out'.[6]

However, in order to be somewhat specific about the kinds of group membership that are being invoked when speakers use *yumi* non-literally, it is necessary to know whether some ingroup memberships are culturally more salient than others. These norms will be underlyingly present for all discourse, and it can be assumed that their general cultural salience will mean that they are easily triggered into contextual salience by a conversational gambit.

We can focus on the use of *yumi* in the village (where the majority of the tokens were recorded). Based on ethnographic work in the village (my own, and Rubinstein 1978), two group identities can be identified as of high cultural salience: one is speaker sex; the other is family membership. The salience of these groups seems to be supported by the overall trend in the data. A number of examples were recorded in which women used inclusive pronouns with other women, even when their addressee had not been present at the event being related. In addition, there was some evidence that young men may actively avoid non-literal uses of the inclusive form with a female addressee (Meyerhoff 1998: 214). When men in the village did use *yumi* metaphorically to address a woman, it was in a context in which family membership had become a salient topic.

The corpus also provides examples of metaphorical *yumi* that support the hypothesis that a conversational trigger can elevate the salience of one of these group identities, and thereby affect the selection of a linguistic variant. A particularly interesting example is seen in the reply a young woman, Alis, gives to the researcher in example 3.

Example 3

MM: *Mi no wantem stap long saed blong ol man Amerika.*
     1s no want   stay on side of   pl. man America
Alis: *No, bae yu kam   stap wetem yumi   mifala nomo.*
       no, IRR 2s come stay with   1p.incl 1p.excl only
MM: 'I don't want to stand with the Americans.'
Alis: 'No, you'll just come stand with us.'

Alis juxtaposes both an inclusive and an exclusive pronoun in her reply to me. Prosodically, it is clear that *yumi mifala* is being treated as a compound; this is not a false start and repair. Two group identities are of principal salience at this point in the conversation: locals and visitors. In this context, Alis's use of *yumi mifala* conveys a great deal of non-referential meaning. It suggests that Alis's attitude to her addressee includes her in the family ingroup, and makes clear that this ingroup identity contrasts with the outgroup identity of the visiting Americans.

The distribution of these metaphorically inclusive forms across the whole corpus also supports the thesis that language variation is at times the surface manifestation of deeper processes, such as a desire to reduce uncertainty in interactions. Gudykunst incorporates CAT in his broader account of uncertainty management. He accepts the proposition of, for instance, Giles and Coupland (1991) that accommodation may be used strategically to achieve a speaker's larger goals of reducing uncertainty, or its affective counterpart, anxiety (Gudykunst 1995: 28). But for one reason or another the social categories to which we assign an interlocutor may not be the social categories most salient to them. Paradoxically, then, some attempts at accommodation may inject a degree of uncertainty into an interaction.

The problem is this: Person A wants to accurately assign Person B to a social category, because this will allow A to better interpret and predict B's behaviour. Ultimately, this reduces A's uncertainty and anxiety. However, interactants can only improve their accuracy of group identifications by testing their hypotheses and working out which identity is shaping their alter's behaviour. In this way, CAT becomes a valuable resource. Evidence of accommodation or adaptation can be evaluated in context and, Gudykunst proposes, used to determine what identity is most salient to one's interlocutor, helping to manage uncertainty in the interaction.

This account provides a plausible framework for interpreting the variation back and forth between inclusive and non-inclusive pronouns in the following example (for reasons of space I have abbreviated some of the conversation to highlight the shifts between inclusive and non-inclusive pronouns in Anita's speech).

Example 4

Anita: ***Yumi*** *maredem evri moning.*
1p.incl marry every morning

MM: ***Yu*** *no save livim long ol bi?*
2s no can leave to pl bee

→ A: *No, . . . man i mas mekem. OK* ***yu*** *girap long eli moning.*
no man AGR must make OK 2s get.up in early morning
Yumi- yu *go blong maredem . . . Taem* ***yumi*** *maredem long san, hem i hang*
1p.incl 2s go to marry time 1p.incl marry in sun 3s AGR hang

MM: ***Yu*** *luksave wan man flaoa mo wan woman flaoa o wanem?*
2s recognise one man flower and one woman flower or what

A: ***Yu*** *luksave i gat paoda ya . . .*
2s recognise AGR have powder SPEC

Anita: We (incl.) pollinate them [vanilla flowers] every morning.
MM: You can't leave it to the bees?
A: No . . . someone has to do it. So you get up early in the morning. We (incl.) – you go to pollinate them . . . If we (incl.) do the pollinating in sunlight, it [the flower] will fall.
MM: Do you look for a male and a female flower or what?
A: You find one that has this powder . . .

This exchange is interesting because Anita starts out using the inclusive form to me, clearly a metaphorical use of the pronoun, but when I ask a question using a non-inclusive form, she responds in like fashion. Shortly after, she reverts to the inclusive form (consistent, I would argue, with the community's norms about same-sex inclusiveness). Again I reply with a non-inclusive pronoun *yu*, and again Anita's response accommodates to this form.

This went on to and fro for much of the conversation, as I was unaware of the social significance of alternations between inclusive and non-inclusive pronouns.

One analysis of this exchange is that Anita's variation is caused at least partly by my behaviour. My responses may either create uncertainty and confusion for Anita, or may suggest uncertainty and confusion in my mind. Whereas Anita's use of the inclusive suggests we share a group identity, my responses imply that at the point of speaking I consider identities we do not share to be most salient. Anita's tussle with competing norms — see her second turn (highlighted), and her eventual convergence to the norm I persist with — suggests that Gudykunst may be correct: communicative accommodation is one way in which speakers attempt to reduce instability, or situational uncertainty, in encounters with others.

3.2   Socialising sorrow

The second case study affords a look at variation at the level of discourse strategies. The Bislama phrase *sore* (/sɔrɛ/ 'sorry') or *sore we* (/sɔrɛ wɛ/ 'so sorry', *we* functions here as an intensifier) is preferentially distributed among different groups of speakers.

Rampton (this volume), among others, points out that apologies serve an array of social functions, and this make them tricky to categorise solely in terms of positive and negative politeness (Brown and Levinson 1987). For reasons of space, these facts will not be rehearsed here. Suffice it to say, an apology is not simply an interpersonal act. The phenomenology of an apology involves recognising that an infraction has occurred, accepting one's responsibility for the infraction, and attempting to redress the infraction. Thus intergroup considerations are also integral to apologies.

As with the distribution of pronouns, the intriguing distribution of *sore* cannot be explained adequately without reference to non-linguistic factors. These factors relate to the community's ideologies about certain social identities encompassed by gender roles, and they relate to individual speakers' attitudes to these social identities, and their motivation to associate themselves with them.

In essence, the facts are as follows: *sore* serves three functions in Bislama. First, it is used to apologise for something which has impinged or might impinge on others, for example 'I am *sorry* that I had to say that' or 'I'm *sorry*, I have to take this away'. Second, it is used to express empathy with someone else about a negative experience that person may have had or may be experiencing; for example, 'Thousands of people died in the earthquake; I'm *sorry* for all the little children who have lost their parents' is expressed with *sore*. This empathetic use of *sore* has been extended to use with crying babies. Where, in English, we might say 'There, there' to a fretful baby, Bislama speakers in the village sometimes repeated '*Sore, sore*'. Third, *sore* has acquired the meaning of 'to miss someone or something', so in 'When I leave, I will *miss* you', the second verb is realised by *sore*. While the first two functions have analogues in English 'sorry', this third function seems to be an indigenous innovation (though by no means surprising as it extends regret for something that *is* a loss to regret for a situation in which there *will be* loss).

In principle, the only restrictions on the use of *sore* are those of contextual appropriateness. But in practice the three functions are not uniformly distributed across all speakers. Although the first and third functions were attested in the speech of men and women, during ten months of fieldwork no instances of men using *sore* to express empathy for others were recorded or observed. Obviously, this is not to say that men do not demonstrate feelings of empathy and sorrow for others; it is simply to say that they use other strategies to express their empathy.

Meyerhoff (1999) discusses the significance of this in greater detail than is possible here, interpreting this asymmetry in the distribution of functions in light of local ideologies about the social roles of the users. It is argued that because local ideologies about what constitutes being a 'good woman' include overt displays of nurturing behaviour, overt linguistic routines that display empathy or nurturance have a strategic function for women that they do not have for men. If a woman behaves in ways that establish her as a good exemplar of the social group of women, she may accrue status and generate positive feelings in others towards herself. But because nurturance is not an important property contributing to being seen as a 'good man', the use of *sore* as a marker of empathy is at best neutral for men. Consequently, there is simply not the same incentive for men to use the word in this particular function as there is for women.[7]

In this case, the variation in the community might well be seen as a case of *maximise fit*. There is comparatively high certainty across the community about what *sore* signifies. The analysis proposed here suggests that a woman's use of *sore* to show empathy maximises her fit to the local prototype of womanly behaviour. It is worth noting that in direct contrast to the position outlined here, Deleuze and Guattari (1987: 103) argue that it is a mistake to analyse variation in terms of deviations from a norm or prototype, since the variants are the only things that are real and it is therefore in the variants themselves that the meaning lies. They are quite right that the variants themselves are actual (or real), but I think it is a mistake to dismiss the significance of norms (whether subjectively perceived or objectively monitored) in analysing the social meaning of a variant. In addition, rejecting a role for virtual or idealised constructs like norms or prototypes seems inconsistent with their own more general argument about the speciousness of the virtual–real contrast.

In sum, just as the distribution of *yumi*, a lexical variable, was at least partly motivated by speakers' perceptions of their own and their interlocutors' social identities, similar motivations constrain variation at the level of discourse routines.

So far, we have considered the analysis of two variables. It was suggested that the first reflected the widespread practice of testing hypotheses; the second, the effects of maximising fit. In the next section, a third variable will be examined. This variable explores the limits of analyses based on uncertainty, even though the analysis of the first two variables profited from this perspective. It represents deep structural variation in the morphosyntax of Bislama — a level of structure that it has been argued is unobservable, and therefore resistant to indexing with social factors.

3.3   Spelling out referents: phonetically null subjects

If the subject of a finite clause has already been introduced to the discourse (or is contextually given), it may be realised in Bislama by a pronoun (as in English) or a phonetically null variant. In the second clause in example 5, the subject ('a message for me') is null. Compare the English translation where the pronoun 'which' is required to index the subject.

Example 5

Mi stap wet long wan mesej   blong mi, bae Ø   i   kam.
1s stay wait on   one message of   1s IRR (3s) AGR come
'I was waiting for a message for me, which should come.' (lit. . . . (and) (it) should come.)

There is considerable variability in Bislama in all persons and numbers between pronoun and phonetically null forms of subjects. But there are signs that the system is stabilising. Younger speakers, especially, prefer pronouns when the subject is first and second person, and phonetically null subjects when the subject is third person, as in example 5.

This kind of split in the grammar, where first and second person subjects are treated differently than third person subjects, may be termed a split *pro*-drop system. Why speakers would organise their grammar in this way is an interesting question. In Bislama, it seems that speakers constrain the system according to the level of informativeness in the verb morphology. Third person subject–verb agreement uniquely identifies singular and plural in Bislama, whereas first and second person agreement do not (the interaction between grammatical and discourse constraints on the variable is discussed in Meyerhoff (2000, ch. 6)).

In this section, it will be seen that even though *pro*-drop is principally constrained by grammar and discourse factors, linguistic factors do not account for all the variation observed. Interpersonal or intergroup factors also play a significant role. Patterns of *pro*-drop in comparable strings of conversation differ solely depending on who the speaker is addressing.

The significance of this is two-fold. First, it is further evidence of the part social and psychological motivations play in linguistic variation. Second, it raises questions about the meaning and scope of Labov's (1993) Interface Principle:

> Members of the speech community [socially] evaluate the surface forms of language but not more abstract structural features (1993: 4)

This principle states that because structural (syntactic) variables are usually unobservable, they do not acquire social or stylistic signification.

The data to be examined are two tellings of the same story by the same man. Sale was the senior (elder) man in the family that hosted me during my fieldwork on Malo island. He lived most of his life in villages on West Malo, and at the time of these recordings was in his sixties. Sale was recorded telling the story, first, to the assembled family after dinner, and six months later to me alone. There was no indication that Sale remembered having previously told this story in my presence or that if he did he considered it odd to be repeating it. Rickford and McNair-Knox (1994) show that separate accounts of the same story to different addressees can provide telling information about how intergroup distinctions may be triggered by a change in the conversational context. The data from Sale provide independent support for their findings.

The first telling, to a general audience of his extended family, can be taken to represent a less marked style against which the second telling can be compared. Note that this is distinct from claiming that it is an *unmarked* style (or that any such thing might exist). As a first approximation, let us say that the family context is less marked in the sense that the participants' presumed salient identities are constructed in an ingroup context. By contrast, the identities presumed to be salient when talking to the researcher include identities constructed as a consequence of intergroup contact. Systematic changes between tellings of the story can be attributed to the speaker's sensitivity to changes in the addressee. However, as will be shown, it may not always be possible to determine precisely what aspect of the addressee the speaker is responding to.

Table 2.2 shows Sale uses phonetically null subjects more frequently when addressing a general audience of listeners than when addressing the researcher only.

Table 2.2 Sale's conversation with two different audiences: number of phonetically null subjects as percentage of all clauses

Addressees	Ø subjects	% of all clauses
Extended family	$N = 50$	71%
MM only	$N = 40$	62%
Total	$N = 90$	67%

This data generalises from quite a small sample, of course, but the difference in the frequency is nonetheless statistically significant at the usual level.[8] It seems that the frequency of even a very deep structural variable such as null subjects shows significant sensitivity to changes in the speaker's interpersonal context. As with the *yumi* and *sore* variables, null subjects are partly constrained by the speaker's perception of the interpersonal or intergroup context.

In this case, there are a number of identities that the speaker could be responding to since my position in the speech community was marked in a number of ways — language learner; non-permanent resident; white; younger woman — to give but a few examples (and these were the identities most salient to me; there may have been others that were more salient to Sale). These factors may remain ineffable, since closer examination of the contexts and the linguistic variable tell us comparatively little here. Unlike the variables *yumi* and *sore*, which have their own rich semantics that can help with interpreting the variation, a phonetically null subject lacks inherent meaning. The perceptions and attitudes that might underlie the speaker's use of this particular variable have to be arrived at more circumstantially, and therefore the conclusions drawn must be more tentative.

The test for significance shows that the difference between Sale's behaviour on the first telling of the story and the second is not due to chance, but without more detailed clues about how he perceived the differences in the two speech events, it is impossible to do more than note a change in addressee. John Heritage (personal communication) has noted the possibility (and perhaps necessity) of talk and participant roles being highly laminated. He observes that an effect of this lamination is that at times it will simply be impossible to determine what roles and identities a particular discourse pattern represents. Here, the number of social and interpersonal variables that differentiate the two conversations profile exactly the sort of highly laminated context Heritage is talking about. Clift (1999) makes excellent use of the notion of laminated participant roles (though she does not use this terminology) in her revealing analysis of conversational irony. The discussion here reminds us that multiple and laminated roles are relevant to an understanding of many exchanges, not just discursively marked ones like ironic utterances.

Gallois *et al.* (1988) suggest that speakers employ qualitatively different strategies to signal attunement to intergroup and interpersonal factors. Interpersonal attunement, they suggest, is more likely to be achieved at the level of non-linguistic variables, for example gaze and gesture, while attunement to intergroup factors is more likely to emerge through linguistic strategies. Since the first two variables (*yumi* and *sore*) were specifically analysed as markers of intergroup boundaries, they cannot offer any data relevant to the distinction between domains that Gallois *et al.* hypothesise. The third variable, null subjects, has the potential to provide relevant data, but because the change in Sale's behaviour is ambiguous between attunement to interpersonal factors, and attunement to perceived intergroup differences in his addressees, i.e. the second recording is a highly laminated context, it fails to do so. As difficult as it may be to test, Gallois *et al.*'s (1988) hypothesis is intriguing and merits further empirical investigation; its reduced specificity in Gallois *et al.* (1995: 144–5) is regrettable.

Let us turn now to consider the implications of this data for Labov's Interface Principle ('Members of the speech community [socially] evaluate the surface forms of language but not more abstract structural features'). This will require some clarification of what it means to be 'socially evaluated'. If social evaluation means the variable shows clear stratification between different social groups (which is what Labov's body of work would suggest he meant), then the result in Table 2.2 alone does not contradict the Interface Principle. A complete examination of the subject variable in the wider speech community (Meyerhoff 2000) tested the distribution of its variants for significant correlations with a number of social dimensions that seemed (for independent reasons) to be salient in the village and urban area studied. There was no evidence that the distribution of phonetically null subjects was stratified by speaker sex, region of origin, level of education, language of education, village or urban residence. As noted already, the principal constraints were linguistic.

But if the fundamental difference between using null subjects with third person referents and pronouns with first and second person reflects differences at a highly abstract level of analysis (and such an analysis, analogous to the one presented in Poletto 1996, seems appropriate for Bislama), then Table 2.2 might present a problem for the Interface Principle. It appears that speakers do evaluate this highly abstract structural variable at some level. The evaluation does not demarcate groups at the level of the speech community, but a change in addressee can have a significant effect on a speaker's use of the variants. It seems that the variation in Table 2.2 is the result of interpersonal rather than intergroup factors. Note that this also runs counter to Gallois *et al.*'s (1988) hypothesis that linguistic variables mark intergroup distinctions. An alternative analysis might be to analyse the alternation between phonetically null and overt pronouns as a surface phenomenon. This would allow us to uphold the Interface Principle as formulated. However, this option does not seem to be viable here. As noted, the bulk of the variation is accounted for by linguistic factors, so abandoning a structural analysis of the variable would be a high price to pay.

This looks like strong counter-evidence to a generalisation that has been proposed in some of the variationist literature.[9] It has been suggested (Bell 1984) that a variable exhibits stylistic variation only if the variable is also socially stratified. None of the culturally salient group distinctions in the Bislama speech community exhibited a systematic constraint on this variable. So in this case, stylistic variation is greater than social variation. It remains to be seen whether this pattern emerges for other syntactic variables. It is possible that there is some form of interaction between the 'observability' of a variable and the proposed implicational relationship between interpersonal (style) and intergroup (social) variation.

These conclusions mean that aspects of the Interface Principle remain something of a mystery. For instance, it is not clear why social evaluations might be blind to abstract structure, while interpersonal evaluations are not. Perhaps grammatical variables can always be sensitive to interpersonal, affective factors, while maintaining independence from social or intergroup factors, because the speaker alone has direct access to their grammar, and because judgements of grammaticality are necessarily resolved internally. Clearly, this is an aspect of sociolinguistic theory that needs considerable further study.

3.4   An analysis of variable types

By way of conclusion to this section (being an analysis of several variables), it is worth pointing out how differences in *types* of variables begin to emerge as an important theoretical and methodological issue for sociolinguists. Perhaps more importantly, it is worth noting how some linguists are dealing with these issues at a practical level.

In the 1993 paper, Labov drew a distinction between two kinds of variables, deterministic and stochastic, and considered their implications for the study of all kinds of linguistic variation. By 'deterministic', Labov meant those variables that this chapter has called variables with inherent meaning (such as the inclusive pronoun), and by 'stochastic' he meant variables that have no meaning in and of themselves, but which may acquire (social) meaning probabilistically through association with some non-linguistic factor (for example a higher frequency of null subjects might acquire significance as an ingroup or family marker, or marker of casualness).

Labov was right in pointing out that the differences between the variables have important analytic consequences. When a variable has inherent meaning this becomes an excellent clue as to how interlocutors interpret and select its variants. Conversely, when the meaning is probabilistic only, this task becomes somewhat more delicate. This is reflected in both the nature and the strength of the claims made about speakers' motivations in the last three sections. Yet today, it would be going too far to conclude as Labov did in 1993 that sociolinguists 'have made comparatively few attempts to trace [speakers'] ability to interpret the wide range of social and stylistic variation in the stream of speech' (1993: 18).

In the last decade, sociolinguistics has increasingly theorised language as negotiated and collaborative behaviour. In the past, attitudinal and subjective factors have sometimes been treated as the field's unruly children — preferably sent to their rooms: applied linguistics; conversation analysis; discourse studies; social psychology. However, as contributions to this volume show, forays into sociology, anthropology, and psychology represent a serious intellectual quest for the tools with which to articulate Labov's 'wide range of social and stylistic' factors with the descriptive facts of language variation. Work by Holmes (1997) and Schilling-Estes (1999) provide models of how this theoretical articulation of goals might translate into methods that combine objective, quantitative analyses of data from the speech community with the subjective analysis of individual discourses. Those papers illuminate the way gender and ethnic identities, respectively, may be strategically made salient in conversation.

4   Conclusion: Sociolinguistics and social psychological theory

When Labov showed that social and attitudinal factors exert systematic effects on community-wide patterns of variation on Martha's Vineyard, and hence on the directions of language change, the door was opened for debate over what methodologies or analytical frameworks are most appropriate when considering variation in its wider, social context. It should no more surprise us that there is debate over the most appropriate frameworks for analysing the effects of social variables than that there is debate over the most appropriate structural frameworks for use in analysing the linguistic factors.

The general question posed at the start of this chapter was: to what extent are problems in sociolinguistics problems of the social psychology of language? The chapter then proceeded to examine the role some major theories in the social psychology of language might play in structuring the analysis of socially situated variation.

Section 2 reviewed a number of motivations and accounts for language variation that have been proposed. It was suggested that one way of looking at these motivations is that they express variability in participants' relative certainty about the stability of the situation or who they are and who their interlocutor is. Certainty, it was suggested, can be taken to be both a property of the individual and the situation. It was suggested that the family of behavioural variables well-known in social psychology — the effects of uncertainty management, interactional strategies with strangers, and communication accommodation — also play a role in constraining sociolinguistic variation.

Section 3 examined three linguistic variables, arguing that crucial aspects of variation could only be accounted for in terms of speakers' attitudes towards their own and their interlocutors' social roles and social identities. Even where most of the variance can be explained in terms of syntactic constraints, it was shown that social or psychological factors cannot be ignored. Where semantic cues as to the meaning of the variables exist, it was suggested that a more complete and constrained account of the variation results from an analysis that combines lexical semantics with the social ideologies of the community in which the variation is observed. It was suggested that intraspeaker variation in the use of inclusive pronouns (which exhibited variation in a conversation, or even in a single clause) was consistent with an analysis of uncertainty management. It was suggested that the speaker's response to what appeared to be divergent behaviour by the interlocutor showed that accommodative strategies may be used to achieve the larger end of uncertainty reduction.

It should be clear that no one motivation expressed in terms of (un)certainty accounts for any one variant. Heritage's metaphor of laminated talk and laminated participant roles seems germane. If roles may be laminated, motivations may also be. Women's use of *sore* as a marker of empathy was analysed as a strategy for maximising their identification with valued prototypes of womanly behaviour. The motivation for this was, in turn, given in terms of the social capital that they accrue in doing so. On the other hand, in the case of the variation in frequency of null subjects, the lamination of social roles confounded the analysis.

Undoubtedly, this leaves the study of language variation afloat at a fairly high level of abstraction, not an entirely undesirable place to be, given the abstraction of language itself. In fact, Deleuze and Guattari (1987) argue that sociolinguistics, being considerably more abstract than formal linguistics, comes closer to providing a complete theory of language than formal linguistics does. Notwithstanding Labov's plaint (above) that sociolinguists themselves have not engaged enough with the widest range of factors influencing variation, the field has been at the forefront in attempting to articulate models of language use that are sufficiently abstract (which does not mean unconstrained) that they can embrace non-linguistic as well as linguistic factors.

Although we are currently unable to state precisely what the units of variation are when we are dealing with affective or attitudinal factors, our understanding of these factors is enriched by drawing on the insights and principles of many other fields. The case studies of several linguistic variables presented here indicate that analysing variation in terms of speakers' (un)certainty about the roles and identities most salient in an interaction has the potential to be a fruitful juncture between sociolinguistics and social theory.

Notes

1. For instance, I am grateful to many people for helping me establish shared norms for coherence and consistency in this paper. Principally, Marisol Del Teso, Sally McConnell-Ginet, the editors of this volume, and the participants at the Second Sociolinguistics Roundtable. Thanks, too, to David

Britain, Kirk Hazen, Janet Holmes, Nancy Niedzielski and Natalie Schilling-Estes. The usual disclaimers apply. I extend thanks, too, to the Wenner-Gren Foundation for their support of my fieldwork in Vanuatu (grant #5742), and Sharon Morrie Tabi for her assistance transcribing and analysing recordings. Work on this paper was completed in the stimulating and supportive environment of the Cornell University Department of Linguistics, on an Andrew C. Mellon postdoctoral fellowship.

2. This chapter will not deal with the (undoubtedly important) question of whether social groups are defined externally, or subjectively, or a combination of both processes.

3. There is some evidence that the sociolinguistic account, biased for speaker attention, may be correct. Experiments by Duck *et al.* (1995) showed that if a person very strongly identifies with a prototypical ingroup characteristic, then they make strong distinctions not only between themself and *outgroup* members, but also between themself and *ingroup* members. This finding is neither predicted nor explicable in terms of the meta-contrast principle, and instead suggests that vigorous attention to one contrast (here, self's representativeness of the group prototype) renders other contrasts, and similarities, opaque.

4. Recordings were made on a Marantz PMD 430 using a Sony ECM-F9 (omnidirectional) condenser microphone. As a rule, recordings took place in people's own homes (village), or in the researcher's home (town), before or after a family meal, or during a spontaneous visit initiated by the person being interviewed. The transcribed corpus is over 30,000 words of Bislama. Data on inclusive pronouns and apologies was supplemented by further fieldnotes and untranscribed recordings.

5. Unless noted otherwise, all examples come from the recorded corpus. The following abbreviations are used in interlinear glosses: AGR subject–verb agreement; IRR irrealis mode; SPEC specificity marker; 1s first person singular; 2s second person singular; 3s third person singular; 1p 1st person plural; incl inclusive; excl exclusive.

6. Although the grammatical distinction that is used to express this metaphorical notion of inclusion is clearly a calque from the Oceanic substrate, it is less clear that the metaphorical use of 1p inclusive calques form a substrate discourse grammar. Terry Crowley reports that this use of the inclusive is not familiar to him from Paamese (central Vanuatu) or Sye (southern Vanuatu). Dorothy Jauncey observed few tokens in Tamambo (Malo), i.e. two tokens of the inclusive form *hinda-* being used metaphorically (in an extensive corpus collected over six months). The frequency of its use in Bislama seems to be much higher than in Tamambo.

7. One might ask whether use of empathic *sore* might even be costly for men. Using a discourse strategy that is associated with the qualities of 'good women' might threaten their identity as 'good men'. However, I have no evidence that people in this area see the social identities of male and female as being in opposition to each other in this way. Moreover, as noted, men do demonstrate empathic sorrow with others, e.g. by weeping or exclaiming in dismay.

8. Statistics were calculated with DataDesk 6.0 (software for the Macintosh, Paul F. Velleman 1997). A two-tailed t-test rejected the null hypothesis that the difference in mean frequency of phonetically null subjects with the two different types of addressee was due to chance. T-statistic = 14.78 with 1df, $p = 0.043$.
9. The articulation of this point is due to David Britain; thanks also to Natalie Schilling-Estes.

References

Bell, Allan (1984) Language style as audience design. *Language in Society* 13: 145–204.

Berger, Charles R. and Calabrese, Richard J. (1975) Some explorations in initial interactions and beyond: Toward a developmental theory of interpersonal communication. *Human Communication Research* 1: 99–112.

Billig, Michael and Tajfel, Henri (1973) Social categorization and similarity in intergroup behaviour. *European Journal of Social Psychology* 3: 27–52.

Britain, David (1997) Dialect contact and phonological reallocation: 'Canadian raising' in the English Fens. *Language in Society* 26: 15–46.

Brown, Penelope and Levinson, Stephen (1987) *Politeness: Some Universals in Language Use*. Cambridge: Cambridge University Press.

Bucholtz, Mary (1999) 'Why be normal?' Language and identity practices in a community of nerd girls. *Language in Society* 28: 203–223.

Callary, R.E. (1975) Phonological change and the development of an urban dialect in Illinois. *Language in Society* 4: 155–170.

Clift, Rebecca (1999) Irony in conversation. *Language in Society* 28: 523–553.

Cronen, Vernon E., Chen, Victoria and Pearce, W. Barnett (1988) Coordinated management of meaning: A critical theory. In Yun Kim Young and William B. Gudykunst (eds) *International and Intercultural Communication Annual, vol 12: Theories in Intercultural Communication*. Newbury Park: Sage, 66–98.

Deleuze, Gilles and Guattari, Félix (1987) *A Thousand Plateaus: Capitalism and Schizophrenia*. (Translated by Brian Massumi). Minneapolis: University of Minnesota Press.

Dittmar, Norbert and Schlobinski, Peter (1988) *The Sociolinguistics of Urban Vernaculars: Case Studies and their Evaluation*. Berlin: Walter de Gruyter.

Duck, Julie M., Hogg, Michael A. and Terry, Deborah J. (1995) Me, us and them: Political identification and the third-person effect in the 1993 Australian federal election. *European Journal of Social Psychology* 25: 195–215.

Duranti, Alessandro (1997) *Linguistic Anthropology*. Cambridge: Cambridge University Press.

Freud, Sigmund (1961 [1930]) *Civilization and Its Discontents*. (Translated by James Strachey). New York: Norton.

Gallois, Cynthia, Franklyn-Stokes, Arlene, Giles, Howard and Coupland, Nikolas (1988) Communication accommodation theory and intercultural encounters:

Intergroup and interpersonal considerations. In Yun Kim Young and William B. Gudykunst (eds) *International and Intercultural Communication Annual, vol 12: Theories in Intercultural Communication*. Newbury Park: Sage, 157–185.

Gallois, Cynthia, Giles, Howard, Jones, Elizabeth, Cargile, Aaron C. and Ota, Hiroshi (1995) Accommodating intercultural encounters: Elaborations and extensions. In Richard L. Wiseman (ed.) *International and Intercultural Communication Annual, vol 19: Intercultural Communication Theory*. Thousand Oaks, CA: Sage, 115–147.

Giles, Howard and Coupland, Nikolas (1991) *Language: Contexts and Consequences*. Pacific Grove, CA: Brooks/Cole.

Giles, Howard and Smith, Philip (1979) Accommodation theory: Optimal levels of convergence. In Howard Giles, Robert N. St. Clair, Peter Trudgill, William Labov and Ralph Fasold (eds) *Language and Social Psychology*. Baltimore: University Park Press, 45–65.

Goffman, Erving (1959) *The Presentation of Self in Everyday Life*. New York: Doubleday.

Gordon, Elizabeth (1997) Sex, speech, stereotypes: Why women use prestige forms more than men. *Language in Society* 26: 47–64.

Gudykunst, William B. (1995) Anxiety/uncertainty management (AUM) theory. In Richard L. Wiseman (ed.) *International and Intercultural Communication Annual, vol 19: Intercultural Communication Theory*. Thousand Oaks, CA: Sage, 8–58.

Hachimi, Atiqa (in press). Shifting sands: Language, gender and change in Moroccan Arabic and Moroccan society. In Marlis Hellinger and Hadumod Bussmann (eds) *Gender Across Languages: International Perspectives of Language Variation and Change*. Amsterdam: John Benjamins.

Haeri, Niloofar (1996) *The Sociolinguistic Market of Cairo: Gender, Class, and Education*. London: Kegan Paul.

Hogg, Michael A. (1996) Intragroup processes, group structure and social identity. In W. Peter Robinson (ed.) *Social Groups and Identities: Developing the Legacy of Henri Tajfel*. Oxford: Butterworth-Heinemann, 65–93.

Holmes, Janet (1997) Women, language and identity. *Journal of Sociolinguistics* 1: 195–223.

James, Deborah (1996) Women, men and prestige forms: A critical review. In Victoria L. Bergvall, Janet M. Bing and Alice F. Freed (eds) *Language and Gender Research: Rethinking Theory and Practice*. London and New York: Longman, 98–125.

Kahneman, Daniel and Tversky, Amos (1973) On the psychology of prediction. *Psychological Review* 80: 237–251.

Kahneman, Daniel and Tversky, Amos (1979) Prospect theory: An analysis of decision making under risk. *Econometrica* 47: 263–292.

Kroch, Anthony S. (1978) Toward a theory of social dialect variation. *Language in Society* 7: 17–36.

Labov, William (1966) *The Social Stratification of English in New York City*. Washington DC: Center for Applied Linguistics.

Labov, William (1972) *Sociolinguistic Patterns*. Philadelphia: University of Pennsylvania Press.

Labov, William (1993) The unobservability of structure and its linguistic consequences. Paper delivered at NWAVE 22, 16 October 1993. University of Ottawa, Ottawa.

Meyerhoff, Miriam (1998) Accommodating your data: the use and misuse of accommodation theory in sociolinguistics. *Language and Communication* 18: 205–225.

Meyerhoff, Miriam (1999) Sorry in the Pacific: Defining communities, defining practices. *Language in Society* 28: 225–238.

Meyerhoff, Miriam (2000). *Constraints on Null Subjects in Bislama (Vanuatu): Social and Linguistic Factors*. Pacific Linguistics. Canberra: Australian National University.

Oakes, Penelope (1996) The categorization process: cognition and the group in the social psychology of stereotyping. In W. Peter Robinson (ed.) *Social Groups and Identities: Developing the Legacy of Henri Tajfel*. Oxford: Butterworth-Heinemann, 95–119.

Oakes, Penelope, Haslam, S. Alexander and Turner, John C. (1998) The role of prototypicality in group influence and cohesion: contextual variation in the graded structure of social categories. In Stephen Worchel, J. Francisco Morales, Darío Páez and Jean-Claude Deschamps (eds) *Social Identity: International Perspectives*. London: Sage, 75–92.

Poletto, Cecilia (1996) Three kinds of subject clitics in Basso Polesano and the theory of *pro*. In Adriana Belletti and Luigi Rizzi (eds) *Parameters and Functional Heads: Essays in Comparative Syntax*. Oxford: Oxford University Press, 269–300.

Rickford, John and McNair-Knox, Faye (1994) Addressee- and topic-influenced style shift. In Douglas Biber and Edward Finegan (eds) *Sociolinguistic Perspectives on Register*. Oxford/New York: Oxford University Press, 235–276.

Robinson, W.P. (1985) Social psychology and discourse. In Teun A. van Dijk (ed.) *Handbook of Discourse Analysis: Volume 1, Disciplines of Discourse*. London: Academic Press, 107–144.

Rosch, Elinor (1975) Cognitive reference points. *Cognitive Psychology* 7: 532–547.

Rubinstein, Robert L. (1978) *Placing the Self on Malo*. Unpublished PhD dissertation, Bryn Mawr University.

Sankoff, David and Laberge, Suzanne (1978) The linguistic market and the statistical explanation of variability. In David Sankoff (ed.) *Linguistic Variation: Models and Methods*. New York: Academic Press, 239–250.

Schilling-Estes, Natalie (1999) Situated ethnicities: Constructing and reconstructing identity in the sociolinguistic interview. *University of Pennsylvania Working Papers in Linguistics (Selected papers from NWAV[E] 27)*. 6: 139–151.

Simmel, Georg (1971 [1908]) The stranger. In Donald N. Levine (ed.) *On Individuality and Social Forms: Selected Writings*. Chicago: University of Chicago Press.

Sunnafrank, Michael (1983) Attitude similarity and interpersonal attraction in communication processes. *Communication Monographs* 50: 273–284.

Tajfel, Henri and Turner, John C. (1986) The social identity theory in intergroup behaviour. In Stephen Worchel and William G. Austin (eds) *Psychology of Intergroup Relations*. Chicago: Nelson-Hall, 7–24.

Trudgill, Peter (1972) Sex, covert prestige and linguistic change in urban British English. *Language in Society* 1: 179–195.

Trudgill, Peter (1974) Linguistic change and diffusion: description and explanation in sociolinguistic dialect geography. *Language in Society* 3: 215–246.

Trudgill, Peter (1986) *Dialects in Contact*. Oxford: Blackwell.

3

Sociolinguistics, cognitivism, and discursive psychology
Jonathan Potter and Derek Edwards

1   Introduction

How can sociolinguistics be related to social theory? This is a complicated question for a range of reasons. Obviously what one understands to fall under the purview of sociolinguistics is one issue; precisely which social theory we are talking about is another. A further complication is whether we consider the relation between sociolinguistics and social theory to be additive or agonistic. For example, on the one hand, van Dijk's (1997) volumes on discourse studies map out an additive approach where various topics — ideology, semantics, register, cognitive representation, and so on — are treated as complementary modules that can be articulated together to contribute to a larger picture. On the other hand, some strands of ethnomethodological conversation analysis provide instead a wholesale respecification of topics, methods and questions. In conversation analysis, for example, the attempt is often not to relate institutions, as prior existing and clearly identifiable phenomena, with the more ephemeral waxing and waning of talk; rather institutional realities are treated as *constituted* in talk in a variety of ways as participants construct and orient to institutional goals and identities (Drew and Sorjonen 1997; Heritage 1997).

In this chapter we will be taking on a discursive psychological perspective, which itself draws heavily on ethnomethodological conversation analysis. So we will be pressing respecification rather than addition in the relation between sociolinguistics and social theory. That is, rather than joining up pieces of an existing jigsaw more neatly we will be attempting to paint a rather different picture. However, we wish to avoid simply reiterating the kinds of arguments about the role of social categories and social context in analysis that have been developed in this area by Sacks (1992), Schegloff (1997) and others. Instead, we will focus in particular on the topic of cognition and its role in sociolinguistics and social theory. Our aim will be to show how the additive model breaks down when considering cognition, and therefore to provide further support for a general respecification.

Much of sociolinguistics has developed against a backdrop of linguistic and sociological themes, and has therefore had little need to develop a formulated and explicit account of cognition. Nevertheless, it is common to find some version of 'perceptual-cognitivism' assumed in sociolinguistic research; that is, the idea that human activities are performed on the basis of cognitive processes of some kind acting on perceptual input, and governing behavioural output. Where cognition is addressed more explicitly, such as in the field of discourse processes (Graesser *et al.* 1997), the standard conceptions of cognitive psychology have often been adopted unchanged, with the research task treated as relating two things: features of language (grammar, lexical items, etc.) and inner cognitive processes.

Ironically, as sociolinguists look toward social theory, they are often dealing with perspectives that make the very same cognitivist assumptions. Other contributors to this volume have drawn on theorists such as Habermas and Bourdieu who, in the course of developing broad social theories, make a number of consequential assumptions about cognitive representations and processes. We do not have time or space here to map out these assumptions in any detail; but we hope to show at least that this would be a fruitful enterprise and that our arguments would have broader implications for those theories.

We are, obviously, aware of the huge research literature in cognitive psychology, cognitive science and social cognition that takes a perspective very different from our own. And, of course, the literature in discourse processes, including a range of contributions to van Dijk (1997), also makes starkly different cognitivist assumptions from the one we have developed. In the course of a range of publications, our argument has been that, for the most part, the research reported in this literature has not *tested* cognitivism against alternatives; rather, cognitivism has been *presupposed* in the detail of research practices. It is striking, for example, that much cognitive psychology uses discursive materials (as both 'input' and 'output') but ignores their specifically discursive features. Put another way, cognitive psychology has overwhelmingly worked with a view of discourse untouched by (the later) Wittgenstein and Sacks. Discourse is treated as an abstract logical and referential system — language — rather than a locally-managed, action-oriented, co-constructed resource.

Part of the difficulty is that theoretical assumptions have become sedimented into method. For the most part, cognitive psychological methods (using experiments, vignettes, questionnaires and so on) act as a systematic machinery for wiping out the practical, indexical, reflexive features of discourse that discursive psychologists argue are fundamental. We have not space here for surveying the arguments for and against these claims — for some examples in the cognitive psychological domains of language, memory and attribution see the debates expressed and described in Conway, 1992; Edwards and Potter 1993, 1999; Schmid and Fiedler 1999. The general point we would take from this work is that the nature of discourse is inadequately theorised, and this inadequacy will cause problems for any sociolinguist attempting to simply bolt on a cognitive 'level of analysis' to a linguistic one.

In this chapter we will take a discursive psychological approach to cognition (Edwards 1997; Edwards and Potter 1992; Potter and Edwards in press). This will involve neither assuming the theorising of current cognitive psychology nor presupposing an implicit perceptual cognitivism. Discursive psychology provides an alternative theorisation of both language and cognition. Instead of considering 'language' an abstract object with systemic properties, the focus is on texts and talk in social practices (discourse). Instead of considering 'cognition' as a collection of more or less technical inner entities and processes, the focus is on how mental phenomena are both constructed and oriented to in people's practices. Discursive psychology starts with action and understands the use of words, modalities, metaphors, and so on in terms of the way that talk and texts are oriented to action. Likewise, it treats the huge thesaurus of mentalistic terms that people have available to them as a resource for doing action: persuading, justifying, accounting, flirting and so on. In this ambition, it blends into, and draws on, a range of work in ethnomethodology and conversation analysis (such as Coulter 1990; Goodwin and Goodwin 1996, 1997; Lynch and Bogen 1996; Peräkylä 1995; Suchman 1987).

A central feature of discursive psychology is its coordinated reworking of the manner in which both cognition and reality (or better, 'cognition' and 'reality') are dealt with analytically (Edwards 1997; Potter 1996). Its caution against literal readings of cognitive descriptions is paralleled by its caution against literal readings of external worldly descriptions. In effect, both the mental world and the rest of reality are reformulated as discursive constructions. This is not to claim that nothing exists under the skull or out in the world, but that research on talk and texts as a medium for action will get into tangles by starting with the objects formulated and oriented to in talk and relating the talk to those objects. The reward for this radical conceptual reformulation is analytic coherence.

What we mean by 'analytic coherence' is a situation where talk and texts are no longer being compared to 'the world' and 'cognitive objects' in a way which obscures the comparison's dependence on prior, but largely hidden, discursive constructions of those entities by researchers. Instead, talk and texts are studied in their own right for how they are constructed and organised, and their orientation to action, whether they involve descriptions of actions ('flirting'), situations ('a bar'), persons ('my wife'), or cognitive states ('jealous') (Edwards 1998; Potter 1998a). Moreover, such descriptions work with close inferential relations between (what would traditionally be understood as) inner and outer realms (Potter et al. 1993). Describing an 'angry feeling' can be part of establishing the nature of an event as problematic; describing details of a person's 'insensitivity' can be part of establishing and justifying the speaker's 'anger'. These interrelationships are crucial in interaction, and yet they are just the kinds of relations that are broken up in many of the research methods of traditional cognitive psychology. The kind of analytic coherence that we are trying to achieve will allow those relations to be mapped out.

The rest of this chapter undertakes two closely related tasks. First, it will consider the way that cognition has been conceptualised in sociolinguistic work. Second, it will show the way that cognition is reconceptualised in discursive psychology. Our general argument will be against sociolinguistics adopting an uncritical cognitivism, either directly or in its embedding in broader social theories.

Clearly the question of how cognition has been dealt with in sociolinguistics is a very broad one with a range of different answers. We have chosen to approach it by focussing on Michael Stubbs's (1997) chapter on language, experience and cognition in the recent *Handbook of Sociolinguistics*. One reason for this is that it is a high-quality statement by a major figure in a major collection. Another is that he gives detailed examples from four important topic areas (racism, courtrooms, science and sexism) to illustrate his case. It thus provides an opportunity for some detailed reworking of our own. We hope that this will be taken as a compliment to the sophistication of Stubbs's work and that it will be apparent that our argumentative exposition is designed to make the issues as clear as possible. At the same time we are aware that Stubbs's chapter is not representative of all sociolinguistics, and that our arguments are much more in tune with other strands of work. With each of Stubbs's examples we will attempt to show how it can be understood in terms of discursive psychology rather than taken in cognitivist terms as evidence of cognitive processes and entities lying behind the talk.

2   Sociolinguistics and cognition

Stubbs's chapter starts by highlighting potential trouble in dealing with cognition; he shows acute awareness of a range of dangers in framing the relation between language and cognition. Despite this, he does not find it easy to escape from cognitivist stories. Like us he emphasises the need to go beyond language structure to focus on language use. However, his general conceptualisation of the issue is a more traditionally cognitivist one. He is concerned with 'relationships between language, thought, and culture' (1997: 358) and with the way in which 'language *mediates* experience' (1997: 364, emphasis in original). He is happy to assert that for most of us, at least some of the time, 'language *influences* thought' and the question is 'the linguistic mechanisms at work' (1997: 364, emphasis in original).

Note the way that Stubbs cannot rid himself of the picture of some kind of influence processes taking place between two different realms. He does not himself mark the distinction at the surface of the skull — but that is very much the taken-for-granted currency of cognitivism. For discursive psychology, instead of starting with a relation between realms, the question is how cognitive terms and orientations figure in interaction. This is not merely an arbitrary analytic preference on our behalf; what we have tried to document over the past few years is the way that ignoring the practical use of cognitivist discourse leads to a range of consequential confusions. Stubbs explores four areas for considering language–thought relations: racist discourse, courtroom discourse, science and sexism. Let us consider them in turn.

2.1   Racist discourse

Stubbs's argument concerns the role of new terms (such as *Scheinasylanten*, a German word for 'apparent/sham political asylum seekers') in sustaining and encouraging racism. Such 'lexical creations crystallize thoughts, make them easy to refer to, presuppose the existence of such things, and therefore facilitate stereotyped reactions' (1997: 366). As Stubbs would probably be the first to admit, examples of this kind do not *demonstrate* an influence process from language to thought. Yet, not only does it not demonstrate the phenomenon, the example *presupposes* it. It assumes that there are such things as racist thoughts that may be 'crystallized' or 'referred to' by particular terms and lead to 'stereotyped' (itself a term from cognitive social psychology) reactions. Part of what gives such constructions their suasive character is the fact that the discourse of thinking is itself amenable to both cognitive and non-cognitive uses. If you ask someone what their thoughts are on some topic you will most likely get, and most likely expect to get, a collection of discursive claims and propositions. They will be rather unlikely to tell you about fleeting images, short-term memory stores or activations in the PN neurones.

The problem with such examples is that they can be understood perfectly sensibly in discursive rather than cognitive terms. For example, we do not have to speculate about entities and processes under the skulls of Germans using the term *Scheinasylanten* to appreciate that it provides both description and evaluation in a compact package which is likely to facilitate making racist claims and, as Stubbs notes, presupposes the very existence of such people. The point is that *Scheinasylanten* can be understood from a discursive psychological perspective as a descriptive term with a range of racist uses (although discursive psychologists would, of course, wish to study those uses rather than speculate about them in the abstract or by way of made-up examples). Any cognitive consequences would have to be established, and this would surely involve going beyond the everyday cognitive thesaurus of words such as 'thinking', metaphors such as 'crystallising', and the semi-technical linguistic detritus of academic disciplines which includes terms such as 'stereotyped'.

It is not that issues of cognition are irrelevant for the study of racism; far from it. Talk and writing about issues of race, discrimination, and related matters is suffused with cognitive concerns. However, a discursive psychological perspective takes these as its topic. For example, the notion of 'attitude' is a technical concept in social psychology; yet, when someone is talking about race it may be a direct practical concern as to whether they are treated as having 'racist attitudes'. Wetherell and Potter (1992) studied the way in which middle class Päkehä (white) New Zealanders made critical claims about minority groups. One way to produce such claims is as elaborate, vivid description where evaluations are carefully tied to the (constructed) evaluative object, and treated as intersubjective or corroborated, rather than delivered as features of the speaker's own psychology. Speakers are here avoiding the discourse of 'attitudes' and its emphasis on potentially culpable individual preferences (Potter 1998b).

More generally, Wetherell and Potter (1992) mapped out the way a wide range of psychological notions — influence, information processing, stereotypes, and the notion of prejudice itself — became elements in the production and management of talk about race. Note the way this inverts the conventional practice in social research. Instead of trying to understand racist talk and action in terms of cognition, it is showing how racist talk and action can be sustained using cognitive notions. Far from cognitive notions being required to do adequate analysis, the analysis is facilitated by focussing on situated practices rather than cognition, where cognitive categories and concerns feature as part of those practices, as ways of talking, and of doing things with words.

2.2   Courtroom reality construction

The second topic area is courtroom discourse, and in particular the construction of reality in courts. Stubbs is interested in 'cases where lexical choices create frames of reference with their own internal logic, and influence perception and memory' (1997: 366). For example, he cites work by Danet (1980) on the language of a trial where a doctor had been accused of manslaughter for performing a late abortion. This emphasised the significance of descriptions — *the foetus was aborted* vs *the baby was murdered* — for the outcome. And he cites Loftus and Palmer's (1974) famous study where people shown a film of a traffic accident gave different descriptions according to terms in the questions about it such as *hit, collide, smash* and *bump*. For example, people who were asked about the cars *smashing* into each other were more likely to say that they saw broken glass on the road.

Picking up from Loftus and Palmer (1974), Stubbs searched a large (120 million) database of words to extract 'the most frequent collocates of words in the lexical field of "hit" '(1997: 367). This identifies varied, often metaphorical, uses of *hit* (*earthquake, hard, jackpot, recession*) while *smash* tends to connote crime and violence (*bottles*, *glass*, *looted*, *window*, *windscreen*) — although in this list only *looted* seems to strongly support the argument. Stubbs's conclusion is that recurrent wordings can 'fix and transmit cultural meanings . . . encode stereotypes and shared assumptions' (1997: 368). Again, the ambiguity over the cognitive status of 'meanings', 'stereotypes', and 'assumptions' contributes to the sense that the argument has implications for relations between language and cognition, while not spelling out what such implications are. Our point is that the plausibility of such arguments falls away when they are examined in detail.

More significantly, the phenomena discussed here are very much the province of discursive psychology. The studies by both Danet (1980) and Loftus and Palmer (1974) show the world-constructive and consequential role that descriptions play in actions. However, showing that descriptions are world-constructive and consequential is not the same as demonstrating that any particular *cognitive* processes or entities are involved. Most importantly, we do not need to know about any such entities or processes to find the important phenomena, to study them, and to identify their implications. The analytic preference of discursive psychology is to study the use of descriptions in natural discourse, where their involvement with particular actions is more easily identified, and the temptation to abstraction into linguistics, in one direction, and cognition, in another, is more easily resisted. Let us try and illustrate this with an example of our own.

In the following case a suspect/interviewee 'A' is telling a police officer 'B' of his involvement in a fight. The interviewee has been accused of starting the fight by 'punching' another man on the head. (See also Edwards 1997: 244–5.) The issue at stake here is, roughly, why did A 'punch him in the head'?

Example 1

(Data from Auburn *et al.* 1995: 375.)

1 A: 'cos I was off dancing and I was just dancing around and I was
2   dancing with this girl and like I've just clipped this boy's head
3   (1.0) and as I as I've clipped him I've gone oh sorry mate
4 B: when you say you've clipped by accident d'you mean
5 A: yeah well I'm not gonna hit someone on the head on purpose am I
6 B: Yeah
7 A: and he's come across all like that and I've gone all right there's
8   no need to be like that and he pushed me so we just started fighting
9   and his mates got up and there was about four of them I think

In this example we are not faced with relations between single words and particular outcomes, as with the Loftus and Palmer study, nor do we have abstract statistics of collocation, as in Stubbs's own study. Rather we have a sequence where one term (*punched*) is used by a police officer, and other terms (*clipped*, *hit*) are used by the suspect. Considering these terms in their sequential location allows us to examine how A's action is played out through the alternation of event descriptions. A's re-formulation of his action from *punch* to *clip*, and the explicit contrast between *clip* and *hit* (line 5), are part of his activity of disclaiming responsibility. *Clip* alternates with *punch* and *hit* to downgrade the contact made, as well as its deliberateness, and thereby reduce the attributional implication that it was enough to cause a fight, and for him to be responsible for that fight. These empirical, interactional details show the way the participants themselves are drawing causal inferences from event descriptions.

It is important to be clear here. It may seem that we too have drifted down a cognitivist path when we talk of the participants 'drawing causal inferences'. Yet we are treating causal inferences as an activity done, and oriented to, in discourse — an activity done in the first instance *by participants*. It is handled and managed, as a participants' concern, through circumstantial descriptions such as 'just dancing around', 'just clipped', the narrated apology 'oh sorry mate' (lines 1–3), and the direct causal invocations 'by accident' and 'on purpose' (lines 4 and 5). Thus we *are* committed to the implications of intentionality that follow from the identification of activities in discourse. Yet we are *not* committed to a cognitivist account of intentions, an account that treats them as mental events preceding talk and action. Such an account would be susceptible to Wittgensteinian criticisms of approaches that take intention as a referent for an inner state (Anscombe 1957; Wittgenstein 1980; Coulter 1990). Nor are we committed to a cognitivist account of inferences. While it is no doubt true, and indeed necessary, that the participants here have brains, neurones, lattices of connecting axons and so on, we do not need to assume that there is any particular representation or process in cognitive stuff, however technically specified, that counts as a 'causal inference' (some biocomputer symbolisation of an 'if x then y' variety, perhaps).

Furthermore, we do not need to make a judgement about *particular* cognitive states to explain the interaction here. The identification of actions and inferences depends on an analysis of discourse and the various orientations displayed in it. Note, for instance, how B picks up the causal implication of A's use of the word *clip* in line 4, and how A ratifies that implication in line 5. Thus discursive psychology draws on the same analytic resources provided by the sequential, recipient-organised nature of interaction that have been used so successfully by conversation analysts (Heritage 1995). For more developed analyses of examples of this kind, see Edwards (1997).

2.3   Scientific reality construction

Stubbs (1997: 369) describes science as an area 'where concepts and syntax seem to have developed together' and where 'this development is amenable to empirical text analysis'. He leans heavily on Halliday and Martin's (1993) study of scientific language, which he describes as starting:

from two clear facts. (1) Scientific and everyday language are very different: e.g., it is well known that certain syntactic features, such as passive and nominalization, are common in scientific language. (2) Scientific and everyday world views are very different, indeed science often rejects common-sense understandings. (1997: 369)

What Halliday and Martin are taken to be attempting is a '*functional*' account of scientific discourse, but not one that is functional in the manner of discursive psychology. It is functional in that it is 'looking for a cognitive *explanation* of the heavily nominalized style of science' (1997: 369, emphasis added).

We have a range of problems with Halliday and Martin's (1993) study and Stubbs's use of it. However, the important issue here is what is being claimed about language and cognition, and in particular the influence of the latter on the former. Let us put to one side the implications for the historical development of scientific discourse that arise from this account. For if the heavily nominalised style of science is to be explained as a consequence of thinking scientifically, then it would be important to demonstrate that it was not merely imported from legal discourse. Historical studies have suggested that scientists such as Robert Boyle looked to the law for models of empirical justification in the mid seventeenth century (Shapin and Schaffer 1985). Do some of the stylistic features of scientific writing reflect this disciplinary emigration? Do they reflect the legalistic, judgemental nature of scientific publishing decisions where a jury of one's peers has become modern peer review? That would be a consequential line of research for verifying these claims. However, that is not an enterprise that we are able to tackle here. Moreover, the difficulties we have with Halliday and Martin are more direct.

First, take the two 'clear facts'. The way they are constructed, to set *language* over against *views* and *understandings*, makes it seem that what is being described are straightforward parallels between language and cognition. Yet, as we noted in the previous sections, terms such as *view* and *understanding* allude to cognition, but in their normal use are not equivalent to the sorts of mental processes and representations that are the currency of cognitive psychology. They are cognitive by innuendo only; they do not rely on cognitive objects or processes as cognitive psychologists understand them, to make sense.

Second, the 'clear facts' themselves are far from clear. Halliday and Martin (1993) studied scientific *texts*, formal writing, and compare this to a generic, rather under-specified everyday language. The trouble here is that scientific language is far from confined to formal texts. Studies of scientific discourse have found that there are wide differences between the way scientists talk at the lab bench, or when they are interviewed by sociologists, and how they write in journal articles (see for example Gilbert and Mulkay 1984; Lynch

1985; Myers 1990). When scientists are talking to one another about experiments, observations and colleagues, their talk is not suffused with passives and nominalisations. Note the significance of this. If the role of scientific language was cognitive, emerging out of and sustaining scientific thinking, we would expect this form of talk, this *register*, to be involved when scientists are practising science itself rather than (merely) representing it in formal written reports.

From a discursive psychological perspective we can ask why it might be that this particular kind of language is used in scientific *articles*. Put another way, can we identify plausible *practical* reasons for this kind of writing? Two complementary possibilities have been suggested (Potter, 1996). First, the impersonality provided by passivisation and nominalisation may reduce conflict in an area of life where conflict is commonplace or even essential, and where it could considerably distract from the business at hand. Second, such constructions enable descriptions to be produced which minimise the actions and commitments of the writer; the scientist becomes almost a bystander while the data take on a textual life of their own, agents which are able to point, show or imply. That is, the formal discourse of scientific articles is rhetorically oriented to constructing the factual out-there-ness of scientific phenomena. This suggests that the character of scientific writing is at least as plausibly explained by its interactional and persuasive role than by any congruence with the cognitions of individual scientists when they are designing experiments, developing theories and so on.

This leads to a further problem with Halliday and Martin's (1993) 'clear facts'. Although the formal writing of scientists may be very different from the kind of informal talk that takes place in a telephone call between friends, it is similar, in certain ways, to other areas of non-scientific discourse. For example, a search through a year's US radio and television news on CD-ROM shows that passive constructions such as 'it was believed' are commonplace. Potter (1996) has suggested that the detailed operation of these constructions may be to do with the complex set of issues surrounding fact construction, footing and accountability that arise in news reporting. Such constructions report beliefs, which may be crucial to the general news narrative, while avoiding potentially problematic attributions of that belief either to the news organisation or its agents, or to possibly interested parties to the story. The detail is less important here than the broad point that when considering constructions such as these *in context*, as parts of *narrative*, as attending to issues of *accountability*, as managing concerns with *footing*, we can start to identify specific activities that are being done which make sense of why they take the form that they do, in the context that they appear. What seemed on superficial examination to be an esoteric discourse of science may be better understood as a generic discursive form for constructing talk and texts in complex social settings. An appeal to some cognitive realm beyond that is unnecessary and misleading.

2.4   Sexism

Stubbs's final example is rather less developed than the other three. Even though it is presented as a further exploration of relations between language and cognition, it mainly describes frequencies of usage of words such as *his* vs *theirs*, or *boy* vs *girl* in spoken English and children's literature. Again, the inferences about the role of cognition are made more by implication or assumption, than by spelled-out argument about identifiable cognitive entities, states and processes. For example, Stubbs writes that sexist language 'uses lexical and grammatical resources to represent the world from the point of view of the male' (1997: 370). This alludes to the perceptual cognitivism, but does not spell out the 'point of view' metaphor. It is not unusual for such metaphors to be used to highlight certain features of practices without buying a specific mental ontology.

As before, we should emphasise that our concern is not that the distribution of constructions such as *his* and *theirs* is not important; the point is *how* it is important. Is it through its influence on some inner stuff — for example mental stereotypes, prototypes, representations — or is it necessary to go beyond that to study the involvement of particular constructions in practices? For discursive psychological work on sexism, the focus has been more on the way accounts are constructed to simultaneously present unequal employment situations as natural and inevitable, and to present the speaker as caring and egalitarian. That is, the concern has been with the practical role of discourse. Let us illustrate this with some examples.

Wetherell, Stiven and Potter (1987) studied the way men talked about women's career opportunities during open-ended interviews. In contrast to much previous work on this topic, the attempt was not to understand how what was said might be a clue to some underlying cognitive entity — an attitude or stereotype of women's career advancement. Rather, the interviews gave them the opportunity to provide extended descriptions, explanations and judgements as they dealt with a range of questions and comments from the interviewer. Close analysis of the interviews found a regular pattern. On the one hand, the men supported the *principle* of women's career opportunities and attacked discrimination based on gender. On the other hand, the men offered a wide range of *practical* reasons for the failure of women to reach full employment equality, including references to such concerns as childcare, tradition, and emotional unsuitability to stressful work. Note the significance of this pattern. These men have the ability to affirm *both* support for women's employment equality (in principle) *and* support for continued inequality (because of important practical concerns). They could be 'unequal egalitarians', supporting the unequal status quo yet displaying themselves as non-sexist through their abstract support of egalitarian principles.

Take another discursive study in this tradition. Gill (1993) studied the way radio controllers accounted for the low representation of female DJs when interviewed about the topic. Her findings repeated the general pattern in the Wetherell *et al.* (1987) study; the controllers supported the *principle* of equality yet drew on an elaborate repertoire of practical reasons for not appointing more women DJs. However, in this study the participants were describing their *own* recruitment practices rather than addressing hypothetical examples. It is notable that they constructed accounts to present the lack of recruitment as a product of external factors rather than their own desires; for example, few women apply, women do not have the appropriate skills, or listeners do not like women's 'shrill' voices.

In both of these studies the focus was on the way accounts were built to make a situation of inequality appear natural, inevitable or at least justifiable. Neither focusses on the particular terms used. However, Speer (2000) has studied talk that drew on potentially heterosexist terms (queer, butch, dyke). She showed the way that speakers attend, in a range of different ways, to potentially negative implications. These speakers were simultaneously managing issues of identity and assigning blame and responsibility. Her conclusion is that psychological work on heterosexism tends to obscure such flexible discursive practices and reify such discourse phenomena into stable, causal attitudes within individuals. For us, the interest is in the way a cognitivist account of this discourse becomes problematic when the practical and action-oriented nature of the talk is allowed to enter the research. These studies start to show the value of studying sexism in terms of a range of practical tasks that people are performing with their talk and texts.

Cognitivism has the same dangers in research on sexism as in the work on racism. It risks reducing a social phenomenon, sustained through a range of practices, to features of individual psychological operation. This is a complex area in which there are deep and delicate issues to do with the management of analytic and political concerns (see Edwards, forthcoming; Wetherell and Potter 1992; Wetherell 1998; Kitzinger and Frith 1999). Our view is that cognitivism is likely to compound the confusions here.

3 Sociolinguistics, cognitivism and discursive psychology

We hope that Michael Stubbs will not mind us using his handbook chapter in this way. It allowed us to deal with one of the most up-to-date and canonical examples of the manner in which sociolinguists deal with cognition. We have attempted to do three things with it. First, we have tried to demonstrate that the substantive claims about the relation between language and cognition can, in every case, be questioned. Second, we have tried to show that the writing draws on an under-theorised cognitivist image of the relations between the inner stuff of cognition and the observable phenomena of talk and texts. Third, we have tried to show that this inner stuff is itself rarely theorised specifically (using the technical apparatus of social cognition, for example) but is alluded to by the use of metaphors such as 'crystallise' and ambiguous terms such as 'thinking'. More generally, we have tried to take the four topics, which Stubbs treats as paradigms for cognitive interpretation, and show how the phenomena can be, and have been, tractable to a discursive psychological analysis in terms of the involvement of discursive constructions in practices.

What lessons do we draw from this for sociolinguistics? There is an interesting parallel here with arguments about cognitivism in psychology. One of the features of psychological research methods is that although they are so dependent on discourse, they break that discourse up into vignettes, tick boxes and so on. That is, they systematically strip off the indexical, rhetorical features of discourse that discursive psychologists, and other researchers in the conversation analytic and ethnomethodological tradition, have shown to be fundamental. Once talk is separated from its action orientations in this way it becomes much easier to treat it as an expression of underlying cognitive processes and states. Without dealing with them in detail, there is a danger that traditional collocation and distributional techniques, for example, can lead to cognitivist conclusions for the same reason. They take words out of their sequential and rhetorical context, thus allowing them to be more easily imagined as products of underlying cognitions.

Our wariness of cognitivism leads us to be wary also of the kinds of large-scale social theories that have been proposed as enriching sociolinguistics or connecting it to broad social and political issues.

Take Bourdieu for example. He has frequently been identified as a social theorist who can make important links to sociolinguistics. And his notion of habitus — roughly dispositions that generate practices, perceptions and attitudes — has been treated as particularly important, as has the idea that there is a specifically linguistic habitus — the particular dispositions involved in language use, including voicing, the use of the lips and so on. It might appear that the notion of habitus avoids the pitfalls of cognitivist accounts we have highlighted because of its emphasis on dispositions which are prior to, and generate, perceptions, attitudes, etc. However, his account of practice is strikingly similar to mainstream cognitive psychology where cognition is not conceptualised as restricted to explicit terms or propositions, and certainly not to conscious images or representations. Rather it presupposes that there is some psychological system that is developed over time and enables storage, processing and the generation of output.

Moreover, it is striking that, for all his emphasis on practice, Bourdieu equally gives precedence to visual perception and the role of schemata in producing 'meaning'. To illustrate these strands in his thinking we have highlighted some of the cognitivist tropes in an illustrative extract from his work:

> The *perception* of the social world is the product of a double social structuring: on the 'objective' side, this *perception* is socially structured because the properties attached to agents or institutions do not make themselves

available to *perception* independently, but in combinations whose probability varies widely [. . .]; on the 'subjective' side, it is structured because the *schemes* of *perception* and *evaluation* . . . express, in a more or less transformed form, the state of symbolic relations of power. . . . [The] plurality of world *views* . . . is linked to plurality of *points of view* . . . [and] to all the *cognitive strategies of fulfilment* which produce the *meaning* of the objects of the social world by going directly beyond *visible* attributes by reference to the future or the past. (Bourdieu 1991: 234–5, italics added)

Bourdieu is an interesting and sometimes exciting theorist, and we are not suggesting that his work has no value for sociolinguists. However, we would caution against an uncritical adoption of some of the assumptions his work makes. In particular, it seems to end up with a surprisingly traditional notion of the psychological individual bringing their linguistic habitus to a particular social context. For the reasons developed above, we believe that such assumptions would lead to analytic incoherence if his work were uncritically bolted on to a detailed analysis of discourse. We suggest that analysts will benefit from adopting a stance that presupposes neither cognition nor reality but addresses both as they are constructed and oriented to in discourse. This path may seem to duck some of the big concerns of social theory, but we believe it to be interesting, analytically coherent, and fruitful.

References

Anscombe, G.E.M. (1957) *Intention*. Oxford: Blackwell.

Auburn, Tim, Willig, Carla and Drake, Sue (1995) 'You punched him, didn't you': Versions of violence in accusatory interviews. *Discourse and Society* 6: 353–386.

Conway, Martin (ed.) (1992) Developments and debates in the study of human memory. *The Psychologist* 5: 439–461.

Coulter, Jeff (1990) *Mind in Action*. Oxford: Polity Press.

Danet, B. (1980) 'Baby' or 'fetus': language and the construction of reality in a manslaughter trial. *Semiotica* 32: 187–219.

Drew, Paul and Sorjonen, M-L. (1997) Institutional dialogue. In T.A. van Dijk (ed.) *Discourse as Interaction (Discourse Studies: A Multidisciplinary Introduction, volume 2)*. London: Sage, 92–118.

Edwards, Derek (1997) *Discourse and Cognition*. London: Sage.

Edwards, Derek (1998) The relevant thing about her: Social identity categories in use. In C. Antaki and S. Widdicombe (eds) *Identities in Talk*. London: Sage, 15–33.

Edwards, Derek (forthcoming) Analysing racial discourse: A view from discursive psychology. In H. van den Berg, H. Houtkoop-Steenstra and M. Wetherell (eds) *Analyzing interviews on racial issues: Multidisciplinary approaches to interview discourse*. Cambridge: Cambridge University Press.

Edwards, Derek and Potter, Jonathan (1992) *Discursive psychology*. London: Sage.

Edwards, Derek and Potter, Jonathan (1993) Language and causation: A discursive action model of description and attribution. *Psychological Review* 100: 23–41.

Edwards, Derek and Potter, Jonathan (1999) Language and causal attribution: A rejoinder to Schmid and Fiedler. *Theory and Psychology* 9: 823–836.

Gilbert, G. Nigel and Mulkay, Michael (1984) *Opening Pandora's Box: A Sociological Analysis of Scientists' Discourse.* Cambridge: Cambridge University Press.

Gill, Ros (1993) Justifying injustice: Broadcasters' accounts on inequality in radio. In E. Burman and I. Parker (eds) *Discourse Analytic Research: Repertoires and Readings of Texts in Action.* London: Routledge, 75–93.

Goodwin, Charles and Goodwin, Marjorie H. (1996) Seeing as situated activity: Formulating planes. In Y. Engeström and D. Middleton (eds) *Cognition and Communication at Work.* Cambridge: Cambridge University Press, 61–95.

Goodwin, Charles and Goodwin, Marjorie H. (1997) Contested vision: The discursive constitution of Rodney King. In B.-L. Gunnarsson, P. Linell and B. Nordberg (eds) *The Construction of Professional Discourse.* London: Longman, 292–316.

Graesser, A.C., Gernsbacher, M.A. and Goldman, S.R. (1997) Cognition. In T.A. van Dijk (ed.) *Discourse Studies: A Multidisciplinary Introduction, Volume 1: Discourse as Structure and Process.* London: Sage, 292–319.

Halliday, M.A.K. and Martin, J. (1993) *Writing Science: Literacy and Discursive Power.* London: Falmer Press.

Heritage, John C. (1995) Conversation analysis: Methodological aspects. In U. Quasthoff (ed.) *Aspects of Oral Communication.* Berlin and New York: De Gruyter, 391–418.

Heritage, John C. (1997) Conversation analysis and institutional talk: Analysing data. In D. Silverman (ed.) *Qualitative Research: Theory, Method and Practice.* London: Sage, 161–182.

Kitzinger, Celia and Frith, Hannah (1999) Just say no? The use of conversation analysis in developing a feminist perspective on sexual refusal. *Discourse and Society* 10: 293–316.

Loftus, Elizabeth F. and Palmer, J.C. (1974) Reconstruction of automobile destruction. *Journal of Verbal Learning and Verbal Behaviour* 13: 585–589.

Lynch, Michael (1985) *Art and Artefact in Laboratory Science: A Study of Shop Work and Shop Talk in a Research Laboratory.* London: Routledge & Kegan Paul.

Lynch, Michael and Bogen, David (1996) *The Spectacle of History: Speech, Text and Memory of the Iran–Contra Hearings.* Durham, NC: Duke University Press.

Myers, Greg (1990) *Writing Biology: Texts in the Construction of Scientific Knowledge.* Madison: University of Wisconsin Press.

Peräkylä, Anssi (1995) *AIDS Counselling: Institutional Interaction and Clinical Practice.* Cambridge: Cambridge University Press.

Potter, Jonathan (1996). *Representing Reality: Discourse, Rhetoric and Social Construction.* London: Sage.

Potter, Jonathan (1998a) Cognition as context (whose cognition?). *Research on Language and Social Interaction* 31: 29–44.

Potter, Jonathan (1998b) Discursive social psychology: From attitudes to evaluations. *European Review of Social Psychology* 9: 233–266.

Potter, Jonathan and Edwards, Derek (in press). Discursive social psychology. In P. Robinson and H. Giles (eds) *Handbook of Language and Social Psychology.* London: Wiley.

Potter, Jonathan, Edwards, Derek and Wetherell, Margaret (1993) A model of discourse in action. *American Behavioural Scientist* 36: 383–401.

Sacks, Harvey (1992) (ed. G. Jefferson) *Lectures on Conversation. Vols. I and II.* Oxford: Basil Blackwell.

Schegloff, Emanuel A. (1997) Whose text? Whose context? *Discourse and Society* 8: 165–187.

Schmid, Joanne and Fiedler, Klaus (1999) A parsimonious theory can account for complex phenomena: A discursive analysis of Edwards' and Potter's critique of non-discursive language research. *Theory and Psychology* 9: 807–822.

Shapin, Steven and Schaffer, Simon (1985) *Leviathan and the Air-pump.* Princeton, NJ: Princeton University Press.

Speer, Susan (2000) Talking gender and sexuality: conversations about leisure. Unpublished PhD, Loughborough University.

Stubbs, Michael (1997) Language and the mediation of experience: Linguistic representation and cognitive orientation. In F. Coulmas (ed.) *The Handbook of Sociolinguistics.* Oxford: Blackwell, 358–373.

Suchman, Lucy (1987) *Plans and Situated Actions: The Problem of Human–Machine Interaction.* Cambridge: Cambridge University Press.

van Dijk, Teun A. (ed.) (1997) *Discourse Studies: A Multidisciplinary Introduction* (2 vols). London: Sage.

Wetherell, Margaret (1998) Positioning and interpretative repertoires: Conversation analysis and post-structuralism in dialogue. *Discourse and Society* 9: 387–412.

Wetherell, Margaret and Potter, Jonathan (1992) *Mapping the Language of Racism: Discourse and the Legitimation of Exploitation.* London: Harvester and New York: Columbia University Press.

Wetherell, Margaret, Stiven, Hilda and Potter, Jonathan (1987) Unequal egalitarianism: a preliminary study of discourses concerning gender and employment opportunities. *British Journal of Social Psychology* 26: 59–71.

Wittgenstein, L. (1980) *Remarks on the Philosophy of Psychology, Vols 1–2.* Oxford: Blackwell.

Part

II

Language and discourse as social practice

4

Dynamics of discourse or stability of structure: Sociolinguistics and the legacy from linguistics
Per Linell

1 Introduction: Language and discourse

When general issues of language and discourse[1] have been treated within the language sciences, including linguistics and sociolinguistics, it has become a commonplace that discourse is discussed in terms of dynamic processes and situated construction. Languages, on the other hand, have traditionally been seen in terms of stable, supraindividual systems of units and rules. Yet the relationships between structure and agency are moot points in sociology and sociolinguistics (Carter and Sealey 2000); language as a system is arguably also subject to dynamic variation and change, and there is structure and stability also in action and in discourse across communicative events. It is therefore too simplistic to claim that, in the realm of language and discourse, language equals stability and discourse equals dynamics, even if this view has been attributed to many linguistic thinkers, for example, Saussure (1964 [1916]; cf. Lähteenmäki 1998).

It has proven very difficult to strike a reasonable balance between stability and variation in the analysis of language *and* discourse. In this paper, I will discuss some aspects of linguistics and sociolinguistics against the backdrop of this problematic. Part of the problems reside, I will argue, in the fact that dynamics in general is much more difficult to describe in a veridical and yet systematic way than is stable structure. To some extent, this is accentuated by a general preference for grand, comprehensive and context-free theories of language and society, which leads to problems of coming to grips with the dynamics of context-sensitive talk. My main argument, however, is that the emphasis on structure, especially with regard to systems of linguistic expressions, has a long tradition in linguistics. This is the legacy of the 'written language bias'.

2 Languaging as action, and languages as sets of forms

People encounter language and linguistic phenomena in all the different cognitive and communicative activities of social life. We are immersed in continuities of practices, in which we try to understand and make known phenomena in the world. In doing so, we do not normally focus on language. Instead, language is an abstract phenomenon, often transparent and invisible in the sense that it is the medium through which we perceive, understand and communicate about other things, and it is these latter things, the topics and the interpersonal relations, that we attend to in the overwhelming majority of communicative events. How then can such a transparent and dynamic phenomenon be construed and made visible?

It is fair to say that linguistic phenomena could be, and have in fact been, seen in basically two different ways, as action and as structured sets of forms. According to the first perspective, to speak, that is to indulge in talk-in-interaction, to write and to read, or to use language in modern hybrid media, is to be involved in **action**, acting in and through language. Such a perspective will highlight dynamic processes; as several authors have emphatically stated, discourse is **process** (see for instance Potter *et al.* 1990: 'discourse is a verb').

But as far as the concept of language is concerned, this is not the dominant tradition. Instead, we have become used to saying that a language is a **set of forms**, that is, expressions such as morphemes, words, and syntactic forms, associated with linguistic meanings (plus rules for constructing such forms). So we have at least two major ways of construing or representing language:[2]

Language as a structured set of forms (used to represent things in the world)	Language as meaningful action, interventions in the world, cultural practices

These ways correspond roughly to Dik's (1978) paradigms of formalism and functionalism, as discussed by Figueroa (1994: 22f) in her account of sociolinguistic metatheory. It is also possible to characterise the two perspectives as Cartesian and monologistic, vs Hegelian and dialogistic, respectively (Marková 1982). The former view usually portrays (the understanding of) the world as independent of language; a language is then simply a means for expressing understandings. At the same time, language is seen as primary relative to the situated meanings in communication, the latter being almost entirely secondary and epiphenomenal. The other view, the 'action' view, argues for the interdependence of, on the one hand, language (as co-constitutive of understandings) and, on the other, the world as it is understood. On this view, we intervene directly in social life when we indulge in actual spoken or textual practices. Given this, the term 'language use', which assigns a logical priority to language as a system, would be slightly misleading; some other term might be preferred, such as 'languaging', i.e. a verb form (suggested by Liberg 1990; cf. similar misgivings about the 'static' noun 'memory'; 'remembering' should be preferred, see Middleton and Edwards 1990).

3   Dealing with language: From practical activities to decontextualised theory-building

If it is natural, as I suggested above, to start out from a communicative perspective on language, that is an 'action' view, then properties of linguistic structure are primarily aspects of utterances, and these utterances in turn are in practice always integrated within contexted communicative activities. This is a claim made by adherents of many present-day approaches to language, including 'integrational linguistics' (Harris and Wolf 1998), 'interactional sociolinguistics' (Gumperz 1982), 'interactional linguistics' (Ochs *et al.* 1996), and 'dialogism' (Linell 1998b). The above-mentioned switch within traditional and mainstream linguistics to a 'structure' view, that is, the view still privileged in the language sciences, therefore involved a great conceptual change, comprising both splitting and inversion in Latour and Woolgar's (1986) sense;[3] first, language structure was abstracted out and construed as an autonomous object, then the priority relations were reversed, so that the communicative activities have now become recontextualised as merely involving the application or use of language (or the separate languages) so construed.

That a 'language' is a system of abstract things is an assumption made in linguistics and in the language sciences more broadly. Words are described and understood as mental things, signs or forms (signifying something), rather than as aspects of actions. These views not only dominate linguistics, but have also been important for large parts of related language sciences, including sociolinguistics (see below), and they are predominant in popular, common-sense theories of language. Why?

The major reason, I believe (Linell 1982, 2000), is that our views of language stem from our collective cultural acquaintance with writing and written language, and from attitudes fostered in connection with this. It is reasonable to assume that language could not be seen as a structured set of objects, until cultural communities had got used to writing and literacy. Language and its constituents undergo a process of reification and objectivation, when we, as language users, become acquainted with permanent and visible signs on paper. When compared with talk in interaction, writing is integrated within entirely new types of linguistic practices. That this might entail differences in the kinds of languages used and attitudes towards these has often been ignored in linguistic theory.

Writing has also acquired a much higher status in most societies than talk. Indeed, a popular, common-sense theory includes the notion that speech and spoken language are not real language; they are faulty, foul, impoverished, incomplete, unclear, impure, illogical, incoherent, whereas writing, and written language *are* (or can be) really full-fledged language; they are (or should be) proper, correct, clear, logical, coherent. Written language is the norm or standard, against which spoken language is also assessed.

Similar attitudes prevail in linguistics, for example in the theories of Saussure or Chomsky. There is no structure or orderliness and nothing social in their notions of 'la parole' and 'performance'. Saussure (1964 [1916]: 38) declared:

> Il n'y a donc rien de collectif dans la parole; les manifestations en sont individuelles et momentanées. Ici il n'y a rien de plus que la somme des cas particuliers [. . .].

Chomsky speaks (1965: 58) of the spoken language surrounding a child as having a 'degenerate quality and narrowly limited extent'. This is the absolute opposite of Harvey Sacks's (1984: 22) dictum that 'there is order at all points' of social interaction. The latter could be taken as a basic assumption for sociolinguistics, and yet, as I argue in this paper, sociolinguists have in many respects stood closer to the linguists on many issues.

There are, therefore, some close similarities between scholarly theories and popular views (everyday 'social representations') of language. The explanation is of course that these have evolved under mutual influencing: see Figure 4.1.

Linguists (or rather their predecessors) were engaged in 'practical' projects and activities that were subject to political goals and ambitions. These included inventing and establishing writing systems for different languages (often the

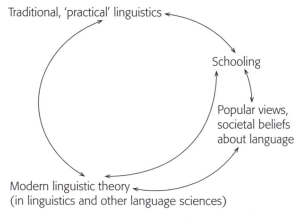

Fig. 4.1.   The circulations and recontextualisations of concepts of 'language'

transposition and modification of alphabetic writing systems already designed for other languages), establishing national standard languages (which
were, most often, new languages constructed above and beyond what existed
beforehand, that is, the divergent, spoken vernaculars), standardising these
written norms (national standards to be used in writing and writing-based
speech), describing language so that people could be taught to read and
write properly, preserving literate (or even holy) language varieties, describing languages so that people could be taught to write (and, less often, speak)
foreign languages and translate texts between languages, among other things.

All this laid the foundation for a scholarly tradition, very much based on
writing and (certain genres of) written language. The 'practical' activities
fostered 'theories' of language, and attenuated versions of these were also
taught in schools and, more broadly, throughout the literate cultures. Schooling activities have always been geared towards teaching how to write correctly, that is, there has been (for good reasons) a normative concern. That
in turn had an impact on how later generations of linguists understood their
task of defining language. Partly the same concepts, attitudes, arguments
and knowledge systems have been 'recontextualised' (Linell 1998a) across
many domains of knowledge, and similar conceptions and ideologies of language have been reproduced (Bernstein 1990). Recontextualisations are
always two-sided. On the one hand, they always, and by definition, involve
fitting material into new contexts with other background premises, and
therefore concepts, arguments and claims will acquire partly new meanings
and have new, and perhaps unexpected, consequences. On the other hand,
words and concepts do not altogether forget their history (Bakhtin 1984: 202).

In the case of linguistics and sociolinguistics, there are many stepwise
recontextualisations dealing with different aspects of language. At the most
comprehensive level, these recontextualisations are part of the grand-scale
change of activities as linguists moved from context-bound 'practical' concerns (see above) to making theoretical claims of (sometimes allegedly) universal validity. The new, theoretical concerns construct a decontextualised
notion of language, liberated from practical applications. On the other hand,
these decontextualising practices are of course themselves context-bound
(Linell 1998b: 279); their homes are in grammar books, language lessons,
logic exercises, etc.

Let us look at a few recontextualising processes. One aspect of these
collective and comprehensive endeavours was the development of the 'sentence' (or 'clause') as the single major syntactic and textual unit of language
(or text). Another point was of course the focus on the notion of (formal)
correctness itself. Correctness is a central notion in the traditional literate
(academic, scholarly) approach to language, and it applies throughout, at
the levels of orthography, grammar and text composition. At the same time,
this serves to point out differences between varieties of language. Many
spoken varieties, in particular those of mundane conversational language,

were portrayed as impoverished and incorrect. The general ideological stance came to be that there exist particular language varieties that are inherently incorrect, bad, improper, foul or uncivilised. Knowledge of language and its varieties became a resource for sorting people into categories, by reference to which language varieties they master or habitually use. These attitudes have also spread to popular views on matters of language (such as Mugglestone 1995). And in research, this prescriptivism 'institutionalises ideas about language which prevent us from seeing and adequately describing' spoken varieties (Coupland 2000: 626).

Modern linguistic theory is, of course, considerably more sophisticated and different on many accounts. Yet it is clearly dependent on 'folk models' of language as well as on older traditions of scholarly activities; tacit assumptions of old traditions (which were largely prescriptive in nature) often stay on, even if the activities now carried out have turned modern and are subject to very different official goals and commitments. Traditional practices of linguists were located in structures of power and ideology, and so are the practices of modern linguists, although in different and often more subtle ways. For example, whereas 'correct language' was traditionally defined in openly prescriptive terms, a language has later often been construed as a well-defined system of forms (an infinite but enumerable set; Chomsky's early 'Syntactic Structures', 1957, view), and correctness ('grammaticality') is then seen as the definitional property, determining whether a proposed string 'belongs to' the language. Here, grammaticality of expression is thus more important than appropriateness (of linguistic actions) to tasks-in-contexts. Grammaticality is construed as an inherent formal property of the language system, which is ultimately dependent on an allegedly innate language capacity; grammaticality is thus no longer 'reflected upon in terms of man-made standards of correctness' (Rommetveit 1988: 37), even though this aspect is in actual fact still there in the background. The effects of such — sometimes very radical — recontextualisations, for instance as regards the notion of unconscious rules (Chomsky), are bound to lead to serious confusion (see for example Zlatev 1997: 32):

> To think that rules [in speakers' 'competence'] await discovery by linguistic theorists is to confuse the appropriate form of explanation of normative phenomena with forms of explanation appropriate only to the physical sciences. (Baker and Hacker 1984: 334)

Two of the most influential linguists of the twentieth century, Saussure and Chomsky (especially the early Chomsky), both contributed in various ways to consolidating the view of language as a set of forms. Saussure set himself the dual task of establishing both language as a system (an autonomous system of *la langue*) and linguistics as a discipline (an autonomous discipline distinct from other scholarly approaches to language, such as philology, psychology and sociology of language, etc.).[4] In Chomskyan linguistics, the idea of language as a separate structure was developed in other ways, as a separate mental organ, or an autonomous module in the mind, housing the ability to organise the system of forms. These scholarly developments have endorsed and radicalised the splitting-and-inversion process referred to above.

Even though the history of modern linguistics has sometimes been portrayed as rather short, there is in fact a long past of constant interplay between common-sense, everyday popular ideas about linguistic matters and dominant scholarly views, models and theories. There are connections between the cultural domains of everyday lay discourse and academic discourse among experts on language. But many theoreticians in modern linguistics seem unwilling to admit their dependence on a legacy of older traditions (or they are quite simply ignorant of the history of their own discipline).

4   Written language systems and spoken language activities

It is easy to oversimplify the differences between speech and writing, and between spoken and written language. One may set up lists of distinctions as in Table 4.1. Such lists[5] decontextualise from many significant aspects, like the many overlapping features of spoken and written language use; indeed, most summaries of this kind simply presuppose an implicit distinction between polar types, such as informal colloquial conversation and expository prose.[6] Barring this, Liberg (1990: 173f.) suggests that the list sets up a contrast between incommensurable entities, that is, between written language systems and spoken language activities.[7] There may be some truth to this. However, my point is, of course, that there is a natural tendency to see

Table 4.1   Written language and writing vs spoken language and speech: some basic differences

Written language and written text (writing)	Spoken language and discourse (speech, spoken interaction)
Persistent	Ephemeral
Static	Dynamic
Discrete	Continuous
Decontextualised	Context-bound
Explicit	Less explicit
etc.	etc.

writing and written language in product terms, and speech and spoken language in action or process terms. And yet, the latter perspective on spoken language has not always been honoured. Instead, we have tacitly accepted the following chain of inferences: written texts are **object-like** (**products** of communicative activities) → language can be seen as systems of objects (building up texts) → language **is** a set of abstract objects → these objects are used also in spoken discourse.

Despite some possible objections to the theory, one cannot but maintain that there has been a 'written language bias' in linguistics, a bias that has persisted in spite of the fact that linguists have now for a long time dubbed spoken language as the primary form of language. Even when they have increasingly moved into studying spoken language and discourse, they have done so with a 'written language bias' in at least two major ways.

First, models and concepts are still by and large those designed for the analysis of written rather than spoken language. So, even if linguists declare spoken language to be the basic medium of language, their use of a metalanguage designed for written language still implicitly points to written language as the preferred variety, that which is the norm and which is worth serious study.[8]

Secondly, writing is also the medium through which spoken discourse is analysed; spoken discourse is translated into written texts, transcripts. Since, by this token, written text is the medium for representing also spoken language, we can assume that it works as a mechanism for activating attitudes to written texts, when in fact we should deal with the ephemeral and dynamic phenomenon of talk-in-interaction.

I would argue that the written language bias is still alive in the language sciences, but it is losing ground. There are now fairly developed alternatives for looking on language and discourse in their communicative contexts. Such dynamic understandings stressing interaction and contexts naturally apply to spoken discourse, but they also recast written communication in a way that is less text- and structure-based. Yet it is interesting that these approaches of constructionism, contextualism, interactionism and dialogism (see Linell 1998b) have been inspired largely from sources outside of linguistics; important names are, for example, Humboldt, Husserl, Mead, Bakhtin, Wittgenstein, Piaget, Vygotsky, Malinowski, Goffman, Garfinkel and Sacks. Pioneers of more functionalist and interactionist approaches in linguistics or sociolinguistics, such as Firth and Halliday, or Hymes and Gumperz, respectively, are dependent on anthropology.

5   The written language bias in linguistics

There are numerous, almost countless, points in linguistics where theories of language are clearly biassed by being modelled, directly or sometimes more indirectly, on writing and written language, or in many cases on certain forms of writing, say expository prose. Such points pertain to virtually all parts of linguistics, and extend far beyond this discipline. Let me cite a few cases from linguistics proper.[9]

1.   Regarding language in general:

* the view that language is the full medium for representing knowledge about the world; in principle, anything can be expressed and communicated in and through a verbal text[10]
* defining language itself; in the analysis of spoken interaction, the boundaries between language (and verbal communication), on the one hand, and paralanguage and 'body language' (non-verbal communication), on the other, are drawn so that the verbal is that part which has a conventional notation in writing.

2.   In phonetics and phonology:

* the overemphasis of phonemic segments (bits and pieces that have regular counterparts in alphabetic writing) at the expense of prosody and paralanguage
* the study of phonetic properties of written decontextualised words, phrases and sentences read aloud (so-called laboratory speech), neglecting the properties of authentic situated talk-in-interaction.

3.   In grammar:

* the overemphasis on sentences (cf. norms for punctuation in writing expository prose) at the expense of other structures (expressions that are not full clauses)
* the analysis of syntactic units as sentences with coherent structures (for example tree structures) that can be inspected at one time (as in the case of written sentences). They are therefore also assumed to be processable by speakers as coherent wholes, rather than incrementally produced and interpreted
* a particular perspective on grammatical ambiguities in written language; some sentences are seen as inherently ambiguous within the grammatical system (language) itself and as being 'disambiguated' by prosody (and contexts) in speech (i.e. one does not contemplate the opposite theory that writing sometimes 'ambiguates' what is unambiguous in situated talk)
* the treatment of 'discontinuities' in spoken discourse (filled and unfilled pauses, repetitions, restarts, etc.) as deviations from ideal delivery and as obstacles to communication, when, in fact, these phenomena may reflect

planning and monitoring activities that provide opportunities for the listener to pace the comprehension process with the speaker's rhythm in making information chunks available.[11]

4.   In lexicology:

- the preoccupation with fixed literal meanings (definitions in terms of necessary and sufficient conditions of a kind commonly found in dictionaries) rather than with flexible and open meaning potentials.[12]

5.   In semantics and pragmatics:

- the preoccupation with truth conditions (an exercise brought to perfection in logic supported by writing) at the expense of situational sense-making and interactional meaning, considerations of politeness and tact, etc.
- the concentration on representational meaning and the expression of beliefs about the world, at the expense for example of practical, instrumental and interpersonal uses of language
- the overemphasis on individual acts at the expense of social interaction, and an excessive reliance on individual intentions in the explanation of utterances (dependent on the analogical assumption that texts have unique authors)
- the view that discourses are consciously planned in advance (rather than being interactionally occasioned and locally produced in an incremental fashion)
- the definition of a semantics, which is relatively autonomous and clearly demarcated, building upon a distinction between linguistic and encyclopedic knowledge. This makes possible a distinction between what it means to understand a particular sentence 'linguistically', that is, as a linguistic item without a context (or in a default context), on the one hand, and to understand a particular situated utterance event in which that sentence is 'used', on the other. The latter is what is always involved in actual communication, but the former reminds us of what could be required when we read a text in a foreign language without any other important communicative context than that of learning that foreign language. We then try to understand what the words and sentences of the text mean at a 'linguistic level' (see Ottosson 1996). In terms of sense-making, this is a rather special activity, quite distant and separate from what is going on in most people's spoken interaction.

The written language bias has led to a focus on structures that linguists expect to find *also* in spoken language and discourse. It therefore has an impact on sociolinguistics, at least those traditions which are not decisively 'interactional' or 'dialogical' in character. But the written language bias may also have influenced social theory in general. It is commonplace to claim (despite the absence of explicit references) that Saussure had his structuralist ideas from Durkheim, that is, linguistic theory borrowed ideas from social theory. But perhaps it is just as much the other way around? Has the notion of language, or linguistic structure, once it has been established, been used as a source of metaphors for conceiving of social and cultural systems? In natural sciences, text-reading was for a long time used as a model for 'reading the Book of Nature'; Olson (1994: ch.8) reminds us that this was the conception of many natural scientists such as Bacon, Galileo, and Boyle. So perhaps one could argue that the model of language also provided a metaphor for sociologists' reading 'the Book of Society'. If there is any truth in this suggestion, it would be another, even more far-reaching effect of the written language bias.

6   The language makers

Many of the points just raised have to do with a striving, on the part of linguists, to establish the autonomy of language and its constituent parts, to emancipate language from real-life cognition and communication (Rommetveit 1988). As I have already pointed out, the autonomy of language was part of Saussure's project of establishing the autonomy of linguistics. It is also consonant with Chomskyan theories of language as a largely autonomous mental capacity.

There can hardly be any doubt that there is 'language' (as well as different 'languages') 'out there' in the social (and individual) lives of people, in the form of tacit knowledge and linguistic routines that transcend single communicative situations. This is what allows speakers to construct, and listeners to comprehend, novel utterances in analogy with old patterns. Participants in communication frequently orient to features of form and meaning, in a reflexive way that presupposes knowledge of language, for instance in repairs and negotiations of meaning. However, in what forms and to what extent there is language out there, as an intersubjective reality, is a moot question. Just as we can safely assume that there is language, we can also be sure that the phenomena involved get strongly changed in and through the linguists' recontextualising activities, as they are 'describing', that is, conceptualising, formulating and indeed codifying languages.

Roy Harris (1980, 1981, 1996, 1997) has consistently argued that language, as described by linguists, is actually a fiction, something that linguists have 'made'. Needless to say, national standard languages are largely scholarly and political constructs. They are 'ideological formation[s]', 'abstract reification[s] and idealisation[s]', a view which is now supported by a 'growing

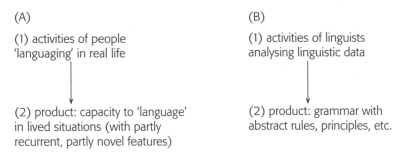

(A)

(1) activities of people 'languaging' in real life

(2) product: capacity to 'language' in lived situations (with partly recurrent, partly novel features)

(B)

(1) activities of linguists analysing linguistic data

(2) product: grammar with abstract rules, principles, etc.

Fig. 4.2.   The incommensurability of language users' and linguists' activities

sociolinguistic literature on language ideology' (Coupland 2000: 624). The same point has also been emphasised by Chomsky, in his later works (for example 1993: 18–19). National standards usually don't have (or at least, didn't have from the beginning) the embodied reality that the spoken vernaculars have. On the other hand, as people orient to written language norms and as distinctions between regional variants are levelled out, these fictions have acquired a different kind of social reality than they had at the outset.

Grammars are in an important sense 'made' by linguists. Indeed, Harris's claims about linguists (and sociolinguists) as language makers are more far-reaching than the point about national standards: exactly how far-reaching is a matter of dispute. If we compare the activities of people experiencing linguistic phenomena in various real-life situations with those of linguists analysing linguistic data, we can set up the contrast outlined in Figure 4.2.

Linguists isolate language, decontextualising it from most or even all social, psychological and environmental factors, while people encounter and live their language as embedded or integrated in communicative practices. Nevertheless, linguists have argued that their 'grammars' (B2) are models of speakers' competences (although Chomsky and others have combined this claim with all sorts of riders). Considering the differences between the activities and contexts of people who are immersed in their 'languaging' and those of linguists in their distanced (and distancing) scholarly activities, such an assumption seems highly unlikely. People learn to master their language, this mastery involving the ability to use utterances in patterned ways as parts of communicative practices in different activity types (see for example Zlatev 1997). Why should they need a very complex grammar of the kind developed by linguists, a grammar which is in fact a syntactic calculus of semantically–pragmatically uninterpreted abstract strings? The generativist theories of language are exceedingly difficult to match with a theory of communication; indeed, Chomsky claimed that communication is an accidental feature of language (in use). One must conclude that linguists and language users don't have the same language (in several senses), and that the analogy drawn between linguistics and the natural sciences as both modelling in similar ways phenomena in the world is largely misleading (see Baker and Hacker quoted above).

7   Sociolinguistics and its linguistic legacy

The claims made here about linguistics and sociolinguistics are deliberately limited to some core features of the mainstream traditions of the discipline(s). They are therefore also a bit lop-sided. In particular, I do not do justice to some currents within linguistics at large, as it now looks some three or four decades after Chomsky entered the academic arena and came to dominate it.[13] As regards Chomsky himself (and his close followers), he has turned away from the task of describing 'surface' languages ('E(xternal) language'), such as English, French or Hebrew. Chomsky's (1995) interest is now, it seems, more decisively on 'minimalist' assumptions of structure ('principles' of universal grammar, core grammars, 'I(nternal) language') associated with the underlying language capacity. The significant entities in a language are now (more abstract) grammatical constructions, rather than sentence types (cf. in this respect 'construction grammar'; Kay and Fillmore, 1999). This also implies much less emphasis on notions like 'grammaticality'.

Of particular interest in present-day linguistics are a number of traditions that are oriented towards 'functionalism' (for a recent overview, see Schegloff *et al.* 1996). Among these is a family of diversified but mutually related approaches within the Firth–Halliday tradition. I cannot review all these here. From a bird's eye view, however, it appears that some of them are quite dependent on what I have called 'the written language bias'. Many seem to be more 'systemic' than 'functional'. The 'Birmingham school' of discourse analysis (such as Coulthard 1992), which has a background in the Halliday tradition, is an interesting case. It adopted models of discourse structure built on hierarchies and slot-and-filler structures reminiscent of models of sentence syntax, and supplemented this with speech act theory. The latter theory (Searle 1969, etc.), probably the most well-known action approach to spoken discourse so far, is not based on analyses of authentic situated talk and interaction, and is clearly monological in nature (Linell and Marková 1993). In general, when discourse analysts have looked for a 'mode of organization' (Hymes 1974: vii) of communicative conduct, and of language as used[14] in discourse, they have often fallen back on structural models of language.

Accordingly, many variants of functional linguistics and discourse theory are still fairly dependent on a formalist conception of language, and they usually lack a full-blown theory of language in the context of communicative action. What, then, is the position of sociolinguistics within all this? Again, it is of course impossible to make a unitary assessment. Some time ago, initiated commentators characterised sociolinguistics in terms of heterogeneity, fragmentation and lack of a theoretical basis (Hymes 1974: 194). Its metatheory was reviewed by Figueroa (1994) two decades later, with special regard to the work of Hymes, Labov and Gumperz. In her monograph, she

makes many penetrating observations, but I would not agree with her contention that it is 'safe to place sociolinguistics within the Hegelian framework and the functionalist linguistic paradigm' (p. 25). Sociolinguistics deals
with variation and regularity in language use, sometimes with interaction
and meaning, but often within a formalist, structural framework rather than
a truly dialogical, contextualist and interactional paradigm.[15] Accordingly, it
seems appropriate to claim that the legacy from linguistics, partly describable in terms of a written language bias, is very influential in the work of
Labov and Trudgill, for instance — that is, forms of sociolinguistics that lean
more towards language than society (see Figueroa 1994: 11).

Both sociology, or social theory in general, and linguistics seem to have
a preference for grand theories. A grand and comprehensive theory could
be briefly characterised as one in which a) one or a few aspects are selected
as underlying others and thus as being uniquely significant, and b) claims
are made for the theory's being universally valid for phenomena within the
knowledge domain, for example all social systems or languages. There are
several strands within linguistics, arguably consequences and concomitants
of the written language bias, that have much in common with the quest for
grand theories. For example, the notion of one system (langue) for each
'language' is partly a linguists' creation (Harris's argument referred to in
section 6), and the search for structural universals, with its realist assumption of language, in Chomskyan linguistics is based on highly abstract (decontextualised) formalist conceptions of structure. As regards sociolinguistics, it
is also fair to say that some traditions, especially those which can be seen as
applications of social and linguistic theories, are clearly affected by the quest
for grand theories. This applies by and large to Labovian sociolinguistics.
At the same time, though, sociolinguistics and discourse theory have sometimes been characterised as collections of 'mini-theories' (see Coupland,
Introduction, this volume). If we look upon communicative construction as
socioculturally and situationally constrained, it is logical to conceive of large
parts of the theories as being located at a 'meso' level, where activity types
and activity systems, organisations and institutions, etc., are defined, rather
than at a 'macro' level of national languages (or universal capacities for
language).

Sociolinguistics has largely dealt with the social and regional variation in
the phonology, morphology and syntax of languages. That is, the starting
point is in a conception of a language derived from linguistics, basically
languages as sets of forms. This is one aspect of the legacy of linguistics.
I would of course not argue that this legacy should simply be thrown over-
board. But there are complementary and alternative approaches. From
a sociocultural point of view, languages cannot be defined exclusively, or
predominantly, in formal and grammatical terms (as unitary, for example
national, languages and varieties thereof). Within activity systems, institutions, organisations and various other communicative communities, 'social

languages' (Wertsch 1991) are largely defined in terms of their vocabularies, as opposed to their phonological and morphosyntactic properties, and the representations of the world(s) that they embody and are embedded within.

8   Can we capture dynamics?

Social, psychological, discursive, linguistic and physical realities are obviously characterised by both stability and change. Language can be seen as structure or as dynamic discourse; in sociology we deal with both social structure and social action, in cultural studies with both culture and cultural practices. But the world view that dawns upon us when we consider how we look upon language is one in which stability is in focus, and dynamics is marginalised. It is a picture of a stable and shared world with some residuals of undetermined aspects to be contextually negotiated and determined in specific situated interactions. This **structure-in-focus view** posits a plethora of underlying structures beneath what on the surface appears to be more vague, ambiguous, changing and only partially shared.

When we deal with social and cultural phenomena, and with language and discourse, it is possible that we should reverse the focus–background relationships from the structure-in-focus view to a **dynamics-in-focus view**. That would involve an epistemology of dialogism (see for example Marková and Foppa 1990; Linell 1998b). We then assume, for example, that we live in a dynamic, only partially shared and fragmentarily known, dialogically constituted world, in which relatively stable features (such as those of language and social representations)[16] are emergent across series of communicative events. Recurrent linguistic routines are of course developed by ordinary members of the language communities, and then lived by them. But structures of language have been articulated, transformed, enhanced and endorsed by institutions and also supported by artifacts. Science is clearly one such powerful institution, and (mainstream) linguistics is a particular kind of a disciplined, socially situated tradition of decontextualising practices. Fish (1989: 9) formulated such an idea in his incisive wording: 'Meanings that seem perspicuous and literal are rendered so by forceful interpretive acts and not by properties of language'.

Language and social representations are clearly *relatively stable* phenomena, that is, relatively stable as compared to singular situated discourses. Following Rommetveit (1974) and others, we could look at the meanings of linguistic expressions as meaning potentials, which, when used together with contextual resources, help actors to make sense in situated discourse. Social representations, too, are potentialities to evoke particular types of discourses, actions, attitudes, etc. Though relatively stable across communicative events, social representations are not static; they are communicatively constructed, socially distributed, circulated in real life, varying in foreground–background relations, and subject to various kinds of recontextualising practices in different contexts. Common-sense conceptions, as shown above, are themselves a case in point.

To return to my initial questions, why are dynamics, change, vagueness and openness so difficult to account for and make visible? The reasons have undoubtedly to do with the fact that structures of language are the products of particular activities of description and analysis, scholarly and other, which involve definition and stabilisation. I suggest that these reasons are of three kinds: a) deep-seated, conceptual ones, b) historical, traditional ones pertaining to the specific legacy of linguistics, and c) practical, technical ones:

a)   At the most general level, scientific generalising analyses inevitably involve reduction and categorisation of data into recurrent abstract patterns. In this endeavour, there is an explicit and conscious striving to identify reasonably stable and objective structures, and also to search for grand theories.

b)   In the history of the language sciences, there is a more specific tradition which has seen written language as the norm both in real life and in scholarly attention. This has generated models of language which cannot treat spoken language and discourse properly. Language is not portrayed as being in motion, but as arrested and even as inert by nature.

c)   The medium for expressing analytic products is writing, diagrams, tables, formulas, etc., which are bound to freeze or paralyse phenomena in motion. It is quite plausible that a real change on this point necessitates an extended use, also in the publications of research results, of excerpts from audio- and video-recordings (rather than just transcripts) together with written descriptions and depictions, such as on CD-ROM. Another intriguing idea is that the remedy might involve the adoption of new representational media, such as computer-supported visualisation of dynamic movements.

Notes

1.   This paper was read at the Roundtable on Sociolinguistics and Social Theory, Gregynog Hall, Newtown, Mid Wales, 7–9 July 1997. A revised version was given in the Department of Applied Linguistics at Jyväskylä University in October 1997. I thank the audiences present on the two occasions, and the editors of this volume, for valuable comments and advice.

2.   A third sense of 'language' is obviously 'language faculty', which can be understood as the ability to acquire and use a specific language (or several such languages) in verbal communication and cognition (in talk-in-interaction, reading, writing, thinking).

3. Splitting and inversion are, according to Latour and Woolgar (1986), common features of scientific activities; aspects of the phenomena observed are abstracted (by splitting an integrated phenomenon) and reinterpreted, and often reified, in terms of ('theoretical') entities or principles underlying the observable data.

4. Wagner (1996: 97), apropos social representations in general, points to the construction of the representation and the construction of the object (of representation) as two aspects of the same project.

5. Cf. Linell (1982: ch. 2), where, however, I treated the matters discursively, rather than actually reducing them to a mere list (as claimed in a critique by Liberg, 1990).

6. See Biber (1988) for arguments and ample empirical evidence.

7. For similar critique, see Pettersson (1996).

8. See, in addition to Linell (1982, 2000), also Kress (1994: 18), and Taylor (1997: 59–60 et passim) on 'scriptism'.

9. For many more (in total: 101) points, see Linell (2000).

10. See, for example, work by Kress & van Leeuwen (1996) on comparisons of elementary text-books in the physical sciences from the early and late 20th century. Fifty years ago pictures were just illustrations of what was also and already communicated through the verbal texts. Such a principle is no longer true of today's pedagogical materials, in which visual representations have more powerful communicative functions, some of which could hardly be mirrored in discursive verbal accounts.

11. Taylor (1997) discusses primarily this point as an example of 'scriptism'.

12. Notions like 'meaning potentials' or 'semantic potentialities', rather than fixed word meanings, have been proposed by several linguists of various functionalist persuasions, for example semanticists interested in semantic change (Bréal), Bakhtinian theories (Lähteenmäki 2000) Prague structuralists like Karcevskij and Mukarovsky (see Marková 1992), and in addition of course Michael Halliday (e.g. 1975, where he uses such a notion in the explanation of how children 'learn how to mean'). A major piece of work on this point is Rommetveit (1974).

13. In addition, within linguistics at large, there has been a broadening of interests both inside certain neo-Chomskyan approaches and, more characteristically, outside these. New foci of interest include empirical studies in typological variation and in working with large corpuses of real language data ('corpus linguistics'); studies of non-standard varieties, such as child language, pidgins and creoles, and of languages for 'specific purposes' (e.g. professional varieties); extensive research on spoken language; applications of action-based theories; and cognitive linguistics compatible with connectionist theories (Zlatev 1997) (here Chomsky's new minimalism has moved a bit closer).

Nevertheless, my stance is, although I cannot argue it here, that a good deal of this research still exhibits a 'written language bias'. New versions of formalist conceptions of language are now often supported by computer-based metaphors and can be found in cognitive science, neurolinguistics and computational linguistics, where a formal language, with no substantial semantics, provides the basis for computations and calculi. Dialogical, interactionist conceptions are still rare.

14. Cf. the remark on the concept of 'language use' in section 1 above. Cf. also Figueroa (1994: 14, n.1).

15. The latter characterisation would fit the 'interactional sociolinguistics' of John Gumperz (e.g. 1982). It goes without saying that his position has inspired the dialogal approach to talk and interaction laid out in e.g. Linell (1998b).

16. Social representations is used here as a descriptive cover term for knowledge and assumptions (especially of a common-sense type), belief systems, attitudes and dispositions to act, ideas and ideologies, etc. within different domains of life. Such structures have often, just as structures of language, been portrayed in rather static terms. I assume, however, that a constructionist account of social representations is possible (e.g. Moscovici 1988, Billig 1993, Wagner 1996, Marková 1996).

References

Baker, Gordon P. and Hacker, Peter M.S. (1984) *Language, Sense and Nonsense.* Oxford: Blackwell.

Bakhtin, Mikhail M. (1984) *Problems of Dostoevsky's Poetics.* Translated and edited by Carol Emerson. Minneapolis: University of Minnesota Press.

Bernstein, Basil (1990) *The Structuring of Pedagogic Discourse. Vol. IV: Class, Codes and Control.* London: Routledge.

Biber, Douglas (1988) *Variation across Speech and Writing.* Cambridge: Cambridge University Press.

Billig, Michael (1993) Studying the thinking society: social representations, rhetoric, and attitudes. In G. Breakwell and D. Canter (eds) *Empirical Approaches to Social Representations.* Oxford: Clarendon Press, 39–62.

Carter, Bob and Sealey, Alison (2000) Language, structure, and agency: What can realist social theory offer to sociolinguistics? *Journal of Sociolinguistics* 4: 3–20.

Chomsky, Noam (1957) *Syntactic Structures.* The Hague: Mouton.

Chomsky, Noam (1965) *Aspects of the Theory of Syntax.* Cambridge, MA: MIT Press.

Chomsky, Noam (1993) *Language and Thought.* London: Moyer Bell.

Chomsky, Noam (1995) *The Minimalist Program.* Cambridge, MA: MIT Press.

Coulthard, Malcolm (ed.) (1992) *Advances in Spoken Discourse Analysis.* London: Routledge.

Coupland, Nikolas (2000) Sociolinguistic prevarication about 'standard English'. Review of Tony Bex and Richard Watts (eds), (1999) 'Standard English: the Widening Debate'. *Journal of Sociolinguistics* 4: 622–634.

Dik, Simon (1978) *Functional Grammar.* Amsterdam: North-Holland.

Figueroa, Esther (1994) *Sociolinguistic Metatheory.* Oxford: Pergamon.

Fish, Stanley (1989) *Doing What Comes Naturally: Change, Rhetoric, and the Practice of Theory in Literary and Legal Studies*. Durham, NC: Duke University Press.

Gumperz, John (1982) *Discourse Strategies*. Cambridge: Cambridge University Press.

Halliday, Michael (1975) *Learning How to Mean: Explorations in the Development of Language*. London: Edward Arnold.

Harris, Roy (1980) *The Language Makers*. London: Duckworth.

Harris, Roy (1981) *The Language Myth*. London: Duckworth.

Harris, Roy (1996) *Signs, Language and Communication*. London: Routledge.

Harris, Roy (1997) From an integrational point of view. In G. Wolf and N. Love (eds) *Linguistics Inside Out: Roy Harris and His Critics*. Amsterdam: John Benjamins, 229–310.

Harris, Roy and Wolf, George (eds) (1998) *Integrational Linguistics: A First Reader*. Oxford: Pergamon.

Hymes, Dell (1974) *Foundations in Sociolinguistics. An Ethnographic Approach*. Philadelphia: University of Pennsylvania Press.

Kay, Paul and Fillmore, Charles (1999) Grammatical constructions and linguistic generalizations. The *What's X doing Y?* construction. *Language* 75: 1–33.

Kress, Gunther (1994) *Learning to Write*, 2nd edn. London: Routledge.

Kress, Gunther and van Leeuwen, Theo (1996) *Reading Images: The Grammar of Visual Design*. London: Routledge.

Lähteenmäki, Mika (1998) On Dynamics and Stability: Saussure, Voloshinov, and Bakhtin. In M. Lähteenmäki and H. Dufva (eds) *Dialogues on Bakhtin: Interdisciplinary Readings*. University of Jyväskylä: Centre for Applied Language Studies, 51–69.

Lähteenmäki, Mika (2000) Between Relativism and Absolutism: Toward an Emergentist Definition of Meaning Potential. In F. Bostad et al. (eds) *Bakhtinian Perspectives: Thinking Culture Dialogically*.

Latour, Bruno and Woolgar, Steve (1986) *Laboratory Life: the Construction of Scientific Facts*. Princeton, NJ: Princeton University Press.

Liberg, Caroline (1990) *Learning to Read and Write*. (Dissertation). (RUUL, 20). Uppsala: Department of Linguistics.

Linell, Per (1982) *The Written Language Bias in Linguistics*. (Studies in Communication = SIC, 2). Linköping: Department of Communication Studies. (Also available at: http://eng.hss.cmu.edu/langs/Linell/Linell.html)

Linell, Per (1998a) Discourse Across Boundaries: On recontextualizations and the blending of voices in professional discourse. *Text* 18: 143–157.

Linell, Per (1998b). *Approaching Dialogue: Talk, Interaction and Contexts in Dialogical Perspectives*. Amsterdam: John Benjamins.

Linell, Per (2000) The Written Language Bias in Linguistics: Its Nature, Origin and Transformations. MS. Linköping: Department of Communication Studies.

Linell, Per and Marková, Ivana (1993) Acts in discourse: From monological speech acts to dialogical inter-acts. *Journal for the Theory of Social Behaviour* 23: 174–195.

Marková, Ivana (1982) *Paradigms, Thought and Language*. New York: Wiley.

Marková, Ivana (1992) On structure and dialogicity in Prague semiotics. In A. Heen Wold (ed.) *The Dialogical Alternative: Toward a Theory of Language and Mind*. Oslo: Scandinavian University Press, 45–63.

Marková, Ivana (1996) Towards an Epistemology of Social Representations. *Journal for the Theory of Social Behaviour* 26: 177–196.

Marková, Ivana and Foppa, Klaus (eds) (1990) *The Dynamics of Dialogue*. New York: Harvester Wheatsheaf.

Middleton, David and Edwards, Derek (eds) (1990) *Collective Remembering*. London: Sage.

Moscovici, Serge (1988) Notes towards a description of Social Representations. *European Journal of Social Psychology* 18: 211–250.

Mugglestone, Lynda (1995) *'Talking Proper'*. Oxford: Oxford University Press.

Ochs, Elinor, Schegloff, Emanuel A. and Thompson, Sandra A. (eds) (1996) *Interaction and Grammar*. Cambridge: Cambridge University Press.

Olson, David (1994) *The World on Paper*. Cambridge: Cambridge University Press.

Ottosson, Ulf (1996) *Kausalitet och semantik*. ('Causality and Semantics'). (Dissertation). Göteborg: Nordistica Gothoburgensia, 19.

Pettersson, John Sören (1996) *Grammatological Studies: Writing and its Relation to Speech*. (Dissertation). (RUUL, 29). Uppsala: Department of Linguistics.

Potter, Jonathan, Wetherell, Margaret, Gill, Ros and Edwards, Derek (1990) Discourse: noun, verb or social practice? *Philosophical Psychology* 3: 205–217.

Rommetveit, Ragnar (1974) *On Message Structure*. London: Wiley.

Rommetveit, Ragnar (1988) On Literacy and the Myth of Literal Meaning. In R. Säljö (ed.) *The Written World*. Berlin: de Gruyter, 13–40.

Sacks, Harvey (1984) Notes on methodology. In J.M. Atkinson and J. Heritage (eds) *Structures of Social Action: Studies in Conversation Analysis*. Cambridge: Cambridge University Press, 21–27.

Saussure, Ferdinand de (1964 [1916]) *Cours de linguistique générale*. Paris: Payot.

Schegloff, Emanuel A., Ochs, Elinor and Thompson, Sandra A. (1996) Introduction. In E. Ochs *et al.* (1996) *Interaction and Grammar*. Cambridge: Cambridge University Press, 1–51.

Searle, John (1969) *Speech Acts*. Cambridge: Cambridge University Press.

Taylor, Talbot (1997) *Theorizing Language: Analysis, Normativity, Rhetoric, History*. Amsterdam: Elsevier.

Wagner, Wolfgang (1996) Queries about social representation and construction. *Journal for the Theory of Social Behaviour* 26: 95–120.

Wertsch, James V. (1991) *Voices of the Mind: A Sociocultural Approach to Mediated Action*. London: Harvester Wheatsheaf.

Zlatev, Jordan (1997) *Situated Embodiment: Studies in the Emergence of Spatial Meaning*. (Dissertation). Stockholm: Department of Linguistics.

5

Discourse, accumulation of symbolic capital and power: The case of *American Visions*
Adam Jaworski

1 Introduction

This chapter is concerned with discourse as the principal site and the means of power enactment and power struggle in social life. It combines interactional sociolinguistic and discourse analytic approaches with the work of Pierre Bourdieu (1977, 1986, 1991, 1993), Michel Foucault (1978, 1980) and Anthony Giddens (1991) in social theory, and Michael Baxandall (1985) in history of art. My discussion of power is illustrated by a case study of the discourses in and around a television art programme (*American Visions*), in which an art critic (Robert Hughes) claims expert knowledge and uses it to legitimise (or not) artists or works of art and to endow them (or not) with symbolic capital. In other words, I examine here the discursive means deployed by an art critic in order to exert his influence within the field of cultural (artistic) production as the consecrator of artists and their guarantor of symbolic capital.

I begin with a brief outline of the notions of 'power' and 'status' in socio-linguistics and social theory. Next I summarise the basic tenets of Baxandall's (1985) and Bourdieu's (1986, 1993) ideas, which form the main theoretical backdrop for my discussion, and draw parallels between them. Then, I analyse a few texts and finally conclude by remarking on the 'politics of taste'.

2 Power

In traditional sociolinguistic research, power has been treated as an attribute of interacting individuals. For example, Brown and Gilman (1972 [1960]) conceptualise power as an asymmetrical dimension of dominance by one person over another in types of relationships in which one of the participants can be described as 'superior in rank', 'stronger', 'older', 'wealthier', etc. than the other. Likewise, Brown and Levinson (1987: 77) argue that interactional power has two overlapping sources: 'material control (over economic distribution and physical force) and metaphysical control (over the actions of others, by virtue of metaphysical forces subscribed by those others).' Consequently, communicative behaviour, for example, the choice of a pronoun of address as in the Brown and Gilman study (showing deference or familiarity), or type of redressive action present in performing a Face Threatening Act (Brown and Levinson 1987) depends, in part, on the perceived characteristics of the interactants as powerful or powerless, and on the (non-)reciprocity of use of the linguistic and non-linguistic signs of power (Hodge and Kress 1988).

Others have approached power as a more dynamic concept. For Ng and Bradac (1993), for example, power is linked to conversational influence and control which are negotiated and achieved through interactional work between social actors. These authors postulate (1993: 61) three principal domains of interactional power: 'the structure of talk exchange (who speaks and for how long), its content (topic and focus), and the evaluation of the content'. Conversational influence and control may be enacted or resisted in hierarchically structured communicative events such as classroom interaction or media interviews, in which the social roles of teacher–pupil and interviewer–interviewee are determined pre-discursively, or they may emerge through talk in 'unstructured', that is informal, spontaneous conversations among peers.

Watts (1991) links power with status and asserts (p. 55) that 'power is exercised on the basis of higher status'. Relative status, in turn, is determined by an individual's position in a hierarchy depending, among other characteristics, on his/her level of education, wealth, age, sex, mental and physical abilities. However, the values attached to these characteristics are culturally and socially dependent, so the power potential of individuals must be viewed in relation to specific contexts of interaction.

The question of power and the role of language in its enactment in social life has been at the top of the research agenda in Critical Discourse Analysis (CDA), or Critical Language Study (see for example Fairclough 1989, 1993, 1995; Hodge and Kress 1988; van Dijk 1993; papers in Caldas-Coulthard and Coulthard 1996). At the heart of this approach lies the 'constructionist' approach to social relations, processes, and to social life in general (for example, van Leeuwen 1993). Because social reality is not treated by CDA as an objective and static given, its aims go beyond a 'mere' description of social life. Fairclough explains that, for him, the term 'critical' means:

> discourse analysis which aims to systematically explore often opaque relationships of causality and determination between (a) discursive practices, events and texts, and (b) wider social and cultural structures, relations and

processes; to investigate how such practices, events and texts arise out of and are ideologically shaped by relations of power and struggles over power; and to explore how the opacity of these relationships between discourse and society is itself a factor securing power and hegemony . . . In referring to opacity, I am suggesting that such linkages between discourse, ideology and power may well be unclear to those involved, and more generally that our social practice is bound up with causes and effects which may not be at all apparent (Bourdieu 1977). (Fairclough 1993: 135)

CDA's view of social life and political struggle is grounded in social theoretical work of such authors as Pierre Bourdieu, Michel Foucault and Anthony Giddens, who have placed discourse at the centre of their work although they have not engaged in close textual analyses of any kind. In Bourdieu's (1986, 1991, 1993) theory of social practice, language is related to his notion of *habitus*, that is, internalised group norms or dispositions whose task is to regulate and generate the actions (practices), perceptions and representations of individuals, and to mediate the social structures which they inhabit. Two important and interrelated aspects of habitus are that it reflects the social structures in which it was acquired and also reproduces these structures. Thus, a person who was brought up in a working-class background will manifest a set of dispositions which are different from those acquired by a person from a middle-class background and these differences will, in turn, reproduce the class divisions between both individuals (and their groups).

For Bourdieu, language is a locus of struggle for power and authority in that some types of language (styles, accents, dialects, codes, and so on) are presupposed to be 'correct', 'distinguished' or 'legitimate' in opposition to those which are 'incorrect' or 'vulgar'. Those who use (in speaking or writing) the varieties ranked as acceptable, exert a degree of control over those with the dominated linguistic habitus (Bourdieu 1991: 60). The field of linguistic production, however, can be manipulated in that the symbolic capital claimed by the authority of 'legitimate' language may be reclaimed in the process of negotiation 'by a metadiscourse concerning the conditions of use of discourse' (1991: 71). In sum,

the habitus . . . provides individuals with a sense of how to act and respond in the course of their daily lives. It 'orients' their actions and inclinations without strictly determining them. It gives them a 'feel for the game', a sense of what is appropriate in the circumstances and what is not, a 'practical sense' . . . (Thompson 1991: 13)

In my discussion of the discourses in and around *American Visions*, I assume that Hughes, other art critics, artists shown or mentioned in the programme and the viewers (presumed by me to be largely middle-class, professional adults) constitute the core group that tacitly accept the rules of play within the field of artistic production, of which this television programme constitutes a part. Various individuals' involvement in the programme as author, interviewees, reviewers, viewing public, and so on, allows them to pursue different goals, for example aesthetic or educational, as well as seeking (in varying proportions) to accumulate symbolic (and economic) capital by producing the series, participating in it, or watching it. All of these activities can be viewed as part of this discourse community's habitus.

Foucault's model of power is 'productive' (Mills 1997). For him, power is dispersed throughout all of social relations and as a force which prevents some actions but enables others (such as the power to show resistance by a minority member). However, power is not defined as a set of attributes characterising any one person, but 'as a set of potentials which, while always present, can be variably exercised, resisted, shifted around and struggled over by social agents' (Hutchby 1999: 586). For example, Foucault (1978) argues that around the eighteenth century, a proliferation of discourses about sex and sexuality was incited institutionally (mainly through the church and schooling system), which allowed the 'agencies of power' to exert control over individuals. 'An imperative was established: Not only will you confess to acts contravening the law, but you will seek to transform your desire, your every desire, into discourse' (Foucault 1978: 21). Thus, discourse does not exist in a social and political vacuum but occupies the same space as power and is the means for exercising it and for constituting different versions of individuals' subjectivity (see also Silverman 1987). For example, Foucault argues that since the eighteenth century, children's sexuality was not 'simply' suppressed, but that a certain version of acceptable sexuality was constructed for children:

> Doctors counselled the directors and professors of educational establishments, but they also gave their opinions to families; educators designed projects which they submitted to authorities; schoolmasters turned to students, made recommendations to them, and drafted for their benefit books of exhortation, full of moral and medical examples. Around the schoolboy and his sex there proliferated a whole literature of precepts, opinions, observations, medical advice, clinical cases, outlines for reform, and plans for ideal institutions. (Foucault 1978: 28)

Another important aspect of Foucault's (1980) view of power is that it is explicitly linked to *knowledge*. The creation of knowledge about a subject involves the struggle of a number of competing versions of the 'truth' about it, and the constitution of new subjectivities for individuals and/or their subjugation. For example, the existing body of knowledge about 'men', 'women', 'India', 'Africa', and so on constitutes these subjects in terms of dominant power paradigms (cross-gender relations, colonial exploration). Furthermore, the individual is not conceived of as an autonomous entity which is acted upon by the forces of power (via discourse); 'the individual is seen as an effect of power, not that which is acted upon by power' (Mills 1997: 22).

In my discussion I demonstrate that although the players in the field are equipped with certain characteristics (such as wealth) marking them pre-discursively as powerful or powerless, they actualise their power potential by deploying specific, local discursive strategies, which are subject to negotiation, acceptance, resistance or rejection. Also, the notion of the 'discourses of power' striving to constitute the dominated individual's subjectivity is highly resonant in my data. Especially in the field of contemporary art, which is viewed by many lay observers as in need of being 'explained' to them (probably on the false assumption that in pre-modern/ist art everything is 'clear'), the art critic can easily position an artist as 'genius' or 'fraud'.

The association of power with knowledge is echoed by Giddens' (1991) emphasis on the pervasiveness of *expert knowledge* in high modernity, or late capitalist societies. According to Giddens, pre-modern societies did produce experts, but there were relatively few technical systems, which required individuals (especially in small societies) to rely on them in everyday life. Experts enjoy a privileged status because it is based on exclusivity:

> Expert knowledge in pre-modern and modern systems concerns the accessibility of expert skills and information to lay actors. Expert knowledge in pre-modern cultures tends to depend on procedures and symbolic forms that resist explicit codification; or, when such knowledge is codified, it is unavailable to lay individuals because literacy is the jealously guarded monopoly of the few. Preservation of the esoteric element of expert knowledge, particularly where this element is separated from 'skills and arts', is probably the main basis of whatever distinctive status experts achieve. (Giddens 1991: 30)

Expert knowledge (combining into expert systems) has clear implications for power relations as it creates a degree of reflexivity which influences the individual to 'the core of the self' (Giddens 1991: 32; see also Fairclough 1993). For example, Giddens invokes the early socialisation of children, which increasingly depends on the instruction from the experts such as paediatricians and educators, rather than traditional, societal norms handed locally from generation to generation. The parallels between this example and Foucault's analysis of the expediency of institutional power and control over children's sexuality since the eighteenth century seem obvious. As will also become clear in this chapter, the assertion of status in discourses on art rests to a great extent on claiming exclusive or 'better' expert knowledge than that represented by one's peers.

In sum, I rely on a number of related and interlinked social theoretic notions (*habitus, field, power/knowledge, subjectivity,* and *expert knowledge*) in order to examine how the artistic order of discourse (admittedly, a very small part of it) becomes a locus of power struggle and a means for the accumulation of symbolic capital (the term *orders of discourse* is used after Fairclough 1989, 1992).

3   Power and symbolic capital in art history and social theory: Baxandall and Bourdieu

According to Baxandall (1985), when one talks about a (representational) picture, however clearly and vividly, one's listener will not be able to reconstruct the picture from the description. There will always be visual aspects of the picture, such as colour sequences, spatial relations, proportions, and so on, which will be left out from the description, not least because language is not best equipped to represent all the nuances of the visual medium (see Kress and van Leeuwen 1996). What one describes, then, is some kind of mental image which develops in one's mind after seeing a picture, or 'what one offers in a description is a representation of thinking about a picture more than a representation of a picture' (Baxandall 1985: 5). Thus, the language of art criticism is of necessity limited, indirect and metaphorical (see Baxandall 1991 [1979]).

On the other hand, one may make a comment about a picture in its presence, when it is seen by both speaker and hearer, but then, Baxandall argues, the language is not descriptive but demonstrative, pointing to particular elements of the picture. However, descriptive or demonstrative talk about pictures does not constitute their explanation or interpretation.

In the interpretation of works of art, Baxandall sees the greatest advantage in adopting a historical/teleological approach, in which one must consider the totality of circumstances which led to the creation and consumption of a work of art. However, in explaining pictures we largely depend on their (imperfect) descriptions. In Baxandall's (1985: 1) words, 'description is the mediating object of explanation'.

As far as the type of painting which Baxandall (1985) is interested in (mostly European painting of the last 500 years), the painter's *Charge*, the initial impetus to paint, is 'to make marks on a plane surface in such a way that their visual interest is directed to an end' (Baxandall 1985: 43). As this type of pictorial Charge is rather general and featureless, so as to be of little interest when discussing specific artists or works of art, it is far more interesting to examine the painter's *Brief*, which involves the questions of why certain pictures are painted and attended to. For example, a painter's Brief may be to find a solution to a painterly problem or to react to an earlier artistic tradition. These elements of the painter's Brief can be set by the artist him/herself in relation to the paintings which s/he knows, likes and dislikes.

However, the artist is not entirely free to set his/her own Brief. S/he operates in a totality of constraining circumstances: the actual (art) market institutions such as galleries, museums, exhibitions, dealers, art journals, art programmes on television and radio, and so on. These market institutions impose formal, rigid structures on the artist and determine his/her Brief (that is, they contribute to the *why* certain pictures are produced and consumed) as they embody some more or less explicit assumptions about what painting is or how it should be. Additionally, the forms of these institutions need not correspond to the current aesthetic tendencies in a culture but often represent remnants of earlier traditions, or they represent structures typical of other markets, such as clothing, antiques, precious metals, and so on, which need not have specially developed for the purpose of the art market (Baxandall 1985: 49).

Apart from the rigid patterns and practices of these market institutions, artists function as social beings in cultural circumstances, which involves reciprocity of relations between them and the cultural systems in which they operate. To account for these types of relationship, Baxandall introduces the notion of the *troc* and explains it as follows:

> In the economists' market what the producer is compensated by is money: money goes one way, goods or services the other. But in the relation between painters and cultures the currency is much more diverse than just money: it includes such things as approval, intellectual nurture and, later, reassurance, provocation and irritation of stimulating kinds, the articulation of ideas, vernacular visual skills, friendship and — very importantly indeed — a history of one's activity and a heredity, as well as sometimes money acting both as a token of some of these and a means to continuing performance. (Baxandall 1985: 48)

Baxandall uses his framework to discuss, among others, aspects of Picasso's work at the beginning of the twentieth century, especially his move towards what is known as his 'Cubist' period. Picasso's Brief at that time was partially a reaction to the earlier Impressionist programme and a search to solve such problems as how to represent a three-dimensional reality in a two-dimensional surface or how to address the question of priority of form over colour. Apart from these *personal* elements, Picasso's Brief was influenced by the Paris (art) market and how he fitted into it. Picasso was determined at that time (approximately between 1906 and 1910) to retain the status of an individualist, that is, to embrace the institutional market structures which allowed him to act as 'a conspicuously individual talent' (Baxandall 1985: 56) and avoid being part of a group movement. This involved marketing his works through individual dealers (first Vollard and later Kahnweiler) and by abstaining (together with Braque) from participating in the group exhibitions, discussions and manifestos produced by the 'minor' Cubists: Albert Gleizes, Jean Metzinger and Robert Delaunay.

Finally, and most relevantly in these considerations, Picasso's Brief (the motivation to paint the way he did) was aided by Apollinaire's writing about his art, which was full of admiration and praise. Even though Picasso, Braque and Kahnweiler later admitted that they had considered Apollinaire to be a poor critic, Apollinaire's writing performed an important ideological and moralist function in the upkeep of Picasso's Brief. Baxandall puts it rather succinctly:

> One would bet Picasso believed the things Apollinaire rhetoricised [about him] long before he had heard of Apollinaire or even visited Paris, but Apollinaire's articulation of them would have sharpened and confirmed them just a little. It is always fortifying to hear your feelings stylishly verbalized by someone you like. And while such things as Apollinaire articulated are inadequate as art criticism, taken *en troc* by a man with his own sharp vision for pictures they play a part, how large one cannot and need not measure. (Baxandall 1985: 58)

Baxandall argues, then, that artists' work is strongly influenced by the discursive practices of their social environment: art institutions, art critics and personal friends. Such discourses are not some 'objectivised' accounts and descriptions of art and art practices, but, more often than not, an impressionistic and highly personalised expression of likes and dislikes, which is partly affected by the vested interests of all parties involved.

In his theory of social practice, Bourdieu (1986, 1993) contextualises art (including literature) as products of one's (or group's) *habitus* (see above). The explanation of works of art requires an analysis of the entire field of cultural production which comprises 'the set of social conditions of the production, circulation and consumption of symbolic goods' (Johnson 1993: 9), its history and structure, and the relationship of the field of cultural production to the field of power.

The works of art in the field of cultural production, just as other human actions in other fields (political, educational, and so on), compete in the field of power for *symbolic capital*, that is, for prestige, consecration, recognition, and so on. Access to symbolic capital is unequal and depends on one's cultural competence as well as on the legitimising practices of the dominant classes: *judgements of taste*, *symbolic violence* (such as violence of silence), familial and formal educational transmission of dominant cultural patterns, and so on. In other words, and importantly for this chapter, the creation of the *belief* of what constitutes a work of art and what its price is, is a result of the relationship between the field of cultural production and the field of power. The study of such beliefs and of their emergence must be related to the discourses about works of art, which are produced by art historians, journalists, art dealers, academics, and artists themselves.

How can we relate Baxandall's work to that of Bourdieu? Very generally, Baxandall's advocacy of the historical explanation of pictures, with reference to the artist's Charge and Brief, market of institutions which s/he operates in and the system of *troc* exchanges which s/he enters and chooses to entertain, corresponds to Bourdieu's claim that

> an art which ever increasingly contains reference to its own history de-mands to be perceived historically; it asks to be referred not to an external referent, the represented or designated 'reality', but to the universe of past and present works of art. (Bourdieu 1986: 3)

Baxandall's notion of the artist's Charge is that of his/her locating his/her individuality in relation to other paintings, and his notion of the artist's Brief centres around a motivation for solving specific artistic problems, setting new programmes and advancing specific pictorial forms. Artists function within fairly rigid structures of institutional markets (corresponding to Bourdieu's field of cultural production), and gain what Bourdieu refers to as symbolic capital — approval, prestige, friendship, sometimes money, etc., as a result of the indeterminate and fluid *troc* exchanges, as defined by Baxandall.

Both Bourdieu and Baxandall attribute a significant role in the artists' (or their works') accumulation of cultural currency (Baxandall) or symbolic cap-ital (Bourdieu) to the mediating nature of discourses about art produced by art critics, art dealers, journalists and academics. I have already quoted Baxandall's example of how Apollinaire assisted Picasso in the maintenance of his Brief through his press accounts full of praise and admiration. Like-wise, Bourdieu recognises that artistic mediators produce the meaning and value of the work, create the 'creator', excluding 'bad' painters from the field of painting by choosing whether to write (or not) good or bad reviews of their work, and so on. An important aspect of all artistic mediators' activity is that they also operate in the field of power and they aim to accumulate as much symbolic capital as possible, usually at each other's expense. In con-sequence, the more powerful the critic is (with the most symbolic capital accumulated) the more legitimising or authenticating powers s/he has over artists and their works.

4   Stated aims of *American Visions*

Robert Hughes, the Australian-born art critic for *Time* magazine, has worked in the USA since 1970. He is the author of several books on different aspects of Australian, American and contemporary art, and he has written and pre-sented two well-known television series on art for the BBC: *The Shock of the New* (1981) and *American Visions* (1996). The latter was shown in Britain on BBC2 in eight parts between 3 November and 29 December 1996. Excerpts from *American Visions* and several other texts (such as press reviews) are analysed in this chapter. The latter texts provide us with a meta-discursive commentary on Hughes's strategies of 'doing' art criticism, and we also gain evidence of the impact not only of the contents of his programme but also of his style of narrating art. We start by examining Hughes's own rationale for making the programme in an article he wrote for the *Sunday Times* to coincide with the beginning of the television series:

> American Visions wasn't conceived as being purely about art; it is about America too. We wanted, in eight hours, to pose and keep reframing a general question: what can we say about Americans from the things they have made. How do these images act in the developing story of American experience? (Hughes 1996: 5).

There is a slight problem of interpretation in relation to Hughes's claims that his programme is intended to go beyond art. It is fairly safe to assume that art critics' role is to *judge* works of art (numerous examples could be cited). Does Hughes mean then that he is going to pass judgement on the works of art, or not? If we follow Baxandall's distinction between the 'explanatory' and 'descriptive' approaches in art criticism, Hughes may mean either. On the one hand, he has the option of the historical functional approach to the 'explanation of pictures', which takes into account the artist's *Brief* and his/her *troc* relations. This approach is also consistent with Bourdieu's idea that the explanation of works of art needs to take into account the relations within the field of cultural production. The other option for Hughes is to adopt a 'descriptive' approach to the works of art, which, to use Baxandall's (1985: 5) quote again, 'is a representation of thinking about a picture more than a representation of a picture'.

An early indication that Hughes has gone for the latter option (of course a degree of 'blending' of both approaches is not impossible), combined with a strong preference to express personal opinion about individual artists, comes from the same article in the *Sunday Times*, in which he comments on the need for making a selection of artists to be discussed in *American Visions*, because television is not 'definitive'. Then, as if making an excuse for leaving out certain names from the programme, he implies that those who did not make it to the programme are as worthy as those who did.

> Half the American artists who are my personal favourites didn't make the final cut... Arshile Gorky, for instance, or the mature work of Isamu Noguchi, or the living sculptor Martin Puryear. (Hughes 1996: 5)

It would be naive to assume that the limitation of time is the only factor responsible for the selection of artists. In a historical survey of art like *American Visions*, the act of selection itself is a commentary on the relevance and importance of some artists over others, and it performs the function of ennobling some works of art vis-à-vis those which are effectively silenced (see also Bourdieu's *violence of silence*). The critic's role and importance in this process is especially apparent when we realise that not only 'Half the American artists who are my personal favourites didn't make the final cut', but a good few who are *not* Hughes's favourites did. However, as I demonstrate later, the inclusion of Hughes's least favourite artists in the programme does not imply his intention to endow them with any amount of symbolic capital.

5   Accumulation and display of symbolic capital by an art critic

Before I discuss the means by which Hughes apportions symbolic capital to others, it is useful to reflect on his own positioning within the field of art criticism. Hughes assumes the role of a 'consecrator' of some artists (while 'desecrating' others) and ensures that his own position to do so cannot be questioned. To this end, his promotional article, quoted above, serves also to assert unequivocally his authority among other television art critics. The article is introduced by the following editorial note, which focusses on Hughes's central strategy: positive self-presentation at the expense of other-bashing.

> Robert Hughes, the Time magazine critic, whose epic series on American culture begins on BBC2 tonight, lambasts programme-makers on both sides of the Atlantic for television's lamentable coverage of the visual arts. (Editorial Note; Hughes 1996: 4)

This note sets the tone and the objective of the article. Hughes is introduced here as an art critic for *Time* magazine, which, undoubtedly, to many readers carries a guarantee of respect and professionalism. Then, the note asserts Hughes's authority by introducing a radical and sweeping idea that the level of art programmes produced in the UK and the US is 'lamentable'.

Further in the article, Hughes ridicules and dismisses some art critics (and briefly praises others), most notably deriding Sister Wendy Beckett. By doing so, it seems that the more he takes symbolic capital as an art critic away from her, the more he appropriates it for himself:

> I feel an allergy to this caravan-dwelling, relentlessly chatty pseudo-hermit with her signature teeth, trundling through the museums like a small black cone on invisible castors. Sister Wendy is to art what Beatrix Potter's Mrs Tiggy-Winkle is to nature, except that, whereas Mrs T-W was a moral teacher of some magnitude and severity, Sister W B trades on her own eccentric cuteness. Who will forget the lady declaring in front of a Rubens crucifixion that she finds the picture very hard to take, since it represents 'the death of someone I love'? (Hughes 1996: 4–5)

In the above passage, Hughes distinctly states his personal aversion to Sister Wendy ('I feel an allergy'). He emphasises her unorthodox habits ('caravan-dwelling') as if they were threatening to the journalistic Establishment, and perpetuates a common, negative stereotype of women being too talkative ('relentlessly chatty'). He undermines her commitment to a declared way of life ('pseudo-hermit'), ridicules her outward appearance ('her signature teeth') and style of dress and size ('small black cone on invisible castors'). Hughes trivialises Sister Wendy by comparing her to a fictitious, non-human character ('Beatrix Potter's Mrs Tiggy-Winkle'), and making the comparison negative for Sister Wendy ('Mrs T-W was a moral teacher of some magnitude and severity, Sister W B trades on her own eccentric cuteness').

Hughes does not stop here. He continues his exercise in self-assertion by invoking a derisory image of Sister Wendy (admittedly, an easy target for mockery and humiliation), by criticising her style of talking about art:

> The good nun's work has nothing to do with explaining the art of painting as such. What she tells are upbeat iconographic stories. Here is Venus with the lovely fluffy pubic hair; there's Mars strapped into his armour, he's about to take it off and they're about to get it on, and Venus' husband, the crippled Vulcan, is lurking in the background steaming with jealousy. This is all very well, and it suits television's preference for simplified narrative, but it doesn't take you very far into the painting. Her humility before dear God and wonderful Art is cloying, near megalomaniac, and pitched at a 15-year-old level; and although it's defended as a way of roping in people who wouldn't ordinarily think about art, I'd rather watch the sheepdog trials. (Hughes 1996: 5)

In this extract, Hughes begins with a patronising term of reference ('The good nun'), questions and ridicules her credibility ('nothing to do with ex-plaining the art of painting'), relevance ('What she tells are upbeat icono-graphic stories'), her personal beliefs ('her humility before dear God and wonderful Art is cloying, near megalomaniac') and target audience ('pitched at a 15-year-old level'). All this is accompanied with a parody of her style and another statement of personal antipathy ('I'd rather watch the sheepdog trials'), which works like a kind of coda in relation to the opening declara-tion: 'I feel an allergy'.

There is no question about the prevailing negativity of these declarations. By contrast, the implication for the reader is that Hughes's own professional position in the world of television art criticism is to be held in unquestion-ably high regard. Such activities provide an ideal illustration of Bourdieu's (1993: 75) remarks on the accumulation of symbolic capital in the field of cultural production:

> For the author, the critic, the art dealer, the publisher or the theatre manager, the only legitimate accumulation consists in making a name for

oneself, a known, recognised name, a capital of consecration implying a power to consecrate objects (with a trademark or signature) or persons (through publication, exhibition, etc.) and therefore to give value, and to appropriate the profits from the operation.

By stating or implying that he represents everything that Sister Wendy does not, Hughes places himself in the authoritarian position of a credible, knowledgeable and thus trustworthy art critic: *the* expert (cf. Giddens quoted above). Through the very act of undertaking a critique of another art critic, and by casting her as incompetent, Hughes leads his readers to believe that he is the one to offer cool, rational, in-depth, serious, respectable commentary on art. Hughes consecrates his own right to consecrate (or not) others in *American Visions*.

6 Hughes's endorsement from within the field

There is no doubt that a single-authored panorama of an artistic tradition will reflect its author's individual taste, preferences, biases and prejudices. This is an inevitable by-product of all journalism, which is neither good nor bad in itself. According to Bourdieu (1986), one's disposition to voice such opinions results from one's habitus and it involves specific position taking in the field of power. In this sense, personal opinions can also be seen as having strong social underpinnings due to the nature of habitus shared with other members of one's social group; in Hughes's case, presumably the members of the middle class in the technologically advanced English-speaking countries with a conservative interest in contemporary art.

As has been noted earlier, the stated aim of *American Visions* is the exploration of 'Americans from the things they have made. How do these images act in the developing story of American experience?' (Hughes 1996: 5). However, if we look elsewhere, we are told by another critic (in what can be seen as an instance of Baxandall's *troc* exchange) that the remit of the series goes further than that:

> Described as a look at the American story seen through the lens of its art, the series contains irritations as well as good jokes, subjects which go on too long, and others on which you wish Hughes would say more. (Dunkley 1996: 19)

Dunkley's metacommentary on *American Visions* implies that Hughes's approach to the programme is overly personal, more so than is apparent from Hughes's own declaration of his aims. This apparent mismatch is not necessarily perceived as problematic by Dunkley or other critics. In fact, another critic reviewing *American Visions* argues that Hughes's singular voice and pronouncement of his verdict on the artists presented in the series is the programme's greatest asset. He even complains that there is not enough of such evaluative commentary:

> At the end of every programme, there's the faintest sense of something missing. I would venture two possibilities. The first is that Hughes' sharp talent for the superlative has been blunted on one of its edges. So that while he is still able to deploy a recruiting trumpet-blast for the art he loves (last night he convinced you to fall in love with Falling Water, Frank Lloyd Wright's astonishing cantilevered house), the art he doesn't gets away relatively unscarred. Discussing Georgia O'Keeffe, for example, he was equivocal about her talents, hinting that her fame was a result of gender politics as much as her own achievements. But he finished by describing her as a 'very considerable painter', an unusually inert phrase for such a muscular writer. (Sutcliffe 1996: 19)

The only matter that Sutcliffe finds objectionable in the programme is Hughes's apparent lack of balance in countering his praise with condemnation. Interestingly, what he finds lacking is forceful criticism. The mention of art which Hughes does not like getting away 'relatively unscarred' suggests that 'scarring' is good and desirable. Whether this is an adequate perception of Hughes's weighing of his opinions is not relevant. More importantly, Sutcliffe endorses such evaluations, which are not only expected of Hughes but, as it seems, of the whole genre of art criticism.

Sometimes, the reviewers of *American Visions* resort to strategies of evaluating Hughes the critic in ways similar to the ones he uses in his scathing attacks on Sister Wendy Beckett. For example, in an overall positive review of the programme, a reviewer signals his disagreement with Hughes's assessment of a particular point, and interestingly finds it easier to disagree with him by making an unfavourable comment on his outward appearance:

> It was only when *the bulky Hughes (who wore the same pale-blue shirt throughout)* — having visited the Lincoln Memorial — turned on more modern forms, that I began to take issue with him. (Aaronovitch 1996: 16; emphasis added)

In sum, the press reviews of *American Visions* are not only 'objective' accounts of the merits of the programme in question, but they also engage in controlling the cultural capital of its author.

7   Praise and condemnation in *American Visions*

It appears that Hughes's most radical and controversial evaluations of American art relate to twentieth-century art. For this reason, and due to limitations of space, I restrict my discussion to several artists from that period as presented in the last three parts of the programme.

The artist who scores the highest with Hughes is Edward Hopper. Hughes describes him as 'the greatest American Artist of the 1930's', and adds:

> He was a man of extreme painlessness, straightforwardness and tact of feeling. He was candid but his candour always holds a certain mystery. He's a painter that I trust absolutely. (*American Visions*, Part 6)

Hughes makes his pronouncement on Hopper with great solemnity. But despite the serious tenor of Hughes's declaration of 'absolute trust' in Hopper, it may sound to some almost as emotional as some of Sister Wendy's attributed narrative style, so much criticised by Hughes. And besides, what does a statement that Hopper 'was a man of extreme painlessness, straightforwardness and tact of feeling', actually have 'to do with explaining the art of [Hopper's] painting as such' (cf. Hughes 1996, quoted above)? We could argue that it has nothing to do with explaining anything about Hopper's paintings. Hughes produces the above statement on camera, without referring to or showing the viewer any particular painting. This can be said to be a typical example of what Baxandall calls 'descriptive' language, which reveals nothing about any specific detail of Hopper's art or his intention to paint specific pictures. Here Hughes does not go beyond representing to the viewers his respectful (mental) image of Hopper.

Another artist accorded high status by Hughes and with a unique place in American art is Jackson Pollock:

> But how to transcend the surrealist model? The artist who really seemed to have done it by his death in 1956 was Jackson Pollock. And American culture never got over its surprise of producing him. (*American Visions*, Part 7)

The exceptional place of Pollock in American art is further asserted by Hughes in his reference to the artist's death in a car crash, as if it was a planned art event. Although this may be a piece of spectacular journalism, this does not seem to give much insight to the lay viewer about the relationship between surrealist art and Pollock. Then, Hughes turns to religious metaphors to talk about Pollock, or, more precisely, about his current standing among younger artists:

> Anyone who thinks that American modernism doesn't have its religious aspect should come here, see the light and be converted. This is the studio once used by Jackson Pollock and Lee Kresner in the village of Sprigs on Long Island. It has since been preserved as a shrine. None of Pollock's actual paintings are here but instead you have the holy coffee cans, the miraculous brushes and the sanctified shoes. I don't know whether young

artists come here in search of transformation, poof, you're a genius, but nothing is impossible. In any case, this is the sanctum sanctorum. The floor preserves the drips left by the master, the ones that went off the edges of the canvas. (*American Visions*, Part 7)

The above quote may be perceived as rather unexpected 'for such a muscular writer' (Sutcliffe 1996: 19; quoted above). Sutcliffe clearly conjures up an image of Hughes as the leading macho art critic (whatever that may mean) rather than a metaphysical 'softie'. Why then does Hughes use all the religious imagery and metaphors which, uncannily, remind us of Sister W B, too? The shrine of Jackson Pollock is visited by his worshippers — 'young artists', who, may or may not believe in the metaphysical powers of the place itself.

Of course, we cannot assume that Hughes *really* believes that any miraculous transformations of young artists do take place there. Instead, he uses subtle irony, which, in this case, is relatively gentle due to its anonymous collective target ('young artists'). Thus, Hughes is safe with this quasi-religious praise for Pollock, as the act of worship is not entirely his, and visually, the drips of paint left on the coffee cans, the shoes and the floor are not unlike those on Pollock's canvases.

By contrast, other abstract painters fare less well. For example, consider the disparaging pronouncement which Hughes makes about Barnett Newman. The following is an extract from Dunkley's review of *American Visions* referred to above. As has been mentioned, Dunkley is very much in favour of Hughes's proclamations of artistic worth or insignificance of specific works of art. Therefore, he seems to revel in Hughes's ironic criticism of Newman.

The following quote begins with Dunkley's overt praise for Hughes in one of the episodes of the series:

> There is a moment in programme seven when it is difficult not to leap from the old green sofa cheering. Showing us around Barnett Newman's series of canvases called 'Stations Of The Cross' with their sub-Mondrian straight black lines on white, Hughes declares: 'As documents of early minimalism they are not without interest, but as a narrative of the suffering and passion of Jesus Christ they're utterly absurd. Newman once said "I thought our quarrel was with Michelangelo." Well bad luck Barney. You lost!' That sort of left to the jaw, delivered with a grin, is too rare. (Dunkley 1996: 19)

Dunkley's opening and closing sentences liken the experience of watching *American Visions* to that of a boxing fight. Of course, that the subject matter is highly esoteric abstract art transforms the egalitarian in-groupness associated with sporting events to elitism and suggests a discourse community within which Dunkley positions himself as 'expert' and Hughes's peer ('team mate').

It is revealing that most reviews of *American Visions* have focussed on such evaluative representations by Hughes of artists' (in)significance by commonly invoking Hughes's machismo or bullishness ('muscular writer', 'left to the jaw'). The value of the series (at least in the eyes of other art journalists) seems to be measured not by the quality of Hughes's critical reflection but the significance and delivery of his personal likes and dislikes. Yet, not surprisingly, in a review of *American Visions* in an arts magazine (*tate*), as opposed to those in non-specialist press, one of Hughes's critics states that the dismissal of Newman's *Stations of the Cross* series 'is unproductive and appears simply bad tempered' (Wyver 1997: 72). What this comment seems to be suggesting is that some art critics are sceptical at treating Hughes's jabs at individual artists as art criticism, if art criticism is taken to mean *interpretation* of works of art through discussion of artists' Brief and *troc* relationships.

In the remaining part of this section I analyse in some detail a more elaborate example of Hughes's dismissal of another artist's (Jeff Koons) work. Apart from his usual voice-over and on-camera commentary, Hughes includes a short interview with Koons, which gives us an opportunity to examine a piece of interactive discourse use in the series.

Hughes cannot deny Koons's prominent, although admittedly controversial, position in the contemporary American and international art scene, and he introduces him as 'egregious Jeff Koons'. Then he continues with the following presentation of Koons's person and his art:

A former bond trader whose ambitions took him right through kitsch and out the other side, into a vulgarity so syrupy, gross and numbing that collectors felt challenged by it. Sometimes his work was at least memorable . . . He didn't make his own stuff, of course — no doubt Koons couldn't carve his name on a tree. He had European souvenir factories to do that, creating delicious porcelain treasures to his design, like *Michael Jackson With Bubbles* and *Leonardo's St John*. This little piggy [close up of the head of a porcelain pig] went to market in a big way, for Koons sees himself as a spiritual artist. Accusing him of hype is like rebuking a fish for being wet. (*American Visions*, Part 8)

This passage serves as a definitive and unequivocal dismissal of Koons as a credible artist. Hughes uses a hyperbolic account of Koons's transition from his non-artistic past to being the champion of *bad taste*. He creates here a subjectivity for Koons which is based on freakishness and aberration, while his observation that 'Sometimes his work was at least memorable' positions Hughes as an objective and credible expert.

Hughes implicitly questions the legitimacy of Koons's commercial success by implying that his work is bought by collectors who feel 'challenged' by Koons's work, which is not a typical response to a 'normal' artist. Moreover, by introducing a third party (challenged collectors), Hughes distances the artworld establishment (including himself) from having anything to do with Koons's commercial success. A divide is created by Hughes between US (art connoisseurs) and THEM (collectors), construing the latter as rather naive and unknowledgeable.

Another characteristic strategy is sarcasm, exemplified towards the end of the extract, when Hughes combines the imagery of a nursery rhyme (a trivial, low-culture genre with mass appeal) with the close-up of a pig's head in one of Koons's sculptures, namely Leonardo's St John. The sculpture is based on a religious painting by Leonardo, which allows Hughes to add irony (again) to his statement that 'Koons sees himself as a spiritual artist'.

Furthermore, Hughes works up his negative evaluation as if it followed from the 'facts' of Koons's lack of any artistic skills. He also employs a host of lexical choices with explicit negative connotations, at least in the context of discussing 'high art', 'kitsch' being probably the strongest of them all. Interestingly, Hughes creates a sense of lexical and semantic cohesion through his word choice, by referring to Koons's work as 'syrupy' and 'delicious', which have strong consumerist associations and give an impression that Koons's work may be bad for one's 'aesthetic health'.

Finally, sanctified by the art market and the 'collectors', Koons is completely desecrated by Hughes. He is excluded from the field of 'legitimate' artists by a reference to his 'real' trade ('former bond trader') and lack of artistic skills ('He didn't make his own stuff, of course', 'Koons couldn't carve his name on a tree'). Koons's work is presented as the complete antithesis of 'rightful' art, as 'kitschy', 'vulgar', 'syrupy', 'gross' and 'numbing'.

The short narrative about Koons's work quoted above serves as an introduction to a brief interview[1] filmed in Koons's studio, in front of an unfinished sculpture showing a giant toy-like pussycat in a sock. The interview recycles all the major themes of criticism raised by Hughes in his introduction: superficiality, pretence of spirituality and lack of artistic skills.

Example 1

1 **Hughes:** hi Jeff [**Koons:** hello] a: kitten (.) in a giant sock (.) tell me about it
2 **Koons:** uh this is one of my new newer works that I I'm:: creating (.) and I think that uh
3 it's a piece that's working in a kind of a very classical tradition of a a crucifixion (.)
4 and this is very open it's more fun loving in a way (.) and uh also deal with
5 spiritual things=
6 **Hughes:** =well I don't see much spirituality there yet I see: a very large and playful pussycat
7 in a sock but how are you going to inject spirituality into this image?
8 **Koons:** I'm gonna give the the cat a little more Bambi-like eyelashes=
9 **Hughes:** =ah: very spiritual Bambi, yeah=
10 **Koons:** =and I think that the flowers are really quite beautiful they are very very Baroque
11 I try to make works [clears throat] pardon me that are very generous I try to be as
12 generous as I can be with myself=

13 **Hughes:** =what do you mean by generous? I mean what you know how is this more
14   generous say than er:: er:: some other kind of sculpture? what's what's generous
15   about it?
16 **Koons:** well I think that it it's communicating ah:: love it's communicating happiness uh:
17   and it does not alienate anyone I think that a young child could come in here a
18   five year old child uh could look and find some pleasure and some enjoyment and
19   I hope that it's something po:sitive for human kind
20 **Hughes:** have you ever actually done any carving or modelling?
21 **Koons:** uh no [**Hughes:** no] no when I was a a child I: did some mo:delling=
22 **Hughes:** =what with plasticine or modelling clay?=
23 **Koons:** =[slightly impatient] with plasticine but now we're working here in my New York
24   studio and I have a staff of artists that I work with which uh er:: really quite
25   phenomenal
26 **Hughes:** so you think the stuff up but you don't make it
27 **Koons:** ah:: that's correct I have to oversee everything here I have to make every decision
28   otherwise I'd have no relation to it at all

Hughes starts his interview with an apparently 'open' question (line 1), which invites Koons to give a gloss on his sculpture. However, Hughes seizes the first opportunity there is to interrupt and challenge Koons. First, he disagrees about his perception of the pussycat, calling it devoid of any spirituality (line 6), then uses sarcasm to dismiss a popular culture image (Bambi) as an inconceivable reference to spirituality (line 9), and rapidly changes the topic of conversation from discussing the pussycat sculpture to questioning Koons's use of the term 'generous' (lines 13–15). Then Hughes changes the topic rapidly again, and questions Koons about his modelling skills (line 20). This is not a question for information, as Hughes has already asserted that 'no doubt Koons couldn't carve his name on a tree'. And when Koons answers the question in the negative, as Hughes must have expected, but adds that he used to model as a child, Hughes concentrates on the minute and irrelevant detail whether Koons had modelled 'with plasticine or modelling clay?' (line 22). That the question seems irrelevant and meant to debase Koons is evidenced by the manner with which Koons answers it with a whiff of impatience in his tone (line 23), and resumes his calm tone promptly to explain that he employs other artists to do work for him (a fact known to most people who are familiar with Koons's work). Hughes seizes one more opportunity to return to the idea of Koons's lack of artistic skills referring disparagingly to his work as 'stuff' (line 26), to which Koons gives an affirmative answer and emphasises his conceptual involvement in the production of his work.

Apart from the first 'open' question, the remaining turns by Hughes in this conversation are intended to dominate his interviewee. He interrupts Koons four times (lines 6, 9, 13, 22), disagrees with him (line 6), ridicules with an ironic remark (line 9), rapidly changes topics (lines 13, 20), refocusses the conversation on irrelevant detail (line 22) and forces Koons to admit to a well-known but potentially embarrassing lack of artistic skill (line 26).

Gaining interpersonal power over Koons in the interview is an important meta-strategy for Hughes because this not only allows him to debase, dismiss and ridicule Koons, but, if successful, it also makes him 'believable' to his viewers. Hughes's agenda on Koons is set out in his narrative, and he is not likely to change it in the course of the interview. Thus Hughes sets an agenda for dismissing Koons and does so in the narrative prior to the interview. Status relations being established in this way, the viewer may be easily convinced that Hughes has the upper hand in the interview that follows. As Meehan (1990: 160) observes: 'all people define situations as real; but when powerful people define situations as real, then they are real "for everybody involved" in their consequences'.

In sum, Hughes engages in two types of power relations: one, at the level of the interaction, which helps him to gain interpersonal power over Koons, and two, at a more general level of social relations, positioning himself as a powerful player in the field of cultural production. These two types of power correspond to two kinds of relations which hold between different types of discourse and social practice, as summarised by van Leeuwen (1993: 193):

> There is discourse as itself, (part of) social practice, discourse as a form of action, as something people do to or for or with each other. And there is discourse in the Foucauldian sense, discourse as a way of representing social practices(s), as a form of knowledge, as the things people say about social practice(s).

8 Conclusion

This chapter has examined a small selection of data derived from a television programme and from some of its reviews. My main thesis has been that the programme's author and presenter engages in a number of strategies which allow him to claim symbolic capital for himself, with a view to being able, as an art critic, to apportion symbolic capital to others. I have also argued that as part of this process, he engages in the acquisition of status, which, in turn, reinforces his position in the wider political field of power (Bourdieu 1991).

The processes of status (self-)apportionment and (de-)legitimisation of works of art are constituted in discourse. The domain of social life from which this paper has drawn its data lies in the field of artistic production, and therefore a combination of art-critical and social-theoretical positions, with a Critical Discourse Analytic approach to the language of art journalism, are useful in unravelling the mechanisms of position taking by the actors in the field of cultural production.

The meta-commentary on *American Visions* quoted throughout the paper has also provided a useful insight into the saliency of the strategies of status manipulation in the programme. Therefore, we can argue that Hughes's strategic use of discourse in the series is to some extent *marked* (unexpected or noticeable). In her model of code choice and markedness, Scotton (1983) argues that participants in a speech event share a knowledge of which of the linguistic choices available to them are unmarked and which are marked, and that the choice of the unmarked variant (in a particular context) indicates the speaker's intention to preserve the status quo as far as the speaker's and addressee's relative positions are concerned, while the choice of a marked form signals the desire to challenge the status quo.

If we accept that one of Hughes's aims in *American Visions* is to establish himself as a star expert on American art, and that some of the contemporary (and past) artists' positions are reassessed, we can conclude that the series is at least in part meant to upset the status quo (whatever it may be), and that some of Hughes's choices for the presentation of his subject matter may be marked, and hence more noticeable than others.

A parallel can be drawn here between *American Visions* and some news interview programmes, in which interviewers step out of the expected (un-marked) 'neutrality' frame for conducting the interview (see Clayman 1992; Greatbatch 1992, 1998; Heritage 1985; Heritage and Greatbatch 1991) and subsequently this fact may become a newsworthy item in itself (Clayman and Whalen 1988/89). These authors analyse a nine-minute interview of George Bush by Dan Rather on the CBS Evening News. The interview gradually departs from the canonical question–answer turn-taking system and moves towards a more conversational mode in which Rather abandons his unmarked 'neutrality' stance of the interviewer, while Bush starts pursu-ing his own agenda and assumes speaking rights going beyond answering the interviewer's questions. Consequently, Rather is branded by the media as 'rude' and bullying Bush, who, on the other hand, is perceived to have discarded in the interview his image of a 'wimp'.

Likewise, Harris (1991) analyses an extract from a 1977 television inter-view between Brian Walden and James Callaghan (then British Prime Min-ister), in which Walden's questioning sequence seems 'to overstep the bounds of interviewer "neutrality"', disrupting the structure of pre-allocated turns and acting as personal assertions in what has essentially become an argument in which participants state opposing views' (Harris 1991: 81).

The interviewer's change of frame from 'information seeking' to 'argu-mentative' led to the breakdown of the interview, which in itself became a newsworthy item causing much public criticism of the interviewer 'suggest-ing that there are fairly strict limits on the extent to which an interviewer can force a politician to provide what he (the interviewer) considers a satis-factory answer to a particular question' (Harris 1991: 81).

It is tempting to see the Koons interview analysed above in a similar way, with Hughes's blatant attacks on the artist's work (made manifest by persistent interruptions and topic changes), and the latter slowly losing his patience, although never openly retaliating. Again, support for treating this interview as marked (especially Hughes's bullishness) comes in the form of a meta-commentary on this exchange, which appears in an interview with the artist Barbara Kruger (*Art in America*, October 1997), who dismisses it as an example of gratuitous criticism that artists face often from haughty critics.

What is then the role of the art critic in a programme oriented towards a mass television audience? So far, most of my analysis points to the highly biased, evaluative discourse style of Hughes's discourse on art. On the one hand, he praises some artists for the emotional effect on him of their painting (Hopper, for instance), and for the long-lasting nature of their legacy (e.g. Pollock). On the other hand, he debases other artists (such as Koons), by ridiculing their work, their skills and intentions, as well as the taste of the collectors who happen to buy their work. For the most part, Hughes's art criticism is oriented towards creating a ranking system, a league table of his favourite artists, which brings us back to the work of Baxandall and Bourdieu, who treat the discursive practices of the field of artistic production as related to the accumulation of symbolic capital. To reiterate an earlier quote, this is then necessary for a player in the field to give him/her the power to 'consecrate objects . . . or persons . . . and therefore to give value, and to appropriate the profits from this operation' (Bourdieu 1993: 75).

But Bourdieu points also to another important aspect of cultural practice, the politics of *taste*. For Bourdieu, taste is a means of classification of objects and of those who do the classifying (which effectively means everyone). 'Social subjects, classified by their classifications, distinguish themselves by the distinctions they make, between the beautiful and the ugly, the distinguished and the vulgar, in which their position in the objective classifications is expressed or betrayed' (Bourdieu 1986: 7). Given the evaluative tone of Hughes's commentary we can also argue that the main function of *American Visions* is the (re)production of *taste* in art. Of course, taste, whether in relation to food and drink, or the aesthetic reactions to music, visual arts, etc., is not the same sensation, objectively given to all individuals. Just as there are individual, social, cultural, political, religious and other sources of variation in the perception and communication of gastronomic taste (for example mineral water, see Kress 1997; chocolate, see Piroelle 1997) there are no givens in appreciating works of art. The likes and dislikes in art are equally shaped by our personal, social and cultural histories, and form part of our habitus. Taste is an attribute of our class membership, and once established is unlikely to undergo major changes.

Therefore, *American Visions*, as well as other programmes and publications on art, (re)produce inter-group relations in society with all their divisions and incompatibilities, positions of dominance, submission and control. An interest and appreciation of art, and a degree of knowledge about art, are more likely to predispose some members of the viewing public to watch such programmes as *American Visions* and to reinforce the division between Self and the Other who does not. This also makes *American Visions* a programme for the *insiders*, those in the 'know'. For example, when Hughes mentions the relationship between Pollock and surrealism (see above), there is no offer of the historical explanation of this link and why it is important in understanding Pollock's work. The addressees of the programme are assumed to possess this knowledge, which creates a sense of in-groupness among those who know and excludes those who don't. Examples of a similar type could be multiplied. Hughes does not teach the lay public of American art. Rather, he speaks to the members of his own community of discourse reinforcing the elitist ethos of art, and imposing a particular view of 'acceptable' and 'unacceptable' art on the members of this community.

Acknowledgement

I thank Nik Coupland and Dariusz Galasiński for useful comments on earlier versions of this chapter. Any remaining errors and inadequacies are my own.

Note

1. The following transcription conventions are used in this extract:

(.)	short pause
=	contiguous speech
[clears throat]	commentary on context or non-verbal features of talk
:	lengthening
::	perceptibly longer lengthening

References

Aaronovitch, David (1996) Television: Decision 97? First to the barber wins: What will Blair be found doing in No 10? Having his hair cut, presumably. *The Independent*, 10 November 1996. No. 1538. 16.

Baxandall, Michael (1985) *Patterns of Intention: On the Historical Explanation of Pictures*. New Haven: Yale University Press.

Baxandall, Michael (1991) The language of art criticism. In S. Kemal and I. Gaskell (eds) *The Language of Art History*. Cambridge: Cambridge University Press, 67–75. (First published 1979 as The language of art history in *New Literary History* 10: 453–465.)

Bourdieu, Pierre (1977) *Outline of a Theory of Practice*. Cambridge: Cambridge University Press.

Bourdieu, Pierre (1986) *Distinction: A Social Critique of the Judgement of Taste*. Translated by Richard Nice. London: Routledge.

Bourdieu, Pierre (1991) *Language and Symbolic Power*. Ed. John B. Thompson, translated by Gino Raymond and Matthew Adamson. Cambridge: Polity Press.

Bourdieu, Pierre (1993) *The Field of Cultural Production: Essays on Art and Literature*. Ed. Randal Johnson. Cambridge: Polity Press.

Brown, Penelope and Levinson, Stephen C. (1987) *Politeness: Some Universals in Language Usage*. Cambridge: Cambridge University Press. (First published 1978 in E.N. Goody (ed.) *Questions and Politeness*. Cambridge: Cambridge University Press.)

Brown, Roger and Gilman, Albert (1972 [1960]) The pronouns of power and solidarity. In P.P. Giglioli (ed.) *Language and Social Context*. Harmondsworth: Penguin, 256–282. (First published 1960 in T.A. Sebeok (ed.) *Style in Language*. Cambridge, MA: MIT Press, 253–277.)

Caldas-Coulthard, Carmen and Coulthard, Malcolm (eds) (1996) *Texts and Practices: Readings in Critical Discourse Analysis*. London: Routledge.

Clayman, Steven E. (1992) Footing in the achievement of neutrality: The case of news interviews discourse. In P. Drew and J. Heritage (eds) *Talk at Work: Interaction in Institutional Settings*. Cambridge: Cambridge University Press, 163–198.

Clayman, Steven E. and Whalen, Jack (1988/89) When the medium becomes the message: The case of the Rather–Bush encounter. *Research on Language and Social Interaction* 22: 241–272.

Dunkley, Christopher (1996) Arts: An American tale artfully told. *The Financial Times* 30 October 1996 (1190), 19.

Fairclough, Norman (1989) *Language and Power*. London: Longman.

Fairclough, Norman (1992) *Discourse and Social Change*. Cambridge: Polity Press.

Fairclough, Norman (1993) Critical discourse analysis and the marketization of public discourse: The universities. *Discourse & Society* 4/2: 133–168.

Fairclough, Norman (1995) *Critical Discourse Analysis: The Critical Study of Language*. London: Longman.

Foucault, Michel (1978) *The History of Sexuality: An Introduction, Vol 1*. Translated by Robert Hurley. London: Penguin. (First published 1976.)

Foucault, Michel (1980) *Power/Knowledge: Selected Interviews and Other Writings, 1972–1977*. Ed. C. Cordon. Brighton: Harvester Press.

Giddens, Anthony (1991) *Modernity and Self-identity: Self and Society in the late Modern Age*. Cambridge: Polity Press.

Greatbatch, David (1992) On the management of disagreement between news interviewees. In P. Drew and J. Heritage (eds) *Talk at Work: Interaction in Institutional Settings*. Cambridge: Cambridge University Press, 268–301.

Greatbatch, David (1998) Conversation analysis: Neutralism in British News Interviews. In A. Bell and P. Garrett (eds) *Approaches to Media Discourse*. Oxford: Blackwell, 163–185.

Harris, Sandra (1991) Evasive action: How politicians respond to questions in political interviews. In P. Scannell (ed.) *Broadcast Talk*. London: Sage, 76–99.

Heritage, John (1985) Analyzing news interviews: Aspects of the production of talk for an 'overhearing' audience. In T. van Dijk (ed.) *Handbook of Discourse Analysis*, Vol. 3. London: Academic Press, 95–119.

Heritage, John and Greatbatch, David (1991) On the institutional character of institutional talk: The case of news interviews. In D. Boden and D.H. Zimmerman (eds) *Talk and Social Structure*. Cambridge: Polity Press, 93–137.

Hodge, Robert and Kress, Gunther (1988) *Language as Ideology*. London: Routledge.

Hughes, Robert (1996) If art moves, why animate it? *The Sunday Times (10)*. 3 November 1996, 4–5.

Hutchby, Ian (1999) Power in discourse: The case of arguments on a British talk radio show. In A. Jaworski and N. Coupland (eds) *The Discourse Reader*. London: Routledge, 576–588. (Originally published in *Discourse & Society* 7/4: 481–497.)

Johnson, Randal (1993) Introduction. In P. Bourdieu *The Field of Cultural Production: Essays on Art and Literature*. Cambridge: Polity Press, 1–25.

Kress, Gunther (1991) Critical discourse analysis. *Annual Review of Applied Linguistics* 11: 84–99.

Kress, Gunther (1997) On the semiotics of taste: The chains of meaning. In A. Piroelle (ed.) *La Représentation Sociale du Goût*. Dijon: PRIsM, 93–112.

Kress, Gunther and van Leeuwen, Theo (1996) *Reading Images: The Grammar of Visual Design*. London: Routledge.

Meehan, Hugh (1990) Oracular reasoning in a psychiatric exam: The resolution of conflict in language. In A.D. Grimshaw (ed.) *Conflict Talk*. Cambridge: Cambridge University Press.

Mills, Sara (1997) *Discourse*. London: Routledge.

Ng, Sik Hung and Bradac, James J. (1993) *Power in Language: Verbal Communication and Social Influence*. Newbury Park, CA: Sage.

Piroelle, Ann (1997) Communication and interculturality: The case of chocolate. In A. Piroelle (ed.) *La Représentation Sociale du Goût*. Dijon: PRIsM, 129–148.

Scotton, Carol Myers (1983) The negotiation of identities in conversation: A theory of markedness and code choice. *International Journal of Sociology of Language* 44: 115–136.

Silverman, David (1987) *Communication and Medical Practice: Social Relations in the Clinic*. London: Sage.

Sutcliffe, T. (1996) Television review. *The Independent* 9 December 1996. No. 707, 19.

Thompson, John B. (1991) Editor's introduction. In P. Bourdieu *Language and Symbolic Power*. Cambridge: Polity Press, 1–31.

van Dijk, T.A. (1993) Principles of critical discourse analysis. *Discourse & Society* 4/2: 249–283.

van Leeuwen, Theo (1993) Genre and field in critical discourse analysis: A synopsis. *Discourse & Society* 4/2: 193–223.

Watts, Richard J. (1991) *Power in Family Discourse*. Berlin: Mouton de Gruyter.

Wyver, John (1997) Review of *American Visions. tate: The Art Magazine* 11, Spring 1997, 71–72.

6

Co-membership and wiggle room: Some implications of the study of talk for the development of social theory[1]
Frederick Erickson

---

1 Introduction

In the last fifteen years there has been a movement within sociolinguistic theory to connect the processes of oral and written discourse with general social processes at the level of political economy and history. Some examples of this trend are found in the work of Fairclough (1989, 1992), Gee (1990, 1992), and in the appearance of a new journal titled *Discourse & Society* (and this brief listing is only intended as illustrative). While earlier theoretical and empirical work in sociolinguistics considered relationships between language and society (hence the origin of the term 'sociolinguistics' itself), the newer approaches, in what might be called discourse studies, are characterised by a focus on the influence upon local social action of general social and cultural processes, especially as they involve social class, ideology, and the distribution of power in society. Earlier sociolinguistics did not focus so directly upon issues of power and ideology, especially concerning the reproduction of class position in modern societies.

Since 'discourse' has become a generative metaphor in social theory within the most recent academic generation, it should be no surprise that proponents of the newer discourse studies within sociolinguistics have drawn upon the work of social theorists such as Foucault, Bourdieu, and Habermas, who have developed notions of discourse in their studies of relations between general and local social processes. In the present volume, several chapters, particularly 1 and 5, refer extensively to their work. (For my purposes in this chapter, the approach of Habermas goes beyond the bounds I am setting and so I will not include Habermas in the following discussion.)

There has also been some influence of sociolinguistics on the development of social theory, especially regarding studies of oral discourse. For example, Bourdieu has cited Goffman, Garfinkel, Gumperz, Labov and various conversation analysts and fairly early in his career he spent a year with Goffman as a visiting scholar at the University of Pennsylvania. In addition, the 'structuration theory' of Giddens draws upon both Goffman and conversation analysis as sources of insight into the conduct of everyday interaction by means of 'practical reason', outside discursive or reflective awareness.

In the new approaches to discourse studies within sociolinguistics, the attempt to consider issues of power and social class as they are at work within the conduct of local discourse practices is both necessary and laudable. Yet as we attempt to connect the workings of history with the work of talk in immediate social interaction, a note of caution should be sounded. The relation between social theory and sociolinguistic discourse studies need not be monologic; that is, sociolinguistics need not adopt general social theory uncritically, especially if that might lead sociolinguists to buy into a view which assumes that general social processes drive local discourse practices in a 'top-down' kind of determinism. (I see such determinism especially in Fairclough's articulation of his version of 'critical discourse analysis', and will comment on this later in the chapter.) Rather, sociolinguistic studies of oral discourse can be a source of criticism that informs general social theory development. It seems to me that the close analysis of what particular interlocutors do interactionally suggests that the currently dominant conceptions of social and cultural reproduction leave too little room for possibilities of interruption of hegemony within local social action. People don't act in speaking exactly as general social theory predicts, and this can be understood as more than just variation that is due to random error. It can be seen as having to do with what Goffman (1983) identified as matters of the *interaction order*. Moreover, what interlocutors do locally can be seen as not only influenced by the wider society but as also influencing it. Accordingly, I want to argue here that influence from sociolinguistic discourse studies upon social theory can be as important for the future development of both fields as has been the influence of general social theory upon discourse studies in sociolinguistics recently.

2   Bourdieu, social reproduction, and examples from studies of education

As a way into these issues we can take a page from the sociology of education over the last thirty years. A guiding theme has been to identify the conditions under which social class position is reproduced across generations. From the work of Basil Bernstein (1961) and Michael F.D. Young (1971) up to the present, the contention has been that cultural differences in ways of speaking (and of valuing and desiring) are distributed across social classes so as to make school achievement harder for working-class students and easier for upper middle-class students. Working-class student speech and self-presentation are viewed as inappropriate by teachers in schools, and thus school experience and school knowledge becomes alienating for working-class students. In contrast, the speech styles and interests of upper middle-class students are seen as consonant with what the school expects and requires.

With the publication of Bourdieu and Passeron's essay on reproduction — it appeared in English in 1977 — the metaphor of cultural capital was introduced. Working-class students lacked such capital and upper middle-class students possessed it. Bourdieu's theoretical project has involved showing social actors as doing something other than simply following rules — what Garfinkel (1967) called being a 'cultural dope'. Growing up in a particular class position, persons learn a stable set of dispositions — the *habitus* — which Bourdieu defines as a stable set of dispositions that lead them to take action strategically in ways that are outside reflective awareness. (This conception derives from Merleau-Ponty's emphasis on the recursive, embodied, and intuitive character of daily practice (Merleau-Ponty 1945/1962: 139–145). It is akin to the insight of linguists that knowledge of phonology and syntax is held and acted upon preconsciously.)

Bourdieu's notion of habitus allows for agency on the part of the individual social actor — it is founded in a critique of the notion of social action as rule following (in *Outline of a Theory of Practice* he contrasts marriage strategies to marriage rules (1977: 58–71) and says of the habitus that it 'is the source of . . . series of moves which are objectively organized as strategies without being the product of a genuine strategic intention' (1977: 73). Within the immediacy of the routine practice of daily life social actors are seen as making choices rather than as following rules.

Yet the consequences of the strategic choices made outside discursive awareness are still overdetermined and their ultimate result is the maintenance of existing class position. Bourdieu's view is that the learned dispositions of the habitus are initially acquired early in life (in the family before school attendance) and while chronologically ordered in subsequent periods of acquisition, they are structurally similar because of similarities from one successive stage to the next: 'the habitus acquired in the family is at the basis of the structuring of school experiences . . . the habitus transformed by the action of the school, itself diversified, is in turn at the absis of all subsequent experiences . . . and so on, from restructuring to restructuring change little after that' (Bourdieu 1972: 188, quoted and translated by Wacquant in Bourdieu and Wacquant 1992 note 87 p. 134). They are the result of the everyday experience that comes with class position, and Bourdieu assumes that such experience is unitary within social classes:

The objective homogenizing of group or class habitus which results from the homogeneity of the conditions of existence is what enables practices to be objectively harmonized without any intentional calculation or conscious reference to a norm . . . because they are the product of dispositions which, being the internalization of the same objective structures, are objectively concerted that the practices of the members of the same group, or in a differentiated society, the same class, are endowed with an objective meaning that is at once unitary and systematic . . . (Bourdieu 1977: 80–81)

Bourdieu grounded his research program upon a conception of socially limited agency (in an attempt to avoid the determinism of structuralists, particularly Lévi-Strauss, and at the same time to avoid the unlimited voluntarism of Sartre, the phenomenologists, and rational choice theorists):

I wanted initially to account for practice in its humblest forms — rituals, matrimonial choices, the mundane economic conduct of everyday life, etc. — by escaping both the objectivism of action understood as a mechanical reaction 'without an agent' and the subjectivism which portrays action as the deliberate pursuit of a conscious intention, the free project of a conscience positing its own ends and maximizing its utility through rational computation. (Bourdieu and Wacquant 1992: 121)

In responding to critics he continues to deny that his theory is too determinist:

Habitus is not the fate that some people read into it. Being the product of history it is an *open system of dispositions* [italics are the author's] that is constantly subjected to experiences and therefore constantly affected by them in a way that either reinforces or modifies its structures. It is durable but not eternal! Having said this, I must immediately add that there is a probability, inscribed in the social destiny associated with definite social conditions, that experiences will confirm habitus, because most people are statistically bound to encounter circumstances that tend to agree with those that originally fashioned their habitus. (Bourdieu and Wacquant 1992: 133) (*Note the hedge in the last sentence of this citation.*)

The dispositions of habitus relate to the field of status competition in which they are employed (the 'field' being a particular configuration of power/cultural capital and ways of acquiring it — distinctively differing status-competitive game-like arenas such as law, academia, medicine, the arts, finance — Bourdieu and Wacquant 1992: 94–98). As conditions in a field change (and in the 'market' within which the field is embedded), so does the pattern of habitus necessary for competitively successful play in it.

Thus, Bourdieu would argue, his model of societal process does allow for the possibility of social change.

But there is a trap here. The influences upon change in Bourdieu's models come always in the direction from higher levels to lower ones — from market to field to habitus — and not in the reverse. This, together with the emphasis in his empirical work on what he called in the quote above 'the social destiny associated with definite social conditions', leads him to show us example after example — in fields such as public education, university education, the arts, the Church — how the overall result of the exercise of agency by persons (following the dispositions of habitus as an intuitive 'sense of the game') is that they end up maintaining existing class positions, for themselves as individuals and for society at large. This leads numerous critics to read him as too much of a determinist, despite his protestations to the contrary (see for example the discussions in Collins (1993) and in Alexander (1995)). Similar criticism applies to Fairclough's (1989, 1992) encyclopedic surveys of issues in critical discourse analysis. In the numerous examples of written and oral discourse he provides as illustrative material — from everyday circumstances of conversation, from professional settings, from advertising, and from cinema and broadcast media — in every instance the direction of influence in social change is from the macro-social to the micro-social; from discursive formations to local discursive practice. Thus while Fairclough's theoretical approach in critical discourse analysis does allow for change, change is only shown empirically as operating in a top-down way.

A classic study along these lines is Paul Willis's *Learning to Labour* (1977). British working-class young men — 'the "lads"' — are shown in this ethnographic study as resisting their teachers as a way of affirming a working-class male identity. It is not simply that they lack cultural capital that middle-class students possess. Rather, they construct their school careers through resistant identity work — in Ray McDermott's (1974) terms they are 'achieving school failure' — in order to maintain a kind of dignity in their own eyes. But the tactical achievement of saving face in the short run (I will have more to say later on Goffman's notion of 'face' and its implications) is self-defeating in the long run, for it locks 'the lads' out of employment opportunities beyond the shop floor (and as jobs on the shop floor disappear, 'the lads' grown to adulthood are further disenfranchised). Both Bourdieu and Giddens cite Willis's example, and in the United States we find scholars such as Ogbu (1974) and Fordham (1996) who take a line similar to Willis with regard to the school achievement of African Americans.

I have a sense that Bernstein, Young, Willis, and Bourdieu (and Fairclough as well) are right in the sense that they are describing the conduct and consequences of gatekeeping judgement as it happens under usual circumstances — the 'default' conditions by which variation in sociolinguistic performance is assessed ideologically in late capitalist societies. I expect this is the case not only for the gatekeeping that takes place in schooling but also in other kinds of gatekeeping situations, such as doctor/patient interviews, job interviews, lawyer/client interaction. In each of these one can find power asymmetry and cultural style that is invidiously judged, especially when one of the parties is middle-class and the other is working-class. It is not that these analyses are totally wrong, or that social theory which explains class reproduction in these terms is entirely wrong. But it does not tell the whole story.

3   Hegemony and its discontents

What's left out of the picture that Willis and others present? Simply put, it is that some sociolinguistic and ethnographic research shows that there is more variation in the communicative and interactional behaviour of working-class and middle-class people than the general social theory accounts for, and also that there are special circumstances of what can be called the micropolitics of social encounters such that ways of speaking and of acting non-verbally which might ordinarily be regarded by others as inappropriate can be overlooked and not taken to count against the person behaving in such a way. Ironically, the study of social and cultural reproduction has become so efficacious that it cannot account for any change happening in society — or it argues that change is only a surface appearance. Yet social change does happen, even in the absence of revolutionary transformation of society. (Consider, for example, the changes in the legal status of women that have taken place in Western societies in the last hundred years. In spite of enduring patterns of gendered habitus in division of labour within the domestic sphere, for example wives continuing to do more 'housework' than their husbands, real change has come in domestic life as women became legally capable of owning property, and in the sphere of civil society, change has come as women gained the right to vote and exercised it.)

Moreover, change happens even within schools — those institutions which social theorists have identified as key sites for social reproduction rather than transformation. Turning again to educational research for examples, there are scholars in the United States (such as Ladson-Billings 1994, Mehan *et al.* 1996, and see the commentary by Trueba 1988) who report on working-class African-American and Latino students who, rather than simply resisting the white/Anglo cultural hegemony of schooling and disaffiliating from school achievement, find a way both to affirm their ethnic/racial identity *and* do well in school. In addition Mike Rose's recent book (1995) documents successful instances of teaching and learning by inner-city teachers and students in classrooms throughout the United States. In a classic study of class and school achievement in Australia, Rob Connell *et al.* (1982) found that working-class students they interviewed could, for the most part, remember some teachers they liked and with whom the students thought they had done better academically. Admittedly most teachers were not like that, yet some were. How to account theoretically for this variation? It may take place in a minority of cases, but it can be seen to be happening.

Putting close analysis of actual instances of face-to-face interaction in the foreground of research attention helps us understand how social change can take place — within processes of social reproduction — particularly as change happens within processes of local interaction that are accomplished intuitively. This is to say that a revised notion of habitus allows us to see it as a site for potentially transformative as well as reproductive local action. To understand the workings of processes of innovation within convention we need first to consider ways in which neither persons nor the social situations in which they encounter one another are entirely fixed unitary entities.

4   The liability of social identity and sociolinguistic repertoire

Increasingly we are coming to see that individuals are unitary neither in their overall social identity nor in their sociolinguistic repertoires. As Goffman (1961) and Barth (1969) observed some time ago and as the discussion in Ochs (1993) reiterates and extends, persons bring to sites of interaction many more potential attributes of social identity than actually become relevant in any particular encounter. For example, one can be simultaneously college-educated, an engineer, a church-goer, the mother of three young children — one of whom has leukemia, local officer in a political party of the moderate left, child of divorced parents, owner of a Border Collie, member of an immigrant minority group, person in their thirties who worked on an assembly line as a young adult, and woman who is bisexual. These attributes are located on various dimensions of identification. Which particular aspects of identity — or particular combinations of them — will become salient within a given encounter is something that interlocutors point to behaviourally during the course of their interaction together. At one moment some attributes may be made relevant and salient and at other moments some others may become salient, but the full multiplicity of aspects of social identity rarely become salient simultaneously in a single social encounter. I will elaborate on this below in a discussion of contextualisation as an interactional process. For now it is sufficient to say that social identities of the moment are constructed/accomplished through the conjoint actions of interlocutors during the course of interaction, and social identity in this constructivist sense is what I have called elsewhere performed or situated social identity (Erickson and Shultz 1982: 16–17, 27–34).

Just as the social identity of a person is not fixed, but can be thought of as a set of potentials that are actualised in a particular situation of interaction with others, neither is that person's overall sociolinguistic repertoire a unitary phenomenon, independent of the ecological influence of participation with interlocutors in the on-line conduct of interaction. Through on-line, real-time participation in interaction as it occurs in a variety of sites of discourse practice — and in a variety of communities or networks of discourse practice — persons have acquired competence in manifold stylistic ways of speaking. After about age five this is true for everyone, regardless of gender, class, or ethnicity, not only in modern societies but also in traditional ones (see Goodenough 1976 on this point). Even as a child grows up in a small village some time is spent in sites of discourse practice where those practices differ from those in the child's nuclear family. That diversity in the experience of immersion in discourse practices in various sites is a characteristic and foundational feature of modern urban life. (Indeed each household is not sociolinguistically unitary in its discourse practices because of differences in the life experiences of its members.) Because of this, people in interaction are able to switch styles to accommodate one another, should they choose to do so. They may be more familiar and fluent in a register learned at home in early childhood but they are not simply constrained by that register as they interact with others later in life.

In some regions of their overall sociolinguistic repertoire persons may have full competence, in others only partial competence. Thus interlocutors possess masteries of multiple sets of communicative practices and they can employ differing aspects of their sociolinguistic repertoire, not only across various social situations but also from moment to moment within a given social situation. This is to say that our notion of sociolinguistic repertoire and of sociolinguistic competence needs to be a differentiated one, taking a broad view of code- and style-shifting. Such a view is consistent with current work that emphasises Bakhtinian hybridity as inherent in sociolinguistic competence and repertoire (see for example, Rampton (1995, and this volume) Woolard (1999), and Spitulnik (1999)). It is also consistent with earlier work on speech style and style-switching — consider the example presented by Blom and Gumperz (1972) in which Norwegian villagers in a post office switched back and forth between local and national standard dialect within conversations as topics changed. Consider as well the work of Mitchell-Kernan (1972) demonstrating that African-American speakers of Black dialect also demonstrate in their speech knowledge of standard English.

5   Context and contextualisation

In the previous discussion I have been considering three fundamental characteristics of the practice of interaction — (1) that the social identity of interlocutors is neither predetermined at the outset of an encounter nor fixed during its ensuing course, (2) that the cultural performance knowledge possessed by each individual is diverse, and (3) that use of various identities and various styles of communicative performance is potentially available to all interlocutors at all times. These three enable and make necessary the overall interactional process that Gumperz (1982, 1992) has called *contextualisation*. Certain surface features of talk — including prosody, lexical choice, linguistic code choice, phonological variation in speech style such as that between 'careful' and 'casual' speech and other aspects of register choice — function in conversation as cues which point to the context of interpretation or interpretive frame within which the utterances of the moment are to be understood. Because interlocutors relate to each other in interaction as an ecosystem of mutual influence, when one party cues a new attribute of identity as salient for the moment, such as gender, or professional status, or ethnicity, the qualitative character of the relationship among the interlocutors changes — in Goffman's terms a change of 'footing' occurs (see Goffman 1983 and the discussion in Drew and Heritage (1992: 8–10)). Differing aspects of the interlocutors' social identities are highlighted as 'footing' changes, for example from a focus on the professional status of one of the parties to their gender or ethnicity, or from a focus on gender to professional status.

If the attributes of identity that interlocutors bring to a given situation of interaction are multidimensional and not entirely obvious or fixed at the outset, so is the situation itself multidimensional. There is enough ambiguity, indexicality, and contingency in any social situation that its character can shift as the interaction plays out. A situation of friendly rivalry can turn in a moment into one of bitter competition. A situation of chance meeting between strangers as they occupy adjacent seats in an airplane or train can become one in which the two parties avoid interaction, or engage only in a perfunctory exchange of pleasantries, or enter into a confessional exchange of intimacies that they would ordinarily withhold from friends and family.

Admittedly there are usual and exceptional ways such encounters play out, and a tendency toward the typical gives interaction in everyday life considerable predictability. (Moreover, asymmetries of power and of material and cultural resources in society make certain routines easier to accomplish than others in a given encounter — they influence or define a line of least resistance, a set of default conditions and procedures. This, in part, accounts for the typicality with which certain kinds of social relations are recurrently played out in social encounters. My argument here should not be taken to imply that the inherent liability of identity-framing and style-shifting is totally unconstrained.) Predictions of the typical and expectable cannot be absolute, however, because the conduct of everyday life is fundamentally contingent from moment to moment. Hence our schemas for the conduct of interaction are not entirely specified; there are default routines that may apply in a given encounter but they are not even sketched as a plot outline or on a story board, let alone being written out fully, as in a play script. Rather, to engage in social interaction (which is to experience contingencies successively as they present themselves from moment to moment, including the contingencies successively present in the verbal and non-verbal actions other participants are taking) is to undertake a process of filling in a sketch, in concert with the other interlocutors present in the scene. Interlocutors in their speaking and listening activity are continually co-constructing their interaction on-line in real time. Thus to engage in interaction with others can be likened to climbing a tree that climbs you back.

In sum, what is apparent when we take a close analytic look at the practice of actual interaction among real persons is that both the persons and the situations in which they interact are never fully determined. They are continually in production, under construction, through the boot-strapping processes of contextualisation, shifts in footing, and adaptation by interlocutors to each other's actions that are being discussed here.

This is to say that the practice of *discourse* (in the limited sense of talk and in the larger sense of the construction of identity and identification by persons in relation to their interlocutors — see Gee 1990: 143–145) is always and most fundamentally a matter of local production. The resources employed in such production are not all local in provenance, however. The most fundamental of these resources is that of language itself, with its resonance of power relations and ideology. Following Bakhtin (1981: 293) we can say that the words we use in speaking are 'half someone else's' and in uttering we expropriate them for our own uses. As Voloshinov puts it (1929/ 1986: 95):

> any utterance, no matter how weighty and complete in and of itself, is *only a moment in the continuous process of verbal communication* [italics are the author's]. But that continuous verbal communication is, in turn, itself only a moment in the continuous, all-inclusive, generative process of a given social collective.

Yet the word, once expropriated, is *used*, and in use the particular word is transformed somewhat by the work that is being done with it. In its use as an actual resource within the contingent local circumstances of practice it is not quite the same entity as it is when it is sitting, as it were, in the societal bank of words as a potential resource. As Voloshinov observes (1929/1986: 68), *'what is important for the speaker about a linguistic form is not that it is a stable and always self-equivalent signal, but that it is an always changeable and adaptable sign.'* [Italics are the author's.]

Vygotsky uses a slightly different but related metaphor. Following Marx he sees words, and language more generally, as cultural tools (Vygotsky 1934/1994, Rockwell 1999). Tools change in the material circumstances of their recurrent use — the spade is worn away by the earth it is used in, and change happens even in symbolic tools during the course of their actual use. (Just as for Marx, work is continually constituting the worker — in musculature, in bone growth, in desires, in ideologies — it is also constituting the worker's tools within the practice of their use.)

The constitution of a cultural tool in its use and of the worker in working is not a matter of deliberate awareness on the part of the worker, however. Rather, the tool is used in practice intuitively, as in Merleau-Ponty's and Bourdieu's conception of *habitus* and in Giddens' notion of *practical consciousness* (Giddens 1984: 6–7, 41–45). Yet if one looks closely at the on-line, real-time conduct of such practice in the conduct of talk it is apparent that it is not bound simply to repeat itself automatically. This contradicts Bourdieu's assumption of the stability of habitus and of its influence upon practice. Within its recursiveness and dailyness, local practice can be seen to entail both lability and stability.

6   Bricolage and co-membership in discourse practice

A way to understand how intuitive and recursive discourse practice can be a site of subtle change is to think of discourse practice as *bricolage* — making novel use of pre-existing forms to accomplish uniquely local functions. (Ironically, this is to make use of an insight about practice from Lévi-Strauss, the doyen of French structuralism whom Bourdieu took on as his antagonist in his essay *Outline of a Theory of Practice* (1977). *Bricolage* is the practice of the *bricoleur*, the French all-purpose handyman (Lévi-Strauss 1966: 16–17). A jack-of-all-trades, the bricoleur uses pre-structured materials to do whatever work at hand needs doing. For example, a bricoleur might take a piece of surgical tape to wrap around a water pipe to stop it from leaking. The surgical tape is pre-structured for a certain functional use, but it gets used by the bricoleur creatively to perform a different function within the immediate circumstance of practice. As Lévi-Strauss points out (in his argument he draws an invidious contrast between primitive and modern thought), the bricoleur (by analogy to a primitive thinker) doesn't transform the materials that are used, as would an engineer (modern thinker), nor does the bricoleur transform the overall job of work to be done by design of a thoroughgoingly new system, as someone with more power in society might — an engineer, an architect, a venture capitalist, an administrator, a policy maker. But bricolage nonetheless can be seen as a source of innovation in that it expropriates and then makes use of certain materials to accomplish different purposes from those for which the materials were originally intended.

As the term is used currently in cultural studies to illuminate processes of intuitive, non-deliberate innovation in the production of popular culture, bricolage involves juxtapositions of elements from differing cultural traditions (that is, bricolage in this sense is a synonym for syncretism). The elements from these differing sources are brought together in novel combinations and this makes a new style. Illustrative examples include the development of jazz through mixing of elements from West African and Western European musics, the evolution of French cuisine from that of Tuscany within the practices of the apprentices to the cooks brought to Paris from Florence by Marie de Medici, and the bricolage of the origins of Christianity from within Judaism. In each of these examples, the process of innovation through bricolage took place in co-constructed real time interaction — playing music, cooking in a royal kitchen, and worshipping and engaging in religious talk are all activities that are accomplished through social interaction. I should emphasise, however, that I am not assuming these innovations were done deliberately — people were not setting out in their daily practice to create new music, cuisine, or religion. But that is what happened through their intuitive, recursive practice of bricolage.

Considered as bricolage, innovation can be seen not as creation *ex nihilo* but as a novel re-use of pre-existing elements. What is 'new' in such innovations is only a tiny percentage of the whole. What makes for novelty is the new combination of forms, not the formal elements themselves. The new juxtaposition of elements makes for a change from the way in which each is seen separately. This is a kind of re-framing.

One way in which bricolage is employed in the conduct of oral discourse involves the signalling of social identity. Because interlocutors possess multiple social identities and can point to these identities by a variety of communicative means in contextualisation cues, interlocutors have at their disposal rich resources for interactional bricolage as they establish and change footing from moment to moment. Thus the process of contextualisation in conversation can be seen as related to bricolage, in that both involve re-framing that results in re-interpretation. An aspect of contextualisation that has especially powerful consequences for changes in footing in encounters among strangers (or among near strangers, as is so often the case in routine bureaucratic encounters) is what in my previous work I have called *situational co-membership* (Erickson and Shultz 1982: 17, 35–37).

Co-membership is established within the local conduct of interaction as interlocutors reveal to one another aspects of common background, some of which, such as gender, ethnicity/race, or social class, may be obvious at the outset of interaction, as was and is in the UK the identity badge of the 'old school tie'. Other aspects of commonality may be more ambiguous, yet be conventionally revealed fairly early on through some aspect of communicative performance style, for example shared sexual orientation and, under certain societal circumstances, shared religious or political affiliation. Other aspects of co-membership are not obvious at all and are only revealed through the content of talk, for instance both parties having a third party as an acquaintance in common, both having been the youngest siblings in their families of origin, both sharing interests and experience in popular or high culture activities, in physical fitness, in hobbies. The interlocutors may find one another to be recently bereaved, or recently unfortunate or fortunate in romance. When one or more of these diverse kinds of commonalities are revealed during the course of talk, a change in footing can take place. Before the moment that co-membership is revealed the encounter may be bureau-cratically neutral in tone, and after that moment the encounter may become more cordial. The relationship of superordination–subordination between the interlocutors may shift, not probably to reverse itself, but to become less extreme than in the moments before the revelation of co-membership.

A relationship of increased solidarity among interlocutors seems to obtain after co-membership has been established. The addition of co-membership features to those features of social identity already salient in the scene is a kind of innovation accomplished locally by the interlocutors — it is a bricolage construction within just that occasion of interaction and for just those moments, not something that will be done in the same way again with other interlocutors. It is a 'value-added' feature of the scene at hand.

The construction of co-membership, like shifts in speech register or in language-switching in bilingual contact situations, is for the most part done outside conscious awareness. It is not a strategy in the strict sense of the term — it is what intuitively feels right. This kind of 'feels right' move, as an intuitive sense of the game, is reminiscent of Bourdieu's notion of the work-ings of the habitus. But co-membership moves and other kinds of interactional bricolage, unlike the habitus as Bourdieu conceives it, do not necessarily reproduce the status quo, although they may do so. As local innovations they can be reproductive — as in the aphorism 'the more things change the more they stay the same' — but they can also be innovative, albeit within a local world of small compass and plenty of constraints. Co-membership work within an encounter can thus be seen as an aspect of habitus that is open to the possibility of innovation in directions that are potentially transformative as well as potentially reproductive. This is to consider the habitus and non-deliberate local practice in a new light, as a site for change.

What is the relationship between the local establishment of situational co-membership and the wider social order? If the default conventions for the conduct of bureaucratic encounters are hegemonic, that is, tending toward reproduction of existing power relations as they obtain in society generally, then some re-framing, some situated change in the nature and conduct of the local bureaucratic encounter, can be counter-hegemonic, that is, having the potential for transforming existing power relations. Or, if they do not have the consequence of transformation outside the local situation of practice they can at least be considered a kind of swimming upstream against the prevailing currents of history, or to take an aerodynamic analogy, a way of making use of existing air currents to move forward — as in piloting a glider (rather than a powered airplane) or sailing a boat into the wind. The counter-hegemonic practice of bricolage, like that of a glider pilot or sailor, is partly deliberate and partly not. It is what Connell (1983) describes as an intuitive distinction between progressive and regressive activity in ordinary social life. Following the metaphor of an uneven playing field, Connell likens the conduct of daily life to walking along a hillside. Without much reflection, through proprioceptive feedback, in the presence of social gravity one is able to get a sense of whether one is walking more uphill or downhill. This is done within the practice of walking itself rather than through a process of rational planning.

6.1   An example from a study of gatekeeping interaction

In the previous section I claimed that the intuitive establishment of co-membership within the conduct of everyday interaction can be a means for counter-hegemonic practice. That is what is apparent in some data I have from a study of practices of interaction and of social gatekeeping in encounters between academic advisors and students in junior colleges in the United States. *Gatekeeping situations* are found as a general class of encounters between a tactically powerful person with institutional authority and expertise and a less powerful person, often a client, in situations in which certain interests of the client are at stake. Examples include interaction between physicians and patients, job interviewers and applicants, auto mechanics and car owners, as well as academic advisors and students. In the practice of gatekeeping interaction there is variation in how such encounters unfold. It can be important for the client how active the gatekeeper becomes as an advocate on his/her behalf.

In some of my early work, published first in Erickson (1975) and more fully in Erickson and Shultz (1982), I studied inter- and intra-racial and ethnic interaction in the gatekeeping situation of academic advising interviews in American junior colleges. Akin to the British 'further education' schools, these were attended predominantly by working-class students. I videotaped and filmed sets of naturally occurring interviews in which a given counsellor spoke alternately with students whose race and cultural communication style was similar to or different from the counsellor. Usually six or seven interviews with each counsellor were filmed. A total of 54 such interviews were filmed, and 25 of them were analyzed in very great detail in what we would now call discourse analysis, or interactional sociolinguistic microanalysis. I called it then 'microethnography of communication'.

What I found was only partly what I had anticipated. I expected that the greater the difference in interaction style — the greater the cultural difference in ways of speaking and listening between the interlocutors — the greater would be the discomfort and miscommunication in the interviews and the harsher would be the judgements of the gatekeepers. This expectation was confirmed in roughly two-thirds of the cases. But in a special subset of the cases (7 out of 25, or 28%), certain aspects of difference in communication style did not seem to make a negative difference. Yet these same kinds of difference in communication style had in the other cases been associated with negative emotional tone and negative interpersonal attribution.

Interactional 'mistakes' and stumbles, in other words, seemed sometimes to be overlooked while at other times they were not. The overlooking — the more charitable rather than less charitable readings of an interlocutor's performance — happened in those interviews where, in spite of racial or ethnic difference, the interlocutors revealed situational co-membership. What follows is a transcribed example, the encounter that was highest in co-membership of any in the set we studied. The two interlocutors are Frank, the counsellor, and Sal, the student. At issue in the example were not cultural differences in communication style but interactional awkward moments of a different sort that might have been treated much more negatively than they were by the counsellor. The first awkward moment occurred as the student revealed that he had received a failing grade in a course in his major field of study. The second awkward moment occurred as the student answered the counsellor's question incorrectly, thus revealing that he was confused about a discourse routine he could have been expected to know.

NB: Transcription conventions are as follows: most utterances are transcribed as breath groups, with the prosaically stressed syllable containing the tonal nucleus appearing at the left margin.

.	when preceding a syllable this indicates a pause less than a half second; when following a letter at the end of an utterance, indicates falling, declarative intonation
. .	approximately half second pause; a 'comma' pause
. . . .	full second pause; a 'period' pause
/	abrupt termination of speech, or 'latching' — no gap or overlap in the alternation of speaking between interlocutors
?	rising, question intonation

Example 1: Transcription from an academic advising session

```
(1)  C:                    Let's have some
(2)       grades  .        .        last se-
(3)       mester  . .               data
(4)       processing  one            oh
(5)       one      what did you get for a
(6)       grade
(7)  S: B
(8)  C:                            Data
(9)       processing       one     e-
(10)      leven
(11) S: F
(12) C:                            data
(13)      processing  . .          that's your
```

(14)   major   .   .   data
(15)   processing   .   .   .   .
(16)   right?
(17) S: yeah   well   I   just
(18)   talked to him   he
(19)   said it was because of excessive
(20)   absences
(21) C: good for
(22)   you! .   .   good for
(23)   you.   .   .   .   .
(24)   Mat'   two   oh
(25)   one?
(26) S: B
(27) C: .   .   .   and
(28)   gym
(29) S: B
(30) C: one full hour of
(31)   gym   .   .   or not
(32) S: (nods, indicating 'yes')
(33) C: (looks at student and smiles)
        you wrestlin'?
(34) S: naw   .   .   I have a bad
(35)   knee .   .   I just had it
(36)   operated on
(37) C: (smiles)   you
(38)   sure it was the knee
(39) S: it sure
(40)   was   .   .   I got a big
(41)   cut   and a scar to
(42)   prove it
(43) C: OK .   .
(44)   this semester
(45) S: this semester
(46) C: English one oh
(47)   two?
(48) S: a
(49)   C   .   .   probably a
(50)   C
(51) C: (smiles)
        you are a student here   .   .
(52)   registered in the school?
(53) S: (nods, indicating 'yes')
(54) C: OK   English one oh
(55)   two   .   .   right?
(56) S: yeah
(57) C: Math
(58) S: naw   .   .   I didn't
(59)   take   math
(60) C: did you
(61)   register for it?

(62) S: no I   registered for
(63)   speech instead of math
(64)   cos' I/
(65) C: /now you don't have to
(66)   drop your math class now . .   you're not
(67)   registered . .   see if you're
(68)   registered in it 'n you just didn't at-
(69)   tend you're going to receive an
(70)   F at the end of the se-
(71)   mester
(72) S: naw . .   I didn't get a
(73)   class card for it
(74) C: OK . .
(75)   Alright . .

There are a number of points in this discourse sequence that strike us as odd. Perhaps the most salient is the counsellor's response (at 12/13 and 21/22) to the student's saying he had gotten a failing grade in a course in his major field of study.

In prosody and facial expression as well as in the content of his talk the counsellor was being ironic in saying 'data processing — that's your major' (12–13) and 'good for you!' (21–22), meaning his comments as criticism rather than as compliment. That much seems obvious, interpretively. But why would the counsellor react in this way, stating his criticism indirectly through irony? Why would he not express concern and disapproval more directly upon hearing of Sal's failing grade? To understand this we must move to another level of inference and consider circumstances that are not immediately apparent in the scene but which can be inferred as being pointed to indexically by the interlocutors within the ongoing conduct of discourse.

As the interview proceeded the counsellor continued with the routine procedure of asking the student the courses he had taken and the grades he had received in those courses. After mentioning the student's gym course — the last item in the routine sequence of questions about courses — the counsellor asked (33) 'You wrestlin'?'

This can be read as a kind of bricolage — an indexical contextualisation cue invoking a co-membership that involves complex embedding. The counsellor, who was Italian-American, had been a teacher in a Roman Catholic high school in the city before coming to work at the public junior college as an academic advisor. He was the wrestling coach at that high school, and Sal's older brother had been a member of the wrestling team. After the counsellor had left for his new job at the junior college, Sal had also wrestled in high school, and the counsellor was aware of this. While Sal's brother was on his high school wrestling team, the counsellor had met Sal's parents and Sal himself. This is how he knew why Sal had an anomalous name — Salvatore Morales. In an interview session in which the counsellor reviewed the videotape of his encounter with Sal the counsellor said, 'He's Italian —

his father's Mexican but his mother's Italian so I think of him as Italian.' (At this time in Chicago people of southern and eastern European ancestry tended to refer in ordinary conversation to their own ethnicity and to that of others by a nationality label (such as 'Italian', 'Polish') rather than by the more formal hyphenated form ('Italian-American', 'Polish-American').

Alternatively the counsellor could have said, 'He's Mexican — his mother's Italian but his father's Mexican', or 'He's part Mexican and part Italian.' Instead the counsellor chose (not necessarily deliberately) the most solidary of those possibilities. He made use of the opportunity provided by Sal's mother's ethnicity to define Sal in relation to himself as a fellow Italian-American. This too can be seen as bricolage — taking advantage of one similarity (mother's ethnicity) as grounds for solidarity rather than taking advantage of one difference (father's ethnicity) as grounds for social distance with Sal.

In asking 'You wrestlin'?' the counsellor was pointing indexically to many aspects of his and Sal's shared background. From Sal's point of view, perhaps the most salient of these may have been the counsellor's acquaintance with Sal across a number of years and with Sal's brother, father, and mother. It is possible that, within the counsellor's bricolage construction of grounds for charitable reading of Sal's actions in the interview, Sal's status as a fellow Italian-American was salient as well, and perhaps even Sal's status as a fellow Roman Catholic.

Whatever the sets of particular attributes that were salient for Sal and the counsellor, the overall frame of co-membership that was established in this encounter seems strong and continuously maintained across the course of the whole encounter. Thus even the appearance of misfortune, in the report by Sal of the injury to his knee, could be used by the counsellor (at 37–38) to make another indirect criticism of his getting a failing grade:

Example 2

```
    (33) C: (looks at student and smiles)
            you wrestlin'?
    (34) S: naw  .   .    I have a bad
    (35)    knee  .   .    I just had it
    (36)    operated on
→   (37) C: (smiles)              you
→   (38)    sure it was the knee
    (39) S:                    it sure
    (40)    was  .   .   I got a big
    (41)    cut    and a scar to
    (42)    prove it
```

My interpretation here is that the counsellor, by pausing, smiling, and then saying 'you sure it was the knee' with special prosodic emphasis on the word 'knee' was implying 'you sure it was the knee and not your head . . . because you got an F in a course in your major field.' The student, by responding to the question about his knee not as an ironic one but as a 'straight' question, may have been indicating that he had not realised the irony of the question, or the student may have been parrying that irony with a response of disingenuous innocence. But either interpretation of the student's response underscores the lightness, the indirectness, of the counsellor's irony. Thus the counsellor can be seen here as treating a serious infraction relatively lightly. Even though the student had just reported receiving a failing grade in his major field of study, the counsellor was responding with minimal negativity.

This tendency by the counsellor to treat infractions by the student charitably rather than non-charitably continued as the topic changed from courses taken and grades received by the student in the previous semester to courses in which the student was enrolled in the present semester:

Example 3

```
      (43) C: OK  .   .
      (44)     this semester
      (45) S:  this semester
      (46) C:  English one oh
      (47)     two?
      (48) S:                            a
  → (49)     C  .      .     probably a
      (50)     C
  → (51) C: (smiles)
               you are a student here   .   .
  → (52)     registered in the school?
      (53) S: (nods, indicating 'yes')
  → (54) C: OK     English one oh
      (55)     two   .   .      right?
      (56) S:  yeah
```

At (49) the student had answered 'a C, probably a C' in answer to the counsellor's question 'English one oh two?' at (46). This was a mistake on the student's part — a failure to recognise a new response form for the answer slot in the new question–answer discourse routine that had been initiated by the counsellor at (43–44) when he said 'OK, this semester.' In the routine appropriate for answering questions about courses and grades taken in the previous semester, the customary way to answer the question was by naming the final grade received in that class. But for courses being taken in the present semester no final grade had yet been received and so the appropriate answer could not be the letter name of a grade but rather, a 'yes' or 'no' (yes, I am enrolled in the course, no, I am not enrolled). That the student may not have realised this shift in the answering routine could be indicated by his utterance at (45) in which he repeated what the counsellor had just said: 'this semester'. (Although this was said by the student without question intonation it could be taken as a request for clarification.) At (51) the counsellor held the student responsible for his discourse mistake, 'you are a student here . . . registered in the school?' but as in the previous cases of mild rebuke it is done implicitly and with irony. The counsellor could be read as saying something like 'Sal, you have been here long enough to know that when we switch to talking about courses in the current semester the correct answer form is "yes" or "no".' Then at (54–55) the counsellor steered the student by implicit clues to the right answer form. He repeated his prior question: 'English one oh two . . . right?' following the question by a pause and the prompt, 'right?' Then the student finally answered in the correct form 'yeah' at (56).

The pattern of the counsellor's minimising negativity in reacting to the student's infractions continued as the counsellor asked about the next course that appeared on the student's academic record in the file and the student responded that he had not taken that course:

Example 4

```
       (57) C: Math
       (58) S: naw  .  .  I didn't
       (59)      take math
→ (60) C:                 did you
→ (61)      register for it?
       (62) S: no I    registered for
       (63)      speech instead of math
       (64)      cos' I/
→ (65) C:        /now you don't have to
       (66)      drop your math class now  .  .  you're not
       (67)      registered  .  .            see if you're
       (68)      registered in it 'n you just didn't at-
       (69)      tend you're going to receive an
       (70)      F at the end of the se-
       (71)      mester
       (72) S: naw  .  .           I didn't get a
       (73)      class card for it
       (74) C: OK  .  .
       (75)      Alright  .  .
```

The counsellor's response to the student's somewhat ambiguous revelation at (58–59) 'naw I didn't take math', was first to ask, at (60), 'did you register for it' and then, at (65), to state why he had been concerned that the student not be registered — if not registered he did not need to drop the course but if registered he would have had to drop the course. This pragmatic advice is in marked contrast to the way in which this counsellor reacted when other students revealed that they had dropped courses. His more usual approach was to give a little speech justifying the taking of the course — it's a required course, it's necessary as a prerequisite for a subsequent course in a sequence, it presents knowledge that is inherently valuable for you. Those justifications were a way of urging the student to try the course again in the next semester. But in this case the counsellor did not do that. He simply checked to be sure the student was not registered for the math course so that he did not have to go through the bureaucratic procedure of dropping that course. Again, an infraction (or at least an irregularity) on the part of the student was treated in the most positive light possible. Consistently, by his use of irony rather than a more direct kind of negativity, the counsellor was doing what Goffman (1967: 47) called 'face-work' — maintaining the student's dignity in spite of the numerous ways in which what the student was doing (interactionally, as well as in terms of his student career) did not fit the standard expectations of the junior college.

To understand the various instances of paradoxical positiveness by the counsellor that I have been discussing here, we must look beyond what was being said explicitly by the counsellor and the student in the encounter itself. One condition beyond the encounter was pointed to indexically by the counsellor through his question about wrestling — the high level of co-membership between himself and the student, his familiarity with the student and his situation. (I use the word 'familiarity' deliberately here, for the relation of co-membership that was established I consider to be that of quasi-kinship.) But there was another condition that bore on the student's situation in life and because it was known to the counsellor as well as to the student it bore on their conduct within the academic interview. This was a condition of the wider world — a matter of big-letter History, and it provides other grounds for the bricolage work of the counsellor that manifested communicatively as charitable reading and face-work by the counsellor on behalf of the student.

The year was 1970 and the place was the United States. At that time the United States was still engaged in what was called then the 'War in Viet Nam'. The student was old enough to be drafted for the war. At the time his interview with the counsellor was filmed the student was enrolled for a seventh semester in a course of study which was normally completed in four semesters.

The counsellor knew this. He was colluding in the young man's attempt to continue as a student in an inexpensive junior college. Term after term the counsellor allowed the student to register for courses, failing some courses and dropping others, making use of the societally and institutionally legitimated status of student to avoid being conscripted and to stay out of the war in Vietnam. The student's organisational career may seem on the surface to have been irrational, but at a deeper level it made profound sense. It was a bricolage of implicit, unspoken resistance to the workings of social processes at the level of society and of history — a bricolage involving the invocation of co-membership as a footing for their relationship within the gatekeeping encounter.

7   Implications for social theory and for sociolinguistic research

What the counsellor and the student were doing together is a kind of local activity that is also the making of history. It was one small moment in the actions of struggle and resistance by many agents as practitioners — Vietnamese and American — whose bricolage eventually stopped US involvement in the civil war in Vietnam. But if this was counter-hegemonic resistance it does not appear to be a kind that was deliberate. It was not theoretically articulated as a revolutionary project by either of the two interlocutors. My guess is that had I asked the counsellor about his general position on the war in Vietnam he might have said he was in favour of it. But he was helping Sal stay out of the draft, using a kind of bricolage that did not require reflective awareness to accomplish the practice. This was indexical foot-dragging rather than the deliberate and public actions of a revolutionary vanguard.

The reason I am emphasising the non-deliberate character of this innovation is that it provides an alternative to the more conventional view in social theory of the process of social change — the possibility of altering the otherwise absolute reproductive effects of non-deliberate dispositions and 'feel for the game' in the conduct of social life that Bourdieu claims for the habitus. The usual assumption is that if social change is to take place, local social actors must be disabused of their false consciousness — they must develop reflective awareness of their situation and deliberately stop behaving in ways that work against their interests. Bourdieu takes this line:

> one can utilize such analyses precisely to step back and gain distance from dispositions . . . reflexive analysis, which teaches that we are the ones who endow the situation with part of the potency it has over us, allows us to alter our perceptions of the situation and thereby our reaction to it . . . At bottom, determinisms operate to their full only by the help of unconsciousness, with the complicity of the unconscious. (Bourdieu and Wacquant 1992: 136)

Fairclough, in a programmatic statement on 'critical discourse analysis', also allows for the possibility of change, both at the level of society and of discourse practice, but he too presumes that conscious reflection is necessary if the hegemonic tendencies in what he calls 'orders of discourse' (akin to Foucault's 'discourse formations') are to be interrupted through *critical language study*:

one of my purposes in writing [this book] was to help increase consciousness of how language contributes to the domination of some people by
others, because consciousness is the first step to emancipation ... [and
there is a role for] those who act as catalysts in the raising of consciousness: there must be people who have the theoretical background to enable
them to act in this way, as well as sharing the experience of the oppressed
to a sufficient extent for them to be accepted as catalysts. (Fairclough
1989: 233, 234)

In my viewing session interview with Frank he did not say that he
was helping keep Sal out of the draft because of his principled objections
to the war in Vietnam. Now, 29 years later at this writing, I cannot go back
and ask him. Frank's advocacy on behalf of Sal appears to have been intuitive
rather than discursively reasoned, yet what Frank did moved in a counter-
hegemonic direction. He was not acting toward Sal in the expectable way as
a gatekeeper.

If there is more variation in gatekeeping judgements than first meets the
eye, then an implication is that the totalising accounts of social theorists
such as Bourdieu and Foucault are only partially correct. What accounts for
the apparent 'time out' circumstances of gatekeeping judgement that I and
others have identified? The local construction of co-membership by interlocutors appears to provide, by means of relatively intuitive bricolage rather
than of more thoroughgoing and deliberate innovation, a kind of 'wiggle
room' within which hegemonic reproduction can be partially interrupted,
or slid around. The significance of this for general social theory is that the
slippage is not just that of random variation; of noise in the system. Rather,
I want to argue, the wiggle room of bricolage that inheres in the use of
cultural tools within the contingencies of local circumstance in ways that are
purposive and adaptive, yet are outside conscious awareness, is inherent in
the conduct of local social action as practice.

Why inherent? Because, as Goffman maintained throughout his career,
and especially in the discussions in *Encounters* (1961), in the essay 'The
neglected situation' (1964), and in his posthumously published essay 'The
interaction order' (1983), immediate social interaction within encounters
constitutes a social order that needs to be considered as distinct, with an
integrity that is its own, at least in part. He uses the metaphor of osmosis
through a membrane to indicate the partial boundedness of an encounter
(Goffman 1961: 19–31). What is salient for participants within the frame of
the encounter, in addition to their instrumental business, is the collective
maintenance of individual dignity (see the discussion in Rawls (1987), and in
Collins (1988: 46–50)). Given the fragility of that dignity at every turn in
interaction it is necessary for interactional partners to collaborate in maintaining it, through the avoidance of interactional moves which are face-
threatening and through the taking of one another's 'fronts' at face value.

One of Goffman's earliest papers, first published in 1955 and republished in 1967, was titled 'On face work'. In it he noted, 'One's face then, is a sacred thing, and the expressive order required to sustain it is therefore a ritual one.' (Goffman 1967: 19). He claims that participants in encounters are accountable to a moral order indigenous to the encounter itself; what Goffman would call in his final essay *the interaction order*. While issues of power and ideology from the wider society beyond the encounter become present within it — leaching through the semi-permeable membrane of mutual attention by which the encounter is sustained — they are present within the encounter in tandem with the interests of the participants in maintaining an interaction order (and this entails the mutual presentation and preservation of self through face-work). The wider social order's pressures, while not absent within the frame of the encounter, do not overwhelm or supplant the ritual action and moral exigencies of the interaction order.

The wiggle room of co-membership and face-work through interactional bricolage can be seen as aspects of the inventive resourcefulness of interlocutors in maintaining the interaction order within the moment-by-moment conduct of interaction. If these processes of mutual self-protection are indeed inherent within local interactional practice then any theory of general social and cultural reproduction that claims to relate to practice needs to take account of them. Commenting on Foucault's totalising conception of power, Giddens takes a Goffmanesque tack in *The Constitution of Society*:

> The point is not just that human beings resist being treated as automata, something which Foucault accepts: the prison is a site of struggle and resistance. [Giddens is discussing here Foucault's essay on the prison, *Discipline and Punish* (1979).] Rather it is that Foucault's 'bodies' are not agents . . . unless subjected to the most extreme deprivation of resources, capable agents are likely to submit to discipline only for parts of the day — usually as a trade-off for rewards that derive from being freed from such discipline at other times. (Giddens 1984: 154)

A few pages later (1984: 157) Giddens paraphrases this criticism and invokes Goffman's notion of face directly by saying 'Foucault's bodies do not have faces.' In leaving no room for face-work by local agents the analytic scheme of Foucault, by which he connects general and local social processes, leads us to collapse entirely the distinction between the general and the local; to reduce knowledge to power. A parallel line of argument can be applied to Bourdieu when, using the trope of causal analysis, he names aspects of status (such as gender, level of education, class origins) as

> variables [which] intervene at every moment in the determination of the objective structure of 'communicative action' . . . the form taken by linguistic interaction will hinge substantially upon this structure, which is unconscious and works almost entirely 'behind the backs' of locutors. In

short, if a French person talks with an Algerian or a black American to a WASP, it is not two persons who speak to each other but, through them, the colonial history in its entirety, or the whole history of the economic, political, and cultural subjugation of blacks (or women, workers, minorities, etc.) in the United States (Bourdieu and Wacquant 1992: 144)

This is taking a good idea just a bit too far. The good idea is that the weight of history does bear on (and live through) the persons engaged in local discursive practice. It is reasonable to say, following Bakhtin's metaphor, that the words they speak must be expropriated for local use and still in their use they continue to carry whiffs of allusion to, and resonances with, the wider social world and the patterns of social interest out of which the word has been expropriated. That far we need to go in connecting general discourse formations with the local discourse practices of actual social actors. But to go on to say that what is invoked in the talk of local social actors who are members of superordinate and subordinate groups is 'colonial history in its entirety' or the 'whole history of economic, political, and cultural subjugation' is a reduction that is unwarranted (see Alexander (1995) on Bourdieu's tendencies toward reduction). It seems to me more reasonable to say that, granting the influence of the weight of history on local social action, discursive practice in everyday life is a richer, more multidimensional matter than that. One way in which it is more multidimensional is that local discourse practice entails effort to maintain an interaction order as well as to do whatever other communicative work presents itself within the circumstances at hand.

Just as we should not take Bourdieu too far, so we should not take Goffman too far. His contentions about the integrity of the interaction order and the partial boundaries of encounters may have limitations in their application. It may well be that in situations of institutionalised power asymmetry between interlocutors, such as gatekeeping encounters, some of the constraints on face-threatening moves that obtain in ordinary conversation are reduced. Avoidance of face threat thus would become an option rather than a constant in the conduct of interaction. Taking such an option may account for the impoliteness and lack of solidarity between interlocutors that can characterise interaction in gatekeeping encounters, for example when teachers embarrass students by asking probing questions of them in front of the whole class, or when physicians interrupt patients' stories of their presenting complaint by asking an abrupt question, or when job interviewers 'stop and frisk' by close interrogation the previous work history of a job applicant. These may be the 'default' conditions of gatekeeping. Moreover, there may be cultural differences in propensity to avoid face threat — we must remember that Goffman restricted his primary research focus to middle-class Caucasian Americans. (I recall an interview I conducted with a Vietnamese physician who was applying for a program of clinical certification (residency) in order to be able to practise medicine in the United States. He said, 'I realize now that in Vietnam we used nurses as extra body parts — as extensions of our hands. Do you suppose if I did that here American nurses would be offended?' I assured him that they would be.)

Yet, at least in the United States, not all teachers and job interviewers embarrass students or job applicants with close questioning, and not all physicians interrupt their patients rudely, regardless of the physicians' and patients' race, gender, or social class. There can be individual differences in tendencies to employ face-threatening moves in gatekeeping encounters. Moreover, as I have found in my own research, some gatekeepers may use face-threatening moves with some of their clients but not with others. The case of Sal and Frank was an instance in which Frank used irony to avoid direct face-threat. But with some other students Frank was much more face-threatening. The argument I am making is not that 'agency' in the conduct of the counsellor's discourse practice was inherently either counter-hegemonic or hegemonic. It is a fallacy to conflate 'agency' with freedom (and hence with progressive, transformative practice) and 'structure' with constraint (and hence with regressive, reproductive practice). Rather, the point is that because local circumstances are contingent and persons are not automata, local social action inherently involves agency, whatever the tendencies or consequences of those actions might be — see the discussion in Alexander (1995, and 1998: 214–216).

The option for interlocutors to adopt a footing of mutual solidarity seems available continually and is acted upon some of the time, even in situations such as gatekeeping in which what Goffman claims as ordinary constraints on face-threat are lessened somewhat. Sociolinguistic microanalysis can show us how the more and less solidary kinds of relations among interlocutors come to happen interactionally — we still do not have a good way of accounting for why this happens — why interlocutors are sometimes more and less cordial, more and less charitable in their 'readings' of one another — within occasions of interaction and from one occasion to the next and when the interlocutors come from similar demographic backgrounds or different ones. The variability in how local interlocutors treat one another is empirically apparent but not yet well explained theoretically. Further research and theory development seems warranted.

To sum up, I have proposed a conception of the nature of local social action in discourse practice which allows for non-deliberate innovation as well as non-deliberate conformity; for practice that tends in counter-hegemonic directions as well as for practice that tends in the direction of hegemony. This suggests for social theory construction that we need a more probabilistic, less totalising way of accounting for social and cultural production and reproduction.

A suggestion of this line of argument for sociolinguistic work is that we should not simply adopt our social theory uncritically, in whole cloth, from theorists such as Bourdieu or Foucault. For empirical work in sociolinguistics an implication is that we should not stop our data collection and data analysis too soon. It may be that the hegemonic story is the usual one. But by collecting video or audio records of naturally occurring gatekeeping situations, and analysing not just a few examples but many, we may begin to discover more of the 'variance' in the conduct of gatekeeping than presently tends to be reported. Are there other sources of wiggle room besides co-membership to be found within the construction of local interaction? That is a possibility, but we will not see it in sociolinguistic microanalysis unless we go looking for it. If we assume at the outset that it is not there we surely will not find it. However if upon further investigation one quarter of the instances of interaction we collect and analyse do not fit the traditional model that current social reproduction theory leads us to expect (as has been the case in my own research), that would be important to determine. Close analysis of such discrepant cases would seem warranted, both for the furtherance of empirical work and for theory construction in sociolinguistics.

8   Conclusion

Is there more intuitive contestation of hegemony, more resistance that is not self-defeating, occurring in mundane interaction 'on the ground', than some social theory has led us to expect? I do not mean to suggest that immediate social interaction can take place entirely outside the social gravity that is the weight of history and the weight of asymmetry in the distribution and exercise of power in society. That would be a kind of sociolinguistic Thatcherism or Reaganism, a naive neo-liberal account of social process in which voluntarism entirely supplanted determinism. When local interaction happens according to the usual 'default' conditions we can expect hegemonic processes to be at work and we can expect that sociocultural reproduction, as characterised by social theorists such as Bourdieu and Foucault or by discourse analysts such as Fairclough, will take place without interruption. But because of the nature of local discourse practice such as bricolage, and the wiggle room that bricolage provides, default conditions may not always obtain within local interaction and thus the weight of history may not apply uniformly in all local cases.

If the argument I am presenting here by recalling Goffman turns out to be correct — that the resourcefulness of bricolage which maintains an interaction order is inherent in the co-construction by interlocutors of discourse in local social interaction — then we must both disagree and agree with what Bourdieu, Foucault, and Fairclough have claimed about the ways in which large-scale social forces determine the conduct of everyday life and everyday discourse. Our stance toward them can and should be that of appreciation as well as of critique. They show us many ways in which the weight of history manifests itself in the conduct of local discourse. But they fail to consider that local encounters may be partially bounded. If in the practice of everyday life the interaction order is indeed interposed between the individual agent and large-scale social forces we must ask why the interaction order appears to have more and less salience for interlocutors in differing local interactional circumstances. In terms of the main concerns of this chapter we must ask why the non-solidary 'default conditions' of gatekeeping seem to obtain strongly in some gatekeeping encounters but not nearly so strongly in others. It is useful and necessary to show how the distribution of power and advantage in the general society relates to the conduct of discourse in face-to-face interaction, and how that in turn is entailed in processes of social and cultural reproduction. Yet in so doing it is important not to reduce discourse to power, nor to reduce the local interaction order to the general social order.

Note

1. This chapter was written while the author was a Fellow at the Center for Advanced Study in the Behavioral Sciences. I am grateful for financial support provided by the Spencer Foundation's grant to the Center, Grant # 199400132. The transcribed example comes from research on social interaction in gatekeeping encounters supported by the National Institute of Mental Health, Center for Studies of Metropolitan Problems, Projects MH18230 and MH21460.

References

Alexander, J. (1995) The reality of reduction: The failed synthesis of Pierre Bourdieu. In J. Alexander (ed.) *Fin de Siècle Social Theory: Relativism, Reduction, and the Problem of Reason*. New York: Verso, 128–217.

Alexander, J. (1998) *Neofunctionalism and After*. Oxford: Blackwell.

Bakhtin, M. (1981) *The Dialogic Imagination*. (Translated by Caryl Emerson and Michael Holquist). Austin, TX: University of Texas Press.

Barth, F. (1969) *Ethnic Groups and Boundaries: The Social Organization of Culture Difference*. Boston: Little, Brown.

Bernstein, B. (1961) Social class and linguistic development: A theory of social learning. In A.H. Halsey, J. Floud, and C.A. Anderson (eds) *Education, Economy, and Society*. New York: Free Press.

Blom, J.P. and Gumperz, J. (1972) Social meaning in linguistic structure: Code switching in Norway. In J. Gumperz and D. Hymes (eds) *Directions in Sociolinguistics: The Ethnography of Communication*. New York: Holt, Rinehart, & Winston.

Bourdieu, P. (1977) *Outline of a Theory of Practice*. Cambridge: Cambridge University Press.

Bourdieu, P. and Passeron, J.C. (1977) *Reproduction: In Education, Society, and Culture*. Beverly Hills, CA: Sage.

Bourdieu, P. and Wacquant, L. (1992) *An Invitation to Reflexive Sociology*. Chicago: University of Chicago Press.

Collins, J. (1993) Determination and contradiction: An appreciation and critique of the work of Pierre Bourdieu on language and education. In C. Calhoun, E. LiPuma, and M. Postone (eds) *Bourdieu: Critical Perspectives*. Chicago: University of Chicago Press, 116–137.

Collins, R. (1988) Theoretical continuities in Goffman's work. In P. Drew and A. Wooton (eds) *Erving Goffman: Exploring the Interaction Order*. Oxford: Polity Press/Blackwell, 41–63.

Connell, Rob (1983) *Which Way is Up?: Essays on Sex, Class, and Culture*. London: Allen & Unwin.

Connell, R., Shenden, D., Kessler, S., and Dowsett, G. (1982) *Making the Difference: Schools, Families, and Social Division*. London: Allen & Unwin.

Drew, P. and Heritage, J. (eds) (1992) *Talk at Work: Interaction in Institutional Settings*. Cambridge: Cambridge University Press.

Erickson, F. (1975) Gatekeeping and the melting pot: interaction in counselling encounters. *Harvard Educational Review* 45: 1: 44–70.

Erickson, F. and Shultz, J. (1982) *The Counselor as Gatekeeper: Social Interaction in Interviews*. New York: Academic Press.

Fairclough, N. (1989) *Language and Power*. London: Longman.

Fairclough, N. (1992) *Discourse and Social Change*. Cambridge: Polity Press.

Fordham, S. (1996) *Blacked Out: Dilemmas of Race, Identity, and Success at Capital High*. Chicago: University of Chicago Press.

Foucault, M. (1979) *Discipline and Punish: The Birth of the Prison*. New York: Random House/Vintage Books.

Garfinkel, H. (1967) *Studies in Ethnomethodology*. Englewood Cliffs, NJ: Prentice-Hall.

Gee, J. (1990) *Social Linguistics and Literacies: Ideology in Discourses*. London: Falmer.

Gee, J. (1992) *The Social Mind: Language, Ideology and Social Practice*. New York: Bergin & Garvey.

Giddens, A. (1984) *The Constitution of Society: Outline of the Theory of Structuration*. Berkeley and Los Angeles: University of California Press.

Goffman, E. (1961) *Encounters: Two Studies in the Sociology of Interaction*. Indianapolis: Bobbs-Merrill.

Goffman, E. (1964) The neglected situation. In J. Gumperz and D. Hymes, *The Ethnography of Communication*. Special issue of *American Anthropologist* 66: 2: 133–136.

Goffman, E. (1967) *Interaction Ritual: Essays on Face-to-Face Behavior*. New York: Doubleday Anchor.

Goffman, E. (1983) The interaction order. *American Sociological Review*: 48: 1: 1–17.

Goodenough, W. (1976) Multiculturalism as the normal human experience. *Anthropology and Education Quarterly* 7: 4: 4–7.

Gumperz, J. (1982) *Discourse Strategies*. Cambridge: Cambridge University Press.

Gumperz, J. (1992) Contextualization and understanding. In A. Duranti and C. Goodwin (eds) *Rethinking Context*. Cambridge: Cambridge University Press, 229–252.

Ladson-Billings, G. (1994) *The Dreamkeepers: Successful Teachers for African American Children*. San Francisco: Jossey-Bass.

Lévi-Strauss, C. (1966) *The Savage Mind*. Chicago: University of Chicago Press.

McDermott, R.P. (1974) Achieving school failure: An anthropological approach to literacy and social stratification. In G. Spindler (ed.) *Education and Cultural Process*. New York: Holt, Rinehart, & Winston.

Mehan, H., Villanueva, I., Hubbard, L., and Lintz, A. (1996) *Constructing School Success: The Consequences of Untracking Low Achieving Students*. Cambridge: Cambridge University Press.

Merleau-Ponty, M. (1945/1962) *Phenomenology of Perception*. London: Routledge & Kegan Paul.

Mitchell-Kernan, C. (1972) On the status of black English for native speakers. In C. Cazden, V. John, and D. Hymes (eds) *Functions of Language in the Classroom*. New York: Teachers College Press.

Ochs, E. (1993) Constructing social identity: A language socialization perspective. *Research on Language and Social Interaction* 26: 3: 287–306.

Ogbu, J. (1974) *The Next Generation: An Ethnography of Education in an Urban Neighborhood*. New York: Academic Press.

Rampton, B. (1995) *Crossing: Language and Ethnicity among Adolescents*. London: Longman.

Rawls, A. (1987) The interaction order sui generis: Goffman's contribution to social theory. *Sociological Theory* 5: 3: 136–149.

Rockwell, E. (1999) Recovering history in the study of schooling: From the Longue Durée to everyday co-construction. *Human Development* 42: 115–128.

Rose, M. (1995) *Possible Lives: The Promise of Public Education in America*. New York and London: Penguin Books.

Spitulnik, D. (1999) The language of the city: Town Bemba as hybridity. *Journal of Linguistic Anthropology* 8: 1: 30–59.

Trueba, H. (1988) Culturally based explanations of minority students' academic achievement. *Anthropology and Education Quarterly* 19: 3: 270–287.

Voloshinov, V. (1986 [1929]) *Marxism and the Philosophy of Language*. Cambridge, MA: Harvard University Press.

Vygotsky, L. (1994 [1934]) The problem of environment. In R. Van der Veer and J. Valsiner (eds) *The Vygotsky Reader*. Oxford: Blackwell.

Willis, P. (1977) *Learning to Labour: How Working Class Kids Get Working Class Jobs*. Westmead (London): Saxon House and Tavistock.

Woolard, K. (1999) Simultaneity and bivalency as strategies in bilingualism. *Journal of Linguistic Anthropology* 8: 1: 3–29.

Young, M.F.D. (1971) *Knowledge and Control: New Directions for the Sociology of Education*. London: Collier-Macmillan.

Language, ideology and social categorisation

7

Age in social and sociolinguistic theory
Nikolas Coupland

1   Introduction

Age is sociolinguistics' under-developed social dimension.[1] Sociolinguistics has, for example, made an outstanding contribution to gender research, providing one of the cornerstones of modern feminist scholarship. Ethnic and race-related cultural patterns and differences and politics are, similarly, focal concerns in sociolinguistics with diverse and compelling literatures. Theoretical and empirical research centring on social class was, especially in the UK, one of the discipline's earliest, and ultimately most controversial, passions. By comparison, sociolinguistic research on age and ageing is, with only a few specific exceptions, rare. The most important exceptions are paradigms that have dealt with early parts of the life course — language development, variation and use in childhood and in adolescence, early bilingualism, and language use in educational settings. As this suggests, sociolinguistics has conceptualised the process of ageing mainly in relation to changes in early life — maturation and the acquisition and deployment of communicative competences.

When sociolinguistics has taken its data from adult populations, age as a social issue has generally been neutralised. That is, adulthood hasn't been construed as 'a life-stage', but rather as an unmarked demographic condition whose marked alternative is youth. It has usually been assumed that adulthood (implying young and mid-adulthood) is the empty stage upon which the social dramas of gender, class and ethnicity are played out in their various contexts. As Eckert says, in sociolinguistics, 'only the middle-aged are seen as engaging in mature use, as "doing" language rather than learning or losing it' (1997: 157). There has been little interest in the social experiencing of adulthood, its relational demands and opportunities, or its identificational possibilities. But language is undoubtedly central to the lived experience of age and ageing, and age is as potent a dimension of social identity as gender, class or race. The politics of age and ageism, often mediated by language, impinge sharply on social life, and show signs of becoming both more prominent (in 'an ageing society') and more diverse.

When we consider *old age*, which is my main concern here, the sociolinguistic slate is almost entirely clean. An important exception is the 'apparent time' methodology (see Labov 1972, 1994) for studying language change in progress. This is the methodological device that captures language and especially dialect change by sampling the speech of different age cohorts at one point in time. For the apparent time device to work, sampling older informants has of course been an essential part of empirical designs, in documenting how specific patterns of linguistic usage have changed either quantitatively or qualitatively across successive generations. Beyond the language change paradigm, though, it is difficult to identify any substantial body of research driven by the wish to explore old age as a sociolinguistically significant life stage. The apparent time device uses old people as informants heuristically rather than focally.

There are many reasons for the absence of sustained, focal interest in the sociolinguistics of ageing. One reason, as colleagues and I have previously suggested (Coupland, Coupland and Giles 1991), is the climate of veiled antipathy that surrounds the very concepts of ageing and late life in contemporary Western society. In this regard, unfortunately, sociolinguistics is more of a barometer of societal ageism than a force for understanding social ageing. The relevant theoretical concept is *gerontophobia*. Since we all age, and fear its implications, repression is a predictable response (Becker 1973), individually but perhaps also institutionally. This explanation imputes a critical naivety to sociolinguists, perhaps unfairly. But it is quite striking how even the most committed and libertarian theorists of gender, race and class can sometimes be blind to the social politics of age — a point also made by Woodward (1995: 88).

A second, related reason is the sequestering of research issues to do with ageing into social policy and social services/welfare research literatures. Social gerontology, which has recently contributed important new critical and theoretical treatments, is a rapidly growing discipline (see the range of sources drawn on below). But it has had to resist the assumption that social ageing is an inherently 'applied' concern — in that narrow and limiting sense of 'applied' that excludes theory. That is, it is has been too readily assumed in the past that research on late life must address 'the social problems of old age' and their remediation. It would be foolish to deny that certain health and social problems *are* probabilistically associated with old age. But to preset an agenda for ageing research in terms of such problems, and these alone, is to contribute to social disenfranchisement, when processes of disenfranchisement are part of the proper agenda for critical research.

A third reason may be the highly diverse social environments of old age in western societies. We might legitimately ask whether the old are a powerful or a powerless social group. Is late life a time of fulfilment in retirement or one of penury and social exclusion? Since we all age, and generally fear our own ageing, isn't old age a condition we must accept, the bad along with the good? So where is the moral imperative? It is possibly true that sociolinguistics has been more easily drawn to social themes where it can construe large-scale, near-universal, within-category social inequalities and establish its agenda relative to these boundaries. This would be a blinkered orientation, and there are many reasons to challenge the assumption that any demographic group is essentially defined by its disempowerment, and that this is the required motivating criterion for researching it. There is certainly no shortage of social practices and arrangements that fall within the remit of the term *ageism*, but the fact that not all old people are equally and unremittingly prey to societal ageism should not deflect research interest. In any case, social inequality is not the only motivating issue for sociolinguistics, which should be interested in documenting and modelling the changing social and ideological configurations of late life, as mediated by language.

The further reason for sociolinguistics' neglect of old age in many ways subsumes those mentioned above, and is in line with one of this book's main general arguments. It is that sociolinguistics has operated with an extremely impoverished social theory of ageing, and has not been sufficiently alert to how its own simple, implicit theory has limited its endeavours so far. Age itself may have seemed an uninteresting, almost mechanistically linear demographic dimension, which would be unrewarding except in possibly being able to index graduated linguistic change. On the contrary, modern social theory offers rich insights into ageing as a multi-dimensional and historically shifting human, social and cultural process. Appreciating the theoretical richness of social ageing should expose the importance of a sociolinguistic contribution to the social science of age, and the importance of age to sociolinguistics. Before expanding on this, I shall comment on the social theory that implicitly drives the apparent time method, which defines the sociolinguistic status quo on researching age in mid and late adulthood.

2   Age in the apparent time design

Chambers discusses age-related research in sociolinguistics in his *Sociolinguistic Theory* volume (Chambers 1995: chapter 4). 'Age', Chambers writes, 'exerts an irrepressible influence on our social being. Our age is an immutable social fact' (1995: 146). Unlike social class, where mobility is possible and indeed common, and unlike gender, where gender roles are nowadays 'less confining', Chambers argues (1995: 146) that 'our ages remain fixed', and age 'plays an almost autocratic role in our social lives'. Already, in his introductory comments, we see what appears to be a principled rationale for treating age differently from other social dimensions in sociolinguistics, because of its immutability. In fact, Chambers implies that age is not a truly *social* dimension at all, if by this we mean one that is socially negotiable. He writes that 'By and large, the physical indicators of age are shared by all people in all cultures' (p. 147). If our age is physically imprinted on us, age can indeed appear immutable and its influence 'autocratic'.

Against this backdrop, Chambers then identifies 'the three sociolinguistically crucial ages': the time of first exposure to social pressures from parents and peers; adolescent networks; and early adulthood. It is worth quoting his summary:

> It is clear, in the first place, that vernacular variables and style-shifting develop along with phonology and syntax from the very beginning of acquisition. From that point, there appear to be three formative periods in the acquisition of sociolects by normal individuals. First, in childhood the vernacular develops under the influence of family and friends . . . Second, in adolescence vernacular norms tend to accelerate beyond the norms established by the previous generation, under the influence of dense networking . . . Third, in young adulthood standardization tends to increase, at least for the sub-set of speakers involved in language-sensitive occupations in the broadest sense of the term . . . After that, from middle-age onward, speakers normally have fixed their sociolects beyond any large-scale or regular changes. (Chambers 1995: 158–9)

In this view the assumption that mid and late life are not 'sociolinguistically crucial' is concretised, although this is a theoretical position reached by a selective route. It depends on a prior definition of sociolinguistics as exclusively concerned with dialectal/sociolectal (and within this, mainly phonological) dimensions of language, and on a model of dialects becoming 'fixed for life' by early adulthood. Limits on space preclude me from discussing the limitations of a dialect-only perspective here, also the limitations of a language-centred rather than a user- and use-centred perspective (see N. Coupland 2001a in press). Also we can note in passing that focussing on acquisition prioritises within-culture rather than multicultural or intercultural processes (although Chambers does discuss data from several multilingual settings) and underplays geographical and socio-cultural mobility during adulthood. It also ignores all manner of social-contextual motivations for dialect variation, including variation across speech (including performance) repertoires. In fact, details of so-called 'stylistic variation' receive little attention in Chambers's review generally. (See Coupland 2001a in press; and Rickford and Eckert 2000, for discussion of 'style' in sociolinguistics.)

I am more concerned here with the general, basal theory of ageing which has prevailed in sociolinguistics, and Chambers is rather explicit about it. He distinguishes two kinds of age-related changes that relate to language. One is *sound change in progress*. Small deviations (for example in pronunciation)

from the cultural norm that are sometimes introduced during and after socialisation mean that a community's language tends to change with succeeding
generations. Younger people's speech tends to drift in specific respects away
from that of their older family members, whose speech is assumed to remain
largely unchanged through their lives. Sound change in progress can be
established in 'real time' or in 'apparent time'. Real time studies sample the
speech of the same individuals over time, longitudinally.[2] Apparent time studies
sample different but matched samples of people at different ages, creating an
apparent time-depth effect. Chambers (1995: 147) holds that demonstrating
sound change in progress, as variationist sociolinguistics has done (Labov
1994 is the standard exposition) is 'perhaps the most striking accomplishment of contemporary linguistics'.

The other sort of age-related change, in Chambers's and many other sociolinguists' terms, is *age-grading*, which he says is 'relatively rare' (p. 147).[3] This
is 'maturational change repeated in successive generations' — when people,
of more or less whatever birth-cohort, and their behaviour generally change
as they age. Age-grading is a developmental process which, we might say,
allows individuals to escape their historical and cultural rootedness. It implies
that a chronological age designation, like 'being 47', may *not* reflect membership of a specific culture-bound cohort born 47 years ago and which has
maintained its socialised speech characteristics. Rather, it reflects the changes
that individuals have undergone as they age, individually or collectively, and
the behavioural gap between what one does at age 27 and age 47.

Chambers offers (pp. 188–193) two examples of the apparently rare
sociolinguistic phenomenon of age-grading. One is children regularly using
the form 'zee' (for the last letter of the alphabet) in Southern Ontario,
Canada, then replacing it with 'zed' before adulthood. (Use of the 'zee' form
is speculated to be triggered by *Sesame Street* on TV, accounting for its use
by the very young, who then drop out of using it as they age.) The other
example is the use of glottal stops in Glasgow and elsewhere, based on
evidence in Macaulay's (1977) study. Middle-class 10-year-olds use stigmatised glottal stops but lose this feature by the age of 15. Vocal creak and pitch
are age-graded prosodic and paralinguistic features and certainly mark age,
and in an 'age-grading' sort of way. But Chambers (I think wrongly) says
that creak and pitch 'do not carry any special social significance' (p. 151),
feeling that they cannot be stigmatised because they affect the whole population. Chambers considers that the scarce evidence of age-grading may be
misleading; it might just be that few instances of age-grading have been
noticed by sociolinguists and reported. Age-grading, as a conceptual model
of change, undermines the apparent time perspective, which needs to assume
that speech changes during adulthood are minimal.

Other sociolinguists are much less confident about the preponderance of
cohort effects — the persistence of socialised patterns of language use throughout the lifespan — over age-grading effects. For example, Eckert (1997: 152)

argues that the extent of social contextual changes over an adult's life course will necessarily impact on speech characteristics:

> progress through the life course involves changes in family status, gender relations, employment status, social networks, place of residence, community participation, institutional participation, engagement in the market-place — all of which have implications for patterns of [sociolinguistic] variation.

Eckert reviews several sociolinguistic variation studies which, by revisiting earlier research communities and studying the same or closely comparable populations, have found evidence of both historical changes in the speech of the community (differences between successive cohorts at the same age), but also evidence of age-grading (differences within cohorts between the two times). Cedergren's study of Panama is discussed as a clear instance both by Eckert (ibid.) and in detail by Labov (1994: 94–97); I will not summarise the data and findings here.

Labov's own overview also entertains complex possibilities about linguistic changes in real time and apparent time, and about how our understanding of change in general is hampered by the methodological and practical problems that I mentioned above. Labov suggests (1994: 73) that 'Many well-established sociolinguistic variables exhibit . . . age-grading, where adolescents and young adults use stigmatized variants more freely than middle-aged speakers, especially when they are being observed'. He gives the examples of the stereotyped (dh) variable (in the words *these, them, those,* etc.) in Philadelphia and New York City. But his general conclusion is that there is evidence of considerable stability across the adult life course, particularly in the use of phonological features below the level of speakers' conscious awareness. He writes (p. 112) that sociolinguistic differences generally found 'indicate that generational change rather than communal change is the basic model of sound change'. That is, linguistic change is achieved more by new generations adopting qualitative and quantitative speech features that are different from those used by older generations, rather than by whole communities (including all age groups) simultaneously adopting new features.

3   Damaging extrapolations: 'aged aliens'

In one sense, the success of the apparent time device is its own justification. It has clearly been a key methodological resource for investigating sound change which, as I mentioned above, has been the dominant concern of variationist sociolinguistics. With the caveats expressed, the evidence does indeed suggest that, in relation to dialect, older adults do largely maintain their socialised speech characteristics into later life. But, as Eckert's quoted comments imply, what we might call the *cohort continuity model* is highly inappropriate as a general model of adult sociolinguistic development, because it edits out all manner of socio-relational changes in which language use is predictably implicated. It is in fact a model of *non*-development in adulthood — of stasis. In Chambers's (1995: 193–4) words, 'those inferences [about language change] depend on the validity of a particular hypothesis, namely that the linguistic usage of a certain group will remain essentially the same for that group as they grow older'. Whatever its factual status for dialect change research, the model is potentially damaging as a general theoretical orientation, because it accords with a partial truth (dialect stasis does not imply sociolinguistic stasis) and with a virulently pervasive social stereotype, certainly of late ageing (older people being 'set in their ways' and 'inflexible').

Compare, for example, one non-linguist sociologist's characterisation of the cohort continuity perspective:

> The aged may be seen as travellers in time . . . They have come down to our own time from what we, the younger generations, think of as the distant past, long before we ourselves were born. Some even come from the last century, quite a few from before World War I. In a sense the generational gap is the equivalent to cultural difference. (Westin 1994: 134)

Westin's characterisation captures the social alienation that a strong version of the cohort continuity model imputes, but which Chambers and many sociolinguists (through the filter of a dominant concern with dialect change) take to be the normal case. Westin talks about 'the aged', but if early adulthood defines the end of what is 'sociolinguistically crucial' about age, it follows that, for most of our adult lives, we are relegated to the status of sociolinguistic aliens who seem to 'travel in time'. In this view (but using a slightly more appropriate metaphor), it is 'time' or 'being in time' that 'travels' past us. The assumption that maturation and enculturation 'fix' our sociolinguistic and social selves implies that, as ageing adults, we drift further and further away from the presumed mainstream. Culture, including language usage norms, moves on beyond us. By implication, the older we become, the less culturally attuned to the present we seemingly become. We, presumably, travel increasingly in other people's time. As we see below, this is a dated and damaging model of social ageing.

The 'out-of-time-ness' of old people is, however, a recurrent element of age mythology and of ageist stereotyping in the west. The fund of age-prejudicial referring expressions ('old fogeys', 'old farts', 'old biddies' — see Nuessel 1982, 1984) distances them from the mainstream. Some older people will themselves recycle tropes such as 'I've seen better days' and 'in our day', where the days invoked are non-current, 'long-gone'. In a darkly humorous key, old people may refer to their earlier life stages as 'when I was alive'. A sense of disjunction from present socio-cultural concerns is of course a *potential* effect of a long-lived life. Social arrangements and lifestyles may conspire to dislocate individuals from what is held to be the mainstream. Some older people might in fact value having left the mainstream, in certain respects. But adaptation and socio-cultural 'age-grading', including socio-linguistic adaptation, are equally feasible, *even if* we assume that the cultural core is occupied by youth or young adults. In fact there are many reasons to suppose that older people occupy a more mainstream cultural position nowadays than previously. Also that the core–periphery structure is generally looser than we have traditionally assumed. I shall come back to these issues below.

In any event, the important socio-political point about the out-of-time and out-of-culture status of old age is that, however accurate or inaccurate a claim it is, social dislocation has been institutionally promoted in the west, tending to naturalise the notion of social as well as occupational 'retirement'. As Phillipson (1987) notes, 'The emergence of retirement has been one of the most significant social trends of the past fifty years . . . The *expectation* of retirement at a fixed age (or earlier) now affects the thoughts and plans of millions of men and women [in the UK]' (Phillipson 1987: 156, with original italics). In terms of personal responses, retirement can be either a welcome release from constraint or exclusion from financial security, status, opportunity and a social network. But either way, in the economic framing of human worth that developed within capitalism, it has been occupational activity and 'productivity' that has come to define a boundary between the core and periphery of society.

The pattern of enforced retirement from work at age 60 or 65 (see below), especially as it developed at the height of the mid-modern industrial period in the middle years of the twentieth century, produced what Talcott Parsons (1942: 616) called, in a USA context, a 'structural isolation' from work and the community. Correspondingly, the social category of 'elderly people', criterially defined as those who are no longer 'economically pro-ductive', was in large part created by the new requirement to retire from working at a set age. As Parsons also commented, this structural develop-ment also engendered the view of late life as a 'problem', and triggered the first evidence of resistance against societal ageism.

But before any form of anti-ageist programme or even the notion of ageism itself (Butler 1969; Bytheway and Johnstone 1990; Williams and Giles 1998) could consolidate, developmental social science coined wholesale the-ories of late life based around the notions of 'rolelessness' and 'disengage-ment' (for example Cumming and Henry 1961; Rosow 1974; Phillipson 1987: 178ff.). Cumming and Henry argued that disengagement from de-manding social roles was actually an avenue to *improved* morale in late life. It was portrayed as a natural, desirable and culturally universal condition. Even Erikson's (1980) famous taxonomy of developmental stages of 'identity and the life cycle' posited that each stage of life held out 'appropriate' tasks which needed to be completed before a person can move on to the next stage (see also Blaikie 1999: 7). Later studies, including Phillipson's, stressed the disruptive effects of occupational retirement, and even its propensity to engender 'shock' and 'crisis', and it is evident that retirement is, for many, an undesirable or at least ambivalent social transition. Current sociological theory stresses how the emergence of a retirement norm was part of a wider process of institutionalising the life course (Kohli 1991: 277ff.). The work economy came to define people as either 'productive' (in their young and mid adulthood), or as preparing for this status (through education and work apprenticeship), or as having left this status (retired). These processes imbued the notions of life stages and chronological age with rather rigid meanings, and reified them at the level of social structure and practice. As Kohli suggests, this construction was also conducive to seeing social groups, theoretically, in terms of temporal cohorts, moving in succession through the economy. As Justine Coupland also points out (in a personal note), it is also a predominantly male-focussed construction, because the work economy was, until relatively recently, one in which women were allowed limited participation.

Here we seem to have moved some considerable distance away from the apparent time method and variationist sociolinguistic interests in language change. But it is important to appreciate how the emphases of this sort of sociolinguistics in many ways perpetuate a 'modernist' (as opposed to 'late-modern') model of ageing and the life course — one based on chronological age categories and on tracking the characteristics of successions of age cohorts. The sociolinguistic model we have become familiar with through studies of dialect change presumes a strongly institutionalised and regimented life course, where age-in-years predicts social characteristics. More than that, variationist sociolinguistics has inherited the 'time-travelling' perspective according to which older people are expected to be (and are then shown to be, in certain very specific respects) progressively distanced from contemporary socio-cultural norms. But whereas the modernist perspective constructed retirement from work as the most distinctive alienating moment, variationism has established early adulthood as the onset of cultural alienation, in terms of dialect use. It is important to repeat that variationism has needed to stand by this model, because it is consistent with its most common pattern of results. At the same time, sociolinguistics needs to consider, and contribute, other theoretical models of social ageing, and especially ones more attuned to contemporary, late-modern social arrangements.

4   The new old age: social ageing in late modernity

Theories of late modernity (such as Giddens 1990, 1991) are based on observation of rapidly shifting social patterns and priorities, involving critical reappraisal of traditional social orders. In some discussions, they admittedly also include pockets of millennial ideology and hyperbole. It would be wrong to assume that the social conditions of the early twenty-first century have as yet been comprehensively or convincingly theorised, although some trends are well established.

It has been clear for some time that western societies have moved out of an epoch of full-blooded industrialisation, and developed much more active service economies. Linked to this key shift, traditional, rigid patterns of social organisation, most obviously class and gender configurations linked to occupational roles, have loosened. As a result, late modernity can generally be characterised as a more flexible social order, although by no means necessarily a more liberal or equal one. The growing service sector of the economy requires and gives increasing capital value to the management of social relationships, perhaps to informality and intimacy, and certainly to communication and language (Bourdieu 1991). Cameron (2000), on the other hand, shows how economic priorities can lead to repressive workplace practices, including the scripting of repetitive communication tasks for low-paid workers, for example in fast-food outlets or in telephone sales and other sorts of call-centre work. Developments in communication technology and cheaper travel have broken many of the constraints on how people associate and communicate. Globalising modes of communication are likely to impact on the directions and rates of language change, but may also produce new styles, genres and functions of language. Like all social behaviour, language is also increasingly reflexive (Lucy 1993; Beck, Giddens and Lash 1994; Giddens 1994; Jaworski, Coupland and Galasinski, in preparation), in the sense that we see social life relayed back to us, reformatted, mimicked or analysed, by photographs, radio, video and television, and the new media.

This brief and informal overview is perhaps enough to suggest that the social organisation of the life course is also beginning to take new forms. Giddens (1991: 5) for example, makes the case that social identities in late modernity are best viewed as 'projects'. We reflexively manage our social identities, including our identities in age terms, updating them progressively and particularly at salient life-transitional points:

> The reflexive project of the self, which consists in the sustaining of coherent, yet continuously revised, biographical narratives, takes place in the context of multiple choice as filtered through abstract systems. In modern social life, the notion of lifestyle takes on a particular significance. The more tradition loses its hold, and the more daily life is reconstituted in terms of the dialectical interplay of the local and the global, the more individuals are forced to negotiate lifestyle choices among a diversity of options.

This implies a process of deinstitutionalisation of ageing and of old age, and at least potential access to greater self-definition and social opportunities:

Once institutionalised through retirement, later life is now being dein-stitutionalised. This fracturing suggests that rather than focus on the social construction of the life-cycle, as a fixed set of stages occupied by people of particular age bands, we should analyse the ways in which it is being deconstructed by individual elders, or groups of older people, negotiating their own life courses. (Blaikie 1999: 59)

Blaikie's suggestion is a resonant one for sociolinguistics, because it shows that there is work to be done on the discursive negotiation of life course identities, which sociolinguists are better placed to undertake than others (see below). It is work that contributes directly to the social theorising of age, rather than being conditioned by pre-existing social theories, implicit in its designs. Sociolinguistics can explore the extent to which, and the ways in which, age is (re)negotiated in different settings, under what constraints and with what consequences. This dynamic perspective on identity and age-identity in particular has an established pedigree. It can be found very explicitly, for example, in Mead's (1932) process model of identity, which assumed that the self emerges through interactional experience. A thread of social psychological theory has for some time stressed the on-the-ground, negotiative nature of age-identity (Ainley and Redfoot 1982; see also Taylor 1989). I refer below to some of my own work with colleagues on age-identity in talk.

But late life is not radically freed from all its social constraints by the shifting forms of industrial capitalism. As Blaikie and others point out, the late-modern social order is still heavily structured and unequal, albeit rather less deterministically so. Social differentiation and inequalities persist, but they are visible more through patterns of consumption and other aspects of lifestyle rather than in the social fabric of class heredity and occupational status. Social differences are often referred to as 'lifestyle choices', although *which* groups have the economic resources and the will to choose specific lifestyles and consumer goods remains a crucial question. As fixed patterns of work in adulthood begin to break down, and as people retire earlier, and as leisure becomes more common, more diverse and itself more institution-alised (Coupland and Coupland 1997), retirement certainly loses much of its inherently sequestered nature. Older people — or at least those with adequate resources — can merge with the late-mid-life early-retirers or those in part-time or flexible work who define themselves through possessions, club-membership, travel, sport, socialising and other forms of recreation. In refreshing contradiction of Chambers's essentialist reading of the styles of old age (see endnote 2), Featherstone and Hepworth (1993) comment that dress styles may be becoming 'uni-age', just as they have at various times been 'uni-sex'. But, as mentioned above, it would be naïve to claim that late life as a whole has thrown off its economic and ideological constraints, and opened up an older persons' playground for leisure and self-definition. It is important to keep track of the economics and demography of old age, and to observe the discursive working-through of ideologies in that context. Let us consider economics and demography first.

Irwin (1999) summarises recent demographic data for the UK, where, amongst men aged 60–64 in 1975, 1985 and 1995 respectively, economic participation rates (as they are conventionally called) declined from 84% to 53% to 50% (see also Arber and Evandrou 1997). That is, according to this trend, less than half of UK males aged 60–64 are currently in paid work, compared with well over 80% in 1975. These data graphically illustrate the extent of the social changes we have been discussing, but they also foreground the question of social inequality. So-called early retirement is occasioned by both affluence and poverty, for different sub-groups. Much-discussed data showing the significant increase in the number of 'pensionable' people as a proportion of total populations have clearly established that the post-retirement segment of society is growing rapidly — for example 2.7 to 9.7 million in the UK between 1901 and 1981. But other data (which Irwin discusses) also show that working-age groups, in the UK and in Europe generally, have become significantly *less* equal socio-economically over the last 20 years. This in turn implies that inequalities among post-retirement populations have increased and will continue to do so.

This is an important generalisation. As we have already seen, social theory has tended to orient to ageing in age-categorial terms, attempting to generalise about age cohorts and their social environments. Irwin's perspective reminds us that any age-stratificational model of ageing, and any generalisations about 'the elderly', under-represent important social divisions within this chrono-logically widespread and itself economically highly stratified population. This is also therefore an important qualification of Laslett's well-known distinction between the 'third age' of post-work fulfilment and the 'fourth age', which Laslett called 'an era of final dependence, decrepitude and death' (Laslett 1989: 4). Neither of these 'ages' will be experienced homogenously by age-cohorts. For the poor, the 'third age' will not exist. Sociolinguistics needs to operationalise age in a correspondingly complex way.

Similarly, generalisations about the new economic power and influence of older people in the marketplace need to be qualified. In 1991, in her chapter titled 'Gold in gray', Minkler wrote that 'the elderly population [in the US] . . . is considered the newest exploitable growth market in the private sector' (p. 81). It is undoubtedly true that older people, overall, are more affluent, not least in the UK as a result of increased rates of home ownership through the period of extreme house-price inflation in the late 1980s. Minkler notes (1991: 82) that, in the USA, the incomes of families headed by people aged 65 and above rose by 54% between 1970 and 1986. But she also confirms that 'There is tremendous income variation within the elderly cohort . . . and deep poverty pockets continue to exist' (p. 83). Many older people occupy the socio-economic mainstream nowadays, and can therefore resource the lifestyle choices they make. But, for example in the UK, the steady decline in the (non means-tested) state pension, at a time when many people approaching retirement age are not members of occupational or private pension schemes, leads one to expect increasing poverty as well as increasing affluence in this sector.

5   Ideologies of old age

The changing socio-structural arrangements in which age is embedded should influence social scientific research agenda, but should also be part of them. If we take sociolinguistics to be the study of social life through language, as much as the social study of language change, a wide range of age-related issues presents itself for sociolinguists. Part of this broader agenda for the sociolinguistics of ageing lies in the analysis of ideology — to consider how the changing social meanings and values of old age are conveyed in language and related symbolic practices. Several studies of ageing and later life are first-responses to this challenge (see for example Cole and Gadow 1986; Green 1993; Featherstone and Wernick 1995; Jamieson, Harper and Victor 1997), although they are not sociolinguistic projects, as conventionally defined.

The Cole and Gadow collection, for example, starts from the assumption that the fundamental *meanings* of ageing and of old age are unclear and changing. Our understandings have been obscured, partly, by biomedical concerns that have swamped gerontology (see also Estes and Binney 1991 on the 'biomedicalization of ageing'; and Green 1993). As socio-structural bonds have loosened, asking (in Cole and Gadow's title) 'What does it mean to grow old?' has a very contemporary salience, and we would expect different clusters of responses. At the same time, structures of meaning and value ('discourses' in Foucault's abstract sense — see for example Foucault 1980) can often be more tightly woven than the social conditions they represent and influence. They can act as a repressive force, traditionalising the experience of a social condition even when social circumstances and structures have moved on. The meanings of old age are therefore to be found not only in the economic and lifestyle characteristics of different groups of older people, but also in the recurrent discourses of age that we regularly imbibe and perhaps recycle.

Ageism, in Butler's (1969) original definition of the concept, was the complex of material disadvantages and prejudicial attitudes and predispositions of younger people towards older people (see also Butler 1975). But ageism is probably better viewed as a complex ideological formation — a structured, historically formed set of myths or discourses which endorse the subordinate or marginal positions and qualities of the old. Even more affluent and less structurally constrained older people will be prey to the effects of an ageist ideology, and they may confirm elements of it in their own talk and practices. If we assume that ideologies will occasionally surface as linguistic and visual representations, as part of discourse in the less abstract sense (Jaworski and Coupland 1999), however mitigated or recontextualised, then analysing the discourse of ageism is another key project for sociolinguistics. Several potentially productive sub-themes for a critical, ideological sociolinguistic analysis of ageing and ageism have emerged. My own work with colleagues has addressed some of them, and I also reference some other recent studies. But what follows is more an agenda for future research than a list of completed studies. Because of limits on space, I can only list some key issues here, without extended commentary.

5.1   Gerontophobia and the 'othering' of the old

I referred earlier to a generalised societal gerontophobia — fear of or revulsion at old age, which is the clearest manifestation of ageism. Its psychoanalytic origins are in the repression of death, to which 'deep old age' is a precursor. In an illuminating critical study of responses to artistic and literary images of old age, Woodward (1991) develops an account of the 'unwatchability' of the elderly nude, as a classic gerontophobic impulse. Physical, including physiognomic, characteristics of old age have been recognised as powerful cultural markers (Blaikie 1999: chapters 4 and 6), and probably underlie the most negative stereotyped reactions to old age. Sociolinguistics has not systematically examined linguistic/textual parallels, which may be more mitigated and subtle than visual representations. The 'othering' of older people is an urgent agenda for sociolinguistics (for a review of issues, including gerontological ones, and a suggested taxonomy of 'othering' strategies, see N. Coupland 2001b in press).

We should not expect language practices to be transparent carriers of ageism, however. Alienation through discourse can be achieved by silence or under-representation (see, for example, Rodwell *et al.* 1992), and even by apparently supportive styles and stances (see references below on patronising talk). Featherstone and Hepworth (1995: 30) write that 'The increasing preoccupation in social gerontology with positive aging . . . arises out of the critical belief that we live in an ageist society, one in which the predominant attitude towards older people is coloured by a negative mixture of pity, fear, disgust, condescension and neglect'. We need to read the ideological contexts in which age politics are transacted with some sophistication. Even so, it is also true that even the most transparent forms of ageist reference to old people have yet to be studied systematically (the studies I mentioned above by Nuessel are a useful first contribution).

As this work develops, cross-cultural perspectives will be important, to off-set the tendency for western experiences and shifts to dominate theory. As Srikant Sarangi comments (in a personal note), the development of social theories of ageing actually requires this breadth. The rather static and traditional conceptualisations of age that I commented on above have remained unchallenged for want of considering alternatives. The research themes I am setting out here all need to be contextualised by sociolinguistic research in different cultural contexts. Ethnographic approaches developed within sociolinguistics (Hymes 1974) are well suited to taking on this task.

5.2   Age appropriateness and the (il)legitimacy of old age

As the demography of late life changes and as lifestyle options increase, at least for wealthier old people, a conservative discourse continues to structure old age by imposing norms of age-appropriateness. As I argued above, the traditional cultural order, mainly through its hierarchical occupational structure, dictated set ways of being old, and ways of speaking are no doubt included in them. Retirement has traditionally been constructed as a form of withdrawal — from status, fulfilment and from some sorts of social relationships. Although no sociolinguistic research has taken up this theme explicitly, it seems true that people in retirement have been expected to be less vocal — for example in the political arena. But even in contemporary life, discourses of age-appropriateness are commonplace. There are many discursive ways, not yet systematically examined, in which the potential freedoms of late-modern old age are undermined, for example in media texts, or in humour. Many rock and pop music icons of the 1960s and 1970s are regularly pilloried as 'dinosaurs of rock', 'repaying the debts of yesteryear', and so on. Age boundaries continue to be policed in the popular press, for example through the ubiquitous practice of what we might call age-tagging. People featured in news stories are very commonly introduced by name plus an appositional age-in-years tag ('Mary McGregor, 36'). The discourse function of the age-tag is often to indicate some element of surprise or even indignation at an action linked to an age-category, such as a teenager giving birth or an old person apprehending a burglar. The same textually manufactured disjunction generates headings such as 'Geriatric Mum' or 'Nintendo Granny'. Physical attractiveness and certainly sexuality are generally portrayed as illegitimate in later life (Gibson 1993). The physical 'youthfulness' of Joan Collins, Jane Fonda and others (cf. Blaikie 1999: 107) is not without its detractors, who might argue that theirs is an 'unnatural' or 'undignified' version of later life.

While older people can be penalised for acting out of age, it is unclear what is taken to be the legitimate condition of old age. This is part of the definitional ambiguity of old age. Featherstone (1995: 25 — see also Featherstone and Hepworth 1990, 1993, 1995) argues that contemporary western societies endorse two contrasting sets of images. In the first set are the 'heroes of ageing' who are 'positive' about ageing, in the tautological sense of maintaining 'youthful' habits and demeanour. In the second are those whose physical selves have degenerated to the extent of being incompatible with and disguising their inner selves, the so-called 'mask of ageing'. Neither condition implies that there is a social space which old people can legitimately occupy *as* old people (see below).

We have previously shown how presumed norms for health and wellbeing in later life strongly colour older people's representations of themselves, for example in responses to 'how are you?' questions in varying settings. 'Not bad for 75' and the general strategy of relativising health to presumed, normative decrement with age are conventionalised responses (J. Coupland, N. Coupland and Robinson 1992). Elaborated accounts structured on similar lines are commonly found in medical situations also (J. Coupland, Robinson and N. Coupland 1994). We have also traced the ideological bases of notions of 'premature ageing' and 'anti-aging protection' as they surface in the texts of skin-care product advertising (J. Coupland and N. Coupland 2000; J. Coupland, forthcoming).

5.3   The 'inverted U' stereotype of the life course

The visual image of two bent, huddled old people crossing a road is strongly iconic of old age in the UK, where it still features as a road-sign warning of an 'old people's home'. Physical smallness is a stereotyped (and no doubt, quantitatively, an actual) characteristic of both the old and the young. These groups are often represented as being similar in other ways, for example in terms of incompetence, dependency and societal marginality. We have referred to this association as the 'inverted U' model of the life course (N. Coupland, J. Coupland and Giles 1991; Hockey and James 1993, 1995), and old people are commonly said to be in their 'second childhood'. On the other hand, it may be that children are presumed to be legitimately dependent, and old people to be illegitimately dependent (Hockey and James 1995: 140). Correspondingly, a very active research paradigm has developed accounts of the sociolinguistic infantilisation of old people under the rubrics of 'secondary baby-talking' (Caporael, Lucaszewski and Culbertson 1983), 'over-accommodation' (N. Coupland, J. Coupland, Giles and Henwood 1988) and 'patronising talk' (for example Hummert 1994). This last approach, mainly developed through experimental research in the social psychology of language, takes an explicitly evaluative and political line on 'inter-generational miscommunication'.

5.4   Ageism and anti-ageism

All the themes that I am summarising here help to fill out our understanding of societal ageism as an ideology and a related set of sociolinguistic practices. But as I suggested above, sociolinguistics needs to be cautious in its appeal to the notion of ageism, and needs to develop theory in this area too. For example, ageism is not simply or uniformly 'something done to older people by younger people', as a generational conflict theory would assume, since many of the conventional tropes of intergenerational talk involve older people in a form of self-disenfranchisement ('what can I expect at my age?', etc.). Again, because ageism is an ideological formation and not just a set of prejudicial personal beliefs, it can be conveyed even by well-meaning and would-be liberal people. We have to recognise forms of ageism conveyed, for example, in over-simplistic and romantic images of old age (Achenbaum 1995). There is a recurring semantic that associates late life with warmth and comfort ('golden agers', 'the Golden Girls', 'the sunset years') and another that imputes dignity and wisdom ('senior Citizens', 'seniors'). 'Positive' though these qualities are, they may well have been coined in the knowledge that the circumstances of old age are less than rosy and statusful. In a reflexive sociolinguistic society, these historico-political machinations of reference can often be complex. It is therefore difficult to disentangle 'compensatory anti-ageism' in address or reference from ageism itself (cf. Binstock 1983: 140 on 'compassionate ageism').

In analyses of first-acquaintance conversations between women in their thirties/forties and others in their seventies and older, we found a propensity for younger women to presume speaking rights and conversational access to their older partners, non-reciprocally (N. Coupland, J. Coupland and Giles 1991: chapter 4). The data suggested that the younger women's conversational styles were intrusive or negative face-threatening, and yet some older people approved of them. They read their younger partners' actions as signalling interest in their personal lives, which they welcomed. Age-telling by older people ('I'm seventy-four next month actually') and age-complimenting by younger partners ('Gosh, you don't look it!') is another ritualised intergenerational discourse practice (ibid, chapter 6). These conventionalised responses are denials of ageing, which may well be locally motivated by anti-ageist intents and again they may be well received. But denial of ageing returns us to the issue, mentioned above, of ageism working subtly and often in multiply embedded ways to deny a legitimate social space for old age, with its distinctive advantages *and* disadvantages.

6   Overview

In the above, necessarily eclectic, review I hope to have shown the yawning gap between a highly circumscribed mainstream sociolinguistic paradigm concerned with age (what Chambers 1995 refers to as the study of 'accents in time') and a complex theoretical conception of the sociolinguistics of ageing. Ageing is, with little doubt, a future priority for sociolinguistics.

This is partly because of the much-discussed, massively shifting demography of the life course in the west. As many writers suggest, social science cannot ignore a post-retirement segment of society that outnumbers working adults. But the apocalyptic tenor of many such reports ('we must attend to the looming elderly health disaster and the onward march of the ageing hordes') should not colour research priorities. The general imperative is for sociolinguistics to take on the task of clarifying the radical uncertainty of what social ageing *means*, and how it is negotiated in language and discourse. In western societies the social context will be detraditionalisation and the new politics of age. Other societies will have radically different histories of intergenerational relations and other problems and possibilities.

Sociolinguistic research into ageing needs a socio-political dimension. As I sketched it in the previous section, sociolinguistics needs to address a *disenfranchisement agenda* of old age, much as it has done in relation to social class, gender and ethnic relations. The patterns and modes of disenfranchisement will, however, be distinctive to the ageing domain, and will vary — from one cultural context to another, and from one social group to another within particular societies. The language change paradigm has presented a thoroughly depoliticised perspective on ageing, and this is how Chambers and others can claim that mid and late life are not 'sociolinguistically crucial' periods. Age is undeniably a focus for social inequalities, for the young as well as the old, although I have not considered the former case in this review. Sociolinguistics has demonstrated that power, control and authority are routinely transacted through language. Many older people are socially disadvantaged and poverty in late life still has a structural social basis — for example because the UK still allows the working-age poor to enter retirement without an adequate financial safety-net. However, as I suggested above in commenting on socio-economic trends in the UK and the USA, it will be important not to over-generalise about 'the disadvantaged elderly'. We need to be clear to distinguish the specific older populations for whom disadvantage is socio-economically structured, and the larger number for whom disadvantage is ideologically ascribed. Language will be implicated in both cases.

Beyond issues of disenfranchisement, the *age-identity agenda* is tantalisingly poised for sociolinguistics to explore. In my own work with Justine Coupland and other colleagues I have suggested that age-identity is often nearer to the surface of talk and text than other dimensions of social identification. At least, there are very many social encounters where age is made immediately and obviously salient, and where it becomes a thematic resource for talk. In most public encounters between non-acquaintances, gender, race and class will be covertly negotiated, and their salience and consequentiality will be difficult to read at the surface of talk. But age-work, especially if we mean in the context of young-adult/old-adult interaction, is often overt, for example in the actual telling of age-in-years (mentioned earlier), or in talk about social or personal change. Age can be told because it plausibly claims a dimension of status — experience achieved through longevity, or the presumption of earned respect. But it can also serve to account for incompetence or incapacity or frailty. Another age-related genre we have examined is troubles telling or painful self-disclosure in inter-generational discourse (Coupland, Coupland and Giles 1991; Coupland and Coupland 2000). But these are very specific foci, textually and socio-culturally, and a much wider view is needed. A general finding in the sociolinguistic analysis of age-identity may prove to be that age-values in discourse are radically out of step with the new social conditions of late life in the west.

When sociolinguists write about identity, they often interpret the term in a rather anodyne way, as if 'having an identity' or 'negotiating an identity' were selecting and displaying options from a repertoire of equally plausible alternatives. Antaki and Widdicombe (1998), for example, write about 'using identities' as the unmarked case. Although sociolinguists have always known that identity 'matters', contemporary theorising of identity stresses contingency and how a multiplicity of identificational symbols are both projected and ascribed. There are important and credible claims in these literatures (Duranti and Goodwin 1992 provide an excellent overview). But in the context of ageing, identity work assumes a more profound personal importance than this model proposes. The negotiation of one's identity as an older person subsumes the self-appraisal of one's own worth as a 'time-travelling' person. We readily reach almost ineffable questions such as 'What is it all about?' and 'What sort of a life has it been anyway?'. The word 'essentialist' is commonly used in disparagement of theoretical orientations which fix social identities too rigidly and which are unresponsive to social contextual processes (see, for example, Rampton 1995), and again this is an important insight.

But age-identities *are*, in another sense, 'essential'. They are the products of the evaluative component of our own life narratives (Gubrium 1976, 1993; Linde 1993), the cumulative assessment of where we stand, developmentally — as individuals and in relation to our social environments. This isn't to say that people do not play identificational games with and around their age-identities, or that talk directly exposes our essential understandings of our ageing selves. But, as we have repeatedly found in the geriatric medical discourses we have studied (e.g. N. Coupland and J. Coupland 1998 and in press), identity in ageing ultimately connects to morale and wellbeing. There is an intensity of personal consequence when old people perceive their identities to be spoiled, or their narratives (to use Linde's term) to be 'incoherent' (see Antonovsky 1984).

For three decades, sociolinguistics has assumed that age is mainly of interest as a resource for the study of language change, and then that only some life stages are of interest. We need to discredit the assumption that ageing is only of interest at the margins. In Eckert's words (1997: 157), 'a balanced view of sociolinguistic aging must merge a developmental perspective with a mature-use perspective for all age groups . . . The developmental perspective recognizes that development is lifelong'. Sociolinguistics, I would certainly agree, needs a theory of lifelong ageing rather than a theory of socialisation. But this chapter's review also suggests that it needs to consider a theoretically much richer *change agenda* as well as a longer one. As we have seen, the main conceptual distinction for age-related sociolinguistics at present is between 'real-time' and 'apparent time'. Then there is the further distinction between researching age-cohorts through either 'panel studies' (sampling data from the same informants over time) or 'trend studies' (sampling from different but matched individuals across time periods) (Labov 1994: 77; Eckert 1997: 153). This metalanguage shows how resolutely sociolinguistics has defined its orientation to ageing in terms of cohorts and the analysis of group norms.

In social gerontology, on the other hand, it is acknowledged that the cohort perspective for ageing research has been overplayed. Riley and Riley (1999: 125) in fact refer to the 'fallacy of cohort centrism', which they define as 'erroneously assuming that members of all cohorts age in the same fashion as members of the cohort under scrutiny'. Sociolinguistics has successfully navigated around another fallacy — Riley and Riley's 'life-course fallacy' (ibid.) — the assumption that cross-sectional age-differences must indicate ('internal') processes of human ageing. But it remains 'cohort-centric', asserting that there are universal chronological principles guiding the acquisition and consolidation of cultural norms and practices, such as dialect. As Riley and Riley go on to say for social gerontology generally, social explanation ultimately lies beyond cross-sectional and cohort studies, which entail a neglect of local social structure and its linkage to individual experience:

> The major challenge for future research on age, as we see it, is to examine, not lives or structures *alone*, but the dynamic *interplay* between them as each influences the other. In the continuing dialectic between lives and structures, it is not only lives that change: structures also change. And full understanding requires understanding the linkages — both methodological and substantive — between ageing and the process of change in the surrounding structures. (Riley and Riley 1999: 126–7, with original italics)

As this implies, the experience of ageing lies in how changing social conditions (such as a looser structure for post-retirement lives or structured poverty in retirement) interact with historical cohort experiences (for example being a 'babyboomer' or having built a career under a right-wing political regime) and a host of other social factors impinging on individual identities (gender, class, network, ethnicity, sexuality, and so on).[4] And the forum for all these interactions is discourse.

Sociolinguistics currently proposes that in late adulthood we are, at least in terms of speech-style, pretty much what we were socialised to be. This is a depressing and repressive assumption, even if dialect is only a small part of discursive practice. I argued above that ageism is best seen as a complex ideology, tending to naturalise conservative, repressive models of ageing. But people will accommodate *or resist* these discourses differently and in different ways, as their resources and personal creativity allow. Resistance is being mobilised in increasingly organised ways (Tulle-Winston 1999; see also Wallace *et al*. 1991 on 'senior power' and the Gray Panther movement in the USA). And for those who successfully resist, age itself starts to seem like a metaphorical and ideological ascription. Other than in having our age-in-years thrust before us (decade birthday-cards, enforced retirement ages, the marketing of holidays for 'over-fifties', age-stereotyped humour, etc.), and assuming we can avoid the health and social problems that have been over-stated in the popular account of old age, 'being old' can seem a refreshingly empty category. Healthy and socially advantaged people in later life can establish their own non-traditional identity spaces, *if* they can ward off ageist discourses that interpret age-nonconformity as the illegitimate aping of youth. Alternatively, old age can be constituted as a life stage distinct from mid-adulthood, with unique competences and opportunities. That is, the new old age does not have to be 'youth with wrinkles'. Disadvantaged older people will find it far harder to resist living out the stereotyped attributes of an ageist and gerontophobic society.

The same challenge, more or less, confronts those who research ageing. Researchers need to reset the tolerances on their own conceptualisations of later life. Green (1993), for example, notes how even the term 'life cycle' suggests 'externally set mechanisms' regulating human development and change while metaphors of the 'life course' suggest a passage or journey or convoy, with individuals more actively responsible for their development and social events as the 'landscape' (pp. 131ff.; see also Hagestad and Neugarten 1985: 35). How the object of inquiry is framed in language tends to determine the questions addressed and therefore what we learn from research. In the ageing context, and especially at this early stage of sociolinguistic research into ageing, there are many reasons to avoid all rigid (pre)conceptualisations. We should recognise that old people often are a minoritised and 'othered' social group, but also that there is far more to social ageing than disadvant-age. We should refine our understanding of societal ageism and explain its linguistic/discursive characteristics, but without over-simplifying its moral complexities. We should continue to model ageing in terms of change. But we should recognise that change involves an interplay between human developmental processes, historical cohort influences and the shifting con-texts of social structure and culture, all subject to creative interpretation by people in their other demographic categories. As in the case of language change, these social configurations will certainly leave their mark on speech and language, and there are still large gaps in our knowledge about the sociolinguistic differentiation of age-groups. But a more ambitious agenda would see sociolinguistics operating in the middle of social theoretic con-cerns, examining the voices that express the conflicting meanings of ageing and that will determine our experiences of age in the future.

Notes

1. I am grateful to Justine Coupland, Srikant Sarangi and Angie Williams for their particularly helpful comments on an earlier draft of this chapter. The usual caveats apply.
2. Srikant Sarangi (in a personal note) observes that linguistics generally lacks longitudinal studies. This is no doubt partly because of administrative complexities and cost implications in establishing them.
3. On the other hand, Chambers (1995: 148) characterises the physical and cultural indicators of ageing as overwhelmingly age-graded: '. . . advancing age brings wrinkling skin, weight re-apportionments in chest and abdomen, greying hair and, for men, receding hairlines . . . only old women dress in solid black to go shopping, only young men wear team sweaters, only little girls wear buckled sandals, only teenagers wear ripped jeans, only old men wear felt fedoras to sit in the sun in the park . . .'. These are what Chambers calls 'infallible indicators' of old age, although this account seems remarkably traditional and stereotyped.
4. Westin (1994, quoted earlier) similarly identifies three sets of explanatory factors which relate to human and social time (p. 135), and cohort effects again constitute only one of the three. He distinguishes *ageing effects* (changes related to individual ageing and maturation processes, including health — cf. age-grading) from *period effects* (changes related to significant events in society, or in individual life, during the period between measurements, including social policy changes), and *cohort effects* (the unique historical experiences of people born at a certain time within a cultural group). This taxonomy originally appears in Bengston, Cutler, Mangen and Marshall (1985); see N. Coupland, J. Coupland and Nussbaum (1993) for a related discussion of *inherent*, *developmental* and *environmental* factors in social ageing.

References

Achenbaum, Andrew (1995) Images of old age in America, 1790–1970: a vision and a re-vision. In Mike Featherstone and Andrew Wernick (eds) *Images of Aging: Representations of Later Life*. London: Routledge, 19–28.

Ainley, S.C. and Redfoot, D.L. (1982) Ageing and identity-in-the-world: A phenomenological analysis. *International Journal of Ageing and Human Development* 15: 1–15.

Antaki, Charles and Widdicombe, Sue (eds) (1998) *Identities in Talk*. London: Sage.

Antonovsky, A. (1984) The sense of coherence as a determinant of health. In J.P. Matarazzo (ed.) *Behavioural Health*. New York: Wiley.

Arber, Sara and Evandrou, Maria (1997) Mapping the territory: Ageing, independence and the life course. In S. Arber and M. Evandrou (eds) (1997) *Ageing, Independence and the Life Course*. London and Bristol, PA.: Jessica Kingsley Publishers, 9–26.

Beck, Ulrich, Giddens, Anthony and Lash, Scott (1994) *Reflexive Modernization: Politics, Tradition and Aesthetics in the Modern Social Order*. Cambridge: Polity Press.

Becker, E. (1973) *The Denial of Death*. New York: Free Press.

Bengston, Vern L., Cutler, N., Mangen, D. and Marshall, V. (1985) Generations, cohorts and relations between age groups. In Robert H. Binstock and E. Shanas (eds) *Handbook of Aging and the Social Sciences*. New York: Van Nostrand Reinhold, 304–338.

Binstock, Robert H. (1983) The aged as scapegoat. *The Gerontologist* 23: 136–143.

Blaikie, Andrew (1999) *Ageing and Popular Culture*. Cambridge: Cambridge University Press.

Bourdieu, Pierre (1991) *Language and Symbolic Power*. London: Polity Press.

Butler, Robert N. (1969) Age-ism: Another form of bigotry. *The Gerontologist* 9: 243–246.

Butler, Robert N. (1975) *Why Survive?: Being Old in America*. New York: Harper & Row.

Bytheway, B. and Johnstone, J. (1990) On defining ageism. *Critical Social Policy* 29: 27–39.

Cameron, Deborah (1990) Demythologizing sociolinguistics: Why language does not reflect society. In J.E. Joseph and T.J. Taylor (eds) *Ideologies of Language*. London: Routledge, 79–93.

Cameron, Deborah (1995) *Verbal Hygiene*. London: Routledge.

Cameron, Deborah (2000) Styling the worker: Gender and the commodification of language in the globalized service economy. *Journal of Sociolinguistics* 4, 3.

Caporael, L., Lucaszewski, M.P. and Culbertson, G.H. (1983) Secondary babytalk: Judgements by institutionalized elderly and their caregivers. *Journal of Personality and Social Psychology* 44, 4: 746–754.

Chambers, J.K. (1995) *Sociolinguistic Theory: Linguistic Variation and its Social Significance*. Oxford: Blackwell.

Cohen, S. and Wills, T.A. (1985) Stress, social support, and the buffering hypothesis. *Psychological Bulletin* 98, 2: 310–357.

Cole, Thomas R. and Gadow, Sally (eds) (1986) *What does it Mean to Grow Old: Reflections from the Humanities*. Durham, NC: Duke University Press.

Coleman, P. (1993) Adjustment in later life. In J. Bond, P. Coleman, and S. Pearce (eds) *Ageing in Society*. London: Sage.

Coulmas, Florian (1997) Introduction. In Florian Coulmas (ed.) *The Handbook of Sociolinguistics*. Oxford: Blackwell, 1–11.

Coupland, Justine (forthcoming). 'Time has a nasty habit of catching up with us': Discourses of skin care product advertising. In Justine Coupland and Richard Gwyn (eds) *Discourses of the Body*. (Proceedings of the Fourth Cardiff Roundtable in Language and Communication).

Coupland, Justine and Coupland, Nikolas (2000) Selling control: Ideological dilemmas of sun, tanning, risk and leisure. In Stuart Allan, Barbara Adam and Cynthia Carter (eds) *Communication, Risk and the Environment*. London: UCL Press.

Coupland, Justine, Coupland, Nikolas and Robinson, Jeffrey (1992) 'How are you?': Negotiating phatic communion. *Language in Society* 21: 201–230.

Coupland, Justine, Robinson, Jeffrey and Coupland, Nikolas (1994) Frame negotiation in doctor–elderly patient consultations. *Discourse and Society* 5, 1: 89–124.

Coupland, Nikolas (1997) Language, ageing and ageism: A project for applied linguistics? *International Journal of Applied Linguistics* 7, 1: 26–48.

Coupland, Nikolas (2001a, in press) Language, context and the relational self: Retheorising dialect style in sociolinguistics. In Penelope Eckert and John Rickford (eds) *Style in Sociolinguistics*. Cambridge: Cambridge University Press.

Coupland, Nikolas (2001b, in press) 'Other' representation. In Jef Verschueren, Jan-Ola Östman, Jan Blommaert and Chris Bulcaen (eds) *Handbook of Pragmatics, Installment 2000*. Amsterdam and Philadelphia: John Benjamins.

Coupland, Nikolas and Coupland, Justine (1997) Bodies, beaches and burntimes: 'Environmentalism' and its discursive competitors. *Discourse & Society* 8, 1: 7–25.

Coupland, Nikolas and Coupland, Justine (1998) Reshaping lives: Constitutive identity work in geriatric medical consultations. *Text* 18, 2: 159–189.

Coupland, Nikolas and Coupland, Justine (1999) Ageing, ageism and anti-ageism: Moral stance in geriatric medical discourse. In Heidi Hamilton (ed.) *Language and Communication in Old Age: Multidisciplinary Perspectives*. New York and London: Garland Publishing Inc. (Taylor & Francis), 177–208.

Coupland, Nikolas and Coupland, Justine (2000) Relational frames and pronominal address/reference: The discourse of geriatric medical triads. In Srikant Sarangi and Malcolm Coulthard (eds) *Discourse and Social Life*. London: Longman, 207–229.

Coupland, Nikolas and Coupland, Justine (in press) Language, ageing and ageism: A social action perspective. In P. Robinson and H. Giles (eds) *Handbook of Language and Social Psychology*, 2nd edn. London: Wiley.

Coupland, Nikolas, Coupland, Justine and Giles, Howard (1991) *Language, Society and the Elderly*. Oxford and Cambridge, MA.: Basil Blackwell.

Coupland, N., Coupland, J., Giles, H. and Henwood, K. (1988) Accommodating the elderly: Invoking and extending a theory. *Language in Society* 17, 1: 1–42.

Coupland, Nikolas, Coupland, Justine and Nussbaum, Jon (1993) Epilogue: Future prospects in lifespan sociolinguistics. In N. Coupland and J. Nussbaum (eds) *Discourse and Lifespan Identity*. Newbury Park: Sage, 284–293.

Coupland, Nikolas and Nussbaum, Jon (eds) (1993) *Discourse and Lifespan Identity*. Newbury Park: Sage.

Cumming, E. and Henry, W. (1961) *Growing Old*. New York: Basic Books.

Duranti, Alessandro and Goodwin, Charles (eds) (1992) *Rethinking Context*. Cambridge: Cambridge University Press.

Eckert, Penelope (1997) Age as a sociolinguistic variable. In Florian Coulmas (ed.) *The Handbook of Sociolinguistics*. Oxford and Cambridge, MA.: Blackwell, 151–167.

Eckert, Penelope (2000) *Linguistic Variation as Social Practice*. Maldon, MA and Oxford: Blackwell.

Erikson, E.H. (1980) *Identity and the Life Cycle (A reissue)*. New York: Norton.

Estes, Carroll L. and Binney, Elizabeth A. (1991) The biomedicalization of aging: Dangers and dilemmas. In M. Minkler and C. Estes (eds) *Critical Perspectives on Aging: The Political and Moral Economy of Growing Old*. Amityville, NY: Baywood Publishing, 117–134.

Featherstone, Mike (1995) *Undoing Culture*. London: Sage.

Featherstone, Mike and Hepworth, Mike (1990) Ageing and old age: Reflections on the postmodern life course. In B. Bytheway, T. Keil, P. Allatt and A. Bryman (eds) *Becoming and Being Old: Sociological Approaches to Later Life*. London: Sage, 133–157.

Featherstone, Mike and Hepworth, Mike (1993) Images of ageing. In J. Bond and P. Coleman (eds) *Ageing in Society: An Introduction to Social Gerontology*. London: Sage, 250–275.

Featherstone, Mike and Hepworth, Mike (1995) Images of positive aging: A case study of retirement. In M. Featherstone and A. Wernick (eds) (1995) *Images of Ageing: Representations of Later Life*. London: Routledge, 29–47.

Featherstone, Mike and Wernick, Andrew (eds) (1995) *Images of Aging: Representations of Later Life*. London: Routledge.

Foucault, Michel (1980) *Power/Knowledge: Selected Interviews and Other Writings 1972–1977* (ed. C. Gordon). Brighton: Harvester.

Gibson, H.B. (1993) Emotional and sexual adjustment in later life. In S. Arber and M. Evandrou (eds) (1997) *Ageing, Independence and the Life Course*. London and Bristol, PA.: Jessica Kingsley, 104–118.

Giddens, Anthony (1990) *The Consequences of Modernity*. Cambridge: Polity Press/ Basil Blackwell.

Giddens, Anthony (1991) *Modernity and Self-identity: Self and Society in the Late Modern Age*. Cambridge: Polity Press/Blackwell.

Giddens, Anthony (1994) Living in a post-traditional society. In U. Beck, A. Giddens and S. Lash, *Reflexive Modernization: Politics, Tradition and Aesthetics in the Modern Social Order*. Cambridge: Polity Press, 56–109.

Green, Bryan S. (1993) *Gerontology and the Construction of Old Age: A Study in Discourse Analysis*. New York: Aldine de Gruyter.

Gubrium, Jaber F. (ed.) (1976) *Time, Roles and Self in Old Age*. New York: Human Sciences Press.

Gubrium, Jaber F. (1993) *Speaking of Life: Horizons of Meaning for Nursing Home Residents*. Hawthorne, NY: Aldine de Gruyter.

Hagestad, Gunhild O. and Neugarten, Bernice L. (1985) Age and the life course. In Robert H. Binstock and E. Shanas (eds) *Handbook of Aging and the Social Sciences*. New York: Van Nostrand Reinhold.

Hockey, Jenny and James, Allison (1993) *Growing Up and Growing Old: Ageing and Dependency in the Life Course*. London: Sage.

Hockey, Jenny and James, Allison (1995) Back to our futures: Imaging second childhood. In M. Featherstone and A. Wernick (eds) *Images of Aging: Representations of Later Life*. London: Routledge, 135–148.

Hummert, Mary Lee (1994) Stereotypes of the elderly and patronising speech. In Mary Lee Hummert, John. M. Wiemann and Jon F. Nussbaum (eds) *Interpersonal Communication in Older Adulthood: Interdisciplinary Theory and Research*. Thousand Oaks, CA: Sage, 162–184.

Hymes, Dell (1974) *Foundations in Sociolinguistics: An Ethnographic Approach*. University of Pennsylvania Press.

Irwin, S. (1999) Later life, inequality and sociological theory. *Ageing and Society* 19, 6: 691–716.

Jamieson, Anne, Harper, Sarah and Victor, Christina (eds) (1997) *Critical Approaches to Ageing and Later Life*. Buckingham and Philadelphia: Open University Press.

Jaworski, Adam and Coupland, Nikolas (eds) (1999) *The Discourse Reader*. London: Routledge.

Jaworski, Adam, Coupland, Nikolas and Galasinski, Dariusz (eds) (forthcoming) *The Sociolinguistics of Metalanguage*.

Kohli, Martin (1991) Retirement and the moral economy: An historical interpretation of the German case. In M. Minkler and C. Estes (eds) *Critical Perspectives on Aging: The Political and Moral Economy of Growing Old*. Amityville, NY: Baywood Publishing, 273–292.

Labov, William (1972) *Sociolinguistic Patterns*. Philadelphia: Pennsylvania University Press.

Labov, William (1994) *Principles of Linguistic Change, Vol. 1: Internal Factors*. Cambridge, MA. and Oxford: Blackwell.

Laslett, P. (1989) *A Fresh Map of Life: The Emergence of the Third Age*. London: Weidenfeld & Nicolson.

Linde, Charlotte (1993) *Life Stories: The Creation of Coherence*. New York and Oxford: Oxford University Press.

Lucy, John A. (1993) Reflexive language and the human disciplines. In John A. Lucy (ed.) *Reflexive Language: Reported Speech and Metapragmatics*. Cambridge: Cambridge University Press, 9–32.

Macaulay, R.K.S. (1977) *Language, Social Class and Education: A Glasgow Study*. Edinburgh: Edinburgh University Press.

Mead, G.H. (1932) *Philosophy of the Present*. LaSalle, IL: Open Court.

Minkler, Meredith (1991) Gold in gray: reflections on business' discovery of the elderly market. In M. Minkler and C. Estes (eds) *Critical Perspectives on Aging: The Political and Moral Economy of Growing Old*. Amityville, NY: Baywood Publishing, 81–93.

Nuessel, F. (1982) The language of ageism. *The Gerontologist* 22: 273–276.

Nuessel, F. (1984) Ageist language. *Maledicta* 8: 17–28.

Parsons, J. Talcott (1942) Age and sex in the social structure of the United States. *American Sociological Review* 7: 604–616.

Phillipson, Chris (1987) The transition to retirement. In Gaynor Cohen (ed.) (1987) *Social Change and the Life Course*. London: Tavistock, 156–183.

Rampton, Ben (1995) *Crossing: Language and Ethnicity Among Adolescents*. London: Longman.

Rickford, John and Eckert, Penelope (2000) *Style and Sociolinguistic Variation*. Cambridge: Cambridge University Press.

Riley, Matilda White and Riley, John W. (1999) Sociological research on age: legacy and challenge. *Ageing and Society* 19: 123–132.

Rodwell, G., Davis, S., Dennison, T., Goldsmith, C. and Whitehead, L. (1992) Images of old age on British television. *Generations Review* 2, 3: 6–8.

Rosow, Irving (1974) *Socialization to Old Age*. Berkeley: University of California Press.

Taylor, C. (1989) *Sources of the Self*. Boston: Harvard University Press.

Tulle-Winston, Emmanuelle (1999) Growing old and resistance: Towards a new cultural economy of old age? *Ageing and Society* 19, 3: 281–300.

Wallace, Steven P., Williamson, John B., Lung, Rita Gaston and Powell, Lawrence A. (1991) A lamb in wolf's clothing?: The reality of senior power and social policy. In M. Minkler and C. Estes (eds) *Critical Perspectives on Ageing: The Political and Moral Economy of Growing Old*. Amityville, NY: Baywood, 95–114.

Westin, Charles (1994) Discussion: Some reflections on age and identity occasioned by reading Nikolas Coupland and Justine Coupland's paper. In *Health Care Encounters and Culture* (Proceedings of the 1992 Summer University of Stockholm Seminar, Botkyrka), 129–137.

Williams, Angie and Giles, Howard (1998) Communication and agism. In Michael Hecht (ed.) *Communicating Prejudice*. Thousand Oaks: Sage, 136–160.

Woodward, Kathleen (1991) *Ageing and its Discontents: Freud and Other Fictions*. Bloomington: Indiana University Press.

Woodward, Kathleen (1995) Tribute to the older woman: psychoanalysis, feminism and ageism. In M. Featherstone and A. Wernick (eds) *Images of Aging: Representations of Later Life*. London: Routledge, 79–96.

8

Undoing the macro/micro dichotomy: Ideology and categorisation in a linguistic minority school[1]
Monica Heller

1 Introduction

One of the central problems of social theory has long been that of how to link so-called 'macro' and 'micro' levels of social structure, social organisation and social process. Over the years, many social scientists have suggested that perhaps the macro/micro dichotomy is not the most helpful way in which to understand how the observable dimensions of social life in the here and now are linked to durable patterns which lie beyond the control or the awareness of individuals (see for example Cicourel 1978; Collins 1981; Giddens 1982; Mehan 1987). Conceptualising social life in terms of a dichotomy implies that there are different types of data for each, equally observable (or not, as the case may be), and that, in addition, the linkages should be identifiable. And yet, empirical work fails to identify such types. Instead, Giddens, for example, proposes thinking in terms of structure and action, but in ways which allow structure and action to be in a dialectical relationship to each other, a relationship which itself occurs in the observable patterns of situated social action.

What this means in practical terms is that as social scientists, if we want to understand how social processes work, or how social reality is constructed, we have to work with what is observable in the here and now (that is, social interaction), and with the traces laid down in time and space by those interactions. The problem of linkage between macro- and micro-levels becomes a problem of linkage among social interactions over time and (social) space. In many ways sociolinguistics is particularly well suited to addressing this problem, since it provides tools not only for the analysis of the unfolding of interaction over time, but also for the analysis of the relations among interactions over time, whether towards the past or the future, and with reference to those immediately present or not. In practical terms, this means identifying the nature and social significance of the communicative resources people bring to interactions and call into play there, how they draw on them in the course of interactions, and with what consequences, for them and for others, immediately and over time. In this respect, Gumperz's notion of situated interaction (Gumperz 1982) takes on the methodological dimension of working out what the relevant aspects of 'situating' are: what interactions do we choose to focus on, why, and how? And then, how do we link up the interactions to each other?

In this perspective, sociolinguistics is seen as a form of social science; sociolinguistic theory is a form of social theory. The specificity of sociolinguistics, however, goes beyond method; it problematises language as a form of social action which needs to be understood in its own right, albeit linked to other forms of social action (and social organisation). That is, language is not transparent, nor simply a reflection of social organisation or social processes; it is one of many elements of social process, and a particularly important one, given its centrality in the social construction of meaning. While there are certainly other questions to be asked about sociolinguistic theory (notably, the extent to which language can be understood separately from other forms of social process or not), it is this dimension of language as social action on which I wish to concentrate here.

In what follows, I will lay out a conceptual framework for addressing these questions (a framework which in many ways is built on the work of Bourdieu, Gumperz, Giddens and Cicourel), and then look at some ways in which I have tried to render the process of asking at least some aspects of these questions concrete in the form of ethnographic, sociolinguistic fieldwork in Canada. I will focus on one specific question, one related to the problem of social categorisation, that is, to the ways in which groups are constructed, both in terms of criteria of inclusion and exclusion and in terms of what it means to be a good (or in any case prototypical) member of a group. Here, the process of categorisation has to do with creating Franco-Ontarians (members of a linguistically-defined minority group in Canada's largest province) in what has long been a key site for such work, the French-language minority school.

I will argue that the process of social categorisation in such a school requires constant interactional work directed at resolving tensions among competing interests and between ideological imperatives and countervailing concrete conditions of life. This work involves exploiting prevailing institutionally-defined interaction orders to conduct linguistic monitoring, in order to construct a public face of school life which conforms linguistically to a certain image of what it means to be Franco-Ontarian. Specifically, the nationalist movements beginning in the 1960s have placed an emphasis on the association of monolingualism and nationhood (and French Canada is scarcely alone among linguistic minorities of the Western world to have followed this path; think of Corsica, Brittany, Wales, among others). In French Ontario, this has meant the development of a nationalist consciousness which focusses on fights for social development on the basis of the creation of monolingual institutional spaces (Heller 1994, 1999). While English–French bilingualism is still valued, that bilingualism is held to be a set of parallel monolingualisms, not any kind of mixed variety. This is the view which prevails in schools. A good Franco-Ontarian, in this ideological perspective, is thus one who separates French from English, and who uses only French in Franco-Ontarian institutional spaces like the school. Most Franco-Ontarians (and certainly just about all the ones in the school I will discuss here) do live their lives in both languages, however, and sometimes in one or two others as well. Further, for students, school is one of the few spaces where it is possible to actively display their bilingualism. The construction of a monolingual public face at school must thus be constantly worked at, in order to build boundaries around languages which are constantly in contact, and in order to convince students who live both languages at once that it is in their interests to separate them from each other. Here, a look at how participants in school life work at constructing a Franco-Ontarian school (and thereby, at constructing Franco-Ontarians) shows how language practices in daily life are part of social processes which tie ideology to resources, and social categories to struggles over those resources and their value.

2   Positions, interests and action

At the heart of the problem of social categorisation lie the resources which are valuable to people, whether material or symbolic (Bourdieu 1982). These are what people work for, struggle over, share and steal; they are what make life possible, and even better agreeable, worth living. But things are unequally distributed, whether the resources themselves or the possibility to control the production and distribution of these resources, or the possibility to decide what is valuable and what is not. And so people start out having differential access to resources and their control, and therefore with different sets of interests with respect to maintaining or gaining access to them, or with respect to accepting or contesting the value assigned to them.

Language is a principal means for regulating access to the social networks and situations in which value is assigned to resources and in which those resources are produced and distributed (and through this function, language itself becomes a resource which is more or less valued by speakers and non-speakers of relevant language varieties). It is through the development of linguistic conventions that we construct stable (normal, routine, taken-for-granted) ways of relating to each other and to the material world, and on the basis of which we can therefore define social categories (who is expected to do what, have what interests, wield what kinds of power) and confront and organise new experience (Cicourel 1978; Gumperz 1982).

It is here that language is central to the relationship between social structure and social action, since it is in linguistic practices that we can see how people draw on already established knowledge to reproduce that knowledge (those ways of organising relationships, of building social categories, of producing and distributing resources), or conversely, to build new knowledge. In linguistic practices we can also see traces of the ways in which old, established knowledge acts as a set of obstacles and opportunities for individual or collective action, and ways in which people deal creatively and strategically with them. Finally, we can see traces of immediate consequences, such as whether a person gets to speak or not, whether topics someone initiates get taken up or marginalised, whether or not a speaker elaborates on information he or she has and others want, how people judge each other, and so on (Gumperz 1982).

However, in order to understand the broader significance of local actions, interactions have to be situated in a number of ways. First, we need to know what kinds of communicative resources and sets of interests interlocutors are likely to have, given their social position with respect to the distribution of resources. Second, we need to know to what extent certain kinds of resources are conventionally associated with certain kinds of interactions (like exams, or job interviews), or more broadly what kinds of resources might be at stake where. Third, we need to be able to discover how immediate interactional consequences are linked to longer-term consequences with respect to the access individuals have to resources, mediated through possibilities for participating in social relationships and activities where the circulation of resources is regulated. All of these require ethnographically-informed sociolinguistic methods, that is, methods which allow us both to see how linguistic resources are at work in local interactions, with local consequences, and how those interactions are tied to others, whether through the life trajectories of individuals, through institutional activities and processes, or through the production and reproduction of ideologies which orient both individual and collective action.

3   A question, and some attempts at finding answers

I will now turn to some ways in which I have tried to work out this approach in my own fieldwork. The question which motivates me has a general (universal) formulation, as well as a local, socially and historically contingent one. Indeed, it is difficult for me to imagine how else to proceed, since the approach I have outlined can only build generalisations on the basis of comparison of in-depth analyses of specific configurations of people and resources. The general formulation has to do with the ways in which people connect the construction of social categories (which is another way of talking about identities) with the construction of relations of power. The specific formulation has to do with the ways in which the political mobilisation of French-speakers in Canada works, and with what consequences for what it means to be francophone (or French Canadian, or Québécois, and so on), anglophone (or English Canadian, or Anglo-Québécois, and so on) or members of other social categories, for what kinds of resources members of those categories have access to, and for how and by whom the production, distribution and valuing of those resources is regulated. I happened to get interested in both the specific and general versions of this question for very practical reasons, that is, because they have a concrete impact on my life, but I can imagine other paths into similar kinds of questions. Nonetheless, whatever the path, my point is that these questions are matters that are connected in direct ways to the concrete conditions of people's lives, with all that that entails for what it is like to do this kind of work in this way.

3.1   Picking a site

There are many potential ways into this question, and I have tried several. For the purposes of this paper, I will however limit myself to discussing one, which is how social categorisation and social inequality work in French-language minority education. As a site, French-language minority schools make sense methodologically, because of the role they play in the struggle between francophones and anglophones, as well as among francophones, over who gets to be what, and over who gets what.

Very briefly, shifting economic conditions in Canada after the Second World War made it possible for some francophones to contest the conditions of economic, social and political subordination and marginalisation that most had lived under (albeit not always quietly) for close to 200 years. The political configuration of Canada made it possible for francophones within Quebec to imagine a collective mobilisation which would have as its goal using the apparatus of the provincial government to ameliorate life conditions and life chances of francophones within that territory. This strategy is legitimated on the basis of an ethnic nationalist view of social organisation of states; it requires demonstrating that the Québécois are a people, who therefore deserve a state which will in turn act in the people's interests. This mobilisation, which to a large extent has been successful, at least for the new francophone middle class, is predicated on a redefinition of social categories, from those based on 'race' (the term prevalent in the nineteenth century, although still present in some discourses in that nineteenth-century sense) to those based on state structures. Accordingly, French-Canadians become Québécois, and a million other former French Canadians living in the nine other provinces (and two territories) have to figure out what they are now. It is also predicated on a redefinition of the rules of access to resources previously controlled by anglophones, such that francophone Québécois can gain access to those resources by deploying the communicative resources they already possess (namely French), communicative resources to which they also, as it happens, have privileged access. Thus recategorisation goes hand in hand with a reconfiguration of relations of power. There is much to be said about the interactional dimensions of how this happened (and is happening) in Quebec, but that lies beyond the scope of this paper. Instead, I want to focus on how what happened in Quebec influenced what happened in the other parts of francophone Canada, since that is another place in which the future of the country, and our experiment with pluralism, are at stake.

The most important aspect of Quebec's influence has to do with the political strategy Quebec adopted, and which has been adopted in modified form elsewhere. The political ideology is legitimated on the basis of the notion of the normalcy of monolingual states. Quebec's argument is that francophones will remain disadvantaged unless they can become autonomous in a monolingual francophone social space, defined as the territory controlled by the government of Quebec. Elsewhere in Canada, francophones cannot easily lay claim to a geographical manifestation of such social space, and instead have fought for an institutional basis of organisation of monolingual autonomous zones. The most important of these zones has been the school, largely because schools are, after the family, the most important social institution of social and cultural reproduction. In addition, the family is acting as an institution of reproduction of *la francité* with less and less efficacy as the rates of assimilation and exogamy climb. Finally, since the state took over control of educational institutions from religious institutions, schools have become important sites of confrontation between minority communities and state structures in which they cannot or do not participate.

Thus one set of reasons for doing fieldwork in a French-language minority school has to do with the role of the school as an institution of social and cultural reproduction, and in this specific case with the ideological importance of those kinds of schools in the attempt to construct monolingual francophone social spaces which act as institutions of social and cultural reproduction. At the same time, those institutions are charged with another goal central to the mobilisation project, namely the preparation of francophones to enter the modern world, a world which, of course, currently happens to be dominated by English. In addition, the goal of collective amelioration entails using an institution which is fundamentally a system of social selection to broaden chances of success for the clientele. One important way in which the schools work at providing social advancement is by credentialising bilingualism (in the form of parallel monolingualisms), something which has developed a recent value in the post-secondary studies and job markets, and possibly simply as a form of capital of distinction (in

Bourdieu's sense). Finally, such schools represent the unexpected dilemmas flowing from francophones' attempts at recategorisation. While the claim for autonomy is based on ethnic nationalist ideology (a people deserves a state, or at least a school), the successful wielding of power in a democratic state or institution requires a shift to some form of civic nationalism which uses democratic criteria of inclusion. The contingencies of the labour market, and the value of French–English bilingualism in it, have produced a situation in which social spaces claimed by an ethnically fairly homogeneous group are now also inhabited by people of other origins who got there through a variety of paths, but whose legitimate presence is argued for on the grounds of (at least potentially) shared language (language being democratic in the sense that theoretically anyone can learn one).

A French-language minority school, then, allows for the study of some of the central contradictions of francophone Canadian political mobilisation, and indeed, it turns out, of many other similar post-war movements of linguistic minority liberation. It also allows for the study of the social construction of categories, since it serves as an example of the ways in which categories (which are abstract, and tend to be fictively homogeneous) encounter the contradictions, ambiguities and ambivalences of real life. Finally, it allows for linking institutional (and in this case, national) ideologies to linguistic ones, and to linguistic practices and their consequences for the regulation of access to the institution, to activities or to groups within the institution, and hence for the regulation of access to the resources the school distributes.

3.2   Ideologies and practices

The logic of the Franco-Canadian mobilisation movement, then, entails the construction of monolingual social spaces, and of speakers who separate their French from their English. The first question to ask is how this construction occurs, especially given the processes which militate against it. This is the question I will focus on here. We can equally ask what the consequences of this process are, in terms of social categorisation and social selection, and their role in the distribution of resources and the construction of relations of power; we can ask who benefits from this process and who does not. To answer this second set of questions in a detailed way is beyond the scope of this paper; I will have to limit myself to indicating some ways in which those who have an interest in collaborating with the school accept at least that part of its definition of a Franco-Ontarian school which has to do with the construction of a monolingual space, and thereby profit from what the school has to offer, while others are marginalised both from the process of production of categorisation itself and from what that process regulates.

I will argue that for the school I discuss here, this process occurs in the following ways. First, the entire school system, as directed centrally by the Ontario Ministry of Education, is oriented towards the production of monolingual spaces. We will see how the Ontario Ministry of Education already formulates the schools' ideological orientation, setting up a vision of a school which functions as a monolingual space; this vision is echoed in documents the school itself produces. Below, I will provide by way of illustration short extracts of three relevant documents, two from the Ministry and one from the school.

Two things are worth noting about the ways in which the ideology of monolingual space (and of bilingualism as parallel monolingualisms) is set up: 1) the rationale for the vision is neither social nor political, but cognitive, and therefore universalising (one of Bourdieu's distinguishing characteristics of successful symbolic domination is that it masks its social origins in universalising and normalising terms); and 2) it nonetheless needs to be made explicit, opening up the possibility for supposing that real conditions must be otherwise, or else it would not be necessary to say things this way.

Indeed, it turns out that getting students to conform to this dimension of the school's symbolic order is indeed a problem (albeit less so among university-bound students than their job-market-bound schoolmates), and it is even a problem for teachers themselves. (The reasons for the variation among students have mainly to do with their class positioning, which orients them differently to the value of the linguistic repertoire valued by the school.)

I will show how the prevailing symbolic order of the school, naturalised as 'respect', is translated into an interaction order characterised by sequential turn-taking on a unified floor (and often by the canonical I–R–E (Initiation–Response–Evaluation) format). This interaction order becomes available as a means of exercising control over students' linguistic production and for constructing a public 'on record' discursive space which becomes the only one that counts for ideological reproduction, and the only one for which participants can be held accountable.

Speaking in turn and speaking in French are both central elements of being '*en ordre*'. Disorder must be controlled; this can be done by direct linguistic monitoring (correction and self-correction), and by more subtle discursive means of relegating disorderly elements to a backstage (in Goffman's sense) for which participants can escape responsibility. Those who successfully accomplish this work can participate in the official public francophone space of the school, and benefit from what it distributes (that is, access to credentialised bilingualism and to the newly emerging power structures of Franco-Ontarian society).[2] (I will not be able to show here exactly how this happens; however, it involves the silencing and self-silencing of students who do not play the game by the rules, and indeed their removal — by the school or by their own volition — from school activities; see Heller 1999 for a fuller discussion).

I will begin the story with three illustrations of ways in which the educational system discursively constructs itself as monolingual space. Examples 1 and 2 are from curriculum guidelines produced by the Ontario Ministry of Education for French-language minority schools. These particular guidelines focus on the problem of teaching French and teaching in French in a minority setting, where students are constantly in contact with English, and where many come to school with knowledge of the French Canadian vernacular, but not the standard. Example 3 is from a course selection manual provided by the École Champlain,[3] the Franco-Ontarian high school in which I did fieldwork from 1991 to 1994 (see Heller 1999).

The Ministry document recognises the diversity of the student body, and states that it is important to respect these differences. Nonetheless, it also affirms at several points the importance of developing a sense of 'belonging' (*appartenance*) to the Franco-Ontarian community. With respect to language, it explicitly discusses the school as a monolingual space in itself, and as a key site of linguistic reproduction for the entire community (lines 1–3); it sets up a structurally-based distinction between the kind of French the school values and the vernacular (decontextualised language, which is better for learning, versus the students' spoken French, which is often characterised by influence from English; lines 4–13); and then describes in universalising terms ('additive', a term drawn from social psychology) the kind of bilingualism it favours (lines 14–17). (The original text is in regular font in the left-hand column; the translation is in italics on the right. Where the original was already in English, the corresponding text in the right-hand column is in underlined italics.)

Example 1

From: *Aménagement linguistique en français: Guide d'élaboration d'une politique d'aménagement linguistique* (Ministry of Education and Training of Ontario, 1994, p. 9)

1 — Promouvoir l'utilisation du français	*— Promote the use of French in all*
2 dans toutes les sphères d'activités à	*spheres of activity at school as well*
3 l'école comme dans la communauté.	*as in the community.*
4 — Élargir le répertoire linguistique des	*— Widen students' linguistic*
5 élèves et développer leurs connaissances	*repertoires and develop their*
6 et leurs compétences en français, en	*knowledge of and competence in French,*
7 acceptant et prenant comme point de	*while accepting their spoken French and*
8 départ leur français parlé. Cette	*using it as a point of departure. This*
9 compétence acquise dans l'usage	*acquired competence in the*
10 décontextualisé du français leur	*decontextualized use of French will*
11 permettra de poursuivre avec succès leur	*allow them to successfully pursue*
12 apprentissage toute la vie durant, quel	*learning all their lives in whatever*
13 que soit le domaine d'études choisi.	*field of study they may choose.*
14 — Permettre aux élèves d'acquérir une	*— Permit the students to acquire a good*
15 bonne compétence communicative en	*communicative competence in English,*
16 anglais, dans des conditions qui	*under conditions which promote*
17 favorisent un bilinguisme additif.	*additive bilingualism.*

Example 2 also distinguishes the vernacular from the kind of French the school system values; the distinction is so important that an entire programme (PDF) has been institutionalised in order to cope with it.

Example 2

From: *Programme-cadre: Actualisation linguistique en français et Perfectionnement du Français* (Ministry of Education and Training of Ontario, 1994, p. 25)

1 Le perfectionnement du Français (PDF)	*Perfecting French (PDF)*
2 Raison d'être: Le programme de PDF	*Rationale: the PDF programme is for*
3 s'adresse à des élèves qui s'expriment	*students who express themselves with*
4 avec une certaine aisance dans une	*relative ease in a regional variety of*
5 variété du français régionale éloignée de	*French distant from the language of*
6 la langue d'enseignement et qui	*instruction and who have academic*
7 éprouvent des difficultés sur le plan	*difficulties as a result of their lack*
8 scolaire en raison de leur manque de	*of familiarity with the language*
9 familiarité avec la langue	*of instruction.*
10 d'enseignement.	

The Ministry of Education orients Franco-Ontarian schools to the production of monolingual spaces and of speakers who speak a monolingual, standard variety of French. Example 3 shows how some of these ideas show up in the texts of the specific school in which I conducted fieldwork. It sets up the school as a monolingual space, again responsible not just for itself but for the community as a whole (lines 14–17), and in terms which link the mastery of monolingual varieties to universal values of learning, communication, and self-realisation (lines 17–21).

Example 3

From École Champlain course listing (*Répertoire des cours*) 1992–1993, p. 3.

1 Usage du français: L'École Champlain	*Use of French: Champlain School is a*
2 est une école de langue française. Toutes	*French-language school. All activities,*
3 les activités, qu'elles soient purement	*whether strictly academic, cultural or*
4 scolaires ou qu'elles soient culturelles ou	*recreational, take place in French. We*
5 récréatives se déroulent en français. On	*also expect of you that you speak in*
6 attend également de vous que vous vous	*French to your teachers and fellow*
7 adressiez en français à vos enseignant-e-s	*students; in class and during all school*
8 et à vos condisciples; en classe et pendant	*and extra-curricular activities. The Law*
9 toutes les activités scolaires et	*on Education stipulates that in a*
10 parascolaires. La loi sur l'éducation	*French-language school the language*
11 précise que dans l'école de langue	*of administration and communication is*
12 française la langue d'administration et	*French. A French-language school, in*
13 de communication est le français. Une	*addition to being a teaching institution,*
14 école de langue française, en plus d'être	*is also a source of extension of this*
15 une maison d'enseignement est aussi un	*language and of the culture it transmits.*
16 foyer de rayonnement de cette langue et	*No human being can develop in*
17 de la culture qu'elle véhicule. Aucun	*harmony, can develop his or her full*
18 être humain ne peut se développer	*potential, if he or she does not master*
19 harmonieusement, se réaliser pleinement	*perfectly this tool of thought and of*
20 s'il ne maîtrise pas parfaitement cet	*communication. Each teacher and each*
21 outil de pensée et de communication.	*department will have a policy aimed*

22 Chaque enseignant-e et chaque secteur   *at encouraging you to use only French*
23 auront une politique visant à vous   *in school and in the classroom.*
24 encourager à n'utiliser que le français à
25 l'école et dans les salles de classe.

There is strong ideological pressure to actualise a school in which only French is ever spoken. However, it would seem that there may be some difficulty in realising the goal of creating a monolingual space in the school and of developing bilinguals who act as serial monolinguals. There are a number of reasons for this. One is the fact that this school is located in a large English-speaking city. Everybody, teachers and students, lives in at least two languages. Schools do also tend to build on out-of-school knowledge (especially in subject areas like Geography and Science), and in this town, that comes in English. The difference between adults and students is that adults can more easily separate the two languages, for example by working (as teachers) in French, and using English in the street. Their livelihood is based on their participation in this institution, moreover, and so they have a strong interest in reproducing its ideology. Students' interests vary; some want to collaborate with the school, and are convinced not only that what the school has to offer will be valuable to them, but also that they are able to do well on the school's terms, while others are less sure of this. Nonetheless, displaying bilingualism is important for students, and in their lives the only people who really understand it are their fellow students.

Teachers and students manage these contradictions in a number of ways. The most important one is built around the interaction order of the school. This order is premised, first, on a separation between spaces controlled by the institution and spaces controlled by the students. These spaces have a geographical aspect: classrooms are typically controlled by the school, the grounds by the students. The library, the corridors and the cafeteria are disputed territory, being inside the school but not under direct and constant surveillance by school authorities. These spaces also have a temporal dimension: class time, extra-curricular activity time, student time (lunch, recreation, moving from one class to another). The school tends to focus its attention on the spaces it can most clearly, undisputedly control: class time. The other spaces then function as backstages which permit the containment of otherwise dangerous contradictions. However, even classrooms contain potential backstages, discursively constructed through asides, or by shifting mode (for example whispering), or other means which will be further explored below.

Still, classrooms are the most important site for the construction of a frontstage. Here, a number of things have to be seen to be going on, notably learning and teaching, and the construction of a Franco-Ontarian face. In order to accomplish these, the school appeals to a sense of 'respect' and of 'order'. As in most schools, the typical interaction order is teacher-controlled sequential turn-taking on a unified floor (often, but not always, in I–R–E format), and this is often explicitly linked to the notion of respect and order. As Lise, a teacher of a general level (that is, not university-bound) class, said to her students: *'respecter les autres, ça veut dire lorsqu'une personne qui parle, tu dois apprendre à te taire'* (respecting others, that means when a person who is talking, you have to learn to be silent.) Her colleague Danielle told her general-level class: *'alors vous devriez tous être en ordre. Okay, comme si vous parlez (comme? avec?) Fatima alors vous n'êtes pas en ordre'* (so you should all be in order. Okay, like if you are talking (like? with?) Fatima, you are not in order.) (It is not surprising that almost all explicit representations of order and respect should have been found in general-level classes; these are, after all, the classes where students have least to gain from collaborating with the school.)

Example 4 is a summary written by Lise after lengthy discussions about class discipline.[4] Note that here speaking French (line 5), taking your turn (not interrupting 'unnecessarily'; see line 1) and politeness (line 4) are associated.

Example 4

10th grade *Français général* class, 1991 (from field notes)

1 — interruptions non-nécessaires	— *unnecessary interruptions*
2 — comportement peu désiré:	— *little-desired behaviour:*
3 —— parler sans raison	—— *speaking for no reason*
4 —— impolitesse	—— *impoliteness*
5 — parler une autre langue que le français	— *speaking a language other than French*

Example 5 shows the same association, this time explicitly tied to serial turn-taking, as it occurs in Lise's class. In line 4, Lise responds to Saïd's use of Somali by reminding him to speak French; in line 8, she calls for a unified floor and distributes a turn at talk. This is followed by two students' turns which are ostensibly collaborative in content (they underline Lise's request for silence), but of course they simultaneously violate her request for silence, since they are talk. Moreover, one of the turns is in English. In line 12, Lise has to begin again; the communicative situation being set up (a class presentation by two students, Leïla and Abdi) simply cannot begin until the two prerequisites (a unified floor and use of French) are met. This is underlined again in line 18, after yet another student intervention.

Example 5

10th grade *Français général* class, 1991

	1 Lise:	Zahra (xxx) feuille Saïd tu	*Zahra (xxx) sheet Saïd you*
	2	lui as donné à à	*gave it to to*
	3 Saïd:	oh euh (xxx) (in Somali)	*oh uh (xxx) (in Somali)*
→	4 Lise:	(xx) aujourd'hui vous parlez	*(xx) today you speak French*
	5	en français	

6	Saïd:	d'accord je vais parler	*okay I'll speak French*
7		Français	
→ 8	Lise:	okay alors on écoute Leïla	*okay so we listen to Leïla*
9		et Abdi	*and Abdi*
10	Student:	chut	*shh*
11	Student:	*shut up*	*shut up*
→ 12	Lise:	okay on recommence quand on	*okay we start again when we*
13		fait une présentation orale ou	*do an oral presentation or*
14		un exposé on s'attend	*an exposé we really expect*
15		vraiment à ce que à ce que les	*people to listen*
16		gens écoutent	
17	Rahman:	c'est quoi ça	*what's that*
→ 18	Lise:	ok si vous avez déjà présenté	*ok if you have already*
19		on vous demande alors	*presented we then ask you to*
20		d'écouter aussi on vous a	*listen also we listened to you*
21		écouté hier (vous?) faites la	*yesterday (you?) do the*
22		même chose pour les	*same for the*
23		personnes d'aujourd'hui ok	*people today ok*

Respect and order in this school are, then, tied to serial turn-taking, to unified floors controlled by teachers (especially, but not exclusively, through I–R–E formats) and to speaking French and only French. Of course, the interaction order itself makes it possible to monitor linguistic production, and therefore to work at producing monolingual behaviour. When interactions do follow this convention, talk is available for monitoring. Among other things, it is monitored for form, that is to say, it is available for regulation according to normative pressures to produce monolingual 'good' French. At the same time, this interaction order provides opportunities for coping with contradictions, by separating out the conventional floor of order and respect as the space where monolingualism must be produced, from other kinds of floors which can then constitute alternative discursive spaces. Since some of these are set up as part of pedagogical practice by the teacher herself or himself, these are not always examples of 'disorder'; a science teacher makes a distinction between what students do when they are conducting lab work in small groups, for example, from what they do when she is lecturing or conducting a whole class discussion. A drama teacher distinguishes between presentations to the class and small-group skit practices. Most classes have examples of these potential backstage spaces, in which students can speak English, mix French and English, and so on, as long as they do it in ways which do not threaten the legitimacy of the frontstage space (such as by whispering, keeping their gaze fixed on a small group, and so on).

In what follows, I will show some ways in which teachers use the interaction order to conduct linguistic monitoring, both of their students and of themselves. Examples 6, 7, and 8 show how teacher-controlled sequential turn-taking allows teachers to focus on form rather than content, and in particular to remove influence from English from their students' French.

Example 6 is from a tenth-grade advanced-level French class. The teacher, Martine, is conducting a general discussion, using the I–R–E format, on why reading is a valuable activity, as a way of setting up an upcoming reading activity. Her Evaluation slot (lines 3–4) is used to comment on the English influence on the form of Michel's answer (line 2).

Example 6

10th grade *Français avancé*, 1991

1	Martine:	pourquoi lit-on?	*why do we read?*
2	Michel:	pour relaxer	*to relax*
→ 3	Martine:	pour se détendre, 'relaxer'	*to* 'se détendre' (*relax*),
4		c'est anglais	'relaxer' *is English*

In Example 7, we meet Lise again. Here she has asked students to construct a narrative. One student begins a story, and the next is supposed to add a few sentences, and so on. While the students could organise their contributions themselves, it is in fact Lise who distributes the turns at talk, and who evaluates each contribution, in a modified I–R–E. The story so far concerns a girl who is running away from danger in a car. It is Stéphane's turn; he offers a flat tyre, and Lise's Evaluation slot confirms the content (she has previously rejected other suggestions as inappropriate), but corrects the form.

Example 7

10th grade *Français général*, 1991

1	Stéphane:	elle a un *flat*	*she has a flat*
→ 2	Lise:	elle a une crevaison	*she has a flat*

Example 8 concerns an eleventh-grade Accounting class. A student, Julien, has made a presentation about the financial difficulties of his favourite hockey team, the Québec Nordiques. The teacher, Thérèse, comments on the English influence she perceives in his use of the word *irréalistique* (line 6), using the occasion not just to monitor Julien's linguistic production, but that of a large number of students ('*beaucoup d'élèves*', line 13); that is, as with most such occasions in Western schools, the feedback is intended not for the single student who expressed some form of knowledge, but as a pedagogic moment for the whole class.

Example 8

11th grade, *Comptabilité*, 1994

1 Julien:	Ça veut dire que, lui s'embarquer	*That means that for him to get*
2	là-dedans c'est vraiment un risque	*involved in that, it's really a risk*
3	pour lui. Perdre son poste puis	*for him. To lose his job and find such*
4	trouver une somme d'argent aussi	*a large sum of money, it it will the*

5		énorme, ça ça sera le euh très le	*uh very the it's like a bit unrealistic*
6		c'est comme un peu irréalistique pour	*for the city of Québec*
7		la ville de Québec	
8	Thérèse:	(...) Les mots en -ic hein ? c'est des	*(...) Words ending in -ic eh? they*
9		mots souvent anglais, *realistic*, (xx)	*are often English words, realistic*
10		il y a plusieurs qui l'utilisent comme	*(xx) there are many who use it like*
11		ça. C'est réaliste, euh réaliste,	*that. It's réaliste uh réaliste,*
12		idéaliste, et cetera, mais il y a	*idéaliste, et cetera, but there are*
13		beaucoup d'élèves qui utilisent ces	*many students who use those words*
14		mots-là avec la la terminaison -ic,	*with the the ending -ic, it doesn't*
15		ça n'existe pas en français, ça c'est	*exist in French, that is English (...)*
16		de l'anglais (...)	

The last example in this set is from a tenth-grade advanced-level Science class. The teacher, Aline, is conducting a lesson on natural fibres, as part of a module on polymers. (I have extracted relevant sequences from a long lesson lasting about 75 minutes.) One of the pedagogical principles Aline tries to adhere to is that of building on students' concrete real-world knowledge in order to bring them to broader and more abstract understandings. Of course, this concrete knowledge is likely to be in English. Because Aline would be in contradiction with herself if she explicitly corrected students in ways that obtain much less strongly for French teachers, she does little overt correcting. Instead, she accepts suggestions formulated in English, usually without reformulating them into French. The sequence culminates when Aline begins dictating notes (prior to line 21) which constitute the 'real' part of what it is the students are supposed to learn. It is precisely in this note-dictation sequence that Aline provides the reformulation of English into French (lines 21–25). Aline thus discursively separates the students' contributions as backstage.

Towards the end of the lesson, the teacher-centred interaction order breaks down a little bit, as Aline relaxes at the end of class. The situation becomes even less clearly frontstage, although it remains ambiguous. Students begin to speak more English (lines 46–52); Aline reacts indirectly, initiating a repair (lines 49–50: *les quoi? qu'est-ce que tu dis là?*) which could as easily be about content as it is about form. The student provides a clarification on both fronts at the same time (lines 51–52). Again, Aline does not directly challenge the students' linguistic production; nonetheless, she constructs a frontstage where it is clear that linguistic production should be in French.

Example 9

10th grade *Sciences avancé*, 1991

→	1	Aline:	okay qu'est-ce que c'est que des	*(xx) okay what are fibres?*
	2		fibres?	
	3	Male student:	*Fibre*	*Fibre*
→	4	Aline:	Ouais	*Yeah*
			(...)	*(...)*

5	Aline:	si je commence avec	(pause) *if I start with*
6		les fibres naturels (pause)	*natural fibres (pause)*
7		okay la laine (pause) quelles	*okay wool (pause) what*
8		autres sortes de fibres qu'on	*other kinds of fibres that we*
9		connaît qui sont relativement	*know that are relatively*
10		communs là	*common*
11	Male student:	le coton	*cotton*
12	Aline:	le coton	*cotton*
13	Male student:	(xx)	*(xx)*
14	Male student:	la soie	*silk*
→ 15	Maria:	*wool sheep*	<u>*wool sheep*</u>
16	Several students:	*wool wool*	<u>*wool wool*</u>
→ 17	Aline:	ouais puis un dernier	*yeah and a last one*
		(. . .)	*(. . .)*
18	Aline:	(. . .) à côté de coton et lin on a	*(. . .) next to cotton and linen*
19		pas du tout (discuté du?) lin le	*we haven't at all (discussed?)*
20		quatrième produit naturel, le	*linen the fourth natural*
→ 21		lin *'linen'* en anglais okay	*product linen <u>linen</u> in English*
22		donc ajouter le lin dans votre	*okay so add linen to your*
23		liste de fibres naturels ou de	*list of natural fibres or of*
24		polymers naturels (noise of	*natural polymers (noise of*
→ 25		chairs) le lin *'linen'* en	*chairs) linen <u>linen</u> in English*
26		Anglais	

(There follows a discussion about the properties of materials made from natural fibres, in which the students' real world knowledge of cloth comes into play. Having discussed linen and cotton, they go on to wool:)

27	Aline:	(. . .) quels sont les avantages à	*(. . .) what advantages are*
28		porter de la laine, pourquoi	*there to wearing wool, why*
29		est-ce qu'on aime ça? Parce	*do we like it? because it*
30		que ça	
31	Maria:	ça donne chaud	*it gives [makes you] hot*
32	Aline:	c'est chaud avantage c'est un	*it's hot advantage it's a*
33		bon isolant	*good insulator*
34	Julien?:	désavantage ça pique	*disadvantage it scratches*
35	Aline:	ça pique désavantage okay	*it scratches disadvantage ok*
36		avantage un bon isolant	*advantage a good insulator*
37		désavantage est-ce que ça se	*disadvantage is it easy to*
38		lave facilement ça?	*wash?*
39	All students:	non	*no*
40	Aline:	pas vraiment	*not really*
41	Amanda:	ça (se?) rétrécit aussi	*it also shrinks*
→ 42	Female student:	*(you have to?) handwash (it?)*	<u>*(you have to?) handwash (it?)*</u>
43	Aline:	(xx) donc désavantage se lave	*(xx) so disadvantage is hard*
44		difficilement	*to wash*
		(After a few more turns on the	
		subject of wool, they turn to silk:)	
45	Aline:	c'est très confortable	*it's very comfortable*

→ 46	Marcel:	les *honeymooners* (xx) la soie	*honeymooners (xx) silk*
47		(xx) le *honeymoon*	*(xx) honeymoon*
48		(Female students laugh)	(Female students laugh)
49	Aline:	les quoi? qu'est-ce que tu dis	*the what? What are you*
50		là?	*saying?*
51	Marcel:	*when two people honeymoon*	*when two people honeymoon*
52		(xx) la soie (xx) lune de miel	*(xx) silk (xx) honeymoon*

The next set of examples demonstrate some ways in which teachers monitor their own linguistic production, and separate out their introduction of English from the frontstage production of French. Since the teachers themselves are bilingual, and they must often deal with material in English, there are times when English sneaks into their talk. They separate it out from their 'on-record' talk through a variety of means. One is self-correction, usually accompanied by flagging (examples 10–12). The flagging, of course, sets off the use of English as something outside of the on-record talk, and as something for which the speaker does not want to be held directly responsible. In examples 10 and 12, the teachers use the formulations '*ce qu'ils appellent/ce qu'on appelle*' (what they call/what one calls), which serve to distance the speaker from his or her words (they call it that, not me); in all three examples the teachers explicitly flag words as English (*en anglais*); and in examples 11 and 12 they also point to their obligation to use French ('*je devrais dire*' — I should say).

Example 10

10th grade *Français général*, 1991

1	Lise:	(. . .) euh ce que j'aimerais	*(. . .) uh what I'd like us to do*
2		qu'on fasse vendredi, c'est	*Friday, is for us to meet in*
3		qu'on se rencontre à la salle	*room 155 and then for us to*
4		155 et puis qu'on fasse ce qu'ils	*have what they call 'by the*
→ 5		appellent à la fortune du pot	*luck of the pot' or a* potluck
6		ou un *potluck* en anglais,	*in English, 'la fortune du pot'*
7		la fortune du pot	

Example 11

10th grade *Français général*, 1991

1	Lise:	(. . .) alors ce qu'on va faire	*(. . .) so what we're going to*
2		aujourd'hui, on va sortir les	*do today, we're going to take*
3		textes que vous avez eus hier	*out the texts which you got*
4		sur le futur dépasse souvent la	*yesterday on the future often*
5		technologie [. . .] ça va être uh	*overtakes technology [. . .] it*
→ 6		*timé*, moi je pense c'est	*will be uh* timed, *I think it's*
7		vraiment le le (pause)	*really the the (pause)*
8		chronométré je devrais dire,	*'chronométré' I should say,*
9		mot anglais, okay t'as ton	*English word, okay you have*
10		texte . . .	*your text . . .*

Example 12

10th grade *Géographie avancé*, 1992

	1 Louis:	c'est ça et ce sont des	*that's it and they are*
→	2	(tuyaux?) qu'on appelle des	*(pipes?) what they call*
	3	*pipelines* hein, ce sont des	*pipelines eh, they are*
	4	(xx) des tuyaux qui	*(xx) pipes which*
	5	transportent le pétrole et le	*transport oil and*
	6	gaz naturel de l'Alberta, ce	*natural gas from Alberta,*
	7	sont ce qu'on appelle des	*they are what they call*
	8	*pipelines* (. . .) les oléoducs ce	*pipelines (. . .) 'oléoducs' are*
	9	sont des tuyaux qui	*pipes which transport*
	10	transportent le pétrole alors	*oil while*
	11	que les gazoducs transportent	*'gazoducs' transport what?*
	12	quoi?	
	13 Male student:	le gaz	*gas*
	14 Louis:	(. . .) nous transportons des (xx)	*(. . .) we transport (xx)*
	15	pour la consommation, par	*to use, for*
	16	exemple, pour nos voitures et	*example, for our cars and*
	17	tout ça, on a besoin de pétrole,	*all that, we need oil,*
	18	donc ici à Toronto i ont des	*so here in Toronto they have*
→	19	(xx) des *pipelines* je devrais	*(xx) pipelines I should*
	20	dire des oléoducs pour le	*say 'oléoducs' for the*
	21	pétrole (. . .)	*oil (. . .)*

Another strategy is to get a student to say the English instead of saying it directly. In the following example, Aline is reading from a poster sent by a nearby university. It lists various careers open to students with degrees in chemistry, and is meant to attract students to the university's science programme. The university, however, is English-speaking, and hence its materials are in English. Aline nonetheless decides to exploit its pedagogical potential, which she frames as a preparation for course selection in the upper grades of high school. She then reads the poster out loud, in simultaneous translation. However, she runs into trouble with the very first occupation, analytical chemist; she hesitates, corrects herself, and then goes on (lines 1–3). At line 9, Aline runs into trouble again, this time over 'forensic chemist'. Here she hesitates and paraphrases. Marcel provides the term in English in line 12, and Aline accepts it, since nobody seems to be able to find the translation, and carries on. Still, it is Marcel who has introduced the English onto the public floor, not Aline.

Example 13

10th grade *Sciences avancé*, 1991

→	1 Aline:	ok tu peux devenir um	*analytical chemist for a gas*
	2	*analytical* chimiste	*company you can become a*
	3	analytique pour une	*chemical engineer you can*
	4	compagnie d'essence tu peux	*become uh a salesperson for*

	5		devenir ingénieur chimique tu	*chemical products you can*
	6		peux devenir euh vendeur de	*work for Hydro-Ontario you*
	7		produits chimiques tu peux	*can work like the police*
	8		travailler pour Hydro-	*as a chemist uh*
→	9		Ontario tu peux travailler	
	10		comme les policiers comme	
	11		chimiste euh	
	12	Marcel:	*Forensic*	*forensic*
	13	Aline:	*forensic* ouais tu peux	*forensic yeah you can teach*
	14		enseigner tu peux euh	*you can uh*

In the last example, Lise is teaching a lesson on acronyms. She is trying to find acronyms students might have heard of, or that she herself knows. She comes up with IRA (Irish Republican Army), but then is stuck with the problem of having herself introduced English. She solves the problem by getting a student to say what IRA stands for, and then by soliciting a translation.

Example 14

10th grade *Français avancé*, 1991

	1	Lise:	okay on passe à la partie D.	*okay we go to part D.*
	2		Derrière le masque (pause)	*Behind the mask (pause)*
	3		problème, chacune des	*problem, each of the*
	4		phrases suivantes contient un	*following sentences contains*
	5		sigle un sigle c'est par	*an acronym an acronym is for*
	6		exemple PUMA c'est un sigle	*example PUMA is an acronym*
→	7		ou euh *IRA* c'est quoi	*or uh IRA what is*
	8		*IRA ? Ireland Irish*	*IRA? Ireland Irish*
	9	Male student:	*Republican Army*	*Republican Army*
→	10	Lise:	*army* le *IRA* en français ce	*army IRA in French that*
	11		serait quoi?	*would be what?*
	12	Male student:	l'armée républicaine de	l'armée républicaine de
			l'Irlande	l'Irlande

What we have here, then, is a set of examples which show how participants in the school setting represent their ideologies of language and of schooling, construct them in everyday life at school, and cope discursively with the contradictions between the ideal and the real. The discursive strategies in question build on modes of behaviour which are either functions of community-wide interactional conventions (as is the case for certain kinds of turn-taking, for example, or notions of multilingual politeness), or more specifically functions of cultural ideologies of schooling (such as serial turn-taking as a mark of order and respect, or Initiation–Response–Evaluation as the principal means of tracking learning). These discursive strategies allow participants to either remove contradictory behaviour and beliefs from areas of behaviour for which they are normally accountable, or to construct their own standpoint with respect to that behaviour in ways which remove from them, at least temporarily, the burden of accountability. The end result is that the dominant ideologies, which in turn represent certain sets of specific social and political interests, are reproducible in the school context.

4   Conclusion

What this set of examples shows is the multiple ways in which linguistic practices, indeed linguistic structures, are linked to socially and historically contingent ideologies. These ideologies in turn take two forms: linguistic ideologies, that is, notions people have about language and language practices (cf. Schieffelin 1997; Blommaert 1999); and social or political ideologies. In this case, certain kinds of Franco-Ontarians have a notion of the right kind of bilingualism as parallel monolingualisms, a notion which derives from the specific goals of francophone political mobilisation, and even more importantly from the political strategies adopted to achieve them. At the same time, the political dimensions of such ideologies meet institutional constraints and ideologies, in this case, those relating to the role of the school as an institution of social and cultural reproduction in which the values and practices of certain groups are valued over those of others.

In addition, we can see in these examples how people occupying certain social positions come to have vested interests in the maintenance of sets of linguistic practices, from which in one way or another they benefit. In the long run, those involved in the institution (in particular, teachers and other educators, administrators, and middle-class parents and their children) benefit from its existence, in part by virtue of the fact that it creates its own linguistic marketplace, and in part because it upholds the value of the linguistic resources they possess. Students who come to school from a different position end up being marginalised, in particular those whose class position does not afford them access to school-type French, and whose bilingual practices are of the wrong (that is, too mixed) kind.

The interactional patterns we have seen here have both local and long-term consequences. It has been easier here to show the local consequences than the longer-term ones; however, it is important to raise both as a way to return to the problem of social theory with which I began. The local consequences have to do with the construction of a discursive social space which, as I have said, permits the reproduction of a dominant ideology in the face of major contradictions. In addition, it positively evaluates behaviour conforming to the conventions in place, and devalues and marginalises deviant behaviour, in the immediate sense of blocking access to the floor. That is, it produces people who are silent, or even absent (who listen to their portable CD players instead of to the teacher, or who stay outside smoking instead of coming to class). These local consequences can then be linked to longer-term consequences precisely in terms of patterns of participation, and of moments of decision and evaluation. To do this, it is necessary to follow the experience of individuals, and to see how the interactional experiences in the here-and-now influence short-term decisions like cutting class or, conversely, handing in your homework on time, and longer-term decisions, like dropping out of school or applying to university. It is also necessary to follow the development of institutional practices and structures. In the case that concerns us here, this might include things like how students are directed to the advanced or general level, what kinds of students are recruited and admitted, how the school represents itself in public (for example, what kinds of photos it sends to the local French-language newspaper), or, at a higher institutional level, how the Ministry of Education handles Franco-Ontarian educational management, programming or other activities under its control or influence.

This kind of tracking is one way to operationalise Giddens' notion of linkages, that is, his idea that social structuration is a process consisting of ties among activities and among actors. These ties themselves have to be understood as processes in which resources are at stake and which have (often unforeseen and unforeseeable) consequences, not only for the direct participants, but also for those removed from them in both physical and social space and time. If Giddens is right, then it should be possible to identify empirically not only activities and actors, resources and consequences, but also the ties among them and the way in which those ties produce structuration. My attempt here has been modest and relatively local; it remains to be seen how far we can take such an approach. Nonetheless, my use of such an approach here has allowed me to unpack the workings of at least some dimensions of the construction of ideologies and categories in the realm of Franco-Ontarian life, and to link them to ideologies, institutions and practices related to bilingualism, to nation and State, and to school as an agency of social and cultural (re)production. I understood this as one step towards exploring the extent to which sociolinguistics can contribute to the construction of a social theory in which language is understood as a central component of social action. To do this opens up the possibility of developing a theory of language as social action, and a way of exploring what the nature of social action might actually be.

Notes

1. The research on which this paper is based was funded by the Social Sciences and Humanities Research Council of Canada and by the Ontario Ministry of Education Transfer Grant to the Ontario Institute for Studies in Education. I am grateful to the participants in the project, and to my research

assistants, for their invaluable contributions. The data has been presented elsewhere, in particular in Heller (1999). An earlier version of this paper was presented at the Cardiff Roundtable on Sociolinguistics and Social Theory in July 1997; many thanks to other Roundtable participants, and to the editors of this volume, for their comments.

2. Heller and Martin-Jones (2001) assemble a series of case studies of educational settings where similar problems of institutional and national ideology and language practice arise. However, the precise nature of the problem, and hence its local manifestations, vary according the sociohistorical conditions which prevail; for example, a number of the case studies deal with post-colonial settings where the former colonial language is used as language of instruction in schools where nobody speaks that language. The result tends to be a preference for teacher-dominated I–R–E formats and for codeswitching. While these strategies scaffold student participation, they perversely keep students at a distance from the kinds of linguistic competence they would need in order to do well in school and have access to membership in their societies' dominant groups.

3. All names have been changed.

4. Examples have been drawn from a number of different classes observed over the three-year fieldwork period. There was little difference over time; the major differences divided the symbolically-charged *Français* classes from others where the ideological pressure was lessened; and subject matter relying on outside-school knowledge, such as Science and Geography, from subjects which could be taught in a more self-contained way. Nonetheless, most of the patterns discussed here were widely observed.

References

Blommaert, Jan (ed.) (1999) *Language Ideological Debates*. Berlin, New York: Mouton de Gruyter.

Bourdieu, Pierre (1982) *Ce que parler veut dire*. Paris: Fayard.

Cicourel, Aaron (1978) Language and society: cognitive, cultural and linguistic aspects of language use. *Sozialwissenschaftliche Annalen* 2: 25–58.

Collins, Randall (1981) On the macro-foundations of micro-sociology. *American Journal of Sociology* 86(5): 984–1014.

Giddens, Anthony (1982) *The Constitution of Society*. Berkeley, Los Angeles: University of California Press.

Gumperz, John (1982) *Discourse Strategies*. Cambridge: Cambridge University Press.

Heller, Monica (1994) *Crosswords: Language, Education and Ethnicity in French Ontario*. Berlin: Mouton de Gruyter.

Heller, Monica in collaboration with Mark Campbell, Phyllis Dalley and Donna Patrick (1999) *Linguistic Minorities and Modernity: A Sociolinguistic Ethnography*. London: Longman.

Heller, Monica and Marilyn Martin-Jones (eds) (2001) *Voices of Authority: Education and Linguistic Difference.* Greenwich, CT: Elsevier.

Mehan, Hugh (1987) Language and power in organizational settings. *Discourse Processes* 10: 291–302.

Schieffelin, Bambi (ed.) (1997) *Language Ideologies.* Oxford: Oxford University Press.

9

The social categories of race and class: Language ideology and sociolinguistics[1]
Lesley Milroy

1   Introduction

This chapter discusses differences in contemporary attitudes to language between Britain and the United States. It considers some of the outcomes of these differences with respect both to public debates about language and to the way applied sociolinguists who attempt to combat the effects of negative language attitudes have traditionally set their research agendas. There appears to be considerable slippage between British and American uses of the apparently innocuous term 'standard English', and default understandings of 'non-standard English' are also different. In Britain, unless further specified, the term 'non-standard English' most frequently refers to urban vernaculars spoken by indigenous working class British people (as in Cheshire, Edwards and Whittle 1993), while in the United States the default referent is usually African American English (most famously in Labov's 1969 polemic 'The logic of nonstandard English'). Thus, non-standardness in the two countries appears to be primarily, but of course not exclusively, associated with different marginalised social groups.

Public approbation of standard English and criticisms of non-standard speakers are commonplace in both Britain and the United States, as is the belief that there is one and only one correct form of the language. It is this belief which Lippi-Green (1997), following Milroy and Milroy (1998 [1985]), has described as 'the standard language ideology', which in turn provides a rationale for language-based discrimination against marginalised social groups. However, the kind of public debates about language which are characteristically accompanied by widespread anxiety, panic and irrationality are framed rather differently in Britain and the United States, as scholars who find themselves in each others' countries are usually aware. Although it is tricky to specify the precise character of these differences, it is hard to imagine a long-running controversy in the United States with all the ingredients of the great grammar debate discussed by Cameron (1995: 78–115). Equally, it is hard to imagine the British press focussing over many years on an English Only movement or on whether British Black English should be used as the medium of initial instruction for native speakers of that dialect, as in the Ebonics debate; Pullum (1997) describes the extremely intemperate reaction of the American press to that proposal.

These contrasting public discourses are initially approached by looking at the ways the term 'standard English' is used with reference to a spoken norm, and language attitudes are then discussed as sociolinguistic outcomes of different histories and differentially naturalised social inequalities. Contemporary British and American language ideologies as instantiated in public discourses are exemplified and discussed in relation to this historical context. Finally it is suggested that the outcomes of these divergent national ideologies are evident not only in lay settings but in different scholarly approaches to issues of class, race and ethnicity in applied sociolinguistic research.

2 Class, race and ethnicity

In this chapter, my use and understanding of these key terms is in accordance with Giddens (1990: 205–73) who provides a well-balanced discussion of structures of inequality. *Class* is distinguished as one of four major types of stratification system which promote inequality in society. While the other three (*slavery*, *caste* and *estates*) depend on institutionally sanctioned inequalities, class divisions are not officially recognised, an individual's class position is to some extent achieved, and mobility is a characteristic of stratification by class. In much of the West class consciousness is strong and division of the population into upper, middle and lower classes is popularly accepted as a reasonable description of the stratification system. The major distinction drawn by Giddens between consensus and conflict theories of class (discussed in Milroy and Milroy 1992) is not relevant here.

Ethnic groups are formed by persons who share common cultural characteristics which are wholly learned, typically very early in life. These generally involve a sense of place and of a common history and destiny, a shared religion and culture and a shared language or set of communicative conventions. In practice, most discussions of ethnicity involve minority groups whose members are discriminated against by the majority population. Rampton's insistence on a flexible view of ethnicity is surely correct (1996 and this volume); like class boundaries, ethnic boundaries are non-essentialist and permeable. However, Rampton's criticisms of much sociolinguistic work which employs the concept of ethnicity are surely wide of the mark. The problem seems to be not that boundaries are viewed as hard, as it is difficult to see how they actually are viewed; but social variables generally, including ethnicity, are usually untheorised or undertheorised and used in whatever way is most convenient for the linguistic analytic purpose at hand.

Race is closely associated with ethnicity, in that it refers to physical characteristics which are treated as ethnically significant — most commonly skin colour — while *racism* refers to the false attribution of undesirable inherited characteristics to someone of a particular physical appearance. Giddens points out that the persistently problematic character of race relations in the United States can best be comprehended within an historical context, since from the earliest days the racist views of European colonists were more extreme with respect to the blacks who had been brought to the Americas as slaves than with respect to other non-Europeans, including native Americans. Linking the rise of racism in the New World with slavery and the early period of colonialism, he points out that 'ever since then racial conflicts and divisions have tended to have pride of place in ethnic conflicts as a whole. In particular, racist views separating "whites" from "blacks" became central in European attitudes' (Giddens 1990: 254). Cornel West (cited by Proulx, 1997: 10) vividly characterises the way in which this outcome subordinates other kinds of social divisions in the United States to divisions of race, a pattern which is relevant to the discussion which follows: 'Without the presence of black people in America, European Americans would not be "white" — they would be only Irish, Italians, Poles, Welsh and others engaged in class, ethnic and gender struggles over resources and identity'. Sugrue's (1996) extended analysis of race and inequality both in Detroit and in American 'rust belt' cities conceptualises class as a system which promotes inequality in capitalist societies. In the United States, the class system works along with long-standing patterns of racial segregation and discrimination so that inequality has a disproportionate impact on African Americans. An important distinction between the operation of class in the United States and Britain is the extent and effect of this interaction between race and class.

3   Some beliefs about standard English

Although the term is used a good deal, linguists do not agree on what constitutes standard English. I have suggested elsewhere (Milroy and Milroy 1998) that standardisation is best treated as a *process*, since attempts to locate a specific standard are by definition doomed to failure. Only a dead language can be fully standardised in the literal sense of removing variability, as happens when standardised systems of coinage, weights and measures, or electric plugs[2] are imposed. However, some linguistic channels and levels may be more successfully standardised than others, such that written language is more easily standardised than spoken, and morphological and syntactic systems more easily than phonological ones. It is precisely because phonology is particularly resistant to standardisation that some scholars (such as Trudgill 1991) argue that the spoken standard language is a type of dialect with a characteristic morphology and syntax like other dialects, but that there is no such thing as a standard accent. In this view, the standard is a prestigious system of grammar and lexis which can be realised with any phonology. However, in practice Received Pronunciation (sometimes called 'the Queen's English') is often treated not only by the general public, but also by some professional linguists, as a reference accent and described as 'standard English' (Smith 1996: 65). In the United States, so-called 'network American'[3] is often identified as standard English, although RP and network American are horses of a very different colour. Network American is a mainstream accent associated with the levelled dialects of the Northern Midwest, where salient locally marked features have been eradicated, so that they are commonly perceived as 'colourless' or 'characterless' (Wolfram 1991: 210). Speakers of such dialects commonly describe themselves and are described by others as having 'no accent' (Preston 1996; Lippi-Green 1997). In Britain, it seems to be RP speakers who are typically described in this way, although unlike network American, RP is saliently marked for class and in no sense is or ever has been a mainstream accent. So not only is the term 'standard' used in a generally unsystematic and inconsistent way when applied to speech (as noted by Smith, 1996: 65), but the confusion in Britain between an elite accent and a standard language ensures that it means something quite different in Britain and America.

Preston (1996) demonstrates that American linguists too are inconsistent in their views of the location of standard English in the United States, noting that often these views amount to no more than the individual's personal prejudice. Within the framework of 'folk linguistics' he investigates folk models of language — ordinary people's ideas of where the best variety of American English is spoken. Certainly there does not exist in America a focussed and identifiable reference accent corresponding to Received Pronunciation in Britain. Boston's Brahmin accent (described by Wolfram, 1991) is a high-status variety, but has never received the institutional support accorded to RP, nor its nation-wide geographical distribution.

Preston explores Americans' perceptions of distinctive speech areas in the US and of the 'pleasantness' and 'correctness' of the varieties thus delineated. A perception shared by Preston's informants is the unique status of the American South as a distinct linguistic and cultural area. One Carolina informant represented linguistic divisions in terms of the Civil War: south of a diagonal line running across the United States from North East to South West 'southerners' are to be found; elsewhere reside 'damn yankees'. A Michigan informant identified much the same area, but labelled it as 'Southern' with the pejorative description 'hill-billy' in parentheses. The Great

Lakes area was marked off with the legend 'midwestern English', described parenthetically as 'normal'.

While judgements such as this provide evidence of a shared perception of a neutral, levelled variety in the Northern Midwest, there was little agreement on a single locus of the most correct variety. For example, Southerners identified the Boston area of New England (presumably they had in mind the Brahmin accent) while Michigan speakers identified their own levelled variety as the most correct. However, agreement on the *least* correct variety was much more evident; judges from Michigan, Indiana and from the South itself all reported that this might be found in an area of the South (the geographical extent of which varied somewhat between judges) and in New York City. Thus, the standard of popular perception in the United States is apparently what is left behind when all the non-standard varieties spoken by disparaged persons are set aside. Besides Southerners and New Yorkers, Preston's informants mention Valley Girls, Hillbillies, African Americans, Mexican Americans and Cubans.

These judgements reveal negative attitudes to language quite different from those current in Britain. In America the urban dialects of industrial cities (apart from New York City) generally do not seem to be as stigmatised as the speech of the South, which is associated not only with an historic and divisive conflict but with rural poverty, low intelligence, and a poor standard of education. However, in Britain many separate investigations have confirmed that the most stigmatised varieties of English are those spoken by the working-class population of industrial cities, particularly Glasgow, Birmingham, Liverpool and London (Giles and Powesland 1975; Honey 1989: 51–78; Giles and Coupland 1991).

4   An historical perspective on language attitudes

Since not only ideas of what constitutes standard English, but also the character of linguistic prejudices, are somewhat different in Britain and America, this section explores these differences in relation to different national histories. Giddens (1989: 256) notes that ethnic relations in different countries vary according to different patterns of historical development, and in keeping with his observation, Chambers (1995: 58) and Baugh (1996: 711) have pointed out that greater mobility in New World immigrant countries and the absence of the strongly hierarchical social organisation characteristic of older nations are likely to give rise to different sociolinguistic consequences. Chambers associates the development of a mainstream levelled variety across a wide geographical territory with this pattern of mobility, and Baugh associates the development of a particularly American pattern of linguistic prejudice especially with early colonial social organisation.

In Britain on the other hand, there is an historic association, explicitly rejected in eighteenth-century America, between standard English and high-status speakers. The variety spoken at the royal court was recommended as early as the sixteenth century as the 'best' English, and during the seventeenth century the speech of London or that of the Universities of Oxford and Cambridge is commonly singled out as a model (Smith 1996). The emergence of prescriptivism in its modern form is associated with the activities of eighteenth-century scholars, grammarians and dictionary writers. Important later developments in Britain were the emergence from about 1870 of Received Pronunciation as a class accent, explicitly taught in the public schools (i.e. a network of elite private schools), and the stigmatisation of English urban dialects, apparently from the early twentieth century (see Wyld 1934; Abercrombie 1965; Honey 1989). This development coincided with a period of particularly bitter class conflict in Britain, as described by Crowley (1989: 209ff). More recently, the levelled variety popularly known as 'Estuary English' has apparently extended both geographically (to oust locally marked varieties in a very large area of south-eastern England) and socially in that it is now used by upper-class speakers (see further below). This change in British sociolinguistic structure may be interpreted as reflecting current patterns of mobility following deindustrialisation and the end of the century-long monopolisation of the linguistic market by RP.

In contrast with Britain, we find that in early twentieth-century America the group whose language is particularly stigmatised is not an urban proletariat speaking varieties of English rooted in historically established dialects, but immigrants who are speakers of languages other than English. Here is Theodore Roosevelt's frequently-cited reaction to these groups at a time of massive immigration into America from central Europe:

> we have room but for one language here and that is the English language, for we intend to see that the crucible turns our people out as Americans, of American nationality, and not as dwellers in a polyglot boarding house. (Crawford 1992: 100)

As Crawford notes, Roosevelt's rhetoric is similar to that of the contemporary English Only movement. However, before the nineteenth century, national multilingualism and personal bilingualism were generally accepted in the United States, for several compelling reasons. First, there are two colonial languages other than English in the United States, Spanish having been spoken in the South West and Florida for more than 400 years, and antedating English in these areas. French was spoken in the eastern regions formerly held and populated by the French and is still spoken in parts of the North East and the South. Second, early colonists encountered a large number of indigenous American languages, and finally the large German population of the United States has a particularly long history of effective mother tongue maintenance supported by an institutional underpinning of churches, schools and colleges. Evidence abounds of ready acceptance of multilingualism by members of the first Continental Congress, and of an enlightened priority to spread learning regardless of the scholar's native tongue, exemplified by Benjamin Rush's assertion that 'a man who is learned in the dialect of a Mohawk Indian is more fit for a legislator than a man who is ignorant even in the language of the early Greeks' (cited by Heath, 1992: 23).

Several different discourses can be distinguished in the eighteenth century, as shown by the readings collected by Crawford (1992). Some promoted English as a national language, although not (as it later became) as a symbol of national loyalty and American values. John Adams proposed a language academy '. . . instituted by the authority of Congress, for correcting, improving, and fixing the English language [which] would strike all the World with Admiration and Great Britain with Envy'. (Quoted by Heath 1992: 27.) Since this initiative did not appeal to Americans who wanted to create a state free of the elitism of European monarchies and aristocracies, a rather different kind of thinking promoted the ideal of a classless form of the English language, known as 'Federal English' (Barron 1992). In 1789 Noah Webster argued that it was in the nation's interest to foster the continued divergence of American and British English, and to this end he compiled not only his famous dictionary with its new spelling system, but numerous English language textbooks.

A number of developments in nineteenth-century America appear to have given rise to a political climate where multilingualism became viewed less tolerantly and a philosophy of Anglo-conformity was able to surface. The Gold Rush attracted a wave of Chinese immigrants to the west who inspired violent xenophobia; the annexation in 1848 of the Mexican territories of the South West forced under American rule a large Spanish-speaking population who had been established in the region since the mid sixteenth century. Although the Treaty of Hidalgo was intended to protect their political, civil, linguistic and religious rights, a massive increase in the English-speaking population created a Spanish-speaking minority and transformed the Mexican–Spanish–Indian lifestyle of the region. The resultant cultural conflict produced a series of laws which discriminated against Mexican-American language and culture and affects Mexican-Americans to this day. In 1878 California became the first English Only state; official proceedings were restricted to English and guarantees for Spanish language publications agreed at the treaty of Hidalgo were eliminated.

Nor did the Native American population fare any better in the climate of fear, intolerance and repression accompanying the conquest of the West. The following is an extract from the 1887 annual report of the commissioner for Indian affairs, J.D.C. Atkins:

> Schools should be established which children should be required to attend; their barbarous dialects should be blotted out and the English language substituted. . . . the object of greatest solicitude should be to break down

the prejudices of tribe among the Indians; to blot out the boundary lines which divide them into distinct nations, and fuse them into one homogeneous mass. Uniformity of language will do this. Nothing else will. . . . It is also believed that teaching an Indian youth in his own barbarous dialect is a positive detriment to him. The first step to be taken towards civilisation, towards teaching the Indians the mischief and folly of continuing in their barbarous practices is to teach them the English language. (Atkins 1887: cited by Crawford 1992: 48)

One effect of the cruel policy recommended here was that after years at school children could neither find employment and assimilate to the white mainstream nor find a place in their home communities. Thus, in the late nineteenth century not only the Spanish-speaking population of the South West but also the indigenous population of a previously multilingual United States became victims of a severe and subtle form of discrimination which set them up not only for an invidious sense of inferiority about their own language and culture, but for educational failure and disadvantage in the employment market (Crawford 1992: 323).

Atkins's remarks contrast sharply with those of Rush a century earlier. Furthermore, for Rush language was politically neutral, a means of spreading learning and democratic principles, while by Atkins's time a language ideology had developed such that American egalitarian, democratic ideals and generally proper and civilised behaviour were associated with English monolingualism. This thinking remains evident in the discourse of present-day English Only activists, who see bilingualism both as a social and personal stigma and as a threat to the cohesion of the state.

A further development shaping Anglo-conformist attitudes was the massive surge in immigration from Central and Eastern Europe around the turn of the century as an industrialised capitalist economy developed, and the elaborate class distinctions of Britain are rather different from those which emerged at that time in the industrial north of the United States. According to Rogers and Wilenz (1991), terminology such as 'labor', 'capital', 'working class', 'middle class' became used less and less as Southern black migration to northern cities also began. Successive waves of immigrants formed a new hierarchy, each new wave occupying the lowest position in society. Evaluatively loaded names for racial categories proliferated: *slav*, *hunkie*, *teuton*, *paddy*, *dago*, *polack* and so forth, and a taxonomy of race developed which might be considered parallel to the British taxonomy of class. The manner in which the American analogue to Booth's (1892) classic work on class in London was carried out shows clearly the contrast between American and British social preoccupations around the turn of the century. Booth surveyed working-class London using a set of simple class taxonomies, half above and half below the poverty line. In 1907 the Russell Sage Foundation carried out a survey of Pittsburgh modelled on Booth, but gave up any attempt to impose his categories, settling instead for a number of 'racial studies'. Only in the 1920s with free immigration at an end were attempts made by the Census Bureau, following the English model, to express inequality in terms of a careful gradation of classes (Marwick 1980; Rogers and Wilenz 1991: 249). On the other hand widespread race consciousness and conflict seems to be a relatively recent feature of British life, erupting only in the years following extensive post-World War Two immigration from former colonies. At this point, many immigrants constituted a new, lower social class (Giddens 1989).

Probably the most stigmatised language variety of all in the United States is African American Vernacular English — effectively a working-class Black variety. Both negative attitudes to the variety and the continuing and amply documented discrimination experienced by African Americans whether or not they are AAVE speakers appear, as Giddens notes, to be rooted in the earliest days of colonisation and slavery. Rogers and Wilenz (1991) comment on the interaction in the early American vocabulary of social description between racial categories and class or rank categories. Delegates to the first Continental Congress followed the British practice of labelling social categories as 'sorts': 'the better sort' (that is, the rich), 'the middling sort' and 'the lower sort' (the poor). The fourth category, often obscured as an embarrassment to those creating a model democratic state, was 'Negro slaves'. The Southern slave-holding elite in the pre-Civil War period operated also with a four-tier social system: gentlemen, common planters, white servants and 'negroes' 'so rarely free that the slave relation was on most occasions subsumed in the language of race'. Even after emancipation, this pattern did not change, although for a short period into the 1870s African Americans had the vote and elected national representatives. Heavy immigration to northern cities between 1880 and 1920 gave rise to conflicts for dominance between immigrant groups and older elites, and to labour conflicts which had the effect of crowding out democratic ideals of equal rights in both north and south. African Americans were powerless against 'the tide of reaction which would leave them trapped in chronic poverty, segregation and disenfranchisement' (Rogers and Wilenz 1991: 257).

This brief historical sketch expands somewhat on Chambers's and Baugh's discussion of the different sociolinguistic outcomes of the different histories and social structures of the New and Old Worlds. Particularly, early Americans sought to avoid the inequalities associated with European monarchical societies which gave rise to a class-related concept of the best language, and to develop instead a democratic kind of common language. In the nineteenth century, following the Mexican and Indian wars, the development of the West and the mass migration of African Americans along with large numbers of European immigrants to the industrialised north, inequality was overwhelmingly manifested not in terms of a traditional class structure as in Britain, but in terms of racial and other ethnic divisions. The class system promoted inequality so that African Americans in particular were disproportionately disadvantaged.

5   Language ideology

We turn now to consider a substantial but very varied literature which has emerged over the last ten years or so and which attempts to relate the standard language ideology to large-scale social and political institutions. Lippi-Green discusses ideology more generally — that is, not exclusively in relation to language — with a framework developed by Bourdieu (1991), Gramsci (1985), Foucault (1984) and Eagleton (1991). Ideologies are similar to D'Andrade's (1987) cultural models, discussed by Niedzielski and Preston (1999: 302–324), which are widely-shared beliefs and assumptions about the world. These beliefs and assumptions are treated as if they are obvious facts ('common sense') and are extremely resistant to rational debate. Lippi-Green notes (1997: 64) that ideology entails:

> the promotion of the needs and interests of a dominant group or class at the expense of marginalized groups, by means of disinformation and mis-representation of these non-dominant groups

While there are many possible approaches to ideology, this is the one which we shall adopt here as it fits in well with the standard language ideology, which indeed has the effect of promoting the interests of one group and marginalising those of another. As Lippi-Green notes, the standard language ideology involves the following:

> a bias towards an abstracted, idealized homogeneous spoken language which is imposed and maintained by dominant bloc institutions and which names as its model the written language, but is drawn primarily from the spoken language of the upper middle class. (1997: 64)

Within an explicit framework of ideological analysis, researchers have attempted to explain the processes which allow, without public protest or debate, the language of the least politically and economically powerful social groups to be stigmatised as 'bad', 'incomprehensible', 'sloppy' and worse, and the consent of low-status speakers to these evaluations to be manufac-tured. In Eagleton's memorable phrase (1991: xiii–xiv), 'The study of ideo-logy is . . . an inquiry into the ways in which people may come to invest in their own unhappiness'. Lippi-Green (1997) considers the role of institu-tions in the United States such as the media, the courts, the educational system and the workplace in promoting the standard language ideology and in marginalising the interests of particular social groups. Widespread lan-guage attitudes which are assumed to be nothing more or less than common sense represent the naturalisation of such ideology.

In their review of a very varied interdisciplinary literature, Woolard and Schieffelin note (1994: 62) that negative evaluation of the language of specific social groups ('symbolic revalorisation') 'often makes discrimination on linguistic grounds publicly acceptable, whereas corresponding ethnic or racial discrimination is not'. This is a point also made by Milroy and Milroy (1998), by Lippi-Green (1997) and by Fairclough (1992); Fairclough in particular argues that language is the primary site of social conflict and discrimination, rather than one of several social traits for which individuals suffer discrimination. In the United States as in Britain, evidence can readily be culled from newspaper reports and television programmes, from courtrooms and classrooms, that such legitimised discrimination provides a useful resource for gatekeepers who wish to restrict access to goods and influence, thus affecting people's lives in many domains, both informal and institutional. To highlight the rather different flavours of British and American standard language ideologies, two examples are presented here, taken respectively from a British magazine article and a popular American television show. The feature article 'Can your accent blight your life?' (*Bella*, 24 January 1996) describes the experiences of Helen, a Manchester woman who moved to London in search of employment : '... "in the arts where no-one has a regional accent ... my CV was good enough to get me interviews, but ... as soon as they heard me speak ... I wasn't taken seriously" ... and when Helen finally landed a job with a community theatre project in Islington, North London, she was told she'd only been selected because the area would benefit from a common touch'. Helen meets with similar reactions in casual interpersonal encounters: 'People can't see further than my voice and assume I'm aggressive and common. They think I should own pigeons and have an outside toilet.'

Consider the contrast provided by comments taken from a 1987 WLS-TV screening of the Oprah Winfrey Show, where both studio audience and telephone callers contributed on the topic of African American Vernacular English:[4]

Example 1

2nd caller: Hi, Oprah?
Winfrey: Yes.
2nd caller: I guess what I'd like to say is that what makes me feel that blacks tend to be ignorant is that they fail to see that the word is spelled A-S-K, not A-X. And when they say aksed, it gives the sentence an entirely different meaning. And this is what I feel holds blacks back.
Winfrey: Why does it give it a different meaning if you know that's what they're saying?
2nd caller: But you don't always know that's what they are saying.

Example 2

9th audience member: The problem seems to be that everybody tries to push something down your throat by arrogance. That's not the way to get something done. You could speak your own language, you could have your own way, but don't force someone else to have to suffer and listen to it.

Winfrey: You say what?
10th audience member: Well I'm an accountant and —
Winfrey: Well, wait, wait, let me get back to you. What is causing you to suffer?
9th audience member: Well I think there is a certain way of speaking that has been considered the acceptable way of speaking. And because of that this is the type of language you speak when you're out in the world. If you want to speak Spanish at home that's fine. If you want to speak black with your friends that's fine. But don't insult someone else's ears by making them listen to it.

The comments reported in the *Bella* magazine covertly articulate class prejudice, as is clear from the expressions 'common touch', 'aggressive and common' and the reference to pigeons and outside toilets which stereotypically characterise northern English working-class lifestyles. Some of the comments phoned in to Oprah Winfrey are presented as tolerant of an 'appropriate' variability, such as the ninth audience member's second contribution (but see Fairclough 1992 on the ideological nature of 'appropriateness'). For the most part, however, it is clear that the contributions in Examples 1 and 2 covertly articulate racial prejudice. Lippi-Green (1994) has demonstrated that such covert discrimination is sanctioned even by the legal system; while employers are no longer able to implement overt racial discrimination in hiring and firing, demonstrably implausible linguistic claims that particular ethnic minority speakers are unintelligible (much as in Example 1 above), continue (as, *mutatis mutandis*, in Britain) to provide a publicly legitimised route to discrimination against disfavoured social groups. Woolard (1989: 89) has commented on the strong and 'visceral' nature of language attitudes. We shall look further at some public comments on language which suggest that in Britain, strong gut reactions typically respond to class-related stereotypes, while in the United States they are overwhelmingly associated with race and ethnicity. Clearly, the documentation by Roberts, Davies and Jupp (1992) of language-based discrimination suffered by ethnic minorities in the British workplace shows that we cannot simplistically associate racial discrimination with America and class discrimination with Britain. Nevertheless, the characteristic public discourses in the two countries which instantiate discriminatory language ideologies are very different, and it is these differences which I highlight here.

In America, distasteful public disparagement of African American English is commonplace and often openly racist: consider for example the title of Morse's (1973) article ('The shuffling speech of slavery: Black English') which appeared in a scholarly journal, and the comments of the journalist John Simon:

> As for 'I be', 'you be', 'he be', etc. which should give us all the heebie-jeebies, these may indeed be comprehensible, but they go against all accepted classical and modern grammars and are the product not of a language with roots in history but of ignorance of how language works. (Quoted by Pinker (1994: 385))

Like many such self-opinionated commentators, Simon is inaccurate; African American English is deeply rooted in history, as these forms of the verb BE are directly traceable to (pre-Norman Conquest) Old English. However, the closest British parallel to such unpleasant and nonsensical rhetoric is to be found in response not to British Black English, but to urban working-class or lower middle-class dialects. For while London Jamaican creole is certainly stigmatised, it is not as severely or consistently disparaged as the urban dialects of Liverpool, London, Birmingham and Glasgow (Honey 1989: 51ff). Consider also Wyld's scathing comments (1934: 613–14) on the levelled accents of English cities ('Modified Standards'):

It is urged however, that to introduce provincial sounds into what is intended to be Standard English, addressed to educated people, is distressing and distracting. For the various forms of Modified Standard of towns which reflect class influence, and are of the nature of plain vulgarisms, there is little to be said except in dispraise.

In the United States, 'foreign accents' seem also to be more subject to negative evaluation than in Britain, unless associated with prestigious social groups. Spanish is viewed with particular disfavour (see Example 2 above), as are Asian-accented Englishes (see further Lippi-Green 1997). Such hostile public discourse both underpins and is supported by a fierce and long-standing political conflict, most clearly visible in the so-called 'English Only' movement.

The lobbying effort known as 'US English' emerged in the early 1980s and has remained active, although its precise objectives are unclear. Broadly speaking, it opposes the use at all official levels of languages other than English. Although it originated as and remains essentially an anti-Hispanic, anti-immigrant coalition, it is hostile also to official educational provision for the needs of AAVE-speaking children, as shown by its interventions in the Ebonics debate, which became particularly heated in January 1997. Associated with right-wing political groups, US English has an extremely high public profile, characteristically eliciting and expressing intemperately strong, irrational and polarised reactions. Crawford (1992) provides a useful source book of contributions to both sides of the debate ranging over more than 200 years. Noting the prominence of language policy as an internal issue for the first time in American history in the years following the emergence of US English, Fishman (1992: 166) identifies the English Only movement as uniquely and characteristically American:

No similar legislative effort to redress the internal insults to English, real or imaginary, have surfaced in any other core countries of English, such as England, Australia or New Zealand, all of which have substantial non-English-mother-tongue populations of their own. The general view toward non-English languages in governmental use in these countries is quite benevolent and even supportive in ways undreamt of here.

While this is an overestimate of the level of government benevolence towards minorities in these countries, in Britain at least the language rights of ethnic minorities seldom emerge as a major public issue. However, the legitimacy and acceptability of indigenous British non-standard dialects elicits strong and irrational reactions (see Example 5 below) comparable to discourse on AAE and Spanish in the United States. Linguistic prejudice thus surfaces with quite characteristically different national ambiences. The characteristic British concern with class quite overtly underpins public reactions to so-called 'Estuary English', a variety which is currently spreading both socially and geographically most probably as a reflex of Britain's changing mobility patterns and class structure (see Dorling 1995). For example, the following newspaper headlines are drawn from a wide selection of comparable comments on a topic which received particularly extensive media exposure between 1994 and 1996, following reports of Kerswill and William's work on the emergence of a 'new' dialect in young Milton Keynes speakers (see Kerswill 1996). It is noticeable that these accounts usually focus on phonological details, sometimes treating RP explicitly as a reference accent:

Example 3

Between Cockney and the Queen: 'Estuary English' describes the speech of a growing number of Britons. Poised between RP and Bow Bells it minds its 'p's and 'q's but drops its 't's.' *Sunday Times* (Wordpower Supplement), 28 March 1993.

Example 4

'Britain's crumbling ruling class is losing the accent of authority... the upper-class young already talk Estuary English, the cockneyfied accent of the South-east'. (Neal Ascherson, *Independent on Sunday*, 7 August 1994)

Example 5

Pity the young who converse only in Oik (Peter Tory, *International Express*, Sunday, 7 August, 1994)

Offering intemperately phrased and implausible objections similar in tone to those expressed above by Simon with reference to African American English, Tory writes:

> According to Reading University, this repellent sub-world speech is originating in Milton Keynes . . . All sorts gather there from every corner of the land, most of them making a career out of soldering on microchips and have produced, from dozens of once respectable dialects, a hellish, slowspreading universal yob-tongue.

The focus on class emerges particularly clearly in Bradbury's (1994) description of Estuary English as 'the classless argot'. In reponse to his own question 'Is there today a standard English?' he offers an answer:

> Estuary English, sometimes called Milton Keynes English, seems to be bidding for the position. It seems to have been learnt in the back of London taxis, or from alternative comedians. It's southern, urban, glottal, easygoing, offhand, vernacular. It's apparently classless, or at any rate a language for talking easily across classes. The Princess of Wales is supposed to speak it: graduates cultivate it, presumably to improve their 'street-credibility'.

Interestingly, Bradbury goes on to suggest that the 'classless argot' may be comparable to the English used by American fiction writers: 'Contemporary American fiction . . . is often admired for its vernacular tone and the easy flow of its speech, which is said to compare well with the "literary" language in which the British write many of their novels'. Although Bradbury's discussion is loosely framed, he seems here to be sensitive to the emergence of a relatively socially unmarked levelled variety in Britain, similar to the mainstream American variety which, as we noted earlier, is often described there as the standard language.

The contrasting attitudes underlying these ideologies are neatly summarised by the observation of Patricia Williams, an American lawyer and 1997 BBC Reith Lecturer, that 'The United States deems itself classless with almost the same degree of self-congratulation that Britain prides itself as being free of racial animus' (Karpf 1997). While in fact race and class are demonstrably both socially divisive, and moreover are generally interacting social categories, the greater divisiveness of race in America is suggested by the very much lower interracial marriage rate in the United States, noted by Karpf. To draw this comparison between the US and Britain does not deny the existence of racism in Britain, or of class-prejudice in the United States, where class may be said to be mediated by race; Sugrue (1996) conceptualises the operation of class as a system for promoting inequality in American cities as a complex interaction with long-standing structures of racial segregation so that 'African Americans have disproportionately borne the impact of that inequality' (1996: 5). The consequent contrast between the British and American situations can be illustrated by an adaptation of Haugen's image of the sociolinguistic hierarchy as a layer cake (1992 [1972]: 407). The monarchy and aristocracy constitute an elaborate, visually striking and rather heavy topping on the British cake, which is also rather taller and less broad-based than the American one, narrowing sharply in the upper layers. In both countries, the upper layers are formed by relatively standardised speakers, with successive layers below of rejected and disparaged social groups. But as the knife reaches the lower layers, another difference becomes apparent; in Britain the lowest layer arguably is constituted by speakers of stigmatised urban dialects, and in the United States African American and perhaps some Spanish speakers. These differences in the constitution of the respective national cakes, particularly at the top and the bottom, give rise to the stereotypical perception that the United States is classless and Britain free of racial animus.

In the following sections, historical, social and political factors are identified which underlie these contrasting national sociolinguistic structures and language ideologies.

6   Applied sociolinguistic research in Britain and America

The response of linguists when faced with evidence of language discrimination is generally to state what Lippi-Green (1997: 7) has described as 'the linguistic facts of life'. This involves the assertion of quite uncontroversial (to linguists) principles such as the equality of all languages as linguistic systems; the social nature of beliefs about correctness; the complexity of grammars (as cognitive constructs or as descriptive statements); the arbitrary nature of prescriptions and the inadequacy of prescriptive grammars; the intrinsic variability of language and the inevitability of linguistic change which renders the identification or existence of a single correct variety of English an impossibility. A recent and excellent example of a comprehensive popular work which deals with language prejudice in this way is Pinker (1994). Pullum (1997) and Rickford (1997) contributed to the Ebonics debate with short but linguistically sophisticated contributions in this general tradition.

Sociolinguists generally develop their responses to language discrimination further by describing the social functions of language in relation to its patterned variability. Typically, they associate variability with such constructs as class, gender, ethnicity, and style and point out that attempts to compel all speakers to adopt a single variety are doomed to failure. Lippi-Green, who sets up a framework like this prior to her discussion of language discrimination in the United States, points out that they generally stop short of considering the wider ideological implications of the standard language ideology. Fairclough (1992) suggests that (what he sees as) this limited account constitutes covert prescriptivism in that the sociolinguistic order is misleadingly represented as stable and consensual, when it is the chief domain of hegemonic struggle. Cameron (1995: 115) makes a different and very relevant criticism — that sociolinguists' contributions to the great grammar debate of the eighties and nineties in Britain had little effect because they dealt with language prejudice by arguing about the nature of language rather than tackling the underlying symbolism which drove the debate; the link between grammar and orderliness. In this she is undoubtedly correct; whether or not we accept that cultural models such as the standard language ideology function chiefly to serve the interests of dominant groups and to marginalise subordinate groups, we surely need to accept that the regular patterns of language variation uncovered by sociolinguists are tangential to understanding their power as a widely-held belief system, with considerable social ramifications.

In the remainder of this chapter, we examine the work of a number of sociolinguists which is intended to be of direct practical relevance, usually to educational issues, and also to combat prescriptivism and language prejudice. I shall try to show that distinctive traditions of such applied research in Britain and America also instantiate the patterns of negative evaluation contrasted throughout this chapter. For although British and American linguists with similar applied research interests are often aware of some slippage as they ponder what seem to be comparable research agendas, I am not aware of any discussion in print of the subtle but quite perceptible differences between these agendas. What seems to happen is this. In the United States, applied work on language discrimination overwhelmingly addresses either discrimination against speakers of languages other than English (usually Spanish speakers), or speakers of African American Vernacular English. Although she does not explicitly state such a bias, this is the orientation of Lippi-Green (1997: 104–133) in her chapter on language discrimination in the educational system, and the orientation also of the work she reviews there. It is the orientation of Labov's (1972) applied work, and much of Wolfram's (see Wolfram 1998). Work has certainly been carried out in the United States on issues of language prejudice against speakers of non-standard English dialects (see for example Wolfram and Christian 1980) but it is much harder to find than work on AAVE and Spanish speakers.

In Britain on the other hand, applied work on language discrimination has long focussed chiefly, but again not exclusively, on discrimination against non-standard speakers of British English, particularly in the classroom; Halliday, McIntosh and Strevens (1964) are an early example. Much subsequent British research explores the links between social class and educational success or failure. Sociolinguists in particular have often attempted to counter linguistic discrimination in the classroom by stressing the linguistic, but not the social, equality of all dialects, and recommending tolerance of a child's home accent or dialect, particularly while she is taught to read and write standard English. Amongst the considerable volume of work in this tradition are Trudgill (1975); Cheshire, Edwards, Muensterman and Weltens (1989) where the issue is discussed with reference to a number of European countries; Edwards (1979) who adopts a social psychological approach; Cheshire and Edwards (1993); Cheshire and Milroy (1993).

Macaulay's (1977) account of language and class in Glasgow is designed also to address educational issues, and shows particularly clearly the accuracy with which accent and dialect in Britain indexes class (represented in this work by occupation) and how linguistic discrimination is rationalised by gatekeepers. Comments by employers, school-teachers and college lecturers reveal a sharp disjunction between overt sympathy with disadvantaged people in Glasgow, and an equally overt stigmatisation of working-class Glasgow speech. Macaulay reports a perceived distinction between 'dialect' (which is positively evaluated) and 'sloppy' speech — a distinction which, interestingly, was not reported by Preston who collected numerous folk-linguistic comments in the United States. We saw earlier that urban dialects in the United States are not especially stigmatised as a set, although they are in Britain. It seems likely that the dialect/sloppy speech dichotomy reflects a negative attitude specifically to urban dialects, which are characteristically sharply stratified by class and characteristically undergo rapid change.[5] Such change may well be the stimulus for the judgement of sloppiness; recall Tory's distinction in Example 5 above between 'respectable dialects' and the 'yob-tongue' of Milton Keynes.

During the period of rapid political and social change in Britain during the 1980s and early 1990s, public debate focussed particularly sharply on language, and much recent work emphasises the overtly political and ideological character of this debate, which concerned the place of standard English in a national curriculum (Stubbs 1989; Cameron 1995). Two major government reports appeared in 1988 (the Kingman Report) and 1989 (the Cox Report). Stubbs (1989) remarks on the contrast between their thoughtful and balanced recommendations and public and political comment on language issues. For example, as discussed by Cameron (1995) and Milroy and Milroy (1998), prominent national figures such as the Prince of Wales and the Conservative Cabinet Minister Norman Tebbit link decline in teaching of grammar with falling standards generally and with a more general anarchy and decline in morality, a theme familiar in the history of linguistic complaints.

Although the Kingman and Cox reports have been criticised for their Anglo-centricity and their neglect of the needs of non-native speakers of English (Cameron and Bourne 1989), in this orientation they reflect a perception, rightly or wrongly, that non-standard indigenous speakers of English are the main group in need of adequate educational provision. Although linguistic discrimination on the basis of race or ethnicity of speaker is certainly discussed in Britain, it is simply not such a political hot potato there as in the United States, nor is it the traditional priority of applied sociolinguists. Notable exceptions include the work of Edwards (1979) on the West Indian language issue in schools; the work on bilingualism and language mixing in British, European and American classrooms surveyed by Martin-Jones (1995); the work of Roberts et al. (1992) who document language discrimination in the workplace. Perhaps significantly, Roberts and her colleagues are following a tradition developed by John Gumperz, an American sociolinguist.

In the United States on the other hand, the groups most seen to be in need of special provision are overwhelmingly African American English speakers or Spanish speakers of English as a second language. And as we have noted, politically loaded controversies focus on these groups. Crawford

(1992) presents a number of readings dealing with bilingual educational provision. Major scholars like Dennis Barron and Charles Fillmore became involved in the Ebonics debate[6] of 1997 in much the same way as their British counterparts became involved in the British debate on grammar teaching described by Cameron. The contributions of Rickford (1997) and Pullum (1997) have already been noted. On the other hand, research on dialects of American English and attitudes to those dialects (exemplified most influentially by Preston 1989; 1996) does not appear to feed directly into politically sensitive language and education issues as does the work of social dialectologists in Britain who work on indigenous British dialects.

We see the same contrast between Lippi-Green's (1997) study of language discrimination in the United States and Milroy and Milroy's (1998) discussion of linguistic prescriptivism and its effects. The latter, which in an earlier edition stimulated Lippi-Green's study, is written from a British perspective and framed primarily in terms of status and class issues. Lippi-Green however deals almost entirely with issues associated with race and ethnicity. In short, the general research emphasis in each country tends to erase less socio-politically salient structures of inequality, an erasure which is apparently thoroughly naturalised. Without overt acknowledgement, researchers seem to respond to the political agendas in their respective countries, and indeed interventions of American politicians on language and race issues are comparable to those of British politicians in the distinctively British debate (see Crawford 1992 for many examples). Particularly striking is the similarity of the right-wing British Conservative Honey's (1983; 1998) criticisms of linguists and educationalists to those of the American Republican Huddleston (1992 [1985]). Both oppose special educational provision while adopting a supportive posture to the disadvantaged group in question; Honey suggests that a tolerant attitude towards the use of non-standard dialects (he also includes British Black English speakers) is likely to block the social mobility of non-standard speakers, while Huddleston (1992: 117) presents similar arguments to support his opposition of policies which are tolerant of bilingualism:

> In essence, what a policy of bilingualism–biculturalism does is to segregate minorities from the mainstream of our politics, economy and society because we are not making it possible for them to freely enter that mainstream. We are pushing them aside into their own communities and we are denying them the tools with which to break out.

The effect on sociolinguist research agendas of these somewhat differently slanted ideologies is particularly evident in British and American responses to the early work (1972–75) on language and class of the British educational sociologist Basil Bernstein. Bernstein developed a distinction between an elaborated and a restricted linguistic code, associating the latter particularly with working-class speakers. The differences in expressive language preferences which the codes characterise are said by Bernstein to arise from culture-specific socialisation patterns (not, it should be noted, deficits). The restricted code is fairly consistently described as implicit, particularistic and context-bound, in the sense that speakers rely more upon the immediate context to express meanings. The elaborated code on the other hand was said to be explicit, universalistic and context-free. Bernstein relates preference for a particular code to class-related, culturally different modes of social control, and ultimately different underlying symbolic systems. A number of researchers have suggested that he seems to be describing differences between informal spoken language and the formal spoken styles which are also parasitic upon written discourse (see further Milroy and Milroy 1998: Ch.7; Finnegan and Biber 1994). Bernstein has complained that his ideas have been misapplied and misunderstood, and indeed, as Labov (1969) has pointed out, their capacity to support language prejudice has led to their being filtered through strongly entrenched and institutionally supported belief systems.

Although this is probably an important reason for the impact of Bernstein's work on applied sociolinguistics — almost invariably, sociolinguists have been sharply critical of codes theory — it has been interpreted quite differently in Britain and the United States, along fairly predictable lines. During the sixties and seventies particularly, Bernstein's theories were extremely influential in British teacher training programmes, educational failure being 'explained' with reference to the unavailability of an elaborated code to working-class speakers. In the United States however educators and legislators were developing during the 1960s bilingual education programs in response to concern at the chronic underachievement of Spanish-speaking children, who had previously been exposed to the brutal sink or swim philosophy — that is, forced to learn in a language which they did not understand (Cardenas 1992: 343). In a political climate strongly affected by race riots and the civil rights movement, William Labov was around the same time carrying out his major research on Black English during a period of official concern at the educational underachievement of African American children. Labov (1969; 1972) argued strongly against those who attributed reading problems and a high drop-out rate from school to either the language or the cultural environment of African American speakers, both being seen in some unclearly specified way as deficient. His counter-argument, with which few sociolinguists would disagree, was that Black English was deficient in relation to Standard English if viewed through the filter of white middle-class prejudice, but not as a linguistic system different from and independent of standard English. This so-called deficit/difference controversy was a live one for many years in educational circles (for a review see Edwards 1979). Labov pointed out that language tests routinely used by educational psychologists were constructed on the basis of a set of invalid assumptions about the nature of language. In fact these certainly instantiated a standard language ideology in a situation of long-term racial conflict. But as well as rounding on the American educational psychologists responsible for these tests, Labov interpreted Bernstein's codes theory in terms of the deficit position, which he also viewed as racist. Bernstein and his many admirers (including the British linguist Halliday whose liberal credentials as an early advocate of linguistic equality in the classroom were impeccable) took understandable exception to an implicit accusation of racist overtones in his work. For although many British and other European linguists were critical of codes theory, it was seized upon in Europe precisely because it focussed on class and was interpreted with reference to class rather than to race cleavages (see further Dittmar 1976). Interestingly, although Labov's 1969 polemic is regularly opposed to Bernstein's position in discussions of the difference/deficit hypothesis, little attention has been paid to the rather significant fact that in the United States Bernstein's work was not interpreted in terms of class as it was originally phrased.

7   Conclusion

The purpose of this chapter has been to contrast, with attention to social and historical contexts, the language ideologies of Britain and the United States as instantiated in language policies and language discrimination against particular social groups. While the language standardisation process in Britain is historically associated with a monarchy which has provided a focal point for a strong class system, early American English developed in a more egalitarian context. Thus, network American, often described as a spoken standard, is a levelled *Gemeinsprache*, a focussed mainstream dialect lacking institutional support. In Britain, however, Received Pronunciation, which is often used as a reference accent and even described sometimes as a spoken standard, is quite differently embedded in social structure. Specifically, the norms of RP have in the past been quite explicitly prescribed; moreover, the accent is historically associated with upper and upper middle-class speakers and has enjoyed strong institutional support.

In the United States, rather different language ideologies took shape under the pressure of social and historical developments. The divisions created by slavery in the early colonial period shaped a language ideology focussed on racial discrimination. In Britain on the other hand, long-standing divisions of class erupted particularly fiercely in the early years of the twentieth century and remain evident to this day. In the United States, the need to accommodate large numbers of non-English speakers, both from long-established communities (such as Spanish speakers in the South West) and from successive waves of immigrants, gave rise early in the history of the nation to policies and attitudes which discriminated against these speakers. These policies and attitudes are to this day embodied in a version of the standard language ideology which is negatively disposed to speakers of languages other than English — again an ideology quite different from that characteristic of Britain.

Scholarly approaches to language discrimination — as opposed to political ideologies and laypersons' attitudes — emerge also as somewhat differently oriented in Britain and the United States. These unacknowledged differences emerge particularly clearly in responses to Bernstein's work. The parallel drawn by Abercrombie (1965 [1951]: 13–14) between class discrimination, race discrimination and linguistic ideology provides us with a relevant concluding comment:

> In England standard English speakers are divided by an 'accent-bar', on one side of which is RP, and on the other side all the other accents. And very often the first judgement made on a stranger's speech is the answer to the question: which side of the accent bar is he? . . . The accent bar is like the colour bar — to many people on the right side of the bar it appears eminently reasonable.

Notes

1. Thanks to Rosina Lippi-Green for useful discussion of many of the issues raised here and to Jim Milroy, John Rickford, Theresa Satterfield and Kathryn Woolard for comments on an earlier draft. I am grateful to Paul Kerswill, Dominic Watt and Paul Foulkes for supplying me with relevant material from British press discussions of language issues.
2. In fact this comparison is quite apposite; the Chinese (written) language, currency and weights and measures systems were all standardised simultaneously under the Qin dynasty as part of an integrated policy (Norman 1988: 63).
3. In reality many high-profile American broadcasters speak with regional accents. For example, Walter Kronkite's successor as CBS newsreader is the audibly Texas accented Dan Rather.
4. The transcription here is taken from Walters (1996).
5. This distinction is made also with reference to Cockney:
    'Cockney is the characteristic speech of 'the greatest city of the greatest empire that the world has ever known. But Cockney is such a pariah that not even the philologists have a good word for it. They deny it the status of a dialect and describe it as vulgar speech based upon error and misunderstanding.' (Matthews 1938: x; quoted by Edwards 1993).
6. Particularly in an extended debate conducted by electronic mail through contribution to Linguist List during January 1997.

References

Abercrombie, David (1951) RP and local accent. Reprinted in D. Abercrombie (ed.) (1965) *Studies in Linguistics and Phonetics*. Oxford: Oxford University Press, 10–15.

Abercrombie, David (ed.) (1965) *Studies in Linguistics and Phonetics*. Oxford: Oxford University Press.

Atkins, J.D.C. (1992 [1887]) Barbarous dialects should be blotted out. In James Crawford (ed.) (1992) *Language Loyalties: a Sourcebook on the Official English Controversy*. Chicago: University of Chicago Press, 47–50.

Barron, Dennis (1992 [1987]) Federal English. Reprinted in J. Crawford (ed.) (1992) *Language Loyalties: a Sourcebook on the Official English Controversy*. Chicago: University of Chicago Press, 36–39.

Baugh, Albert C. and Cable, Thomas (1978) *A History of the English Language*, 3rd edn. London: Routledge & Kegan Paul.

Baugh, John (1996) Linguistic discrimination. In Hans Goebl, Peter Nelde, Stary Zdenek and Wolfgang Woelck (eds) *Contact Linguistics: a Handbook of Contemporary Research*. Berlin: de Gruyter, 709–14.

Bernstein, B. (1972, 1973, 1975) *Class, Codes and Control* (3 vols). London: Routledge & Kegan Paul.

Booth, Charles (1892) *Life and Labour of the People of London, Vol. 1*. London: Macmillan.

Bourdieu, Pierre (1991) *Language and Symbolic Power*. Edited by J.B. Thompson. Translated by G. Raymond and M. Adamson. Cambridge, MA: Harvard University Press.

Bradbury, Malcolm (1994) Eschew the Estuary. *The Times* (London), Thursday Sept 1.

Cameron, Deborah (1995) *Verbal Hygiene*. London: Routledge.

Cameron, D. and Bourne, J. (1989) No common ground: Kingman, grammar and the nation. *Language and Education* 3: 147–160.

Cardenas, Jose A. (1992) An educator's rationale for native language instruction. In J. Crawford (ed.) *Language Loyalties: a Sourcebook on the Official English Controversy*. Chicago: University of Chicago Press, 342–351.

Castro, Max (1992) On the curious question of language in Miami. In J. Crawford (ed.) *Language Loyalties: a Sourcebook on the Official English Controversy*. Chicago: University of Chicago Press, 178–185.

Chambers, Jack K. (1995) *Sociolinguistic Theory*. Oxford: Blackwell.

Cheshire, Jenny and Edwards, Viv (1993): Sociolinguistics in the classroom: exploring linguistic diversity. In James Milroy and Lesley Milroy (eds) *Real English: the Grammar of English Dialects in the British Isles*. London: Longman, 34–51.

Cheshire, Jenny and Milroy, James (1993) Syntactic variation in non-standard dialects: background issues. In James Milroy and Lesley Milroy (eds) *Real English: the Grammar of English Dialects in the British Isles*. London: Longman, 3–33.

Cheshire, Jenny, Edwards, Viv and Whittle, P. (1993) Non-standard English and dialect levelling. In J. Milroy and L. Milroy (eds) *Real English: the Grammar of English Dialects in the British Isles*. London: Longman, 53–97.

Cheshire, Jenny, Edwards, Viv, Muensterman, H. and Weltens, Bert (1989) *Dialect and Education*. Cleveland, Avon: Multilingual Matters.

Corfield, P.J. (ed.) (1991) *Language, History and Class*. Oxford: Blackwell.

Crawford, James (ed.) (1992) *Language Loyalties: a Sourcebook on the Official English Controversy*. Chicago: University of Chicago Press.

Crossick, G. (1991) From gentlemen to the residuum: languages of social description in Victorian Britain. In P.J. Corfield (ed.) *Language, History and Class*. Oxford: Blackwell.

Crowley, Tony (1989) *Standard English and the Politics of Language*. Urbana and Chicago: University of Illinois Press.

D'Andrade, Roy (1987) A folk model of the mind. In D. Holland and N. Quinn (eds) *Cultural Models in Language and Thought*. Cambridge: Cambridge University Press, 112–148.

Dittmar, Norbert (1976) *Introduction to Sociolinguistics*. London: Arnold.

Dorling, Daniel (1995) *A New Social Atlas of Britain*. New York: Wiley.

Eagleton, Terry (1991) *Ideology: an Introduction*. London: Verso.

Edwards, John (1979) *Language and Disadvantage*. London: Arnold.

Edwards, Viv (1979) *The West Indian Issue in British Schools: Challenges and Responses*. London: Routledge & Kegan Paul.

Edwards, Viv (1986) *Language in a Black Community*. Cleveland, Avon: Multilingual Matters.

Edwards, Viv (1993) The grammar of southern British English. In James Milroy and Lesley Milroy (eds) *Real English: the Grammar of English Dialects in the British Isles*. London: Longman, 214–238.

Fairclough, Norman (1992) The appropriacy of 'appropriateness'. In N. Fairclough (ed.) *Critical Language Awareness*. London: Longman, 33–56.

Finnegan, Edward and Biber, Douglas (1994) *Sociolinguistic Perspectives on Register*. Oxford: Oxford University Press.

Fishman, Joshua (1992) The displaced anxiety of Anglo Americans. In James Crawford (ed.) *Language Loyalties: a Sourcebook on the Official English Controversy*. Chicago: University of Chicago Press, 165–170.

Foucault, Michel (1984) The order of discourse. In M. Shapiro (ed.) *Language and politics*. New York: New York University Press, 108–138.

Franklin, Benjamin ([1753] 1992) The German language in Pennsylvania. In James Crawford (ed.) *Language Loyalties: a Sourcebook on the Official English Controversy*. Chicago: University of Chicago Press, 18–19.

Giddens, Anthony (1989) *Sociology*. London: Polity Press.

Giles, Howard and Coupland, Nikolas (1991) *Language: Contexts and Consequences*. Milton Keynes: Open University.

Giles, Howard and Powesland, Peter F. (1975) *Speech Style and Social Evaluation*. New York and London: Academic Press.

Gramsci, Antonio (1985) *Selection from Cultural Writings*. London: Lawrence & Wishart.

Halliday, Michael A.K., McIntosh, Angus and Strevens, Peter (1964) *The Linguistic Sciences and Language Teaching*. London: Longman:

Haugen, Einar (1992 [1972]) The curse of Babel. In J. Crawford (ed.) *Language Loyalties: a Sourcebook on the Official English Controversy*. Chicago: University of Chicago Press, 399–409.

Heath, Shirley B. (1992 [1976]) Why no official tongue? In J. Crawford (ed.) *Language Loyalties: a Sourcebook on the Official English Controversy*. Chicago: University of Chicago Press, 220–230.

Honey, John (1983) *The Language Trap: Language, Class and the 'Standard English' Issue in British Schools*. Kenton, Middlesex: National Council for Educational Standards.

Honey, John (1989) *Does accent matter?* London: Faber.

Honey, John (1998) *Language and Power: the Story of Standard English and its Enemies*. London: Faber.

Huddleston, Walter (1992) The misdirected policy of bilingualism. In J. Crawford (ed.) *Language Loyalties: a Sourcebook on the Official English Controversy*. Chicago: University of Chicago Press, 114–117.

Karpf, Anne (1997) Fighting Talk. *The Guardian* (London), G2, pp. 4–5. Jan. 23.

Kerswill, Paul (1996) Children, adolescents and language change. *Language Variation and Change* 8: 177–202.

Labov, William (1969) The logic of nonstandard English. *Georgetown Monographs on Language and Linguistics*, 22, 1–31. Georgetown University: School of Languages and Linguistics.

Labov, William (1972) *Language in the Inner City*. Philadelphia: Pennsylvania University Press.

Labov, W. (1984) Field methods of the project on linguistic change and variation. In John Baugh and Joel Sherzer (eds) *Language in Use: Readings in Sociolinguistics*. Englewood Cliffs, NJ: Prentice Hall.

Lambert, W.E. (1960) Evaluational reactions to spoken languages. *Journal of Abnormal and Social Psychology* 50, 197–200.

Leibowicz, Joseph (1992) Official English: another Americanisation campaign? In J. Crawford (ed.) *Language Loyalties: a Sourcebook on the Official English Controversy*. Chicago: University of Chicago Press, 101–111.

Lippi-Green, Rosina (1994) Accent, standard and language ideology, and discriminatory pretext in court. *Language in Society* 23: 163–198.

Lippi-Green, Rosina (1997) *Accents in Time*. London: Routledge.

Macaulay, Ronald K.S. (1977) *Language and Social Class in Glasgow*. Edinburgh: Edinburgh University Press.

Martin-Jones, Marilyn (1995) Code-switching in the classroom: two decades of research. In Lesley Milroy and Pieter Muysken (eds) *One Speaker, Two Languages: Cross-disciplinary Perspectives on Bilingualism*. Cambridge: Cambridge University Press, 90–112.

Marwick, Arthur (1980) *Class: Image and Reality in Britain, France and the USA since 1930*. Oxford: Oxford University Press.

Matthews, W. (1938) *Cockney Past and Present*. London: Routledge.

Milroy, James and Milroy, Lesley (eds) (1993) *Real English: the Grammar of English Dialects in the British Isles*. London: Longman.

Milroy, James and Milroy, Lesley (1998) Authority in Language, 3rd edn. London: Routledge.

Milroy, Lesley and Milroy, James (1992) Social network and social class: towards an integrated sociolinguistic model. *Language in Society* 21: 1, 1–26.

Morse, J. Mitchell (1973) The shuffling speech of slavery: Black English. *College English* 34: 834–843.

Niedzielski, N. and Preston, D. (1999) *Folk Linguistics*. Berlin: Mouton de Gruyter.

Norman, Gerry (1988) *Chinese*. Cambridge: Cambridge University Press.

Ochs, Eleanor (1979) Planned and unplanned discourse. In T. Givon (ed.) *Syntax and Semantics*, vol. 12. New York: Academic Press, 51–80.

Oprah Winfrey Show (1987) Standard and 'black English'. Nov. 19. WLS-TV (Chicago, IL). Transcript #W309. New York: Journal Graphics, Inc.

Pinker, Stephen (1994) *The Language Instinct*. Middlesex: Penguin.

Preston, Dennis (1989) Standard English spoken here: the geographical loci of linguistic norms. In U. Ammon (ed.) *Status and Function of Languages and Language Varieties*. Amsterdam: Benjamins, 324–354.

Preston, Dennis (1996) Where the worst English is spoken. In E.W. Schneider (ed.) *Focus on the USA*. Amsterdam: Benjamins, 297–361.

Proulx, E. Annie (1997) *Accordion Crimes*. London: Fourth Estate.

Pullum, Geoffrey K. (1997) Language that dare not speak its name. *Nature* 386, 27 March, 321–322.

Rampton, Ben (1996) Language crossing and the problematisation of ethnicity and socialisation. *Pragmatics* 5: 4, 485–513.

Rickford, John (1997) Commentary: Suite for Ebony and Phonics. *Discover* 18(12), 82–87.

Roberts, Celia, Davies, Evelyn and Jupp, Tom (1992) *Language and Discrimination: a Study of Communication in Multi-ethnic Workplaces*. London: Longman.

Rogers, Daniel T. and Wilenz, Sean (1991) Languages of power in the United States. In P.J. Corfield (ed.) *Language, History and Class*. Oxford: Blackwell, 240–263.

Smith, J. (1996) *An Historical Study of English: Function, Form and Change*. London: Routledge.

Stubbs, M. (1989) The state of English in the English state: reflections on the Cox Report. *Language and Education* 3: 235–250.

Sugrue, Thomas (1996) *The Origins of the Urban Crisis: Race and Inequality in Post-war Detroit*. Princeton: Princeton University Press.

Trudgill, Peter (1975) *Accent, Dialect and the School*. London: Arnold.

Trudgill, Peter (1991) *Sociolinguistics*, 3rd edn. Harmondsworth: Penguin.

Walters, Keith (1996) Contesting representations of African American language. *Proceedings of SALSA III*. Austin: University of Texas Press, 137–151.

Wolfram, Walt (1991) *Dialects and American English*. Washington: Center for Applied Linguistics.

Wolfram, Walt (1998) Dialect in society. In F. Coulmas (ed.) *The Handbook of Sociolinguistics*. Oxford: Blackwell, 107–126.

Wolfram, W. and Christian, D. (1980) On the application of sociolinguistic information: test evaluation and dialect differences in Appalachia. In T. Shopen and J.M. Williams (eds) *Standards and Dialects in English*. Cambridge, MA: Winthrop, 177–209.

Woolard, Kathryn A. (1989) *Double Talk*. Stanford, CA: Stanford University Press.

Woolard, Kathryn A. and Schieffelin, Bambi (1994) Language ideology. *Annual Review of Anthropology* 23: 55–82.

Wyld, Henry C. (1934) 'The Best English: a claim for the superiority of Received Standard English'. *Society for Pure English* 4, Tract XXXIX, 603–621. Oxford: Clarendon.

10

Language crossing, cross-talk, and cross-disciplinarity in sociolinguistics
Ben Rampton

1 An initial context for debate[1]

Over the last 30 years or so (and for maybe much longer before that), three very general perspectives have been highly influential in attempts to account for inequalities in the distribution of knowledge, influence and resources within stratified societies. The first perspective, 'the *deficit* position', stresses the inadequacies of subordinate (out)groups and the importance of their being socialised into dominant (in)group norms. The second, with *difference* as its key word, emphasises the integrity and autonomy of the language and culture of subordinate groups, and the need for institutions to be hospitable to diversity. In the third, the focus shifts to larger structures of *domination*, and the need is stressed for institutions to combat the institutional processes and ideologies that reproduce the oppression of subordinate groups. There is obviously a lot of conflict between these interpretations of the basic character of inequality, and different perspectives have gained ascendency at different times in different places. In the debates about race and ethnicity in British education, they are fairly easily recognised as assimilation, multiculturalism and antiracism (Brandt 1986), and in discussions about the global spread of English, they are broadly in line with the views expressed in Quirk (1990), Kachru (1982) and Phillipson (1992) respectively.

More recently, however, a fourth very general perspective has emerged. This view accepts the role that larger social, economic and political systems play in structuring dominant–subordinate, majority–minority relations, but it argues that their impact on everyday experience cannot be easily predicted. Instead, the emphasis is on looking closely at how people make sense of inequality and difference in their local situations, and at how they interpret them in the context of a range of social relationships (gender, class, region, generation, etc.). This perspective is wary of seeing culture *either* as an elite canon, *or* as a set of static ethnic essences, *or* as a simple reflection of economic and political processes; it takes the view that the reality of people's circumstances is actively shaped by the ways in which they interpret and respond to them; and in line with this, it lays a good deal of emphasis on the cultural politics of imagery and representation. In terms of the two areas of language-culture-and-inequality debate mentioned above, this fourth perspective can be seen in debates about pluralism in the UK (and elsewhere) in a book like Donald and Rattansi's *'Race' Culture and Difference* (1992), and it is central in Pennycook's *The Cultural Politics of English as an International Language* (1994). Overall, it is a perspective which tunes with much wider public discussion of 'post-modernity', and preserving the alliteration, it has been summarised as *'discourse'*. These four positions are mapped out schematically in Table 10.1 (see also McDermott and Varenne 1996).

The development of this discourse perspective in the humanities and social sciences has been viewed with some relish in sociolinguistics, where there are now a range of very well established approaches to the close analysis of spoken, written and mediated texts. There has been a feeling that the discipline will be able to contribute its expert understanding of 'grammatical and pragmatic complexity' (Gal 1995a: 409) to traditions of enquiry that have hitherto taken language for granted (cf. Gal 1995b: 173; Billig 1995: 134ff; Harris 1996), and there has also been some expectation that through reciprocation, it will be possible to repair what has often been seen as naivety about social theory in sociolinguistics (Thompson 1984: 100; Hewitt 1986: 200–201; Cameron 1990: 81; Williams 1992: xiii; Bernstein 1996: 149). At the same time, though, there is a worry that these cross-disciplinary relations might be harder to manage than they might seem at first, and that discourse might not be quite as safe a meeting point as it initially appears. As many scholars have pointed out (for example Agar 1985, Fairclough 1992, Scollon and Scollon 1995: Ch. 6), the term 'discourse' is used in a number of different senses, both in grand theory, referring to whole-systems-of-thought-and-action, as well as in nose-to-data accounts of the intricate details of everyday social interaction, and potentially at least, there might be a danger of overgeneralising linguistic models, of assuming syntax-like standards of precision in the study of society, and of shuttling too fast up into grand theory from theories of data (see the comments in Stubbs 1997: 100).

Given its history of incorporating ideas and approaches previously thought to lie 'elsewhere', starting with the early syntheses of linguistics, sociology and anthropology in the 1960s, anxieties about misappropriation might not seem to have a lot of force in sociolinguistics. But in fact even within sociolinguistics, research traditions fluctuate in the extent to which they seek either autonomy or connection, and links can be inept even in periods of openness. Affiliated disciplines are themselves also subject to major change, and so it makes a good deal of sense to keep sociolinguistic relationships with other areas continuously under review.

The question of how sociolinguists can best create and maintain ties with research in sociology, psychology, anthropology, cultural, literary and/

Table 10.1   Four orientations to cultural diversity

Interpretation of linguistic diversity	I. Diversity as deficit	II. Diversity as difference	III. Not diversity, domination	IV. Deficit, difference and domination as discourse
View of culture	Culture as elite canon/standard	Cultures as sets of values, beliefs and behaviours	Culture as reflection of socio-economic relations	Culture as the processes and resources involved in situated, dialogical sense-making
Approach to language	Prescriptivism: norms and standards to be followed	Descriptivism: system and authenticity of non-standard forms	Determinism: language either subordinate to, or a distraction from, structures of political and economic domination	Social constructionism: reality extensively constructed through institutional discourse and discursive interaction
View of research	Neutral, objective, informative	Neutral, objective, advocate	Part of apparatus of hegemony; scientific imperialism	Either regime of truth/discipline, or empowering, giving voice to subjugated knowledges
Descriptive concerns/focus	The canon. The Other lacks culture and knowledge	The Other's autonomy and integrity	Self and Other in larger system	Global and national discourses, diaspora and multi-local sites
Philosophical and political emphasis	Superiority of 'Us'. 'Them' at fault	Relativism. Cultures incommensurable: 'we' can't say 'them' at fault	Power, capitalist oppression. Resistance through the unity of oppressed groups	Power, difference and contingency. 'Them' resists, or sees things differently
Assumptions about the world	Universals and grand narratives: development/modernisation/global markets	Grand narratives maybe, but celebration of the subplots	Universals and grand narratives: imperialism/dependency	Universals and grand narratives disclaimed
Intervention strategy	Assimilation	Multiculturalism	Anti-racism/anti-imperialism	Anti-essentialism
Typical politics	Conservatism	Liberal pluralism	Marxism	Post-modernism

or educational studies is bound to elicit complex and varied answers, and the duration and productivity of inter-disciplinary relationships is sure to involve a host of unpredictable local contingencies (see Coupland 1997; Rampton 1997). Even so, in this chapter, I will try to differentiate three kinds of connection that sociolinguistic research can usefully make with work that (at the time anyway) seems to fall outside the normal disciplinary boundaries. First and most obviously, research outside sociolinguistics can be useful as a form of wider contextualisation for any given project on language in social life, helping to specify the larger environment within which any particular group, institution or practice is located. Second, it can have a deep influence on the underlying assumptions about social reality that shape research in sociolinguistics. Third, it can provide concepts which can be integrated into the analysis and interpretation of specific data, and which may then also serve as a very practical 'bridge' back and forwards between sociolinguistics and the fields where the concepts originate. I shall try to illustrate all three kinds of connection in the course of this chapter, but this list certainly is not offered as an exhaustive account of the kinds of link that are possible, and it comes neither from a fluent and extensive knowledge of the philosophy of science, nor from a particular reading of sociolinguistic researchers who have stood out for ground-breaking cross-disciplinarity (for example, Bernstein, Hymes, Gumperz, or Fairclough). Instead, these points draw on my own experience of research, which, because it has always been driven by 'real-world' problems, has inevitably required quite a lot of reading outside sociolinguistics and which has also in the end involved the formulation of claims about sociolinguistic processes in vocabularies borrowed from elsewhere.

My chapter involves a mixture of three components: (a) a description of my research; (b) an account of how I have tried to update sociolinguistic findings and theories, or to compensate for gaps in them, by referring to sociology, anthropology and cultural studies; (c) an attempt to clarify this cross-referring in terms of the three kinds of connection listed immediately above — cross-referring done to contextualise, cross-referring for ontological orientation, and cross-referring to improve the data analysis.

The development of the discussion is as follows. In Section 2 I draw attention to the distinction between ontology and substantive theory and its implications for our understanding of cross-disciplinary borrowing. After that I provide an initial description of my own research on adolescents in multilingual peer groups in Britain, together with some illustrative analysis of data on 'language crossing' (defined as the use of a language that is not normally thought to belong to you) (Section 3). Section 4 then compares this with the classic work of Gumperz and his associates on intercultural communication ('Crosstalk'). The method of analysis developed by Gumperz *et al.*, 'interactional sociolinguistics', has been a very significant influence in my research, but my findings on ethnicity in interaction turned out to be rather different from theirs, and in a long Section 5, I argue that these

differences point to a major gap in the way that ethnicity has been conceptualised in sociolinguistics. In fact, hitherto dominant notions of ethnicity
are intimately connected with very deep disciplinary assumptions about 'system', 'coherence' and 'community' which many people are now starting to
question. Looking beyond just 'language crossing', I look at the emergence
of sociolinguistic theories and concepts which no longer make these assumptions, and I comment on the ways in which they are connected with debates
about late/post-modernity elsewhere in the social sciences. Section 6 changes
tack and discusses my appropriation of the notions of ritual and liminality.
These provided a great deal of purchase in data analysis, and after describing
how they did so, I try to clarify the mid-level of abstraction at which they
worked and suggest that they may be particularly valuable as 'bridging concepts' between sociolinguistics and other disciplines (Section 7).

2   Ontology vs substantive theory

According to Ira Cohen (1987), ontology consists of very general ideas which
specify the types of fundamental entity occurring in a given domain together
with the ways in which these entities interact. Ontologies provide an essential starting point for any research, and they consist of non-refutable, metaphysical presuppositions about qualities and forces thought to underlie all
of the phenomena being addressed. Cohen cites ideas about the universal
trajectory of social evolution as one example of an ontology, and in many
treatments in pragmatics, the notion of face-needs would be another (Cohen
1987: 275–280; Brown and Levinson 1987: 13–15). In contrast, the details of
Brown and Levinson's politeness theory, the way it ranges, for example, from
'bald-on-record' to 'not-doing-the-FTA (face-threatening-act)', would be seen
as substantive theory, a set of claims that are designed as open to empirical
refutation (though see Brown and Levinson 1987: 8).

The distinction between ontology and substantive theory is not, however,
a necessarily settled one. Disputes arise where one person treats something
as ontological which others claim as the topic of substantive theory, and when
this happens, assumptions about the ontological status of a phenomenon
tend to look reductionist, 'trimming and shaping' 'the diversity that is evident across different societies . . . to preserve the fundamental metaphysical
insights' (Cohen 1987: 277). Something rather like this can actually be found
in arguments between the four perspectives on inequality outlined in the
opening paragraphs, where what seems a non-refutable ontological truth in
the 'deficit' perspective, for example, looks like a highly suspect, empirically
unwarranted overgeneralisation to proponents of 'difference' or 'domination'.
The most recent of the four — the 'discourse' view — looks as if it takes
less for granted, 'allow[ing] the widest possible latitude for the diversity and

contingencies that may occur in different settings' (Cohen 1987: 279), though of course this too can seem reductionist in its treatment of the physical and biological (Aronsson 1997: 54; Livia and Hall 1997: 9–10).

Within the discourse orientation itself, where new prospects for cross-connection seem to have been opening, the unstable distinction between ontology and substantive theory throws some light on two potential difficulties in the way that sociolinguists relate to other kinds of researcher.

In the first place, the distinction points to a rather sensitive ambiguity in the illocutionary force of relatively summary references to work outside the author's own area of credentialled expertise: are such references to work in other fields strategic temporary simplifications, or are they articles of faith? It's obviously impossible to problematise everything when you are working on 'real-world' processes, and when it is something like everyday interaction that is the principal object of analysis, sociolinguists frequently flag up their orientation to wider social processes by citing the work of whichever sociologist or cultural theorist seems best to capture the way that they conceptualise society at large. These cross-references often look rather simple and formulaic to people working in fields where these figures are a central focus of debate, operating as friends or enemies rather than authorities, but since one cannot know everything, there is nothing necessarily shameful about them. In an ideal world, references like these would only ever serve as temporary flags of convenience, pointing to literatures which, with more time (and other lives), the analyst feels it would be worth exploring with the particular data on hand. In practice, though, this is often hard to achieve, and it is potentially rather embarrassing when researchers in one area look as though they are committed to the ontological status of theories that are treated as substantive, and quite possibly flawed beyond repair, in their own heartlands (see Brumfit 1984: 1).

Second and more significantly, difficulties can arise where 'discourse' is itself treated as an ontology in one discipline and as a focus for substantive theory in another. For many sociologists and cultural analysts, discourse is (as I will clarify in Section 5) primarily an ontological premise, a way of rehabilitating agency after structural functionalism (Giddens 1976; Bourdieu 1977). For these researchers, there is more interest in the circulation and effects of discourse than in its internal organisation, and one of the most important consequences of this concern has been the growth of a reflexive awareness of power/knowledge and of the political role of social science (Foucault 1977, 1980). For researchers who see the workings of discourse as very much open to proof and refutation, and who are committed to analysing how the details of particular kinds of text constrain and enable particular kinds of meaning, this can be disappointing (see Bernstein 1990: 3,167). In return, it is not hard for social and cultural analysts to see nose-to-data discourse researchers as unimaginative behaviourists, insensitive to the theoretical potential of their empirical material and maybe even oblivious to their own implication in the very processes they analyse (Thompson 1984: Ch. 3; Hewitt 1992: 38; Williams 1992).

The distinction, then, between substantive theory and ontology suggests certain ways in which researchers from sociolinguistics and elsewhere might misunderstand one another. My own view is that, where they are interested in different objects, there should not be any problem if the substantive theories that sociolinguists work with are different from other social scientists'. They are likely to be able to bring different kinds and amounts of knowledge to bear on claims about, say, text-processing rather than race relations, and in line with this, complaints about sociolinguists not knowing more sociology or anthropology are only fair if sociolinguists make inflated claims to cross-disciplinary knowledge they do not really have. Where, however, disciplines differ in the foundational assumptions that researchers are working with, compatibility and conflict become more serious issues, and complaints (such as Cameron's (1990)) about gaps between the ontologies of sociolinguistics and other areas are much more weighty.

In due course, I will suggest that sociolinguistics is still working through a rather major shift in its ontological premises, and that this is part of a much wider social scientific reorientation towards the conditions and/or theories of late modernity. In fact, we will be able to see this ongoing change in the differences between my findings on interactional ethnicity and the findings of Gumperz and his associates, produced a decade and a half earlier, and to get to this comparative vantage point, it is worth now introducing the research that I carried out.

3   A research project, its data and analysis

The research that I will discuss looked at 'language crossing' into Panjabi, Creole and Indian English, 'language crossing' being the use of a language by speakers who are not really felt to own it (cf. Rampton 1999c). The research tried to provide a detailed acount of the contexts in which these language practices occurred, and to do so, it drew on the methodologies of ethnographic and interactional sociolinguistics (Hymes 1972; Gumperz 1982a; Duranti 1997). This meant paying particularly close attention to four interrelated dimensions of socio-cultural organisation: obviously enough, (a) language, seen both as a central element in social action and as a form of knowledge differentially distributed across individuals and groups; but also (b) the interaction order mapped out by Erving Goffman; (c) institutional organisation, encompassing domains, networks, activity types, social roles and normative expectations; (d) social knowledge specifically as this relates to race and ethnicity (for a full exposition on each of these, see Rampton 1995: Appendix 1). There were two periods of fieldwork focussing on one neighbourhood of the South Midlands of England, with 23 eleven- to thirteen-year-olds of Indian, Pakistani, African-Caribbean and Anglo descent in 1984, and approximately 64 fourteen- to sixteen-year-olds in 1987. Methods of data-collection included radio-microphone recording, participant observation, interviewing and retrospective participant commentary on extracts of recorded interaction, and the analysis was based on about 68 incidents of Panjabi 'crossing' (Panjabi being used by kids of Anglo and African-Caribbean descent), on more than 250 episodes where a Creole influence was clearly detectable in the speech of whites and Panjabis, and on about 160 exchanges where youngsters 'put on' a strong Indian English style of speaking. Three significantly different contexts for language crossing were identified: interaction with adults, interaction with peers, and performance art.

Here is an episode that illustrates some of the ways that adolescents code-crossed in interaction with adults. It comes from a session in which I was playing back some extracts from the radio-microphone recordings that I had made of Asif, Kazim and Alan during their recreation. I had been trying to elicit their comments and responses, but the boys were in high spirits and it was an effort to keep them focussed on what I wanted them to do:

Example 1

Participants: Asif (15 years old, male, Pakistani descent), Kazim (15, male, Pakistani descent), Alan (15, male, Anglo descent), Ben (the researcher/author, 30+, male, Anglo descent).

Setting: 1987. Having recorded these three friends with radio-microphones during their informal recreation, Ben is trying to get some feedback on extracts from the recordings. But the boys are in high spirits, Asif and Alan have just been talking playground Panjabi into the microphone from close up, and Ben is now trying to reestablish their commitment to the listening activity. (For fuller discussion of the linguistic features distinguishing Creole and Asian/Indian English, cf. Rampton 1995: Ch. 3.1 and Ch. 5.)

```
 1 Ben:     right shall I- shall we shall we stop there
 2 Kazim:   no
 3 Alan:    no come ⌈on carry on
 4 Asif:           ⌊do another extract
 5 Ben:     le- lets have (.) ⌈then you have to give me more=
 6 Alan:                      ⌊carry on
 7 Ben:     =attention gents
 8 Asif ((quieter)):   yeh ⌈alright
 9 Alan ((quieter)):       │ alright
10 Asif ((quieter)):       ⌊   yeh
11 Ben:     I need more attention
12 Kazim ((in Asian English)):   I  AM  VERY SORRY BEN JAAD
                                 [aɪ æm veɾi sɒɾi   ben dʒɑːd]
13 Asif ((in Asian English)):    ATTENTION BENJAMIN
                                 [əthenʃɑːn bendʒəmɪn]
14 :       ⌈((laughter))
15 Ben:    │right well you can- we cn-
16 Alan:   ⌊BENJAADEMIN
```

```
17 Ben:   we can continue but we er must concentrate a bit
18        ⎡more
19 Asif:  ⎣yeh
20 Alan:  alright        ⎡(go on) then
21 Asif ((in Asian English)): ⎣concentrating very hard
                               [kɒnsəntɾetɪŋ  veɾi  ɑɾ]
22 Ben:   okay  right
23 :      ((giggles dying down))
24 Kazim ((in Asian English)):  what a stupid (    )
                                [vʌd  ə stupɪd      ]
25 Ben ((returning the microphone to what he considers to be a better position to catch all the speakers)):
          concentrate a little bit-
26 Alan:  alright then
27 Kazim ((in Creole)): stop movin dat ting aroun
                        [dæt tɪŋ  əɹɑʊn]
28 Ben:   WELL YOU stop moving it around and then I'll won't
29        need to (.)   r⎡ight
30 Kazim ((in Creole)): ⎣ stop moving dat ting aroun
                         [dæʔ tɪŋ  əɹɑʊn]
31 Ben:   right okay ⎡
32 Kazim:            ⎣ BEN JAAD
33 Alan:  ((laughs))
34 Ben:   what are you doing
35 Alan:  ben jaa⎡ad
36 Ben:         ⎣well leave (    ) alone
37 Kazim: IT'S HIM that ben jaad over there
38 Ben:   right
```
((Ben continues his efforts to reinstitute the listening activity))

With a view to subsequent discussion, I would like to concentrate on the code-switching into Indian/Asian English (AE).

The episode as a whole can be characterised as a struggle between two different definitions of the situation — very approximately, on the one hand, my research-oriented 'retrospective-participant-commentary-on-extracts-of-recorded-data', and on the other, their 'havin'-a-good-time-listening-to-Ben's-tapes'. The episode begins with the boys saying they are reluctant to finish, and then in lines 5 and 6 I lay down the conditions for continuing with the listening activity, implying that they are making it pretty difficult and that it will be their own fault if we stop. Asif and Alan appear to accept the conditions, and then a small sequence of ritual remediation begins, drawing in a heavily accented Asian English: Kazim apologises in line 12; in lines 13 and 21, Asif declares his allegiance to the kind of behaviour I was asking for (in lines 5 and 7, 17 and 18); and Kazim seems to take my perspective in the muttered disapproval in line 24. But of course none of this can be taken at face value. According to Goffman (1971), in apologies people split themselves into two parts — the self that was guilty in the past, and now the new self that recognises the offence and disavows the self of old. But normally, one would expect people apologising for noisy disorder to signal the split by switching into relatively quiet, serious, sincere voices; in *this* episode the boys apologise for messing around by moving into a conspicuously false accent, accompanying it with an equally contradictory loudness and hilarity.

In addition, of course, it is not just the failure to talk normally that is significant here: the variety they select is also important. More specifically, by using a strong Asian English to feign their respect for my wishes, the boys are invoking long-standing Anglo stereotypes about deferential Indian *babus* — racist stereotypes originally developed during British rule in India but at the time still continuing in circulation through contemporary mass media. So just at the moment when a white adult is trying to bring them back to the task of his choosing, the boys produce a display of mock-compliance with strong symbolic resonances of Anglo-Asian domination — resonances which are well calculated to embarass anyone with a white liberal conscience.[2]

This was a pattern that was often repeated when Panjabi adolescents were negotiating whether and how to participate in activities where a white adult would have some control or influence over them. They switched into an exaggerated Asian English at the threshold of activities like detention or basketball; when they were asking white adults for goods or services; when teachers tried to institute question–answer exchanges; and, as we have seen, when interviewers asked for more concentrated attention. These switches seemed to operate as a kind of probe, saying 'if I'm this, then how will you respond?' They conjured awkward knowledge about intergroup relations and in doing so, the purpose seemed to be to disturb transition to the activity being expected.

There were also at least two other distinctive ways in which young people switched into Asian English, to which I will return in Section 6 below. But before that, I would like to compare the portrait of ethnicity emerging through my analysis of Example 1 with the account of ethnicity produced in the classic work of Gumperz and his associates several years earlier. Once the differences between them have been established, we will be able to detail some rather fundamental shifts in the assumptions of sociolinguistics, and that, in turn, will allow a sharper assessment of the relationship between sociolinguistics and social theory.

4   'Language crossing' vs 'crosstalk'

In the late 1970s and early 80s, there were important interactional socio-linguistic (IS) studies which analysed intercultural 'crosstalk' between Anglos and Asians in the UK (Gumperz, Roberts and Jupp 1979; Gumperz 1982a, 1982b; Roberts, Davies and Jupp 1992). They focussed on workplace encounters between adults who hardly knew each other, who had different linguistic backgrounds, and who had very different degrees of institutional power. There was a certain amount of initial goodwill in these gatekeeping interactions, but this got disrupted by hidden differences in the participants' communicative resources, which, in the end, conjured up negative social images, (re)producing racial discrimination. To the extent that my own research focussed on interactions in England between people with Anglo, Asian and African-Caribbean ethnic backgrounds, it bore some resemblance to these formative IS analyses, but in other respects, there were obvious empirical contrasts. In the data example above, for instance, there were adolescents as well as adults; nearly everyone was born in the UK and everyone spoke fluent English; we were very well known to each other outside this particular interview; and even though I felt rather uncomfortable during parts of the interview, there was a strong element of what Singh *et al.* (1988: 45) call a 'human sense of the joyfulness of speech', contrasting somewhat with the relatively formal and bureaucratic events analysed in the classic IS research.

In the first instance, these more recent data help to update the *empirical* portrait of ethno-linguistic processes between Asians and Anglos in Britain (see also for example Roberts and Sarangi 1995). One of the most important practical contributions from Gumperz, Roberts and others has been to provide a detailed understanding of how unrecognised discourse differences can validate derogatory sociolinguistic stereotypes. Data such as my own adds something about the ways in which these stereotypes can be taken on, foregrounded and reworked. Negative caricatures of ESL users — what Ferguson (1975) calls Secondary Foreigner Talk — lurk with other racist images in the background of the cross-ethnic interactions described by Gumperz *et al.* (Gumperz and Roberts 1991: 47),[3] and in episodes such as Example 1, we can see these images being flushed out and spotlighted, with secondary foreigner talk itself being reconfigured into something one might actually call *tertiary* FT — a language practice where people with migrant or minority backgrounds strategically masquerade in the racist imagery used in dominant discourses about them (see also for example Mitchell-Kernan 1971; Sims Holt 1972; Hill and Coombs 1982; Parmar 1982: 264–5; Pratt 1991).

Gumperz certainly mentions processes similar to this (for instance 1982: 34), and some version of Gumperzian 'metaphorical' codeswitching is indeed essential if we are to account for data such as we find in Example 1 (see Rampton 1995: 278–280). Even so, it is difficult to fit these data into Gumperz and Cook-Gumperz's explicit definitions of ethnicity (1982), and as their explication of ethnicity is both influential and representative of a good deal of socio- and applied linguistics, it is worth reviewing here.

Like a great many other scholars and linguists, Gumperz and Cook-Gumperz identify two notions of ethnicity (1982: 5–6; Fishman 1972: 22–28). The first is an 'interactive ethnicity', which is seen as a tacit cultural inheritance, realised in the distinctive patterns of language use that people acquire in local community networks and in the early years at home. The second notion is more group-for-itself than group-in-itself, and Gumperz and Cook-Gumperz call this 'reactive ethnicity'. This is more self-conscious and can be seen at work in symbolic *assertions* of inherited identity that are strategically activated in different ways and different contexts. Here, rather than being the cultural legacy itself, ethnicity is a contrastive, positional construct which participants use to create, express, and interpret a variety of social and political differences.

Overall, this formulation seems to allow individuals just two options: they can either embrace and cultivate the ethnolinguistic legacy passed on by their parents and grandparents, or they can drop it as a category that is personally relevant to them. But if these were the only two options, then my interpretation of the use of Asian English in Example 1 would not make much sense. If all one could do with ethnicity was turn it up or down, as it were, then these switches to Indian English would have to be analysed as acts of identification with the valued linguistic models provided by an older genera-tion. But this would be difficult to reconcile with any detailed interpretation of the data. If one were to claim that youngsters in this peer group were converging to ingroup adult norms when they switched to Asian English, it would be necessary to overlook the comic irony involved in the way Asian English was used with white adults, as well as the way in which it recycled racist stereotypes of babu Asian English circulating in the mass media and in white culture generally. It would also be hard to reconcile such an inter-pretation with a number of other characteristics that I will outline in Section 6: the use of Asian English as a critical 'say-for', a voice for caricaturing kids who did something wrong (Goffman 1974: 535); its role in racist abuse directed at Bangladeshis; and its ritual organisation overall. It makes much more sense to see these uses of Asian English as a reworking of popular stereotypes, and as a result, it becomes necessary to articulate a *third* notion of ethnicity in sociolinguistics: an ethnicity that is deracinated, represented, and accessed by outsiders, neither group-in-itself nor -for-itself but group-for-someone-else.

This is outlined in Table 10.2, which I will elaborate on in the next section.

5   Late modern ethnicities and sociolinguistics

There has in fact been a great deal of work in sociolinguistics on the ways in which people see and refer to outgroups ('group-for-someone-else'), and this includes research on intergroup stereotypes in the social psychology of lan-guage (for example Ryan and Giles 1982), a burgeoning literature on racist

Table 10.2 Three notions of ethnicity in sociolinguistics

	Ethnicity 1	Ethnicity 2	Ethnicity 3
Otherwise known as	Interactive, experiential, group-in-itself	Reactive, referential, group-for-itself ('us')	Deracinated, represented, group-for-someone-else ('them')
The linguistic and cultural substance of the ethnicity in question	Ingrained linguistic and cultural dispositions and practices, developed over time through face-to-face interaction at home and in local networks	Certain features selected from local or domestic tradition ('Ethnicity 1'), strategically stressed in order to symbolise ingroup membership in multiracial interactions and settings. 'Ethnicity 2' is a selection/simplification/idealisation from 'Ethnicity 1'	Widely or locally disseminated tokens and images of other groups and cultures, generated either within or outside the group depicted, with currency either partially or totally beyond the group's control. 'Ethnicity 3' is an idealisation/reduction/fabrication of the experience entailed in 'Ethnicities 1 and 2'
How do people become aligned with the ethnicity in question?	Individuals have no choice: their identities and conduct are extensively shaped by ethnic experience	Ethnicity can be either positively claimed, or it can be negatively imposed. In racist societies, it can be hard to escape ethnicity as a social category that is potentially relevant to the definition of you	Alignment is voluntary – individuals are attracted to outgroup cultural forms. Otherwise, the outgroup ethnicity either has little personal relevance, or it serves as a negative Other against which the Self is defined positively

Table 10.2 *(cont'd)*

	Ethnicity 1	Ethnicity 2	Ethnicity 3
Illustrative studies	Philips 1972, Heath 1983	McDermott and Gospodinoff 1979, Erickson and Shultz 1982, Gumperz and Cook-Gumperz 1982	Hewitt 1986, Hill 1993, Rampton 1995, Heller 1999, etc.
Emblem	Roots	Routes	Aerials
Complications/problems involved in seeing the ethnicity in question as distinct	In what ways can you really say that on their own, these dispositions and practices constitute ethnic identity rather than class, gender, regional, idiosyncratic, etc. identity? Defining cultural inheritance as ethnicity is in fact a matter of the social processes associated with Ethnicities 2 and 3.	A sense of your own ethnicity arises out of both a sense of other people's ethnicities *and* an awareness of their representations of yours. Sometimes, other people's representations of your ethnicity may be attractive rather than offensive – something you want to embrace rather than reject.	People can get to know, interact, identify and often live with people from ethnic outgroups. In doing so, Ethnicities 2 and 3 can become quite closely tuned.

representations in interviews and media discourse (van Dijk 1987; Wetherall and Potter 1992), as well as the long-standing studies of phenomena like Secondary Foreigner talk mentioned above (Ferguson 1975).[4] The crucial difference, though, between this research and my own is that sociolinguistic research on the representation of outgroups has overwhelmingly assumed that speakers have a relatively stable view of their own ethnic position: they seem to know which in-group they belong to, and the ethnic category they are representing is definitely 'other'. In contrast, in the data illustrated above and exemplified at much greater length in Rampton 1995, people don't sit contentedly in the social group categories that society tries to fix them in, and they don't confine themselves only to those identities that they are expected to have legitimate or routine access to. Rather than simply attributing particular outgroup identities to other people, adolescents also often *claim particular outgroup identities for themselves.*[5] The young people I studied certainly knew whether or not either Creole or Panjabi were used in their homes, but this didn't stop a number of them from, in one way or another, actually affiliating themselves with these languages, seeing them as part of their own youth community speech repertoire (see also Hewitt 1986).

The processes involved in this kind of cross-identification were highly complex, and were sometimes developed through sensitive long-term negotiations about the meaning of category membership in interethnic friendship. At the same time, it is increasingly difficult to ignore the ways in which ethnicities have also been commodified (both now and in the past), with ethnic forms, products and symbols marketised and widely disseminated as desirable commodities, life-style options and aesthetic objects (see for example Hewitt 1986; Hannerz 1992a and b; Hill 1993, 1995; Hall 1995: 201–3; Lury 1996; Urciuoli 1996; Hoechsmann 1997). Language often serves as a major element in the design of these products, and the ways in which both members and non-members of the groups represented react to, reject or buy them are bound to be highly diverse, as is evidenced in Hewitt's 1986 discussion of reggae's complex sociolinguistic impact on adolescents in South London, or Cutler's (1999) account of rap. And yet it is only relatively recently that sociolinguistics has started to adjust its theoretical apparatus in ways which can start to understand the realignments, flirtations and purchases variously involved in processes like these.

In M.L. Pratt's terms, sociolinguistics has generally been much more a 'linguistics of community' than a 'linguistics of contact' (1987), and at least during the 1970s and 1980s, the dominant view was

a)   that language study was centrally concerned with systematicity in grammar and coherence in discourse, and
b)   that these come from community membership — that people learn to talk grammatically and coherently from extensive early experience of living in families and fairly stable local social networks.

Admittedly, sociolinguistics has long fought against the view that language and society are homogenous and it has championed ethnolinguistic heterogeneity, but on encountering diversity and variation, its strongest instinct has been to root out what it imagines to be the orderliness and uniformity beneath the surface, an orderliness laid down during early socialisation (Pratt 1987: 56; Barrett 1997: 190). This instinct can be seen, for example, in the variationist's quest for the vernacular (Gumperz 1982a: 26; Rampton 1992: 46–7); it has led code-switching researchers to look for *conventional* syntactic and pragmatic patterns in the mixed speech of relatively well-established ingroups (Rampton 1995: 280; Woolard 1988: 69–70); and when sociolinguists have looked at intercultural contact, there has been a strong tendency to emphasise the integrity of tradition *inside* particular cultural groupings, the concern being that 'sociolinguistic interference' was likely to occur in cross-cultural encounters where people with very different backgrounds had to interact.

Certainly, there have been alternatives to this 'linguistics of community', and the long-standing ideas of Le Page and Tabouret-Keller (1980, 1985) are one very notable exception. The notion of speech community has itself always been unstable and contested (Hudson 1980; Gumperz 1982a: 26; Rampton 1998), and the idea that social order is as much emergent in interaction as pre-given in stable communities actually has rather deep roots in the discipline (Sapir 1949: 104; Bauman and Sherzer 1974: 8, 1989: xvii–xix; Livia and Hall 1997: 8–9; see also below). More recently, however, attempts to look *beyond* 'straightforward communication' and 'the normal system' (Pratt 1987: 55) have come much more to the fore.

Among other things, a 'linguistics of contact' attends to the heightened metacultural and metalinguistic awareness generated through sociolinguistic encounters with 'difference', and there is increased interest in the ways that, rather like Kazim and Asif, 'speakers have, and act in relation to, ideologically constructed representations of linguistic practice' (Gal and Irvine 1995: 973; also Kroskrity *et al.* 1992; Cameron 1995). Richard Bauman's view of performance as a form of speech where there is 'heightened awareness of both the act of expression and the performer' (Bauman 1986: 3; Bauman and Briggs 1990) constitutes one significant perspective on these processes, as do notions of 'stylisation', 'intertextuality', 'polyphony' and 'double-voicing' (where in addition to 'direct unmediated discourse directed exclusively toward its referential object', speech is also seen as often being very actively oriented to the discourses of other people, which influence and 'enter into the project that the speaker's discourse has set itself' — Bakhtin 1984: 187; Hill and Hill 1986; Rampton 1995: Ch. 8.5). Over time, one of the effects of this emerging perspective might be to revitalise interest in Labovian 'stereotypes', the indexical speech productions which have been traditionally marginalised in variationist approaches that prize 'indicators' and 'markers' for their systematicity (Labov 1972); another would be to treat the notion of 'authenticity' as an ideological construct contributing to the exchange value of cultural commodities (Lury 1996), rather than just as an intrinsic property of tacit practices shaped in unselfconscious local community socialisation (Labov 1980). 'Community' itself remains an important concept in the outlook emerging here, but it is being dramatically recast. On the one hand, its status as an ideological construct is emphasised, together with its symbolic and communicative role in the construction and demarcation of 'imagined' collectivities (Anderson 1983; Pratt 1987: 49; Woolard and Schieffelin 1994; Gal and Irvine 1995; also Gumperz 1962: 34; Fishman 1972: 23), while on the other, researchers concerned with the tacit reproduction of identities, capacities and practice increasingly equate community with co-participation in particular activities ('communities of practice'), shrinking it down to a more manageable size where the manner and extent to which conduct really *is* regular can be established through comprehensive, detailed and often multimodal description (Lave and Wenger 1991; Eckert and McConnell-Ginet 1992; Rampton 1998).

Taken individually, none of these developments is without precedent in sociolinguistics, but cumulatively, they constitute an important shift away from an earlier tendency to hypostasise system, structure and regularity as governing principles with a foundational status that warranted the marginalisation of deviant exceptions. Instead, systematicity is now much less likely to be taken for granted, and there is a concomitant growth of interest in exceptions themselves.

This ongoing change of perspective in fact finds major parallels in a much wider shift in the humanities and social sciences. In sociology and cultural studies, the notion of ethnicity represented in the first column of Table 10.2 ('Ethnicity 1') is open to critical characterisation as 'ethnic absolutism', which Gilroy describes as a restrictive ideology that maintains (a) that a person's ethnicity is fixed from their birth in the early years of home experience, and (b) that ethnicity is the most important aspect of a person's identity, other roles and identities paling into insignificance beside it (Gilroy 1987; Rampton 1995: Ch. 1.2).[6] More generally, there is a growing feeling in sociology that the image of society as a 'compact, sealed [and systematic] totality' is rather uncomfortably based on an idealisation of the nation-state (Z. Bauman 1992: 57), and that 'the reality to be modelled is . . . much more fluid, heterogeneous and "under-patterned" than anything that sociologists tried to grasp intellectually in the past' (ibid: 65). In a period when social totality seems to have been 'dissipated into a series of randomly emerging, shifting and evanescent islands of order' (ibid: 189), the relatively micro focus of research on communities-of-practice looks very well-judged, and at a time when reality is envisaged as an increasingly closed circuit of artifactual images and representations (Baudrillard 1985; Morley and Robins 1995: 38; Castells 1996: 477), much the same might be said of the new attention paid to (artful) performance, stylisation, metapragmatics and language ideology, which all describe the ways in which social, cultural and linguistic representations penetrate practice, dispelling its tacitness. Sociolinguistic studies of cross-group identification synchronise with wider sociological interest in hybridity and mixing, and instead of trying to define the core features of any social group or institution, there is major interest outside sociolinguistics in fragmentation, indeterminacy and ambivalence, in boundaries of inclusion and exclusion, and in the flows of people, knowledge, texts and objects across social and geographical space. Indeed, linguistic notions such as creolisation and translation are sometimes borrowed as metaphors to conceptualise processes like these (see for example Hall 1992: 310; Hannerz 1989: 212; Harris and Rampton 2000).

There are, then, a number of parallels between developments in sociolinguistics and in the humanities and social sciences, and this allows us to provide a more detailed and more fully contextualised characterisation of relations between sociolinguistics and social theory.

Some of the shifts in sociological theory sketched above are driven by claims that western societies are entering a new era, profoundly affected by new information technologies, by a decline in traditional institutions and by the rise of new social movements (see Frazer and Lacey 1993). These claims are empirical, and they form part of substantive theories which are open to refutation (such as Lash and Urry 1994; Castells 1996, 1997). Doing sociolinguistics, one can read accounts like this and agree that they seem to make sense of quite a lot that seems to be going on around one, but it would be difficult to take any really authoritative view on the accuracy of their characterisation of, say, 'disorganised capital' or 'flexible accumulation'. Instead, one tends to be guided by (whatever one can gather of) more expert consensus on the quality of research like this, and to use it as useful wider contextualisation for the much smaller-scale processes one analyses. Over time, it's conceivable that these more micro-analyses might be brought into active interaction with the substantive theories and empirical literatures identified in these contextualising references, but as often as not, the references amount to little more than signposts.

At the same time, however, by no means all of the shifts in social theory are driven by new empirical generalisations. A significant part of what we can call the debate about late- or post-modernity also entails a perspectival change in the assumptions governing research (Frazer and Lacey 1993: 30). Accordingly, it is not only the idea that we're entering a new 'information age' which motivates the general shift of interest from entities-as-stable-unities to dynamic-processes-of-flow — there is also a more general feeling that perspectives reckoning with time and movement are more inclusive and are going to throw new light on old questions, as well as opening up new issues that have been side-lined hitherto. This recent preference for much more processual accounts may result from the refutation of substantive theory in some areas of science, but it translates into sociolinguistics more as an ontology, and my impression is that it's primarily as an ontology that flow-oriented perspectives are influential in the approaches which I described as superseding the 'linguistics of community'.

The assumptions actually composing this ontology may vary slightly in their formulation, but broadly speaking, they entail a commitment to the idea that culture and social reality are both reproduced *and* created anew in the skilled activity of actors drawing on unevenly distributed resources in locally and historically specific circumstances, and that these circumstances are themselves enabling and constraining to different degrees. In sociology and anthropology, these assumptions emerge from a particular sensitivity to discourse and situated practice (see for example Foucault 1962; Berger and Luckman 1966: 172–3; Giddens 1976; Bourdieu 1977; Hall 1996), and this must certainly make them especially congenial to sociolinguists trying to break away from the hypostasisation of system, coherence and community. But there is also a more general point to make about the positions that this ontology offers in wider public debate.

The assumptions I have outlined represent something of the broad orientation to 'discourse' introduced in Section 1 and delineated in Table 10.1 column 4. The table as a whole contrasts 'discourse' with 'deficit', 'difference' and 'domination' as perspectives on diversity, and carrying the logic of this comparison one step further, it looks as though the relevance of this ontology stretches much further than the reorientation it provides for research. It also has implications for one's political response to diversity in education and other social settings (McDermott and Varenne 1996). Indeed, rather in line with Giddens' idea of a 'double hermeneutic' (1976: 162), in which there is a two-way flow between ordinary and academic ways of thinking, this 'discourse' ontology may actually be on the way to becoming something like a new popular common sense.

These different ways of connecting with work outside sociolinguistics — the contextualising, the ontological (and thence the educational/political) — have certainly been important in the research project that the data in Example 1 come from. Paul Gilroy's 1987 book *There Ain't No Black in the Union Jack* was invaluable as a contextualising account of the wider cultural politics of race and class in late industrial Britain; ontological assumptions about the discursive construction of reality made my interpretive claim that adolescent language crossing contributed to the emergence of new ethnicities 'predicated on difference and diversity', transecting the lines of ethnic–genetic descent, much more credible than they might otherwise have been;[7] and following on from the latter, I also tried to spell out some of the consequences for language education (Rampton 1989/90; Leung, Harris and Rampton 1997).

At the same time, though, whatever the verdict on my own research, one can still legitimately query whether on their own, these kinds of connection mean that the relationship between sociolinguistics and sociology or cultural studies is *necessarily* animated, rigorous or argumentative. It is not impossible, in fact, to imagine situations where there is comfy consensus on one or two first principles plus a few cross-references to authors and issues that may be respectable but that the researcher can't really be bothered to pursue. What about more active cross-disciplinary relations, connections which are more obvious candidates for designation with a stronger term like 'cross-fertilisation'?

Productive cross-fertilisation is sure to take many different forms, but once again, I will take a personal line and try to describe what (at present anyway) I think were the most significant other-disciplinary appropriations in my research. More specifically, I will outline the ways in which largely non-sociolinguistic ideas about 'liminality' and 'ritual' contributed to the relatively detailed interpretation of interactional data. To do so, I will first outline their contribution to the way that I described my data on stylised Asian English, and after that, I will offer a methodological characterisation of their role in the process of analysis.

6   Ritual and liminality in stylised Asian English

As I have already intimated, the kind of codeswitching illustrated in Example 1 was not the only way in which adolescents used Asian English. There were also at least two others. (For space reasons, I can only give a very summary account of them here, but they are described at some length in Rampton 1995: Ch. 6.)

One of these occurred during informal everyday activities like standing around in dinner queues or walking around the corridors or playground. Here, Panjabi bilinguals would switch into Asian English to criticise another youngster for being somehow deviant or non-conformist — for example, for having poor taste in music, dressing badly, being fat, saying something stupid, doing something uncool ('get out!'; 'what you do, man'; 'understand English, don't you understand English'; 'eh! this is not middle school'; see Rampton 1995: Ch. 6). Rather than being located as before at the boundary of an upcoming interactional enclosure characterised by white adult control, in these incidents, it was the misdemeanour of a peer that prompted Asian English, which operated as what Goffman calls a 'prime', an attempt to get the (putative) offender to provide a remedy, which they might do by desisting, apologising and/or giving an explanation (Goffman 1971: 154ff, 109–14; Rampton 1995: 145). With any particular impropriety in focus, Asian English seemed to raise questions about the identity of the perpetrator: 'if you do that, then you must be the kind of incompetent that this accent conjures'.

The third distinctive context for Asian English was games, and this produced another radical shift. As has just been mentioned, when used to criticise a peer, Asian English was a voice of negative sanctioning. In contrast, in structured games, this was transformed and stylised AE became a language of *positive* sanctioning. Here, it was used as a language of commentary ('and Kapil Dev is batting now and Aziz is the wicket keeper for Pakistan . . . oh yes, what a ball . . . what a save by the wicketkeeper'); it was used to express praise and encouragement ('very good shot'); and when it was used to announce the score in badminton or a change of suit at blackjack, it helped everyone to get their bearings ('one nil'; 'diamond — d'you want diamond'; 'fifteen you pick up'; see Rampton 1995: 153–156). Asian English still seemed to connote some remoteness from the main currents of multiracial adolescent youth culture, but whereas before this was something to be scorned, in games this detachment became much more altruistic and authoritative. In this context, Asian English seemed to place the speaker at some remove from the competitors' concentrated struggle for advantage: it emphasised rules and ideals which all players had contracted to but which their enthusiasm about winning would always make vulnerable. This third use of AE is typified by Salim's interjection in a discussion about betting in a game of pool: 'no, you no play for money, you play for love'.

In my corpus, then, were three rather different ways in which adolescents with Panjabi backgrounds put on Indian English accents: in the first set of uses, stylised Asian English seemed to ruffle the transition into activities dominated by white adults; in the second, it was prompted by the improprieties of peers; and in the third, it was used in games, positively proclaiming the rules and ideals of play. Much to my surprise, I found that these three kinds of use corresponded with three very general categories of ritual.

Prototypically, rituals are forms of action inextricably linked to actual and potential interruptions in the orderly flow of everyday social life and relations. They orient to issues of respect and disregard, they involve formulaic conduct, they are a salient focus for comment and sanctions, and their mood is often what Turner calls 'subjunctive' rather than 'indicative', characterised by an orientation to feeling, willing, desiring, fantasising and playfulness rather than by an interest in applying 'reason to human action and systematis[ing] the relationship between means and ends' (Turner 1987: 123; Sperber 1975). Rituals may serve either to create, celebrate, elaborate, avoid, mitigate or repair these breaches in the predictable patterns of ordinary social activity, and there are at least three general types. Rituals of *consensus* bind members of a group together as a distinct collectivity, rituals of *differentiation* mark one group off from another, while *anti-rites* are counterposed to dominant systems of categorisation (Durkheim [1912] 1975; Douglas 1966; Bernstein 1975; Turner 1982). These can be aligned with the three kinds of stylised Asian English described above.

With adults, stylised Asian English seemed to serve as an anti-rite, a small destabilising act counterposed to the categories and conduct that the adult would normally be orienting to. In informal interaction with peers, it seemed to serve as a differentiating ritual, focussing on transgression and threatening the recipient with isolation in the marginal zones that AE conjured if the offender did not return to the norms of proper adolescent conduct. In games, it seemed to be a consensual ritual, stepping aside from the competitors' factional interests, focusing on activity-internal boundaries, sequences and junctures, and highlighting the ideals and rules of play rather than their disruption (for fuller discussion, see Rampton 1995: Chs 6.5 and 6.6). Indeed, beyond this correspondence between different kinds of stylised conduct and different kinds of ritual, there also seemed to be a great deal of relevance in the standard anthopological view that collective rituals try to resolve deep social anomalies and contradictions (see for example Turner 1969; Sperber 1975).

When Panjabi adolescents discussed second language Indian English in interviews, it seemed to be a very complex and emotive issue. When they associated Indian English with older members of their families, they objected to the linguistic racism that their relatives experienced ('maybe older [Pakistani and Indian] people don't understand the way that some [white] people sort of really speak slowly to impress other white people around that go "oh god, look at this one" — cos they think they're inferior to them . . . they can talk about equality, but when you go down the bloody shop . . .'). They linked accented English with processes of transition from one country to another, they mentioned translating and interpreting for their parents at home and in public settings, and their stance was generally solidary ('sometimes my mum speaks English, but I laugh cos she can't say it properly . . . she laughs herself'). They reacted ambivalently, however, to the way Asians were represented by white comedians on TV ('you laugh at first but if you think about it, why should they take the piss out of the way we talk'; 'he's good, he's a laugh' — 'he's a big bastard he is, a racialist' [two boys referring to a comedian who put on Asian English accents]), and they also admitted to themselves being racist about Bangladeshis, who were frequently ridiculed with the very same code ('yes I think it is racism, but I just can't help it . . . I'm not as bad as some people'). Putting this interview evidence next to the interactional data, it looks as though the unstable but insistent evaluative charge attached to Asian English was being picked up and reorganised into three broadly distinct forms of interactional ritual, and what was uncertain and contradictory in explicit discussion was being transformed into a ritual symbol which, in contrast, adolescents seemed to use with a high level of consistency and assurance.

Ritual, then, presented itself as a very relevant concept for my data. At the same time, however, the Asian English codeswitched data seemed to fall between both the macro and micro frames of reference within which ritual is most commonly treated.

On the one hand, it was hard to subsume them within the traditional anthropological conception of grand rites — Asian English wasn't restricted to formal collective events specifically given over to 'consecrated behaviour' (such as weddings, funerals, prayers, assemblies or graduation ceremonies — Bernstein 1975; Saville-Troike 1982: 46). It did not seem to be a 'prescribed formal behaviour for occasions not given over to technological routine, having reference to beliefs in mystical being or powers' (Turner 1969: 19; Du Bois 1986: 314).

On the other, it would have been reductive to follow Brown and Levinson's appropriation of the concept and to see Asian English as a routine politeness strategy. In Brown and Levinson's account, consensual rituals are reinterpreted as positive face strategies, differentiating rituals are reconstrued as negative face strategies, and both are treated as alternative choices continuously available to individuals in the ongoing formulation of optimally effective interpersonal utterances (so that, put crudely, speakers are envisaged as asking themselves: 'when I make this request, shall I present myself as an old pal, or as a respectful acquaintance reluctant to impose myself?'). But in the first place, this view of positive and negative face orientations competing on-line in the speaker's inner deliberations says little to the fact that positive/consensual and negative/differentiating uses of Asian English presented themselves as separate public displays (the first in the context of games, and the second in less structured peer interaction). And second, stylised Asian English seemed to show a symbolic orientation to historical and political group experiences that would be flattened out in the theoretical priority that Brown and Levinson give to individual speaker goals and means-and-ends reasoning (1987: 64 et passim).

What was needed, then, was an account of ritual that somehow combined the anthropologist's interest in social symbolism with the orientation to everyday speech in pragmatics.

To try to achieve this, the accounts of action in awkward social moments that Goffman provides served as an indispensable starting point. Brown and Levinson's notion of face comes, of course, from Goffman, and indeed like them, Goffman (1981) regards a ritual orientation to facework as omnipervasive in conduct. He dwells, however, much more fully than Brown and Levinson on what people do in moments when expectations about the orderly flow of respectful social relations are uncertain, jeopardised or relaxed,[8] and this made his work particularly valuable for the analysis of language crossing, much of which seemed to occur at precisely these kinds of non-routine interactional juncture. The boundaries of interactional enclosure, when the roles and identities for ensuing interaction are still relatively indeterminate, were one recurrent context (Goffman 1971: Ch. 7; Laver 1975, 1981; Rampton 1995: Ch. 3.3); open states of talk, self-talk and response cries, all of which constitute time away from the full demands of respectful interpersonal conduct, were another (Goffman 1981: 81,85,99; cf Rampton 1995: Chs 7.5, 10.7); and interactional breaches, delicts and transgressions were a third. We can see this last context if we return to Example 1, drawing on Goffman but also enriching his approach with observations from more macro-sociological accounts of ritual.

As I have already indicated, Example 1 involves a dispute over interactional frames, and within it, the boys switch into Asian English, Creole and Panjabi at moments when transgression and impropriety are focal issues. According to Goffman (1971: 98), at moments like this, we do not just seek some kind of repair to whatever's been damaged or disrupted by the infraction — we look for signs of where the actor stands more generally in relation to social rules and the order we approve. In fact, this happens whenever our sense of the orderly flow of everyday conduct is jeopardised or uncertain, and people often respond to these moments by briefly shifting away from the (appropriately modulated) production of propositional utterances geared to truth and falsity, instead turning to a range of symbolic formulae to intensify the ritual dimension of their conduct: farewell and greeting routines, apologies, thanks, expletives, expressions of dismay or surprise, even proverbs (Drew and Holt 1988). By invoking well-established material authored by tradition, these formulae display an orientation to wider collectivities capable of overriding the temporary disturbance immediately on hand.

Very often, ritual actions are broadly convergent. Words and phrases like 'how do you do' and 'sorry' allow people to establish or to get back on the right wavelength, drawing on a shared cultural inheritance, serving as small affirmations of a dominant social order. But as we have already noted, ritual actions can just as well be differentiating, creating a sense of distance between the participants (see Goodwin 1990), and, particularly significant for the data on hand, in stratified plural societies they can also be opposed to dominant values and beliefs (Lukes 1975; Alexander 1988). This capacity of ritual to combine interpersonal divergence and political dissidence can be seen in the codeswitching in Example 1.

The element of interpersonal divergence is half-concealed in the switches into Indian English: they look as though they are polite, but in fact the symbolic connotations of babu raise uncomfortable questions about white racism. With the Creole in lines 27 and 30, there is no element of surface politeness: the first switch leads to a short run-in, and the code itself is associated with the rejection of illegitimate white power. Much more than simply creating interpersonal distance, these ritual sequences seem to be serving as showcase moments for the boys to play with a wider sense of social positioning. As already suggested, Asian English was a variety that these youngsters felt they were leaving behind, that they associated with an older generation and with newcomers to England. In contrast, Creole stood for excitement and excellence in youth culture which a lot of kids aspired to and which was even referred to once as 'future language'.[9] These perspectives are intricately connected to population movements, to mass media representations and to the politics of race in Britain, and yet here they seem to be highlighted in the prism of interaction, symbolically indexed and actively processed within just a few seconds of talk.

Goffman, then, provides a good deal of purchase on moments when coherence and community are problematic and when our sense of the effort involved in building solidarity, opposition or a social location are intensified.

He himself, though, does not attend much to the socio-historical particularities of symbolisation, and so at this point, I found it useful to draw in the notion of 'liminality' as a way of flagging up the scope for social creativity that these Goffmanian moments actually afforded.[10]

In Victor Turner's account, the idea of liminality was first developed to refer to the middle phase of initiation rites in agrarian societies. After the separation phase (leaving childhood behind), and before incorporation (taking up a new and well-defined position in society), the liminal middle phase of transition is

> a period and area of ambiguity, a sort of social limbo which has few...
> of the attributes of either the preceding or subsequent social statuses or
> cultural states ... In liminality, [everyday] social relations may be discontinued, former rights and obligations are suspended, the social order may
> seem to have been turned upside down. (Turner 1982: 24,27)

But Turner then adapts this notion to industrial urban settings, where, he argues, as well as being 'more idiosyncratic [and] quirky' (p. 45), liminal practices are also often creative, containing social critiques and exposing wrongs in mainstream structures and organisation (p. 54). Here in urban liminality, 'the seeds of cultural transformation, discontent with the ways things are culturally, and social criticism, always implicit in the traditionally [agrarian] liminal, have become situationally central' (p. 45).

The idea of using liminality as a concept in the micro-interactional analysis of ritual was first raised by John Laver in 1975, drawing on both Goffman (1959) and Raymond Firth (1972). But the particular turn which Turner gives to the concept is especially relevant to my own data, where it is impossible to ignore the politics and where speakers seem to be probing away at dominant systems of 'race' categorisation. Beyond that, the concept of liminality has additional value in the way that it allows us to connect language crossing in non-routine *interactional* moments to the way in which language crossing could also occur in *larger* genres, events and relationships such as games, jocular abuse, musical performance and cross-sex interaction. The notion of liminality has or can also be used to characterise all of these phenomena: in games, there is an agreed relaxation of routine interaction's rules and constraints (Handelman 1977; Turner 1982: 56; Sutton-Smith 1982); in joking/ritual abuse, normal considerations of truth and falsity are held in abeyance (Labov 1972; Goodwin and Goodwin 1987); in musical performance, 'the temporal and spatial order of the dominant culture' can be suspended (Gilroy 1987: 210); and in settings where everyday recreation is single-sex and where many parents discourage unmonitored contact between adolescent girls and boys, cross-sex interaction may itself seem special, unusually invested with both risk and promise (see Foley 1990: 33, 70, 95; Shuman 1993: 146; Gillespie 1995: 41). By drawing all these sites together under the heading of liminality, we can in fact come to a much larger generalisation about my data on inter-ethnic language crossing. The fact that adolescents only crossed into other-ethnic languages in moments and events that were liminal, suggests that in the dominant version of world to which they normally oriented, they saw a strong link between minority languages and minority ethnicities — Panjabi belonged to Panjabis, Creole to African Caribbeans, and Asian English to parents and Bangladeshis. So language crossing was not a deconstructionist free-for-all, where ethnicity and race had been emptied of all meaning. Instead, it only seemed safe to question these equations and to try out alternative configurations in periods of liminality when business-as-usual was interrupted.

What of more general questions about the relationship between sociolinguistics and social theory?

7   Liminality and ritual as analytic aids and cross-disciplinary bridges

The way that I used the notions of ritual and liminality could be seen as an example of the theory building that qualitative research is sometimes regarded as best suited to (Hammersley and Atkinson 1983). To clarify this and to explain a little further the purchase that these two concepts do and do not provide, I would like to use this short final section to provide a brief methodological specification of their role in the process of analysis, focussing, for space reasons, mainly on liminality.

In terms borrowed from Erickson's marvellous 1986 paper 'Qualitative methods in research on teaching', liminality can in the first instance be seen as a mid-level 'key linkage' capable of connecting up 'many items of data as analogous instances of the same phenomena' (1986: 148) — in the case here, contexts (moments, genres and events) for crossing that varied quite considerably in their intensity, scale and duration. As such, liminality is a relatively abstract analytic concept. Establishing its relevance certainly involved (an approximation to) the processes of detailed and intensive data-examination that Erickson describes (such as constant comparison of specific instances and the search for discrepant cases), but on its own, liminality is too broad and undiscriminating a concept to answer the first questions that characterise interpretive interaction analysis:

1. What is happening, specifically, in social action that takes place in this particular setting? 2. What do these actions mean to the actors involved in them, at the moment the actions took place? 3. How are the happenings organised in patterns of social organisation and learned cultural principles for the conduct of everyday life? (Erickson 1986: 121)

To address questions such as these, all of the descriptive vocabularies brought together in research traditions such as interactional sociolinguistics (involving for example phonetics, conversation analysis and the ethnography of communication) are an essential first port of call, and indeed, frameworks like these constitute much of the specialist expertise that sociolinguists (broadly defined) can bring as their distinctive contribution to interdisciplinary debate. However, as a higher level concept tying together a host of instances that were first analysed with much more delicate descriptive tools, 'liminality' does allow one to address the later questions that Erickson poses:

4. How is what is happening in this setting as a whole . . . related to happenings at other system levels outside and inside the setting? 5. How do the ways everyday life in this setting is organised compare with other ways of organising social life in a wide range of settings in other places and at other times? (Erickson 1986: 121)

Taking question 4, it was, as I've said, 'liminality' that allowed me to suggest what the common properties might be that made diverse activities like remedial sequences, games and cross-sex banter all hospitable to language crossing, and when one moves to question 5, one can start to see how liminality might serve as a bridging concept to other studies *outside* as well as inside sociolinguistics.

This methodological characterisation of how 'liminality' functioned as a concept in analysis could also be applied to 'ritual'. Together, they form a pair of fairly formal, complementary concepts that can refer to a wide range of different processes and phenomena — liminality points to breaches in the customary flow of social order and relations, and ritual refers to actions oriented specifically to such breaches. Recently in anthropology, sociology and cultural studies, liminality has been a particularly popular concept in discussions of the fluidity and renegotiation of identities, and it has been conceptualised at a number of different levels on the macro–micro scale of social structuring — dances, leisure time, adolescence and particular ethnicities have all been seen as liminal (see Rampton 1999a for fuller discussion). What scholars in other disciplines have (quite understandably) tended to miss, however, is that interaction is itself a constant flow of structured practices that can be breached and interrupted, and because of this, day-to-day life presents dozens of small-scale opportunities for minor adventures into liminality and the reworkings of identity that liminality permits. Brought alongside Victor Turner, Goffman's interaction order itself provides a wealth of possibilities for the kinds of social redefinition and creativity that students of late modernity are particularly interested in, and this is an area where sociolinguistic research on interactional discourse can offer something that is both highly relevant and distinctive.

At the same time, of course, traffic across these two 'bridging concepts' can flow in the opposite direction. Brown and Levinson are themselves aware (1987: 43–7) of the potential for enriching politeness theory with a fuller notion of ritual, and the same could be said of educational discourse analyses, where the treatment of ritual has tended to be both restricted and freighted with negative evaluation,[11] and where the preoccupation with individual cognition and its interactional supports has often led to a neglect of social symbolism, with ritual frequently recoded as 'repetition', 'routines', 'chunks' or 'prefabricated patterns'. One consequence of this is that when students do not seem to be interested by repetitive formal methods of instruction, this is put down to boredom, and the recommended cure consists of more plentiful opportunites for the 'negotiation of meaning'. In contrast, a fuller notion of ritual, drawing on the anthropologist's sensitivity to social symbolism, might suggest that far from being empty of meaning, repetitive form-focussed activities are actually replete with symbolic meanings, that these meanings are *actively alienating* for a lot of students, and that they evoke social horizons, heritages, affiliations and futures in which they feel they have no possible stake (see Rampton 1999b).

Summing up, liminality and ritual can be seen as invaluable nodal points of intersection. Within and across corpora, they can serve as 'key linkages', bringing actions and activities together that are positioned at different levels in institutional organisation and the interaction order. At the same time, they offer themselves as channels for two-way flow between sociolinguistics on the one hand and sociology, anthropology, education and cultural studies on the other. How far they are generally used in this way, either hitherto or in the future, is a question that lies well beyond the scope of this chapter, and it would also be well beyond the terms of my discussion to try to make any authoritative larger claims that this kind of disciplinary cross-referring was always superior to the contextualising and ontological alignments addressed in earlier sections. Even so, judging simply from my own experience as a solo researcher — the situation for members of multi-disciplinary groupings may well be different — my personal guess is that it is concepts with a methodological profile, scope and flexibility broadly comparable to liminality and ritual that are likely to generate the most intense and productive cross-disciplinary engagements.

Notes

1. I am very grateful to the three editors of this volume for an invaluable set of detailed comments that led to the substantial (actually, total) revision of an earlier draft.

2. For a fuller account of my interpretation of switches into Indian English, see Rampton 1995: Chs 3 and 6.

3. Whether or not these ideological 'pre-texts' and stereotypes are given quite enough emphasis has been a matter of some debate (Shea 1994: 360 and Meeuwis 1994: 403).

4. Indeed, if the relevance of ethnicity is negotiated by participants in mixed race interactions, then when one person stresses their ethnic background (as in the 'reactive' view of ethnicity), their addressee is going to make some kind of sense of this in terms of their own models of the speaker's ethnicity.

5. See Rampton (ed.) 1999 for a range of studies examining the ways in which people use language varieties variably felt to be other.

6. There are in fact a number of quite serious problems with the idea of ethnicity as an ingrained disposition. It would be foolish to deny the importance or subtlety of the linguistic and cultural dispositions and practices laid down over time through face-to-face interaction at home and in local networks, and it is also necessary to recognise that some of these patterns are deeply marked with emotional associations. But what are the reasons for assuming that these ingrained patterns are co-terminous with ethnic category membership rather than say class, gender, neighbourhood, family, etc.? If this legacy is called 'ethnic', there is a risk of misrepresenting the personal, social and emotional connotations themselves, which may be much more to do with the memory of particular families, particular individuals, or particular experiences. Following on from this, one also risks misrepresenting ethnicity if one assumes that these resonances are common to everyone who either aligns themself with the ethnic category, or gets ascribed to it. Turning to more sociolinguistic perspectives on this kind of ethnicity, it also highly likely that much of the meaning of these deep emotional connotations is pre-conceptual and preverbal, and so the connection with linguistic data remains very problematic. Lastly, as Gumperz and Cook-Gumperz say, it is essential not to forget the here-and-now context where particular forms are actually being used or discussed. If you forget the context of interpretation itself, there is a danger of mistaking interpretations made in the here-and-now for symbolic meanings inscribed in the linguistic objects there-and-then during the period when they were first acquired — in fact, depending on whatever is relevant to the discourse in which the interpretation is being made, the very same linguistic resources can often be construed in terms of class, gender, generation, region, personality, mood, etc.

7. There was a certain amount of evidence to support this claim, but I certainly did not measure the effects of language crossing by operationalising orientations to 'homogeneous' vs 'heterogeneous' ethnicity on attitudinal rating scales, for example, or on any of the other kinds of measure that have traditionally made fairly immediate sense to policy makers, for instance.

8. Brown and Levinson's communicators generally avoid these, since their model describes the advance procedures that people are prompted to take by their sensitivity to potential rather than actual offence.

9. As elsewhere in this chapter, the description here may seem rather sketchy, but for space reasons, the best I can do is (once again!) to refer the reader to Rampton 1995.

10. Moments of breach to 'the world of daily life known in common with others and with others taken for granted' (Garfinkel 1984: 35) are also obviously particularly important in ethnomethodology.

11. Edwards and Mercer (1987), for example, call learner activities 'ritual' when they seem to be imitative, automatic, inflexible, practical, unreflexive, and designed to please the teacher, and they contrast these unfavourably with 'principled' learning, which is described as creative, considered, flexible, theoretical, meta-cognitive and done for one's own purposes.

References

Agar, M. (1985) Institutional discourse. *Text* 5.3: 147–168.

Alexander, J. (ed.) (1988) *Durkheimian Sociology: Cultural Studies*. Cambridge: Cambridge University Press.

Anderson, B. (1983) *Imagined Communities: Reflections on the Origin and Spread of Nationalism*. London: Verso.

Aronsson, K. (1997) Age in social interaction. On constructivist epistemologies and the social psychology of language. *International Journal of Applied Linguistics* 7.1: 49–56.

Bakhtin, M. (1984) *Problems in Dostoevsky's Poetics*. Minneapolis: University of Minnesota Press.

Barrett, R. (1997) The 'Homo-genius' speech community. In A. Livia and K. Hall (eds) *Queerly Phrased: Language, Gender and Sexuality*. Oxford: Oxford University Press, 181–201.

Basso, K. (1979) *Portraits of 'the White Man': Linguistic Play and Cultural Symbols among the Western Apache*. Cambridge: Cambridge University Press.

Baudrillard, J. (1985) The ecstasy of communication. In H. Foster (ed.) *Postmodern Culture*. London: Pluto.

Bauman, R. (1986) *Story, Performance and Event: Contextual Studies of Oral Narrative*. Cambridge: Cambridge University Press.

Bauman, R. and Briggs, C. (1990) Poetics and performance as critical perspectives on language and social life. *Annual Review of Anthropology* 19: 59–88.

Bauman, R. and Sherzer, J. (eds) (1974) *Explorations in the Ethnography of Speaking*, 2nd edn. Cambridge: Cambridge University Press.

Bauman, R. and Sherzer, J. (1989) Introduction to the second edition. In R. Bauman and J. Sherzer (eds) *Explorations in the Ethnography of Speaking*, 2nd edn. Cambridge: Cambridge University Press.

Bauman, Z. (1992) *Intimations of Postmodernity*. London: Routledge.

Bell, A. (1984) Language style as audience design. *Language in Society* 13.2: 145–204.

Berger, P. and Luckman, T. (1966) *The Social Construction of Reality*. Harmondsworth: Penguin.

Bernstein, B. (1975) Ritual in education. In *Class, Codes and Control III: Towards a Theory of Educational Transmissions*. London: Routledge & Kegan Paul, 54–66.

Bernstein, B. (1990) *Class, Codes and Control IV: The Structuring of Pedagogic Discourse*. London: Routledge.

Bernstein, B. (1996) Sociolinguistics: A personal view. In *Pedagogy, Symbolic Control and Identity*. London: Taylor & Francis, 147–156.

Billig, M. (1995) *Banal Nationalism*. London: Sage.

Bourdieu, P. (1977) *Outline of a Theory of Practice*. Cambridge: Cambridge University Press.

Brandt, G. (1986) *The Realisation of Anti-racist Teaching*. Lewes: Falmer Press.

Brown, P. and Levinson, S. (1987) *Politeness*. Cambridge: Cambridge University Press.

Brumfit, C. (1984) *Communicative Methodology in Language Teaching*. Cambridge: Cambridge University Press.

Cameron, D. (1990) Demythologising sociolinguistics: Why language does not reflect society. In J. Joseph and T. Taylor (eds) *Ideologies of Language*. London: Routledge, 79–96.

Cameron, D. (1995) *Verbal Hygiene*. London: Routledge.

Cameron, D., Frazer, E., Harvey, P., Rampton, B. and Richardson, K. (1992) *Researching Language: Issues of Power and Method*. London: Routledge.

Castells, M. (1996) *The Rise of the Network Society*. Oxford: Blackwell.

Castells, M. (1997) *The Power of Identity*. Oxford: Blackwell.

Cheshire, J. and Moser, L.-M. (1994) English as a cultural symbol: The case of advertisements in French-speaking Switzerland. *Journal of Multilingual and Multicultural Development* 15.6: 451–469.

Cohen, I. (1987) Structuration theory. In A. Giddens and J. Turner (eds) *Social Theory Today*. Oxford: Polity Press, 273–308.

Coupland, N. (1997) Stylised deception: Sociolinguistics, authenticity and the comic rogue. MS.

Cutler, C. (1999) Yorkville crossing: White teens, hip hop and African American English. *Journal of Sociolinguistics* 3.4: 428–442.

Donald, J. and Rattansi, A. (eds) (1992) *'Race', Culture and Difference*. London: Sage.

Douglas, M. (1966) *Purity and Danger*. London: Routledge & Kegan Paul.

Douglas, M. (1968) The social control of cognition: Some factors in joke production. *Man (NS)* 3: 361–376.

Drew, P. and Holt, E. (1988) Complainable matters: The use of idiomatic expressions in making complaints. *Social Problems* 35.4: 398–417.

Du Bois, J. (1986) Self-evidence and ritual speech. In W. Chafe and J. Nichols (eds) *Evidentiality*. New Jersey: Ablex, 313–336.

Duranti, A. (1997) *Linguistic Anthropology*. Cambridge: Cambridge University Press.

Durkheim, E. ([1912] 1975). *The Elementary Forms of Religious Life*. Extracts in W. Pickering, *Durkheim on Religion*. London: Routledge & Kegan Paul.

Eastman, C. and Stein, R. (1993) Language display: Authenticating claims to social identity. *Journal of Multilingual and Multicultural Development* 14: 187–202.

Eckert, P. and McConnell-Ginet, S. (1992) Think practically and look locally: Language and gender as community-based practice. *Annual Review of Anthropology* 21: 461–490.

Edwards, D. and Mercer, N. (1987) *Common Knowledge*. London: Methuen.

Erickson, F. (1986) Qualitative methods in research on teaching. In M. Wittrock (ed.) *Handbook of Research on Teaching*, 3rd edn. New York: Macmillan, 119–161.

Erickson, F. and Shultz, J. (1982) *The Counsellor as Gatekeeper*. New York: Academic Press.

Fairclough, N. (1992) *Discourse and Social Change*. Oxford: Polity Press.

Ferguson, C. (1975) Towards a characterisation of English foreigner talk. *Anthropological Linguistics* 17: 1–14.

Firth, R. (1972) Verbal and bodily rituals of greeting and parting. In J. La Fontaine (ed.) *The Interpretation of Ritual*. London: Tavistock, 1–38.

Fishman, J. (1972) *The Sociology of Language*. Rowley, MA: Newbury House.

Foley, D. (1990) *Learning Capitalist Culture*. Philadelphia: University of Pennsylvania Press.

Foucault, M. (1962) *The Archeology of Knowledge*. London: Tavistock.

Foucault, M. (1977) *Discipline and Punish*. Harmondsworth: Penguin.

Foucault, M. (1980) *Power/Knowledge*. Brighton: Harvester Press.

Frazer, E. and Lacey, N. (1993) *The Politics of Community*. Hemel Hempstead: Harvester Wheatsheaf.

Gal, S. (1995a) Language, gender and power: An anthropological review. In K. Hall and M. Bucholtz (eds) *Gender Articulated*. London: Routledge, 169–182.

Gal, S. (1995b) Language and the 'Arts of Resistance'. *Cultural Anthropology* 10.3: 407–424.

Gal, S. and Irvine, J. (1995) The boundaries of languages and disciplines: How ideologies construct difference. *Social Research* 62.4: 967–1001.

Garfinkel, H. (1984) *Studies in Ethnomethodology*. Oxford: Polity Press.

Giddens, A. (1976) *New Rules of Sociological Method*. London: Hutchinson.

Gillespie, M. (1995) *Television, Ethnicity and Cultural Change*. London: Routledge.

Gilroy, P. (1987) *There Ain't No Black in the Union Jack*. London: Hutchinson.

Goffman, E. (1959) *The Presentation of Self in Everyday Life*. New York: Doubleday Anchor.

Goffman, E. (1971) *Relations in Public*. London: Allen Lane.

Goffman, E. (1974) *Frame Analysis*. Harmondsworth: Penguin.

Goffman, E. (1981) *Forms of Talk*. Oxford: Blackwell.

Goffman, E. (1983) The interaction order. *American Sociological Review* 48: 1–17.

Goodwin, M. (1990) *He-Said-She-Said*. Bloomington: Indiana University Press.

Goodwin, C. and Goodwin, M. (1987) Children's arguing. In A. Grimshaw (ed.) *Conflict Talk*. Cambridge: Cambridge University Press, 200–248.

Grossberg, L. (1996) Identity and cultural studies — Is that all there is? In S. Hall and P. du Gay (eds) *Questions of Cultural Identity*. London: Sage.

Gumperz, J. (1962) Types of linguistic community. *Anthropological Linguistics* 4: 28–40.

Gumperz, J. (1968) The speech community. In *International Encyclopedia of the Social Sciences*. London: Macmillan, 381–386.

Gumperz, J. (1982a) *Discourse Strategies*. Cambridge: Cambridge University Press.

Gumperz, J. (ed.) (1982b) *Language and Social Identity*. Cambridge: Cambridge University Press.

Gumperz, J. and Cook-Gumperz, J. (1982) Introduction: Language and the communication of social identity. In J. Gumperz (ed.) *Language and Social Identity*. Cambridge University Press, 1–21.

Gumperz, J. and Roberts, C. (1991) Understanding in intercultural encounters. In J. Blommaert and J. Verschueren (eds) *The Pragmatics of Intercultural and International Communication*. Amsterdam: John Benjamins, 51–90.

Gumperz, J., Roberts, C. and Jupp, T. (1979) *Crosstalk: A Study of Cross-cultural Communication*. Southall, Middlesex: National Centre for Industrial Language Training.

Hall, K. (1995) Lip service on the fantasy lines. In K. Hall and M. Bucholtz (eds) *Gender Articulated*. New York: Routledge, 183–216.

Hall, S. (1992) The question of cultural identity. In S. Hall, D. Held and T. McGrew (eds) *Modernity and its Futures*. Cambridge: Polity Press, 274–316.

Hall, S. (1996) Introduction: Who needs identity? In S. Hall and P. du Gay (eds) *Questions of Cultural Identity*. London: Sage, 1–17.

Hammersley, M. and Atkinson, P. (1983) *Ethnography: Principles in Practice*. London: Tavistock.

Handelman, D. (1977) Play and ritual: Complementary forms of metacommunication. In A. Chapman and H. Foot (eds) *It's a Funny Thing, Humour*. Oxford: Pergamon, 185–192.

Hannerz, U. (1989) Culture between center and periphery. *Ethnos* 54.3 and 4: 200–216.

Hannerz, U. (1992a) *Cultural Complexity*. New York: Columbia University Press.

Hannerz, U. (1992b) The global ecumene as a network of networks. In A. Kuper (ed.) *Conceptualising Society*. London: Routledge, 34–56.

Harris, R. (1996) Openings, absences and omissions: Aspects of the treatment of 'race', culture and ethnicity within British Cultural Studies. *Cultural Studies* 10.

Harris, R. and Rampton, B. (2000) Creole metaphors in cultural analysis: The limits and possibilities of sociolinguistics. Oxford: Transnational Communities Working Paper Series WPTC-2K-12.

Heath, S.B. (1983) *Ways with Words*. Cambridge: Cambridge University Press.

Heller, M. (1999) *Linguistic Minorities and Modernity: A Sociolinguistic Ethnography*. London: Longman.

Hewitt, R. (1986) *White Talk Black Talk*. Cambridge: Cambridge University Press.

Hewitt, R. (1992) Language, youth and the destabilisation of ethnicity. In C. Palmgren, K. Lougren and G. Bolin (eds) *Ethnicity in Youth Culture*. Stockholm: Youth Culture at Stockholm University.

Hill, J. (1993) Hasta la vista, baby: Anglo Spanish in the American Southwest. *Critique of Anthropology* 13: 145–176.

Hill, J. (1995) Junk Spanish, covert racism, and the (leaky) boundary between public and private spheres. *Pragmatics* 5.2: 197–212.

Hill, J. and Coombs, D. (1982) The vernacular remodelling of national and international languages. *Applied Linguistics* 3: 224–234.

Hill, J. and Hill, K. (1986) *Speaking Mexicano*. Tucson: University of Arizona Press.

Hoechsmann, M. (1997) Benetton culture: Marketing difference to the new global consumer. In H. Riggins (ed.) *The Language and Politics of Exclusion*. London: Sage, 183–202.

Hudson, R. (1980) *Sociolinguistics*. Cambridge: Cambridge University Press.

Hymes, D. (1972) Models of the interaction of language and social life. In J. Gumperz and D. Hymes (eds) *Directions in Sociolinguistics*. Oxford: Blackwell, 35–71.

James, A. (1995) Talking of children and youth: Language, socialisation and culture. In V. Amit-Talai and H. Wulff (eds) *Youth Cultures: A Cross-cultural Perspective.* London: Routledge, 43–62.

Kachru, B. (1982) Introduction: The other side of English. In B. Kachru (ed.) *The Other Tongue: English across Cultures.* Oxford: Pergamon, 1–12.

Kroskrity, P., Schieffelin, B. and Woolard, K. (eds) (1992) Special Issue on Language Ideologies. *Pragmatics* 2.3.

Labov, W. (1972) The reflection of social processes in linguistic structures. In *Sociolinguistic Patterns.* Oxford: Blackwell, 110–121.

Labov, W. (1980) Is there a creole speech community? In A. Valdman and A. Highfield (eds) *Theoretical Orientations in Creole Studies.* New York: Academic Press, 389–424.

Lash, S. and Urry, J. (1994) *Economies of Signs and Space.* London: Sage.

Lave, J. and Wenger, E. (1991) *Situated Learning: Legitimate Peripheral Participation.* Cambridge: Cambridge University Press.

Laver, J. (1975) Communicative functions of phatic communion. In A. Kendon, R. Harris and M. Key (eds) *Organisation of Behaviour in Face-to-face Interaction.* The Hague: Mouton, 215–238.

Laver, J. (1981) Linguistic routines and politeness in greeting and parting. In F. Coulmas (ed.) *Conversational Routine.* The Hague: Mouton, 289–304.

Le Page, R. (1980) Projection, focusing and diffusion. *York Papers in Linguistics* 9.

Le Page, R. and Tabouret-Keller, A. (1985) *Acts of Identity.* Cambridge: Cambridge University Press.

Leung, C., Harris, R. and Rampton, B. (1997) The idealised native speaker, reified ethnicities and classroom realities. *TESOL Quarterly* 31.3: 543–566.

Livia, A. and Hall, K. (1997) 'It's a girl': Bringing performativity back to linguistics. In A. Livia and K. Hall (eds) *Queerly Phrased: Language, Gender and Sexuality.* Oxford: Oxford University Press, 3–18.

Livia, A. and Hall, K. (eds) (1997) *Queerly Phrased: Language, Gender and Sexuality.* Oxford: Oxford University Press.

Lukes, S. (1975) Political ritual and social integration. *Sociology* 9: 289–308.

Lury, C. (1996) *Consumer Culture.* Oxford: Polity Press.

McDermott, R. and Gospodinoff, K. (1981) Social contexts for ethnic borders and school failure. In H. Trueba, G. Guthrie and K. Au (eds) *Culture and the Bilingual Classroom.* Rowley: Newbury House, 212–236.

McDermott, R. and Varenne, H. (1996) Culture, development, disability. In R. Jessor, A. Colby and R. Shweder (eds) *Ethnography and Human Development.* Chicago: Chicago University Press, 101–126.

Meeuwis, M. (1994) Leniency and testiness in intercultural communication: Remarks on ideology and context in interactional sociolinguistics. *Pragmatics* 4.3: 391–408.

Mitchell-Kernan, C. (1971) *Language Behaviour in a Black Urban Community.* Language Behaviour Research Laboratory Monograph 2. Berkeley: University of California Press.

Morley, D. and Robins, K. (1995) *Spaces of Identity: Global Media, Electronic Landscapes and Cultural Boundaries.* London: Routledge.

Parmar, P. (1982) Gender, race and class: Asian women in resistance. In Centre for Contemporary Cultural Studies *The Empire Strikes Back.* London: Hutchinson, 236–275.

Pennycook, A. (1994) *The Cultural Politics of English as an International Language.* London: Longman.

Philips, S.U. (1972) Participant structures and communicative competence: Warm Springs Indian children in community and classroom. In C. Cazden, D. Hymes and V. John (eds) *Functions of Language in the Classroom.* New York: Teachers College Press, 370–394.

Phillipson, R. (1992) *Linguistic Imperialism.* Oxford: Oxford University Press.

Pratt, M.L. (1987) Linguistic Utopias. In N. Fabb, D. Attridge, A. Durant and C. McCabe (eds) *The Linguistics of Writing.* Manchester: Manchester University Press, 48–66.

Pratt, M.L. (1991) The arts of the contact zone. *Profession* 91: 33–40.

Py, B. (1995) Quelques remarques sur les notions d'exolinguisme et de bilinguisme. *Cahier Praxématique* 25: 79–95.

Quirk, Randolph (1990) Language varieties and standard language. *English Today* 21: 3–10.

Rampton, B. (1989/90) Some unofficial perspectives on bilingualism and education for all. *Language Issues* 3.2.

Rampton, B. (1990) Displacing the 'native speaker': Expertise, affiliation and inheritance. *ELT Journal* 44.2: 97–101.

Rampton, B. (1992) Scope for empowerment in sociolinguistics? In D. Cameron *et al. Researching Language: Issues of Power and Method.* London: Routledge, 29–64.

Rampton, B. (1995) *Crossing: Language and Ethnicity among Adolescents.* London: Longman.

Rampton, B. (1997) Retuning in applied linguistics? *International Journal of Applied Linguistics* 7.1: 3–25.

Rampton, B. (1998) Speech community. In J. Verschueren, J.-O. Östman, J. Blommaert and C. Bulcaen (eds) *Handbook of Pragmatics.* Amsterdam: John Benjamins.

Rampton, B. (1999a) Sociolinguistics and Cultural Studies: New ethnicities, liminality and interaction. *Social Semiotics* 9.3: 355–373.

Rampton, B. (1999b) Dichotomies, difference and ritual in second language learning and teaching. *Applied Linguistics* 20.3: 316–340.

Rampton, B. (1999c) Crossing. *Journal of Linguistic Anthropology* 9(1–2): 54–56.

Rampton, B. (ed.) (1999) Styling the 'Other'. Special issue of *Journal of Sociolinguistics* 3.4.

Roberts, C., Davies, E. and Jupp, T. (1992) *Language and Discrimination.* London: Longman.

Roberts, C. and Sarangi, S. (1995) 'But are they one of us?': Managing and evaluating identities in work-related contexts. *Multilingua* 14.4: 363–390.

Ryan, E. and Giles, H. (eds) (1982) *Attitudes to Language Variation.* London: Arnold.

Sapir, E. ([1931] 1949) Communication. In D. Mandelbaum (ed.) *Edward Sapir: Selected Writings in Language, Culture and Personality.* Berkeley: California University Press, 104–109.

Saville-Troike, M. (1982) *The Ethnography of Communication.* Oxford: Blackwell.

Scollon, R. and Scollon, S. (1995) *Intercultural Communication.* Oxford: Blackwell.

Shea, D. (1994) Perspective and production: Structuring conversational participation across cultural borders. *Pragmatics* 4.3: 357–390.

Shuman, A. (1993) 'Get outa my face': Entitlement and authoritative discourse. In J. Hill and J. Irvine (eds) *Responsibility and Evidence in Oral Discourse*. Cambridge: Cambridge University Press, 135–160.

Sims Holt, G. (1972) Inversion in Black communication. In T. Kochman (ed.) *Rappin' and Stylin' Out*. Urbana: University of Illinois Press.

Singh, R., Lele, J. and Martohardjono, G. (1988) Communication in a multilingual society: Some missed opportunities. *Language in Society* 17.1: 43–59.

Sperber, D. (1975) *Rethinking Symbolism*. Cambridge: Cambridge University Press.

Stubbs, M. (1997) Whorf's children: Critical comments on Critical Discourse Analysis. In A. Ryan and A. Wray (eds) *Evolving Models of Language*. Clevedon: Multilingual Matters, 100–116.

Sutton-Smith, B. (1982) A performance theory of peer relations. In K. Borman (ed.) *The Social Life of Children in a Changing Society*. Norwood, NJ: Ablex, 65–77.

Thompson, J. (1984) *Studies in the Theory of Ideology*. Oxford: Polity Press.

Turner, V. (1969) *The Ritual Process*. London: Routledge & Kegan Paul.

Turner, V. (1982) *From Ritual to Theatre: The Human Seriousness of Play*. New York: PAJ.

Turner, V. (1987) *The Anthropology of Performance*. New York: PAJ.

Urciuoli, B. (1996) *Exposing Prejudice: Puerto Rican Experiences of Language, Race and Class*. New York: Westview Press.

van Dijk, T. (1987) *Communicating Racism*. London: Sage.

Wetherall, M. and Potter, J. (1992) *Mapping the Language of Racism*. Hemel Hempstead: Harvester Wheatsheaf.

Williams, G. (1992) *Sociolinguistics: A Sociological Critique*. London: Routledge.

Woolard, K. (1988) Codeswitching and comedy in Catalonia. In M. Heller (ed.) *Codeswitching: Anthropological and Sociolinguistic Perspectives*. The Hague: Mouton de Gruyter, 53–76.

Woolard, K. and Schieffelin, B. (1994) Language ideology. *Annual Review of Anthropology* 23: 55–82.

11

Discourse theory and language planning: A critical reading of language planning reports in Switzerland[1]

Richard J. Watts

1 Introduction

Language planning projects in most states stem from, and also feed into, policy statements on language. Their aim is generally to underwrite political decisions concerning language that have already been made or to provide political decision makers with a 'secure basis' on which to shape language policy. Ideally, of course, the state commissions linguists and sociolinguists to carry out language planning projects and to provide the secure basis needed by the politicians in power, although reality frequently clashes with this ideal. Indeed, even in the ideal cases in which the 'expertise' of linguists and sociolinguists has been sought — and the case that I shall discuss in this chapter is one of these — there is a very real danger of collaborating with or openly opposing ideologies which politically legitimise the social construction of state, ethnicity, citizenship, etc.[2] The policies themselves and the decisions deriving from them, however, may have far-reaching effects on the people for whom they are made, effects which they may not always perceive to be in their best interests.

Much of the literature on language planning (see Haugen 1966; Fishman 1972, 1989; Young 1987; Cooper 1989) is written from a static, structuralist perspective on society, in which social groups, social roles, social institutions, etc. are taken as 'givens' with language mediating between them in some sense. By planning which language varieties are to function in selected social domains (for example education, administration, the media) and what form those varieties are to take, language planners and the political decision makers who use their expertise aim at exercising forms of social control over individual language users and groups of language users. I do not wish to suggest that those aims are not well-intentioned and benevolent, but there is an alternative way of looking at social structures which sees language not merely as an index of those structures but rather as a crucial constitutive factor in constructing social reality (cf. Heller [present volume] for similar comments on this issue within the overall framework of public education).

Sociolinguists engaged in language planning should be prepared to engage with other, post-structuralist social theories such as Bourdieu's theory of the interplay between material, cultural, social and symbolic resources (Bourdieu 1991), social constructivism in the wake of Berger and Luckmann (1969), Foucault's theory of the constitutive role played by discourse in producing and reproducing relationships of power (Foucault 1977), Fairclough's theory of discourse, power and social change (Fairclough 1989, 1992), etc. If they do not engage with this type of social theory, the language planning projects they propose may have little or no effect on the real-life language practices of individuals. If they do engage in them, they may well discover that language planning enterprises are often at odds with social theory. In order to exemplify this incompatibility, I shall give a critical analysis of the competing discourses through which language policies are constructed. I shall discuss one example from an ongoing debate in Switzerland in which competing language ideologies are not only embedded within social practices, but are a crucial aspect of constructing them.

The debate concerns the choice of language subjects in the Swiss cantonal education systems. It is a politically highly-charged issue, one which automatically involves the participants in a struggle not only over the status of languages in Swiss public life, but also, and perhaps more fundamentally, over the teaching of languages in public education. Controversies over the choice of language subjects to be offered in public education are inextricably linked with the other discourses on language in Switzerland, and by identifying those links it should be possible to open up a critical debate on the merits and demerits of the language planning decisions that are taken.

I shall examine two significant documents in the 'language debate', the report published in 1989 by a work group with a view to examining the status of the national languages of Switzerland and making suggestions with respect to their constitutional status (*Zustand und Zukunft der viersprachigen Schweiz* [The Present State and the Future of Quadrilingual Switzerland]) and the report published in August 1998 by a work group appointed by the Federal Committee of Directors of Education to look into the possible revision of language teaching (foreign and mother tongue teaching) in the school system (*Welche Sprachen sollen die Schülerinnen und Schüler der Schweiz während der obligatorischen Schulzeit lernen?* [What languages should Swiss schoolchildren learn during their obligatory schooling?]). The controversy between the two positions represented in these reports is an example of how different social groups can and do consciously attempt to manipulate language policy decisions and linguistic practices.

On one level, then, the 'controversy' involves the choice of language subjects to be offered at primary and secondary levels of public education in Switzerland. On another, more covert level, however, it involves the status of English in relation to the indigenous official languages of Switzerland and the struggle to define the social value of multilingualism in the country.

2   Language ideologies

I shall begin by arguing that any discourse which is carried on at different points in time and by different individuals and groups embodies and constructs an ideology if there is sufficient agreement on a fundamental set of beliefs shared and articulated by the individuals/groups instantiating that discourse (see also Heller, present volume). A discourse on language which represents a coherent set of beliefs about language, a language, a language variety, language use, language structure, etc. can then be called a 'language ideology'.

Work on language ideologies has been particularly productive during the 1990s (see for example Taylor and Joseph 1990; Woolard 1992; Pennycook 1998). Blommaert (1999) contains a range of contributions on language ideological debates which clearly reveal the intimate connection between discourse and discursive practices, on the one hand, and the construction and deployment of language ideologies, on the other.

The nature of that connection, however, has not yet been adequately clarified. Pennycook (1998: 39), for example, sees ideologies, including language ideologies, as being produced through the complex interplay of several discourses, although he does not give a clear indication of how this comes about. Cameron (1990: 92), on the other hand, stresses the importance of analysing individual language users' comments on their own linguistic practices as a way of involving the sociolinguist in the observation and analysis of those practices *as* social practices. She argues that they reveal the social reproduction of language ideologies which come into being and are perpetuated through time by the shared articulation of sets of beliefs about language, thus implying that any discourse is by definition ideological. Fairclough (1992) uses much the same argument.

Language ideologies, then, are constructed by discourses that have language (language attitudes, beliefs, opinions and convictions about language, etc.) as their central theme. So a close interpretive analysis of what is said and what is left unsaid in individual realisations of those discourses should reveal the shared beliefs that go to make up the language ideologies themselves. A critical analysis of the competing discourses should reveal the tensions and values lying behind and feeding into them.

The two reports that I wish to consider reveal much more about the variety of attitudes towards multilingualism and the conflicting values that are attached to it in Switzerland, and towards the status of English in Switzerland, than language planners would lead us to believe at first glance. I shall argue that a critical discourse approach towards language is a particularly fruitful way to tap into the hidden agendas behind LP projects and the policies derived from them. At the same time, however, it raises some rather uncomfortable questions concerning the public role of sociolinguists, which I shall take up in the concluding section of this chapter. Before proceeding with the analysis, however, I shall provide information about the complex linguistic situation in Switzerland in section 3 and give a short layperson's briefing on the planning projects that resulted in the reports that form the data base of the analysis in section 4.

3 Language and language ideologies in Switzerland

3.1 'Quadrilingual' Switzerland?

Switzerland is an officially quadrilingual country, in theory but not of course in individual practice (see Lüdi 1992). The last census in 1990 revealed somewhat uneven statistics with respect to native speakers, 63.6% German speakers, 19.2% French speakers, 7.6% Italian speakers and 0.6% Rumantsch speakers. The most interesting statistic, however, is that non-indigenous languages rose from 6% in 1980 to 8.9% in 1990. The greatest increase has been in the number of native speakers of Turkish, Kurdish and Serbo–Croat, whereas other non-indigenous languages like Spanish and Portuguese have remained relatively stable or have increased only very slightly. The overall increase is undoubtedly the consequence of a steady rise in the number of migrant workers coming to Switzerland from southern, south-western and south-eastern Europe and the number of refugees seeking political asylum in Switzerland. Out of a population of just over 7,000,000 inhabitants, just under 20% are not in possession of a Swiss passport and over 900,000 have a permanent resident's permit.

Switzerland is thus very much more and, at the same time, very much less than a quadrilingual state. It is very much more in that the number of languages used on a day-to-day basis far exceeds the four official languages, but it is very much less in that, with the exception of those born in bilingual homes, those brought up in close proximity to the language borders running through Switzerland or those for whom learning a second 'Swiss' language was a matter of personal survival (i.e. virtually only the Rumantsch speakers), the percentage of fluent speakers of two or more of the official languages is relatively small. Indeed, certain of the non-native languages spoken as a mother tongue have higher percentages of native speakers in the overall population than Rumantsch; for example, Spanish and Turkish have over

1%. The geographical distribution of these language groups across the country and the low social status of their native speakers within Switzerland, however, give them a lower relative symbolic value than Rumantsch.

The status of English in Switzerland is particularly interesting in this respect. Although the percentage of native speakers of English living and working in Switzerland makes up only 0.5% of the total population, the number of L2 and FL speakers of English is very high as a proportion of the total population and is steadily rising. The symbolic value of English in the Swiss linguistic marketplace is thus extremely high.

3.2   The constitutional status of the national languages and the ideology of dialect

The Swiss federal constitution gives official status to three of the four national languages, German, French and Italian, but at present the fourth national language, Rumantsch, although it has in principle been granted a measure of recognition as an official rather than merely a national language by a referendum held in 1996, will only acquire that status once a decision has been made by the Rumantsch speakers themselves as to which variety of the language should be promoted. The reason for deferring the final decision lies in the fact that Rumantsch is a group of five related dialects, some of which are difficult to understand by speakers of other dialects. A written standard, Rumantsch Grischun, was 'invented' from three of the major dialects by the Romance scholar Heinrich Schmid as late as the 1980s, but Rumantsch Grischun occupies a precarious position as a written standard not only because some of the dialects already have a literature of their own but also, and more significantly, because party political interests are involved in the rivalry between recognition of the different dialect areas.

The German-speaking area of the country comprises 17 of the 26 cantons, with four cantons officially bilingual or trilingual (Bern [German–French], Fribourg [French–German], Grisons [German–Italian–Rumantsch] and Valais [French–German]). The avowed 'mother-tongue' of the German-speakers, however, is not a form of standard German but 'Swiss German', which is a cover-all term for roughly 30 mutually intelligible Alemannic dialects of German. The dialects are used throughout the social spectrum in most walks of life, including a large number of radio and television programmes, church services, some cantonal parliaments, frequently in the lawcourts and, significantly, in at least the first two grades of primary school by the majority of teachers. I have argued elsewhere (Watts 1999) that the complex set of attitudes towards standard German and the dialects, on the one hand, and the Rumantsch dialects and the newly created standard Rumantsch Grischun, on the other, constitutes an 'ideology of dialect', in which the dialects and not the standard are used to construct the 'idea of Switzerland' by German speakers, and to a lesser extent by Rumantsch speakers.

Thus although standard German is the declared official language of over 60% of the population, it is hardly anyone's mother tongue. Indeed, it is looked upon by the vast majority of Swiss German speakers as a 'foreign' language, as the language of Switzerland's powerful neighbour to the north of the Rhine, as a symbol of intellectual elitism, of external political power, in a word, as everything that the German-speaking Swiss consider to be non-Swiss. The value of the dialects in most linguistic marketplaces in German-speaking Switzerland is higher than that of the standard, since Swiss German symbolises local patriotism, political decentralisation, a safeguard against possible outside interference in the affairs of Switzerland and the guardian of tradition. On the other hand, communication with French and Italian-speaking compatriots requires a knowledge of and fluency in standard German. It requires a commitment at least to the territorial multilingualism of Switzerland which recognises standard German as one of the official languages.

3.3   The French-speaking construction of Switzerland as a 'nation by an act of free will' and the ideology of multilingual Switzerland

In opposition to the ideology of dialect, a competing language ideology has developed in the French-speaking part of the country which constructs the unwillingness of the German-speaking Swiss to use standard German, particularly in the media and in interethnic social interaction, as a betrayal of the 'idea' of Switzerland as what they refer to as a 'nation by an act of free will'. This counter-ideology also constructs the French-speaking Swiss as more 'patriotic' and more committed to 'multilingual Switzerland' than the German speakers.

The French-speaking Swiss value French as a link to 'la francophonie', as the bridge between Switzerland and Europe, indeed between Switzerland and the rest of the world. In the 1992 referendum on whether Switzerland should join the European Economic Area, the French-speaking section of the population voted overwhelmingly in favour of joining and were unable to understand the opposition to the referendum in the rural German-speaking areas which caused the motion to be narrowly defeated. At the time there was serious political debate about whether or not 'la Romandie', as the French speakers refer to French-speaking Switzerland, should secede from the Confederation. Ironically, however, the Romands are just as fierce local patriots as the German-speaking Swiss and share their abhorrence of centralised government and outside intervention. The ideal of multilingual Switzerland is upheld in the Romandie as a means of counteracting the German-speaking Swiss, as a way of insuring that they have a say in the political processes of the country and as a way of insulating themselves territorially and ethnically against any encroachments from German-speaking Switzerland. There are a number of similarities here with language policy and language practices within the European Union, and, once again, the language that has most to gain from supporting a multilingual policy in order to protect itself from the encroachments of English is French.

In Switzerland, while on an official level Romand politicians and the Romand media complain bitterly about the spread of the dialects and urge their German-speaking compatriots to use the standard, it is my impression that they are unwilling to learn German at school and even more unwilling to use it in German-speaking Switzerland. Attempts to use German in the Romandie are frequently met with a wave of hostile protest.

At the level of federal politics the dominant discourse is one which articulates a set of beliefs in the desirability of retaining the multilingual nature of Switzerland and enhancing the ability of the Swiss to communicate with each other across ethnolinguistic boundaries. I shall call this set of convictions 'the ideology of multilingual Switzerland', and it is an ideology which constructs the ideal Swiss citizen as one who has, or should have, a command of her/his native language (note the problems that arise here with respect to the German- and Rumantsch-speaking Swiss), a good command of one of the other national languages, and knowledge (though perhaps not a working knowledge) of a third language.

The ideology of multilingual Switzerland translates into language teaching policies in the 26 cantonal public education systems in the following way: alongside the L1, a second national language ('*langue nationale 2*' or LN2) is introduced in the fourth or fifth grade (age 11 to 12) followed by a third language (L3) in the fifth or sixth grade (age 12 to 13), which is either a third national language or English. With respect to the languages fostered by and in use in the federal administration, however, the ideology of multilingual Switzerland motivates language policies which aim to inhibit, or even exclude, the high-status, non-indigenous language English in favour of the LN3, which is in this case Italian.

In my analysis of the two reports on the status of language in Switzerland the ideology of multilingual Switzerland is the dominant feature of both examples of discourse on language. In the 1998 report, however, a subtle, but not insignificant, change occurs in that space is given for a competing ideology involving the spread of English which I shall call the discourse of 'the globalisation of English'. These two competing ideological positions are at the heart of the debate, and they allow us to compare Switzerland with other multilingual states in which English is also present (see for example Platt, Weber and Ho 1983; Fraser Gupta 1984).

3.4   The status of English in Switzerland

It is at the interface between the language policy of the federal administration and language teaching in the curricula of the cantonal education systems that the controversy that I wish to illustrate here emerges, and it is centred on the status of the English language in Switzerland. Outside the official language discourses and the ideologies they instantiate there is a further discourse on language which is articulated by a wide variety of interest groups as well as by private citizens in all parts of the country and is focussed on the high market value, both symbolic and material, of a non-national language, English.

It is of course hardly surprising that this discourse should have developed in Switzerland given the 'perceived' significance of English in the world of scientific research, tourism, the 'global economy', etc. It has long been on the agenda of ideological debate in several European countries (see Flaitz 1988; Ammon 1991; Preisler 1999). But it is the interplay between what, following Pennycook (1998), we might call the neo-colonial ideological discourse of 'the globalisation of English' and the other dominant language discourses in Switzerland which make it so significant.

The principal argument in the 'globalisation of English' ideology in Switzerland is that the market value of English is so great that it, rather than an LN2, should be taught as the first non-mother tongue. The avowed aim of those supporting the ideology is to make the Swiss citizen fluent not only in her/his mother tongue but also, at least, in English.[3] The argument is put most forcefully by a majority of influential industrialists and financiers in all three major language areas (leaving Rumantsch out of consideration for the moment), who are therefore the major players on this side of the debate. It also receives considerable support from parents who imagine, rightly or wrongly, that fluency in English will give their children access to material resources and increase their chances of success in the professional world. It is supported by educationalists who see the same kinds of advantage for students in the academic world, and by a number of federal and cantonal politicians who feel that the inevitable integration of Switzerland within the European Union will entail an increase in the overall ability of the Swiss to communicate using English. All in all, therefore, the lobby for the language ideology constructed through this discourse in Switzerland is very powerful indeed.

The presence of English in Switzerland is there for all to see and hear. It can be read on public notices, on advertising billboards and in information sent to customers daily through the mail by firms, advertising agencies, banks, etc. It can be heard (and seen) in television advertising; it is virtually ubiquitous in popular subculture such as pop music of various kinds (rock, soul, heavy metal, punk, rap, etc.) and the snowboarding 'community'; it is the dominant language allowing access to internet services and electronic mail; it can be heard in English language films (at least in the larger towns in which films are not shown in their dubbed version), etc. It has found its way, both lexically and syntactically, into the oral and written language usage of speakers of Swiss German, German, French and Italian in Switzerland. Countless examples could be given and countless anecdotes could be told.

In the following two sections I want to trace a significant shift in the 'official' articulation of the interplay of language ideologies in Switzerland by focussing on the two documents mentioned in section 1, since they are good examples of the discursive sites of the cultural production and reproduction of attitudes towards, and statements about, language in Switzerland.

4   A brief preliminary look at the two reports

The work group whose report *Zustand und Zukunft der viersprachigen Schweiz* (The Present State and the Future of Quadrilingual Switzerland) appeared in 1989 was set up by the federal government and its brief was to analyse the constitutional status of the Swiss national languages and to make a set of proposals to be presented to the National Assembly by the Federal Council (which is effectively the Swiss cabinet of ministers). The ostensible reason for doing so was the alarm felt over the gradual disappearance of Rumantsch. One of the briefs of the work group, therefore, was to suggest concrete measures to maintain the language and to bolster its significance within the overall linguistic landscape of Switzerland. Heinrich Schmid had completed his work on Rumantsch Grischun in the early 1980s and the first ever full professor of Rumantsch language and literature, Iso Camartin, was elected to a chair in the University of Zurich and the Federal Technical University in Zurich at around the same time.

The report was conceptualised as the basis upon which constitutional measures could be proposed to improve the position of Rumantsch, and, logically, it was chaired by the then professor of constitutional law at the University of Bern, the late Professor Peter Saladin. Since the report could only be written within the context of the overall language situation in Switzerland, five professors specialising on matters of language from each of the four language areas were elected onto the work group (Professor Stefan Sonderegger [German], Professor Ottavio Lurati [Italian], Professor Iso Camartin [Rumantsch and German], Professor Roland Ruffieux [French] and Professor Joseph Voyame [French]), the last two, oddly enough, from the French-speaking part of Switzerland. Because of the original orientation towards the maintenance of Rumantsch, the final two members of the work group were Rumantsch speakers and experts on the situation in the Rumantsch-speaking area, Dr. Bernard Cathomas and Dr. Ursina Fried-Turnes.

The final report of the work group, however, goes far beyond this rather narrow brief and reviews the historical development of the language situation in Switzerland, deals with questions relating to the geography and demography of the different ethnolinguistic groups, discusses legal problems arising from the so-called Territoriality Principle, the status of non-indigenous languages (including English) in Switzerland, etc.

As might be expected, the report generally articulates the ideology of multilingual Switzerland, but it also articulates all of the other ideological discourses presented in the previous section. Because it was set up by the federal government, it was politically expedient to focus on the ideology of multilingual Switzerland, and the report tends to take an anti-English language stance, virtually all references to English in the report — and there are many — constructing English as a serious threat to ethnolinguistic harmony in Switzerland, or even holding the spread of English responsible for much of the disharmony perceived by the members of the work group. I shall refer to the 1989 report in section 5 as the Saladin report.

The work group whose report *Welche Sprachen sollen die Schülerinnen und Schüler der Schweiz während der obligatorischen Schulzeit lernen?* (What languages should Swiss schoolchildren learn during their obligatory schooling?) appeared in August 1998 was set up in September 1997 by the Committee for General Education, a subcommittee of the Federal Committee of Directors of Education[4] in Switzerland. It was composed of only four members, two 'educationalists' (Jean-Marie Boillat from the Romandie and Hans-Ulrich Bosshard from German-speaking Switzerland), one Romance sociolinguist (Professor Georges Lüdi from the University of Basel) and a member of the secretariat of the Federal Committee of Directors of Education (Cornelia Oertle Bürki). It was assisted by a large group of experts consisting of professors of linguistics, experts in bilingual education, members of cantonal education departments, etc.

Given the fact that, as we shall see, the status of English as an obligatory foreign language in all education systems in Switzerland constitutes one of the most controversial recommendations in the report, it is all the more surprising that none of the members of the work group itself, nor of the group of experts, was a linguist or sociolinguist specialising in English. It is somewhat difficult to interpret this fact in any logical way, although I suggest that the presence of such a specialist on either the work group or the group of expert advisers might have unnecessarily provoked opposition to the recommendations concerning English from those who uphold the ideology of multilingual Switzerland.

The brief of the work group was to 'develop a concept for foreign language teaching in the schools of quadrilingual Switzerland'. However, since the 1989 report had already endorsed the policy of an LN2 as the first obligatory language subject after the mother tongue followed by the optional choice between the LN3 and English, and had also warned unequivocally of the dangers of admitting English as an obligatory language subject, one can only assume that the two novel suggestions made by the work group, viz. that forms of bilingual education be introduced and that English be introduced as an obligatory subject, were the result of concessions made towards two strong lobbies, on the one hand the lobby for forms of bilingual education and, on the other hand, the very powerful commercial (hence political) lobby for the introduction of English (see section 3.4).

The final report by the work group was presented to the media and submitted to a wide range of educational institutions throughout Switzerland for detailed comment and criticism in August 1998. Reports were to be submitted to the Federal Committee of Directors of Education by the end of September 1998. Again, the work group touched on aspects of all the ideological discourses presented in the previous section, including the 'globalisation of English' discourse. The objectives of each work group were admittedly different, the Saladin report focusing on cementing a multilingual identity for Switzerland and the 1998 report — which I shall henceforth refer to as the 'Lüdi report' — focussing on making the Swiss education systems conform to developments in language education in the EU. Nevertheless, differences in each work group's social construction of the role of English are rather striking.

5   A critical analysis of the two reports: The uneasy presence of English or the necessary presence of English?

The debate over the choice of language subjects in the Swiss cantonal education systems is one which almost inevitably involves the participants in competing discourses. Controversies over the choice of language subjects to be offered in public education are inextricably linked with the other discourses on language in Switzerland which I outlined in section 3, and by identifying those links it should be possible to open up a critical debate on the merits and demerits of the decisions that are taken. In this section I intend to examine the two reports presented in section 4.

5.1   'Summary' (*Kurzfassung*) and 'Foreword' (*Vorwort*) of the Saladin report

One of the problems in comparing the two reports arises from their different lengths. The Saladin report encompasses 458 pages and also includes a summary and foreword of 26 pages. The Lüdi report encompasses only 43 pages, including the preamble. The summary and foreword of the Saladin report thus range over a much broader spectrum of topics than the Lüdi report, the preamble of which is given as a succinct list of points to be dealt with in the body of the text.

The most striking aspect about the summary and foreword of the Saladin report is the language in which the text is couched. We find frequent metaphors taken from the fields of physical force, aggression, competition, escape (or lack of escape), etc. These are set up in the first 26 pages, and they run through the rest of the report almost like a Leitmotif, particularly when the status of English is under discussion.

In comparison with the rest of the report, English is given a much more prominent place in the summary and is presented as an ominous presence threatening the harmonious coexistence of the four national languages within Switzerland. Here are three extracts from the summary and foreword:[5]

> In public life, viz. in politics and the administration, insofar as there is enough evidence at all, language use is closely connected to the relevant language area. Institutions that are organised and operate on a national level generally use the two national languages German and French. The same is true for business and industry. In this area English, which, because of the worldwide interconnections between several branches of industry has become almost indispensable, is providing increasingly important competition for the national languages used as a second language. (pp. vi–vii)

English is presented here as competing for a place as a second language with the national languages, and although the point of view of the text's 'voice' is not overtly critical, it is quite obvious that the world of business and industry is behind this development.

In the second extract, English is listed along with several other factors as being part of what is described as the 'partially dramatic impasse' into which Swiss multilingualism has got itself and with which the Federation will somehow have to deal:

> Our proposals are likely to place the Federation into the situation in which from now on it should cope better with the partially dramatic impasse into which this quadrilingualism has got itself (cues: erosion of Rumantsch, the threat presented by German to Italian in parts of the Ticino and the Grisons 'valli', the 'dialect wave' in German-speaking Switzerland, in general the decreasing ability and willingness to develop mutual understanding between the languages and cultures of our country, the presence of English). (p. xxvi)

The third extract, however, paints an even more ominous picture in which English is overtly presented as a force which might lead to 'a Switzerland with 2½ languages':

> The analysis of the problem sketched out above leads to the question of its projected future development: will everything stay the same as it is at present? Hardly, for the language statistics and developmental tendencies that have been identified so far lead us to expect a change in language usage. Are we approaching a Switzerland with 2½ languages? This would be possible in at least two forms. Alongside the two largest linguistic groups, which would not be in danger with respect to area and substance, the third group, Italian, would be weakened still further, in other words it

would only be half-heartedly present, while the fourth and smallest group would disappear altogether. Or, alternatively, we are approaching a situation in which every Swiss, alongside her/his native language, would have a command of the English language to such an extent that one could consider her/him factually bilingual (measured generously of course). Command of 2 ½ languages would then arise out of an imperfect knowledge of another national language. Or will English even become the language of everyday communication among the Swiss? This cannot be excluded if we take the increasing attraction of this language seriously, as well as certain observations that appear to provide evidence for this state of affairs.

The text voice uses a rhetorical question in the second line to imply to her/his readers that the future of multilingual Switzerland looks grim. It even tries to base its prediction on undefined 'language statistics' and 'developmental tendencies'. The reader is meant to take the prediction as being in some sense scientifically well founded. To begin with, the prediction of a Switzerland with 2½ languages is given substance by reference to a slight reordering of relationships between German, French and Italian. But this is followed by the real danger of a radical reorganisation involving English as a second language and one of the national languages as the unlucky half. An even more threatening scenario is then presented in which English has 'become the language of everyday communication among the Swiss'.

Quite clearly, therefore, the summary/foreword locates the text within the discourse of multilingual Switzerland, and any non-national language, but of course primarily English, is constructed through that discourse as a threat to the harmonious coexistence of the four national languages.

5.2   The preamble of the Lüdi report

The preamble of the Lüdi report starts off by listing the previous sets of recommendations with respect to various aspects of language teaching made by the EDK (Federal Committee of Directors of Education) from 1975 to 1995. It then states its brief:

> On the basis of these previous reports and faced with the declared intention of several cantons to introduce the teaching of English as an obligatory subject at secondary level I [that is from the fifth grade on or at age 12] the Committee for General Education of the EDK, on the basis of a committee decision of 10 September 1997, commissioned the development of a concept for foreign language teaching in the schools of quadrilingual Switzerland ... (p. 3)

The significant point here is that the major reason for the report being commissioned was 'the declared intention of several cantons to introduce the teaching of English as an obligatory subject at secondary level I'. Looking back at the 1989 Saladin report, then, perhaps the fears expressed with respect to the dangers of English were to a certain extent well founded. In addition, the decision to set up the work group may also have arisen from within the discourse of multilingual Switzerland.

The preamble of the Lüdi report then goes on to list the terms of the commission given to the work group:

> In particular basic criteria for language learning at school and a range of models for language learning during the period of obligatory education should be developed, which make statements on and suggestions with respect to
> * goals and the level to be attained in the various languages
> * the point in time at which instruction in the L2 in the various language regions should begin
> * the relationship between mother tongue and foreign languages
> * the order in which and the point in time at which other languages, in particular English and the other national languages, should be introduced
> * the methodological-didactic structuring of language learning and teaching and the time devoted to language instruction (in hours per week)
> * the length of time and intensity of foreign language teaching
> * the quality of different forms of language competence at the end of the primary and secondary I stage of education
> * suggestions for the linguistic and didactic training of teachers. (p. 3)

There are a number of blurred conceptual distinctions in the text of the commission which might be missed if the reader is not familiar with the language situation and language policies in Switzerland. For example, what are the 'various languages' in Switzerland? The four official languages, German, French, Italian and Rumantsch, or these together with a wide range of non-indigenous languages spoken as mother tongues in Switzerland, like Spanish, Portuguese, Turkish, Serbo–Croat, etc. — and of course English? Does the second point refer to the onset of instruction in a second 'Swiss' language or any second language when it refers to 'L2'? What languages in Switzerland are taken to be 'mother tongues'? For example, is it reasonable to think of a dialect as a mother tongue in contradistinction to a standard variety, since that is precisely the way speakers of Swiss German would see things? And are other 'Swiss' languages 'foreign languages' or only those languages that are not indigenous to Switzerland? Why is it that, in point four, English seems to have a privileged status along with the 'official' languages?

The first problem for the work group was therefore to sort out these blurred distinctions and in particular to deal with the final question — the question of English. If I am right in suggesting that the work group was set up by the EDK to find solutions to the mounting pressure on the ideology of multilingual Switzerland from those groups articulating the ideology of the 'globalisation of English' (cf. section 4), that is, industrialists, bankers, parents, professional groups, academics, etc., then there should be clear signs of the tensions arising from these two conflicting language ideological discourses in the Lüdi report.

The first indication of just such a tension is evident in two of the preconditions listed by the work group as the basis for their draft 'concept for foreign language teaching'. The second precondition is derived directly from the ideological discourse of multilingual Switzerland:

> Linguistic and cultural plurality is part of the indispensable historical inheritance of Switzerland and Europe. It is part of our second nature. Taking care of it and protecting it is an explicit goal of Swiss politics (cf. Art. 116 of the Federal Constitution) and of European politics. (p. 4)

However, although this statement clearly belongs to the discourse of multilingual Switzerland, it cleverly introduces a European angle by equating this aspect of Swiss politics with European politics. The European slant to the argument might indeed be able to encompass the demands for English without actually stating so.

In the fifth precondition the need to equip the Swiss through the education system for the demands of increased international mobility and (economic?) globalisation is introduced without any mention of the role of English:

> Knowledge of foreign languages will become more and more important as an additional professional qualification in a world that is characterised by international mobility and globalisation. There is a relationship between sociocultural status and the use of certain FLs. . . . On the other hand, a specific knowledge of FLs will have a direct effect on salary levels with otherwise identical qualifications. (p. 4)

The phrasing of this precondition is taken almost directly from the 'globalisation of English' discourse, but it neatly avoids any mention of English, of what kind of globalisation is being referred to or what the 'specific knowledge of foreign languages' might entail.

5.3   Fear of English and the cultivation of the national languages

The beginning of the main text of the Saladin report focuses on the use of English as the language of globalisation, although the term itself does not seem to have been as fashionable in 1989 as it is today and only sporadically occurs as the adjective 'global' throughout the whole report. The following extract constructs English as a threat to the fragile stability of multilingual Switzerland in a particularly dramatic way:

> Evidence for the linguistic changes caused by our modern society of com-
> munication is provided in the European area by the almost drastic shift in
> status of the national languages in favour of the world language English.
> Global economic constraints, the general development in technology, but
> also mass cultural phenomena have created a situation in which English is
> granted a high priority in all modern states. Particularly in a small country
> like Switzerland, in which a part of the cultural habitus is to learn the
> languages of one's compatriots as far as possible, this attraction and signi-
> ficance of a non-national world language must lead to changes in attitude
> towards one's linguistic neighbours. Since multilingualism is not simply
> a cultural value but, in most cases, just as much a hard and ponderous
> learning process, a tendential development towards the 'lowest common
> denominator' cannot be excluded. For a multilingual nation like Switzer-
> land, however, the prospect of English as that language which the Swiss
> will in the future use to communicate with their own compatriots is any-
> thing but an auspicious development. The price to be paid to gain access
> to progressive society should not be linguistic uniformity entailing a loss
> of the linguistic traditions of one's own country. (pp. 5–6)

The discourse of multilingual Switzerland is explicitly opposed here to the
'globalisation of English' discourse. Some of the argumentation used in this
extract, however, is a little odd. It is said to be 'part of the cultural habitus' of
the Swiss 'to learn the languages of one's compatriots as far as possible'. This
does not quite square with reality, however, as the two contributions to the
theme of multilingualism in Werlen (1993) have shown (Dürmüller 1993;
Franceschini 1993), and as Lüdi (1992) also argues. The spectre of English
being used as a link language among the Swiss in interaction across the ethnolinguistic boundaries is a common theme. But while I do not deny that English
probably is used as a link language in Switzerland, we have little or no empirical evidence on which to base such conclusions (see Andres and Watts 1993).

The Lüdi report tackles the question of English as the international
language of research, business and commerce in the following way:

> The importance of English as the international language of research and
> business has increased for trainees and professionals in every language
> area in the last few years and it will clearly continue to increase. In addi-
> tion, English is increasingly necessary to gain access to information (mass
> media, new technologies) and throughout the world serves as a lingua
> franca among speakers from different linguistic backgrounds. On the other
> hand, its importance is not uniformly great in all of the language areas,
> local regions and professional branches. (p. 7)

There is no attempt here to construct English as a threat to multilingual
Switzerland even though the perspective from which the report has been

written is situated within that discourse. However, there is an attempt to play down the importance of English throughout all areas and in all social domains in Switzerland, whilst at the same time recognising its global importance. I interpret this as further evidence of the tension between the two principal language discourses that motivated the report in the first place and an attempt to accommodate to the ideology of the 'globalisation of English' from within the framework of the wider discourse of multilingual Switzerland.

5.4   The problem of the dialects

As pointed out above, the counter-ideology to the ideology of dialect which is prevalent in the French-speaking part of Switzerland constructs the German-speaking Swiss as 'traitors' to the idea of multilingual Switzerland and the French-speaking Swiss as more 'patriotic' and more committed to that ideology than the German speakers. In the French-speaking areas at least a partial explanation of the shift towards a demand for English rather than German as a second language is derivable from that counter-ideology. Why learn standard German ('le bon allemand'), so the argument runs, if you can never use it with your German-speaking compatriots? The debate over what is commonly called the 'dialect wave' in German-speaking Switzerland has been carried on for several years now between German-speaking and French-speaking Switzerland. It is a favourite theme of complaint in the French-speaking press (see Lüdi 1992) and it is frequently a topic in discussion programmes on radio and television.

The Saladin report is divided on how to treat the dialect ideology. On the one hand, it tries to construct the dialect wave as a natural leaning towards familiar forms of everyday language, which is in no way out of the ordinary:

> The term 'dialect wave' characterises a phenomenon which is neither unusual nor unique in the present day. Basically it is nothing more than the living expression of a diglossic situation in which the two language varieties are struggling to discover the social domains in which they are valid. Developments such as this should be considered as normal phenomena in a living language culture. Yet the word 'wave' correctly indicates that various phases of intensity of the phenomenon have been observed in the course of the 20th century. (p. 139)

On the other hand, the increasing use of the dialects in the non-print media (radio and television) in particular is presented as a danger to Swiss unity and the use of the dialects in everyday life as being a 'marked' cultural phenomenon:

> The most worrying complaint of all is probably the undeniably negative mark placed alongside the 'dialect wave' by the non-German-speaking population of the country. Demographically and economically they are in

any case under the domination of German-speaking Switzerland so that their motivation towards learning the national language German[6] is fading, in particular when their attempts to contact their compatriots on the other side of the Saane [the river that is thought to form the metaphorical border between German- and French-speaking Switzerland] are met with an ever decreasing will and ability to use standard German. A situation like this simply increases the difficulty in approaching what is in any case felt to be a difficult language to learn, the cultural background to which is often not well understood. (p. 142)

Any concern with questions of linguistic and cultural communities in Switzerland today is influenced, not to say marked, by the phenomenon of the so-called 'dialect wave' manifest in German-speaking Switzerland. . . . In several representations of this phenomenon negative aspects are dominant, foremost of which is without doubt the problem of communication between the various language regions of our country which often ends in the reproach that Swiss solidarity is being negated. (p. 139)

The Saladin report goes on to argue that in a situation in which non-German speakers cannot participate in interethnic communication in Switzerland because of the German speakers' reluctance to use a standard form of the language, the natural reaction is to turn to English:

Alongside an increasing alienation between the different areas of the country a disinclination to learn the other national languages is becoming evident together with a shift towards English, which at least at the level of the school is not only felt to be an easier language to learn but also to be considerably more useful. (p. 143)

Note here that the typical justification for this move is that English is constructed as 'an easier language to learn'. The argument that English is in some sense easier to learn than other languages has been commented on repeatedly in the literature, sometimes as a 'fact' which is believed by the author (see Bryson 1990) and sometimes in a considerably more sceptical and critical vein (cf. Bailey 1991; Pennycook 1998).

The Lüdi report, although it appears to be couched within the discourse of multilingual Switzerland, is also trying to argue in favour of introducing English as an obligatory language subject into the cantonal school systems. By doing so, however, he attempts to evade the argument of the French-speaking cantons that increased use of the dialects in German-speaking Switzerland might be instrumental in furthering a move towards English and contradicts the core argument of the 'globalisation of English' discourse (that any move towards English should be furthered) espoused by those professional and non-professional groups by whom it is used to further their perceived interests.

The ideological conflict between the two discourses is neatly side-stepped by the Lüdi report in two ways. Firstly, the term 'dialect' is not mentioned in the report at all, and secondly, a pan-Swiss perspective is adopted in which reference is made to 'local language' and 'standard language'. In the following extract, some of the same points are made as in the extracts from the Saladin report above, but they are veiled by more general references and not constructed quite so obviously as problems:

> The local national language is unavoidable both for social integration and for successful participation in the worlds of school and work. It should be learnt well not only by the indigenous population but also by migrants. In this respect, the diglossic situation in German-speaking Switzerland (and to a lesser extent in Italian-speaking Switzerland) should be considered, which may lead to deficits in the command of the standard language in certain regions and school types. Faced with the connection between socio-cultural status and use of the standard language . . . a regular and through the years an increased use of the standard language in teaching should be given a high priority, particularly in German-speaking Switzerland. (p. 7)

At the same time, however, on the very same page as the extract presented above, the Lüdi report clearly documents its belief in the ideology of multilingual Switzerland:

> Neglecting the national languages German, French and Italian hinders mobility between the language areas and neighbouring states; in addition it represents a danger to the language concord in Switzerland and increases the danger of the language areas drifting apart. (p. 7)

It is somewhat strange here that Rumantsch is left out of consideration as a national language. Obviously it can hardly be used in communicating with people from 'neighbouring states', but it surely is of significance in cases of internal migration. More importantly, however, the two movements which might induce the neglect talked about here are the move towards an increasing use of dialect and the move towards an increasing demand for English. So the report remains strangely ambivalent between support of the ideology of multilingual Switzerland and concessions towards the 'globalisation of English' discourse.

6 Conclusion: A dilemma for sociolinguists

It would of course be possible to continue a comparison of these two reports on the state of languages in Switzerland, since both are particularly rich in statements that reveal contradictions, changes of opinion, hidden tensions and latent controversy. What an extensive comparison would show, however, amounts to a confirmation of the trends discussed in the previous section. It is time, therefore, to return to some of the points presented in the introductory sections of this chapter and to assess what a close analysis of discourses such as the one sketched out here can achieve, how it can achieve it and for whom the results of the analysis may be beneficial.

The first point that should be noted here is that both work groups were set up by political bodies (the federal government in the case of the Saladin report and the EDK in the case of the Lüdi report) to provide political decision makers in Switzerland with a 'secure basis' on which to develop language policy. In both cases 'experts' were sought from among the ranks of academia, not only linguists in the case of the Saladin report, but also experts on constitutional law, and not only sociolinguists in the case of the Lüdi report, but also experts in education. However, as we have seen from the work group presided over by Lüdi, the choice of the members of the work group leaves a lot to be desired if one of its briefs was to reassess the status of English as a language subject in the school systems of the country.

A critical discourse approach to the examples of discourse produced during the processes of language planning projects might help to reveal some of the presuppositions guiding the ways in which those projects are commissioned and carried out. This kind of analysis might bring to light unresolved tensions between opposing ideological positions. Sometimes what is left unsaid is as potent in meaning as that which is said. In the Swiss situation, for example, it is important to see how those tensions can be related back to deeper and longer-lasting tensions between the ethnolinguistic groups in the country and how both the ideology of multilingual Switzerland and the 'globalisation of English' ideology can be used to gloss over or even ignore those tensions. A critical reading of competing discourses thus opens up the interpretive option of assessing a number of alternative discursive practices and tracing them back through time, as long as that reading is soundly situated historically and socially.

The two reports analysed here were presented after a great deal of conscious deliberation among the members of the two work groups, and were compiled, circulated and edited thoroughly before being published. They are thus examples of carefully executed language planning projects, although their aims were somewhat different. One major question which needs to be put with respect to the Saladin report, however, is the extent to which the discourse, in constructing English as a potential danger to multilingual harmony in Switzerland, has actually given an unintended impetus to the alternative 'globalisation of English' discourse. To the extent that this is so, it could be said to have failed in at least one of its objectives.

It remains to be seen whether the recommendations of the Lüdi report will be implemented throughout the country. Reactions from the education authorities are mixed, some (such as Zurich) already moving towards the implementation of obligatory English, others (notably in bilingual cantons) opposing it vehemently.

It appears that no amount of language planning can achieve all the goals set by the political organisations which commission the reports and by the sociolinguists who carry them out. However, one thing is clear, viz. social theory which conceptualises language as simply reflecting social structures and social processes, and not as being a constitutive factor in their very pro-duction, is not particularly helpful in guiding the efforts of sociolinguists in language planning projects. The way in which I have represented language ideologies as being constructed through thematically focussed instantiations of competitive discourses on language also suggests that language ideology needs to be looked at from both a sociolinguistic and a social-theoretic perspective.

It might also appear that I have omitted the concept of power from the discussion. Fairclough (1992) argues that social change is effected through discourse, which is predicated on a relationship of power. Crowley (1989) has also said that language discourses are inherently powerful. At the present point in time the globalisation of English discourse appears to have become as powerful as, if not more powerful than, the discourse of multilingual Switzerland. The only way in which language planning can reverse that trend is by recommending that the state should apply the use of physical force on a national level. Fortunately, that is not an option in Switzerland.

Notes

1. My thanks go to the editors of the present volume, Nik Coupland, Chris Candlin and Srikant Sarangi, for their extremely helpful and perceptive comments on earlier drafts of this contribution. Dealing with those com-ments has helped me to gain a clearer picture of the issues involved in the present 'debate' concerning the status of English in Switzerland. Any last-minute inconsistencies and errors, of course, remain my own responsibility.

2. Cf. Heller (1999) for an excellent discussion of how Canadian linguists, sociolinguists and other students of and researchers into questions of lan-guage in Canada have become caught up in the ideological debate over ethnicity and citizenship in Canada and Québec.

3. If English were introduced as an obligatory language subject at school, Switzerland would come into line with the European Union's two L2s policy in secondary education. There would be one major difference, how-ever. In the EU this policy is designed to protect French in the face of competition from English. In Switzerland it would effectively reduce the significance of French (and of German) as an LN2 ('langue nationale 2') and would fly in the face of the ideology of multilingual Switzerland.

4. Public education in Switzerland is under the control of the 26 Cantons composing the Confederation. In order to coordinate curricula, final school leaving exams, university entry, the transfer of pupils from one Canton to another, and educational policy in general, the Directors of Education in each of the 26 Cantons are members of the Federal Committee of Directors of Education.

5. I have translated all the quotations from the two reports from German into English. In doing so I have not focussed on producing an idiomatic English translation, but have rather concentrated on conveying the essence of what is written. For this reason, the English texts may seem somewhat wooden, although there are times at which the text appears to have been written in a rather journalistic style. If so, I can assure the reader that that is simply a reflection of the style of the original text.

6. The reference here is to standard German rather than the dialect.

References

Ammon, U. (1991) *Die internationale Stellung der deutschen Sprache*. Berlin: Walter de Gruyter.

Andres, Franz and Watts, Richard J. (1993) English as a lingua franca in Switzerland: Myth or reality? In Iwar Werlen (ed.) *Schweizer Soziolinguistik — Soziolinguistik der Schweiz*. Special Issue of *Bulletin CILA* 58 (*Bulletin de la Commission Interuniversitaire de Linguistique Appliquée*). Neuchâtel: Institut de Linguistique de l'Université de Neuchâtel, 109–127.

Bailey, Richard W. (1991) *Images of English: A Cultural History of the Language*. Cambridge: Cambridge University Press.

Berger, P. and Luckmann, T. (1991 [1966]) *The Social Construction of Reality: a Treatise in the Sociology of Knowledge*, 6th edn. Harmondsworth: Penguin.

Bex, Tony and Watts, Richard J. (eds) (1999) *Standard English: The Widening Debate*. London: Routledge.

Blommaert, Jan (ed.) (1999) *Language Ideological Debates*. Berlin: Mouton de Gruyter.

Bourdieu, Pierre (1991) *Language and Symbolic Power*. Edited by J.B. Thompson and translated by G. Raymond and M. Adamson. Cambridge: Polity Press.

Briggs, Charles (1992) Linguistic ideologies and the naturalization of power in Warao discourse. In Kathryn Woolard (ed.) *Language Ideology*, *Pragmatics* 2: 387–404.

Bryson, Bill (1990) *Mother Tongue: the English Language*. Harmondsworth: Penguin.

Cameron, Deborah (1990) Demythologizing sociolinguistics: Why language does not reflect society. In John E. Joseph and Talbot J. Taylor (eds) *Ideologies of Language*. London: Routledge, 70–93.

Cooper, Robert L. (1989) *Language Planning and Social Control*. Cambridge: Cambridge University Press.

Crowley, Tony (1989) *The Politics of Discourse: the Standard Language Question in British Cultural Debates*. London: Macmillan.

Dürmüller, Urs (1993) Themen der Schweizerischen Soziolinguistik im Spiegel der öffentlichen Meinung. In Iwar Werlen (ed.) *Schweizer Soziolinguistik — Soziolinguistik der Schweiz*. Special Issue of *Bulletin CILA* 58 (*Bulletin de la Commission Interuniversitaire de Linguistique Appliquée*). Neuchâtel: Institut de Linguistique de l'Université de Neuchâtel, 79–92.

Fairclough, Norman (1989) *Language and Power*. London: Longman.

Fairclough, Norman (1992) *Discourse and Social Change*. Cambridge: Polity Press.

Fishman, Joshua A. (1972) *Language in Sociocultural Change: Essays by Joshua A. Fishman*. Selected and introduced by Anwar S. Dil. Stanford, CA: Stanford University Press.

Fishman, Joshua A. (1989) *Language and Ethnicity in Minority Sociolinguistic Perspective*. Clevedon: Multilingual Matters.

Flaitz, Jeffra (1988) *The Ideology of English: French Perceptions of English as a World Language*. Berlin: Mouton de Gruyter.

Foucault, Michel (1977) *Discipline and Punish: the Birth of the Prison*. Translated by A. Sheridan-Smith. New York: Vintage.

Franceschini, Rita (1993) Mehrsprachigkeit: Präliminarien zur Auswertung der Sprachdaten der Volkszählung 1990. In Iwar Werlen (ed.) *Schweizer Soziolinguistik — Soziolinguistik der Schweiz*. Special Issue of *Bulletin CILA* 58 (*Bulletin de la Commission Interuniversitaire de Linguistique Appliqueé*). Neuchâtel: Institut de Linguistique de l'Université de Neuchâtel, 93–108.

Fraser Gupta, Anthea (1994) *The Step-tongue: Children's English in Singapore*. Clevedon: Multilingual Matters.

Haugen, Einar (1966) *Language Conflict and Language Planning: The Case of Modern Norwegian*. Cambridge: Cambridge University Press.

Heller, Monica (1994) *Crosswords: Language, Education and Ethnicity in French Ontario*. Berlin: Mouton de Gruyter.

Heller, Monica (1999) Heated language in a cold climate. In Jan Blommaert (ed.) *Language Ideological Debates*. Berlin: Mouton de Gruyter, 143–170.

Lüdi, Georges (1992) Internal migrants in a multilingual country. In Georges Lüdi (ed.) *The Dynamics of Languages in Contact: Linguistic, Sociolinguistic and Sociopolitical Aspects*. Special Issue of *Multilingua* 11(1): 45–73.

Lüdi, Georges et al. (1998) *Welche Sprache sollen die Schülerinnen und Schüler der Schweiz während der obligatorischen Schulzeit lernen? Bericht von der Kommission für allgemeine Bildung eingesetzten Expertengruppe 'Gesamtsprachenkonzept'*. Bern: Schweizerische Konferenz der kantonalen Erziehungsdirektoren.

Pennycook, Alastair (1998) *English and the Discourses of Colonialism*. London: Routledge.

Platt, John, Weber, Heidi and Ho, Mian Lian (1983) *Singapore and Malaysia*. Amsterdam: Benjamins.

Preisler, Bent (1999) Functions and forms of English in a European EFL country. In Tony Bex and Richard J. Watts (eds) *Standard English: The Widening Debate*. London: Routledge, 239–267.

Rumsey, Alan (1990) Wording, meaning, and linguistic ideology. *American Anthropologist* 92: 346–361.

Saladin, P. et al. (1989) *Zustand und Zukunft der viersprachigen Schweiz*. Bern: Eidgenössisches Departement des Innern.

Taylor, Talbot and Joseph, John (eds) (1990) *Ideologies of Language*. London: Routledge.

Watts, Richard J. (1999) The ideology of dialect in Switzerland. In Jan Blommaert (ed.) *Language Ideological Debates*. Berlin: Mouton de Gruyter.

Werlen, Iwar (1993) *Schweizer Soziolinguistik — Soziolinguistik der Schweiz*. Special Issue of *Bulletin CILA* 58 (*Bulletin de la Commission Interuniversitaire de Linguistique Appliquée*). Neuchâtel: Institut de Linguistique de l'Université de Neuchâtel.
Woolard, Kathryn (ed.) (1992) *Language Ideology*. Special Issue of *Pragmatics 2*.
Young, D.N. (ed.) (1987) *Language Planning and Medium in Education*. Rondebosch, South Africa: The Language Planning Institute and SAALA.

Part

IV

Retrospective commentaries

12

'Critical' social theory: Good to think with or something more?
Celia Roberts

1 Introduction

In this brief post-script to the volume, I want to raise some issues which a number of contributors have raised for me as a sociolinguist primarily concerned with real-world problems in institutional settings. So I shall discuss only a few of the chapters which seem to me particularly relevant to my concerns, and leave to John Wilson the much more daunting task of commenting on virtually all of them.

From a real-world perspective the question is, how useful are social theories in dealing with sociolinguistic problems? What status do they have in our thinking and can we and should we make them relevant to the practitioners with whom we are working? The kind of real-world settings and issues that sociolinguists become involved in, such as language planning, policies on ageing, classroom practices and institutional discrimination — to name some of the themes of this volume — tend to position them (or us) within a 'critical' tradition in which issues of social justice and the possibilities of social change are central. This is not to say that sociolinguists who deal with these issues in the real world are primarily engaged in sniffing out political incorrectness from the huge complexities of institutional life. Far from it. But that problems of language and social life tend to revolve around some kind of inequality, and sociolinguists working with practitioners, politicians and ordinary people are usually doing this because they are concerned with inequality. For this reason, I shall concentrate on those chapters which deal explicitly with the work of the 'critical' thinkers — Bourdieu and Foucault — within what has come to be called 'critical social theory' (Calhoun 1995). I shall be asking how these chapters help us to evaluate their contribution to sociolinguistics and then I shall discuss their usefulness, more explicitly, in helping sociolinguists to deal with real-world problems.

2   Good to think with?

Lévi-Strauss's idea that animals are good to think with as well as to eat came to mind on reading these chapters. I began to ask the question, 'Is social theory good to think with and how far can we think with it?' As far as I know Lévi-Strauss was not in any sense a zoologist. His interest in animals was not in understanding their inner workings or their habitats but in their symbolic value in understanding social structure. He borrowed the idea of eating practices to illuminate his own studies. In a similar vein, we can ask how far we have to become social theorists in order to be sociolinguists. And how far can we use social theories as thinking tools without some attempt at assessing their value?

These kinds of questions have been rumbling in the sociolinguistic backrooms for quite a while. Woolard's article (1985) on the role of cultural hegemony in sociolinguistics was an early discussion of the relationship between social theory and sociolinguistics:

> ... Sociolinguists have often borrowed sociological concepts in an ad hoc and unreflecting fashion, not usually considering critically the implicit theoretical frameworks that are imported wholesale ... In other cases (we) have invented or at least elaborated our own favourite explanatory concepts, developing through these what amount to partial social theories to account for our immediate empirical data. (Woolard 1985: 738)

She takes the reproduction theories of Gramsci and Bourdieu — in which class structures are seen to construct practices which in turn feed back into structures — and criticises them for being over-determining. Linking Gramsci's theory of hegemony to Bourdieu's notion of the linguistic market, she argues that the emphasis on formal institutions and on impenetrable hegemonic ideologies fails to take account of the local community practices which she studied in Barcelona. In particular, she suggests (1985: 742) that our attention should be forced back to 'the effects of primary economic relations on arrangements for everyday living and in the informal structures of experience in daily life'.

No doubt, most contributors to this volume would broadly agree with Woolard's position, and the chapters by Frederick Erickson, Monica Heller, Ben Rampton and Srikant Sarangi take up these issues most explicitly. But there are some differences. Firstly, there is a more confident position taken in regard to sociolinguists' own social theories so that they are not sidelined as 'partial theories'. Secondly, these four contributors argue for a more explicit relationship between institutional hegemony and what Woolard calls 'the informal structures of experience in daily life'. Rather than looking at different sites — such as the non-institutional ones which Woolard uses to critique some aspect of reproduction theory — they are interested in the informal experiences within the formal institutions. In looking at the dialogue between formal and informal, they can use and critique Bourdieu in a more nuanced way. There is a third difference, which is perhaps the result of a general increase in reflexivity in the social sciences. Woolard's chapter is reflexive but she is less explicit than Erickson, Heller and Rampton. They talk about the choices they made in drawing on concepts outside sociolinguistics, on research sites and specific types of interaction. Their 'personal anthropology' (Pocock 1975) is acknowledged as part of the discursive and constructivist turn in doing social research. This, in turn, would appear to have an influence on the ways they are drawn to social theory, how far it excites or worries them, how far it makes sense to them as people with certain orientations, values and priorities.

3   Social theories and personal anthropologies

I want to look for a moment at the second of the two differences just mentioned above on 'the informal structures of experience in daily life'. I want to consider how far, in the chapters by Erickson, Heller and Rampton, the informal and daily are researched within the institutional constraints of educational life and the extent to which the social theory used in this research is influenced as much by personal anthropology as any intrinsic value of the theory. In Monica Heller's chapter on social categorisation in Franco-Ontarian schools, the informal and oppositional is conceptualised within the interaction order as backstage work. The prime focus is on the discursive social space in which the dominant ideology can be reproduced. So although the detailed analysis shows creativity and agency in locally-situated interactions, it either serves to reproduce or is in opposition from behind the scenes where the dominant social drama is being played out.

Erickson's chapter is in some ways closest to Woolard's in arguing for the limitations of reproduction theory. He argues that Bourdieu's theories are top-down and quotes 'the social destiny' of habitus in which experience confirms habitus. However, as Woolard says, this is not impermeable, there is success among minority and working-class students in the school system and it is not simply a case of accommodation to the dominant configurations within the interaction order. Reproduction theory might argue that these are exceptions that prove the rule, but Erickson asks how these exceptions come to be and if they are numerically significant, as in his own study of gatekeeping encounters, then how can this be accounted for?

It is the importing of the informal structures of daily life into the processes of self-presentation and evaluation which, unconsciously, produce a different outcome from the expected one. There is more ambiguity in

Erickson's gatekeeping encounters than in Heller's classrooms and so their take on reproduction theory is a rather different one. Local production and the conversationalist bricoleur's creativity allows for significant variety in Erickson's account. Local production for Heller is attuned to wider ideological formations.

Ben Rampton in his chapter and in recent articles has argued for the oppositional and performative as ways of reconceptualising ethnicity in school settings where the linguistic regime is less politically charged than in Ontario. Again, his position seems to be close to Woolard's although the settings in which he examines counter-hegemonic practices are within or associated with formal institutions. Linguistic hegemony is backgrounded while performance aspects of a multi-faceted ethnicity are foregrounded. Bourdieu gives way to Bauman's notions of performance and Bakhtin's heteroglossia.

Ideologies of race, ethnicity and language have had different histories in different contexts (see Milroy, this volume) and these differing histories contribute to researchers' personal anthropologies. These, in turn, affect which social theories they gravitate towards and how they use and/or challenge these theories. So, for example, how research questions are developed, which theoretical concepts have particular resonance and even what methods are used, are decided by the researcher's personal anthropology, embedded, as it is, in particular social and historical contexts. 'So what?' you may ask. Of course what you research depends on your background and interests. The point is that the kind of sociolinguistic research done by those who draw ideas from Foucault and Bourdieu, as the four contributors focussed on here do, is not trying to test theories from some disinterested perspective. Rather, as Rampton says, these sociolinguists interpret and use theory as basic metaphysical presuppositions about the nature of the world. But it is their personal anthropology which leads them to immerse themselves in particular contexts and it is their analysis of data in those contexts over extended periods which produces the sociolinguistic theories which can be convincing to practitioners, policy makers and so on. Such theories have a lot more status than what Woolard rather dismissively calls 'our own favourite explanatory concepts'.

In the fifteen years since Woolard wrote her chapter, sociolinguistics appears to have taken a more confident stance in relation to social theory, if this volume can be seen as representative of the field. Certainly, the four chapters I am focusing on here do not claim social theory as the dominant partner in any integration of social theory with sociolinguistics. Their somewhat different stances on the value of, in particular, critical social theory in relation to their own work, suggest two things. Firstly, that their personal anthropology, combined with the grounded analysis which comes from extended periods in the field, gives their work an authority and relevance which may be framed or given a general context by social theory but does not require it to be 'imported'. Secondly, the extent of the debt of critical social theory depends more upon the particular circumstances of the socio-linguistic research than on the robustness of the theory. The reproduction theories are more 'partial' social theories in Erickson's gatekeeping sites than in Heller's Ontarian classrooms where they have a more extensive explanatory power.

So, I want to argue that 'critical' social theory is good to think with because it can provide warrants for a personal orientation to social justice. It sharpens our political senses and provides illuminating metaphors as thinking tools rather like Lévi-Strauss's animals did. 'The linguistic market place', 'surveillance' , 'habitus', 'orders of discourse' and so on are the tropes which shed light on wider social and cultural processes but, it seems to me, are not necessary in providing a voice of authority to sociolinguistic work and do not take us far when it comes to *doing* sociolinguistics. When we look at the detailed analysis of data presented within the broader frame of 'critical' social theory, the detailed interpretive work draws on sociolinguistic theory, linguistic anthropology and the sociologists of interaction. Of course thinking is a kind of doing, as Monica Heller says (1997: 84):

> I realise that the process of constructing understanding is at the same time a process of doing which one can scarcely control . . .

But since nearly all the chapters in this volume are concerned with the kind of sociolinguistics which is applied to real world settings, 'constructing understanding' involves doing research out in the field and so issues of practical methodology and relevance are raised.

4   Methodology

Taking a qualitative approach to methodology, the so-called 'grand' social theories seem to have influenced sociolinguistics in only indirect ways. In practical terms, as researchers, we have to decide what interactions to focus on, what to do about interactions we have not focussed upon, how to analyse these interactions, and so on. The social theorists from the critical tradition may help to orientate us to certain sites — for example Habermas's notion of the 'lifeworld' and its relation to institutional settings — but my reading of the chapters in this volume, based in real-world settings, suggests that it is researchers' life experiences and sociolinguistic and social interactionist theories (together with practical and technical considerations) which determine their choice. It is to Goffman, to ethnomethodology, to the ethnography of speaking tradition and linguistic anthropology more generally that we turn, and to perhaps the single most important concept welded together from these differing perspectives: 'context' (Duranti and Goodwin 1992). It is theories of context that provide the practical insights for the data collection and analysis of interactions.

For example, Srikant Sarangi's chapter discusses some of the theories of Habermas, Foucault and Bourdieu and relates them to his analysis of psychotherapeutic counselling interviews. Habermas's notion of 'idealised' versus 'distorted' communication frames the discussion of the use of metacommunication to define the situation. But it is assumptions from ethnomethodology and conversation analysis which seem to drive the analysis as the counselling interview is interactionally accomplished. Similarly, Foucault's notion of 'being in language' and Bourdieu's linguistic market place, while being good to think with at an abstract level, do not give us the grounded insights of Sarangi's subsequent analysis. The means by which doctors and patients categorise each other seem to owe as much to Sacks as they do to critical social theory.

I think it's fair to make a distinction here between the kind of data and analytical frameworks used in critical discourse analysis, notably by Fairclough, Wodak and colleagues (Fairclough 1995a, 1995b, Fairclough and Wodak 1997) and the rather different use of critical theories in the four chapters I am focusing on. Clearly Fairclough and his associates find a much closer fit between the kind of data they tend to use, that is, texts from the media and critical social theory, than certainly Erickson, Rampton or Sarangi do. It also seems to be the case that Fairclough is more comfortable with generalisations about social practices, not necessarily grounded in fine-grained analysis, than the contributors to this volume. For example the marketisation of higher education is illustrated with two contrastive advertisements for lecturing posts (Fairclough 1997). The analysis is illuminating but the data is illustrative rather than at the centre of the argument. Media data, whether TV debates, advertising or newspaper articles, are, of course, as the word implies, already doing mediating work. Perhaps this makes it more susceptible to analysis using critical social theory than what we might call the 'messy system' of ordinary talk and interaction. Fairclough's more determinist view of 'discourse making people' finds less purchase in even institutional talk than in the media texts so often used by critical discourse analysts. And yet one might suppose that the talk of institutions would be highly determining.

I want to step away in a different direction, for a moment, from the chapters in this volume to discuss, with another example, the role of social theory for practical thinking about methodology and methods — that of issues of representation in transcription. Critical social theory has given discourse analysts and sociolinguists ideas and metaphors for worrying about transcription as a form of representation, but it was the linguistic anthropologist Eleanor Ochs, whose critique of the conceptualisation of transcription as an atheoretical, technical tool back in 1979, raised the consciousness of sociolinguists. More recently the debate has been pursued by socio- or anthropological linguists such as Green, Franquiz and Dickson (1997), Gumperz and Berenz (1990) and Tedlock (1983). A general concern about the politics of representation informs these debates, rather than any strong linkage between critical social theory and the difficult decisions about how to represent the voices of informants in ways that tell their stories from an emic perspective.

Critical social theory helps us to be reflexive about our methods. But perhaps whether we turn the reflexive searchlight on to issues of transcription, interview methods or any other social science methods, it is as much a matter of bringing our politics of social justice into our work as making strong links between it and social theory. As Briggs has eloquently shown in his critique of traditional interview methods, a reflexive politics can come from engagement in the field as much as from imported theory:

> Just as interview techniques contain hidden theoretical and ideological assumptions, they are tied to relationships of power and control. The same patterns of inequality emerge from the relationship between controlling and subordinate groups within societies, between 'developed' and 'under-developed' societies and between interviewers and interviewees. (Briggs 1986: 23)

Similarly, the arguments about researching on, for and with proposed by Deborah Cameron, Ben Rampton and colleagues (Cameron *et al.* 1992) are grounded in the politics of field relationships and the ethics of fairness and usefulness for relatively disadvantaged groups as much as, if not more than, in 'grand' social theories.

5   Practical relevance

I now want to turn to the other practical issue — that of relevance in the 'real world' and the extent to which critical social theory, which promises an agenda for change outside the academy, contributes to an applied socio-linguistics. And if such change is to come about, is it only at the level of consciousness raising through the public media or is it also through working relationships with practitioners from institutional life outside the academy? Is it, indeed, relevant to talk of practical relevance in a volume which is concerned with linkages between social theory and sociolinguistics? I want to suggest here that thinking about the linkages between social theory and sociolinguistics resonates with some of the current debates about practice and theory.

Again, it is useful to consider Critical Discourse Analysis (CDA) as an example of using critical social theory for a change agenda. Fairclough is quite explicit (1992, 1995b) about using CDA for research *on* sociocultural change, and he suggests (1997) that CDA 'is both researching and doing the politics of language'. In particular, he argues (1997: 13) that CDA has 'acted as a bridge between sociopolitical movements and the academy, giving wider public presence to the perspectives and knowledge of these movements, while bringing theoretical resources to them'. If this is the case, then CDA has raised consciousness but it is more difficult to see its change agenda having an impact on more orthodox socio-political institutions or having an impact on people within these institutions who are represented in this volume.

Several of the contributors to this volume mention applied and practical matters, or it is implied in the problem-solving stance they take on issues of inequality and negative social categorisation (for example, Erickson, Heller, Milroy and Rampton). However, Coupland talks of actively resisting the applied aspects of social research on ageing which construct old age as a problem and discuss how to remedy it. Coupland is, rightly, concerned that it is elderly people who are constructed as the problem, and such stereotyping should be resisted. But it seems wrong to resist all application because of its potential dangers in being part of the problem rather than part of the solution. It is a question of how far the problem orientation, of the kind of sociolinguistics influenced by the critical thinkers mentioned above, is a process of understanding which stops there or whether understanding leads to consciousness raising in an explicit way (Erickson, this volume, and Fairclough in some of his writing) or to more direct programmes of change.

If the problem solving goes beyond understanding within the academy, then issues of the status of knowledge, of values and of relationships all come into focus. For example, taking theory out to practitioners often turns them into consumers of theory in rather the same way as social theorists may see sociolinguists as consumers of social theory. This kind of Goliath and David relationship in which social theorists are privileged over sociolinguists and theory over practice puts brakes on attempts to use critical thinking to create change. With Srikant Sarangi, I have argued elsewhere for a joint problematisation of social and sociolinguistic theory and practice, in which those with broadly similar social values but with different epistemological traditions (sociolinguistics, on the one hand, and practitioners and experts from a variety of institutional backgrounds, on the other) can work together as experts, audiences, resources and agents for change (Roberts and Sarangi 1999; see also Carr and Kemmis 1986, Sarangi and Hall 1997, and Bloor 1997).

It is a long distance from the abstractions of Bourdieuan and Foucauldian discourses to the practical consultancy work which is one aspect of the critical change agenda. And indeed the critical turn in sociolinguistics is not easily integrated into the joint problematisation between practitioners and consultants. There is often the danger of being used as linguistic technocrats (see Linell in this volume on linguistic stability) in what Bloor (1997) would call an 'engineering' interventionist model rather than his enlightenment or critical models. For example, Srikant Sarangi and I found we had to work hard to turn our consultancy role with the Royal College of General Practitioners away from a concern with correlations between ethnicity and exam performance to looking at the interaction order of the exam, from a critical and constructivist perspective, as a topic in its own right. Having done that it was only in the detail of the interactions that we could provide evidence of the ways in which the exam was constructing disadvantage for certain candidates.

One final point about practical relevance. It is often only by undertaking consultancy that sociolinguists have access to data which might otherwise be too confidential, etc. In particular, gaining participant perspective on experiences which are emotionally charged and heavily freighted with anxiety — such as reactions to job interviews or exams — may only be agreed if the participants are convinced that some good will come of it, if not for them, then perhaps for others in the future. Similarly, access to these potentially life-changing gatekeeping interviews and to the assessments of candidates by the assessors is often only possible where the researcher is in some form of consultancy mode. It is here, in sharp focus, that the role of language as discrimination is played out in the real world.

It is also here that some of the critical and post-modern theories of multiple identities, creativity and agency are themselves found to be permeable. Just as it is not a question of total institutions bearing down on hapless individuals, nor is it a question of choice, in a post-modern way, of deciding who you want to be in the interview. For example, in the same RCGP research and in numerous other cases of post-hoc interview conversations, we talked to candidates who had been fully committed to doing well and believed they had done well, and yet were rejected or given low marks because they had failed to play the interview game according to the assessors' rules. It is in the fine-grained detail of situated talk that we try to understand these failures, and in the comparison between this analysis and the assessors' comments. Reproduction theory gives us some pre-suppositions, as does post-modern theory, on ethnicity and identity, but it is in the local context of production and in the history of particular interaction orders that explanation lies.

For example, if we compare Heller's Ontario classrooms with Rampton's South Midlands ones, it is as much the differing histories of linguistic rights debates and the particular circumstances of those classrooms at this juncture in time and social space which could account for their relatively different positions on reproduction theory versus post-modern identity crises. In the same way, Erickson's counselling interviews between counsellors and students, where there was the potential for both sides to share community experiences, can be contrasted with our gatekeeping research where no such 'co-membership' was at all likely and where the interaction order of the exam did not allow for such co-membership to be aired. In these latter cases, there was a more total relationship between success and shared communicative style than in the counsellor gatekeeping data.

So, critical social theories may have soaked into our consciousness and act as a resource for thinking with, but my argument has been that their value is somewhat limited by a number of factors. Firstly, much of our critical response to real-world problems comes from our social justice politics and our ethical experience in the field. We may not necessarily need to integrate Foucault or Bourdieu into our analysis even though they are good to think with (and we could add, rather sceptically, sometimes used more to quote with than to think with). Secondly, the theories which are of practical use to us tend to come not so much from these critical thinkers but from sociologists of interaction, from linguistic anthropology and literary critical theory and, of course, from sociolinguistics itself. Finally, the 'grand' social theories are not quite so 'grand' after all when stripped of some of their pomp by the circumstances of historically contingent but locally produced interaction.

Sociolinguistic theory, it seems to me, emerges from this volume more confidently and in much less of a relationship of subordination to social theory. Coupland argues that social theory frees up our thinking and perhaps it's done a good job in helping sociolinguistic thinking to be more robust, more authoritative as a result. Halliday (1993) argues for 'transdisciplinary research' which would change disciplines as they came into contact with each other. Perhaps, looking back over the last fifteen years since Woolard's paper, sociolinguistic theory has become 'transdisciplinary' and as a result has produced not 'partial social theories' but rounded sociolinguistic theories. On the whole, their grounded quality makes them considerably less impenetrable and more useful in and for the real world. They are good to think with and good to do things with.

Acknowledgements

Many thanks to Nik Coupland and Ben Rampton for their very helpful comments on an earlier version.

References

Bloor, M. (1997) Addressing social problems through qualitative research. In D. Silverman (ed.) *Qualitative Research: Theory, Method and Practice*. London: Sage, 221–238.

Briggs, C. (1986) *Learning How to Ask: A Sociolinguistic Appraisal of the role of the Interview in Social Science Research*. Cambridge: Cambridge University Press.

Calhoun, C. (1995) *Critical Social Theory*. Oxford: Blackwell.

Cameron, D., Frazer, E., Harvey, P., Rampton, B. and Richardson, K. (1992) *Researching Language: Issues of Power and Method*. London: Routledge.

Carr, W. and Kemmis, S. (1986) *Becoming Critical.* London: Falmer Press.

Duranti, A. and Goodwin, C. (eds) (1992) *Rethinking Context.* Cambridge: Cambridge University Press.

Fairclough, N. (ed) (1992) *Critical Language Awareness.* London: Longman.

Fairclough, N. (1995a) *Media Discourse.* London: Edward Arnold.

Fairclough, N. (1995b) *Critical Discourse Analysis.* London: Longman.

Fairclough, N. (1997) Discourse across disciplines: Discourse analysis in researching social change. *AILA Review* 12: 3–17. (*Review of Association Internationale de Linguistique Appliquée*).

Fairclough, N. and Wodak, R. (1997) Critical discourse analysis. In T. van Dijk (ed.) *Discourse as Social Interaction.* London: Sage, 258–284.

Green, J., Franquiz, M. and Dixon, C. (1997) The myth of the objective transcript: Transcribing as a situated act. *TESOL Quarterly* 31(1): 172–176.

Gumperz, J. and Berenz, N. (1990) Transcribing conversational exchanges. *Berkeley Working Papers in Social Cognition* no 68. Berkeley: University of California.

Halliday, M. (1993) Language in a changing world. Occasional Paper no. 13. Sydney: Applied Linguistic Association of Australia.

Heller, M. (1997) Autonomy and interdependence: Language in the world. *International Journal of Applied Linguistics.* Special Issue edited by Ben Rampton, vol. 7(1): 79–85.

Pocock, D. (1975) *Teach Yourself: Understanding Social Anthropology.* London: Hodder & Stoughton.

Roberts, C. and Sarangi, S. (1999) Hybridity in gatekeeping discourse: Issues of practical relevance for the researcher. In S. Sarangi and C. Roberts (eds) *Talk, Work and Institutional Order.* Berlin: Mouton de Gruyter, 473–503.

Sarangi, S. and Hall, C. (1997) Bringing off 'applied' research in inter-professional discourse studies. Paper presented at the BAAL/CUP Seminar on Urban Culture, Discourse and Ethnography, Thames Valley University, London, March 24–5 1997.

Tedlock, D. (1983) *The Spoken Word and the Work of Interpretation.* Philadelphia: University of Pennsylvania Press.

Woolard, K. (1985) Language variation and cultural hegemony: toward an integration of sociolinguistic and social theory. *American Ethnologist* 12:4: 738–748.

13

Who needs social theory anyway?
John Wilson

1 Introduction

Although the invitation to comment on the papers in this volume allowed a freedom to choose between limited (one or two articles) or extended (all) commentary, any choice is fraught with danger. The danger is the relativist one of 'point of view' (Bakhtin 1981), which is also one of the dynamic action-centred issues for social theory itself. I once noted (Wilson 1997) that it was one of sociolinguistics' interesting paradoxes (for another see Wilson 1987) that when it defended the structural equivalence of accents and dialects, it did so within the chosen dialect/accent of the powerful, the educated and the elite (see Cameron 1994; Pullum 1997; Milroy and Milroy 1998). If I try to claim freedom for my working-class accent/dialect in the accent or dialect of the strong and dominant, then, by this very action, I would seem to have accepted the received view that my working-class accent/dialect was unsuitable for the job — hence the paradox. Sociolinguists are, in the main, standard language users, and when they discuss the language of non-standard users they may become like ethnographers observing and commenting on some other tribe. At its best it can pass for Geertz's 'thick' description (Geertz 1993), at its worst for patronising or divisive and ignorant social engineering (Honey 1998).

So here I am at the opening of my own paradox, my own point of view. What I say may fall into the trap, as discussed in Jaworski (Chapter 5), of producing an 'expert view', one in which my interpretation (or is it manipulation?) of others' views, with critical comments and asides, generates for me a Bourdieuan symbolic capital — that is me as expert commentator. In such a position I might influence you the reader to reinterpret (or 'recontexualise', perhaps, to use Linell's term: Chapter 4) the claims of other papers, and as such influence understanding. Or is it rather that my work interfaces with the other papers in a form of textual interaction whereby I construct a textual reality? One which is discursive and therefore open to analysis by Potter and Edwards (Chapter 3) as a reflection of my psychological biases and takes for granted views of not so much what others have meant in what they say, but of what I make them mean by what I say (or is it write?)?

So where do we go and how do we get out? We don't and we can't. Just like Jaworski who accuses an art critic of power manipulation, yet then proceeds to utilise his own power in unmasking this behaviour. Or like Linell who castigates the influence of the written model of linguistic theory in writing, we are always inside and outside our language at the same time. Both Barthes (1996) and Foucault (1996) have noted the contrasting alienation and freedom provided by language. So with Molloy (cf. Foucault 1996: 339), 'I must go on, I must say the words as long as there are words, I must say them until they find me, until they say me'.

2   Social Theory and sociolinguistics

What is Social Theory? In a recent text on this issue Callinicos (1999) suggests that perhaps this is an odd question to ask in modern times, since there is a clear understanding of what a social theory should be about. To social theorists perhaps, but others reacting to or drawing on other ontologies (to take Rampton's stance: Chapter 10) surely owe it to themselves and to others to at least articulate the positioning of their case as social theory as opposed to social contextualisation. Consider Heller's (Chapter 8) claim that '. . . sociolinguistic theory is a form of social theory'. Here she is referring to the way in which interactional options worked through in situated encounters generate questions of Why this here? Why this now? And that answers to such questions permeate upwards (and downwards) through interaction sets to questions of social structure and social action. I'm sure this is true. There is another and similar way to see sociolinguistics as social theory, that is by a process of commutative reasoning. If sociolinguistics is about language in society, and if social theory focusses on the social and what processes organise and structure society(ies) in specific ways, and if language is a central social process then sociolinguistic claims are relevant to social theoretic questions (see Erickson, Chapter 6, also below). So now we can all go home.

Hold on, not so quick! The problem here, of course, is that any subject predicated on social issues now becomes social theory, and at one level of abstraction this must be correct; but it doesn't seem quite right. It doesn't seem quite right because it doesn't really say anything. Social theory may be about explaining social processes of formation, structure and action, but the history of social theory has been about alternative social theories: for example, the neo-scientific; the economic; the evolutionary; the functional; the structural; the interactional; the historical and interpretative; and the post-theoretic theory of social theory. Equally, the history of social theory reflects core paradigms in developing social theory; for example, 'classical social theory' (Durkheim; Weber; Marx); critical social theory (Marcuse;

Horkheimer; Habermas); modern social theory (Parsons; Park; Giddens; Bourdieu) and postmodern social theory (Lyotard; Baudrillard; Foucault). So when we talk of sociolinguistics and social theory we could mean anything from the revitalisation of selected core founders of social theory such as Vico (1668–1744) (via Shotter 1993 directly and Garfinkel 1967 indirectly); to the adoption of the heritage of the critical perspective (see Fairclough 1984; Wodak 1996), wherein social theory provides the background theory for linguistic emancipation.

It was Vico for example who argued that social theory should be centred on the human subject whose actions could only be understood within social contexts of interaction (see comment on Heller above). It is only a small step from here to the foundations of sociolinguistics, when it is claimed that language is a social enterprise best understood in its social context of production. But is this a step we need to take, or one that takes us forward? This is the point perhaps. Making such connections is easy, because there is so much developmental and historical linkage around to connect to (Wilson 2000). But this is not particularly fulfilling and becomes an answer to a question no one really asked. So is Sociolinguistics a form of social theory or not? The answer is, it is if you want it to be.

2.1   From the top one more time

There is a sense in which several of the general themes within the history and development of social theory get worked out in the papers included in this volume, sometimes explicitly, sometimes implicitly. For example, Heller and Watts discuss how higher-level political aspirations impact at the level of multilingualism and bilingualism in producing conflicting outcomes for the educational system and the learning of language(s). Watts compares historically separate reports (1989/1997) on the status of the languages of Switzerland. The 1989 report sets centrally the relationship between multilingualism and the national identity of Switzerland, linking them in defence against the negative effects of the globalising attacks of English. By 1997 the defence was beginning to crumble, as English gained economic, political, and symbolic capital — here the writing was on the wall, and it was in English.

Watts claims that his analysis shows the dynamic, as opposed to static, nature of structural perspectives on society, and how through this ideologies drive agendas of language control, language education and language change. Equally, Heller indicates how particular political and ideological assumptions of what it is to be a francophone create the need for monolingual social spaces within which speakers can separate their French from English. Focussing on minority language school contexts she reveals the lower level (interactional) covert and overt linguistic impact of higher-level political choices and aspirations.

Both papers seem exemplars of the interface of social theory and sociolinguistics. Both link the core sociolinguistic issue of language planning with issues of social theory's concern with the role of power, ideologies, and history as interpretation. But therein lies the danger. The term ideology itself becomes ideologised within an implicit moral order, where some actions seem implicitly critiqued. Description slips into social comment on linguistic struggles for status and control. Outside of idealistic theories of communicative interaction such as that of Habermas (1984, 1987) or the rejectionist nihilism of Nietzsche (1966) through Lyotard (1984), and Baudrillard (1983; 1993), it was ever thus.

The question is not relevance to social theory, but explanation of social theory and its centrality (even indispensability) for the problematics at hand. Watts's work on the higher-level macro impact on potential linguistic choice reflects the way in which societies become affected by external forces of globalisation and capitalism. There is an interesting issue for social theory here, specifically, the historical struggle of states for nationhood and the symbolic value of language in that process. Watts's work highlights this well, but does not tackle it directly, linking instead to issues of linguistic capital echoing Bourdieu (1977; 1992). While I believe this to be innovative and original, as with several papers that also call on Bourdieu there is a general selecting out of components of Bourdieu's overall theory. This theory, I would argue, cannot easily lend itself to such selection, since its force was in providing interrelated dimensions of class accounts of social behaviour.

Bourdieu's starting point in his analysis of social structure is the multidimensional nature of an individual's positioning within social space as social class positioning. Individuals are found to operate within different social fields (arts, academia, law, polity) and these fields are created and defined not in terms of some pre-set notion such as capitalism, but rather in terms of the value attached and distributed to sets of cultural capital. Capital here refers to resources attached to an individual or social position that can be said to carry social influence or currency. Different social fields value different types of resources or currency. In academic fields, for example, cultural capital or knowledge is highly valued, whereas in business economic capital would carry greater value. For Bourdieu culture becomes defined as capital, in terms of goods, symbols, etc., and these in turn are always stamped by social class. In this case class domination becomes possible whereby, in terms of the positioning of differing lifestyles, tastes, and aesthetic judgements, the dominating classes prefigure particular symbolic forms with higher value. Here cultural consumption becomes central to class politics. Particular types of production and consumption are valued by the dominant classes and thus serve to maintain their hegemonic class status. Most interesting in this theory is the way in which this same pattern allows Bourdieu to account for how the dominated classes themselves, in turn, choose and maintain a class-specific habitus with patterns of consumption which produce and maintain their dominated position.

Central to all this, of course, is linguistic capital. And while Watts and Heller weave interesting, clearly argued and intriguing cases of linguistic choice and impact, it is unclear how issues of domination and class play out in both cases. The comparative reports Watts refers to reflect a struggle within the dominant classes themselves, and within the fields of politics and academia. A central question is not only the ideological shifts but also how these are reflected within cultural consumption at different class levels. This is where Heller comes in since her work is more suggestive of the impact of linguistic domination in the context of the classroom, and the structural outcome of the maintenance of linguistic control. I think this stands as quality structural description independent of any specific social theory (although perhaps not social comment).

But perhaps we are asking for too many levels at once, or perhaps the core claims of both papers stand sociolinguistically (as I think they do) independent of Bourdieu or social theory in general. This is the issue. How far do you want to go? In what way could the general concept of political constraint impacting on linguistic choice be anything other than social theory, in its most general sense? But I think if this is so we would need much more history, much more politics, much more economics, and much more sociological theory. On the other hand, perhaps the main points of ideological and political impact on language planning are revealed more in the findings than the avowed social theoretical processes underlying the outcomes. It is not that these are not relevant, but they seem more of a backdrop than a counterpoint. In Rampton's terms (Chapter 10, Section 1), 'research outside sociolinguistics can be useful as a form of wider contextualisation for any given project on language in social life', and there is certainly nothing wrong with that.

2.2   Bottom-up considerations

As I have suggested, via Bourdieu, the same considerations at the level of language planning within states should operate within a range of fields and at different levels of language, at the levels of dialect and accent choice for example. This is an area taken up by Milroy (Chapter 9), who considers the comparative nature of language attitudes in Britain and the USA. She notes that while Britain and America both have dominant language value systems, where certain dialects, accents, and styles of speech are more valued than others, she cites a clear distinction with an emphasis on class difference in Britain, and race or ethnic difference in the United States. At one level of social theoretic abstraction, however, one could argue this is not the point, since domination strategies are roughly the same. We can treat both 'class' and 'ethnicity' as the same within a framework of domination and stratification. Here the dominating classes, via Bourdieu, will select particular dialect forms (ethnic or class) and imbue them with cultural capital and value, while at the same time, and by this very action, selecting out other forms of dialect as having less value. This allows domination to take place, and, within specific fields, value to be withdrawn from those who maintain particular non-standard (less valued) dialect/accent forms. Having said this much, however, Milroy's analysis proves important in descriptively highlighting the way in which particular societies work through the general frame of linguistic domination (that is, ethnicity versus class).

In this sense, and again, the findings seem more sociolinguistic than social theory, although one could argue that what Milroy's survey indicates is the way in which broad social-theoretic claims become worked out at different linguistic levels. Bourdieu is one of several social theorists who treat language as central to their work (see also Habermas 1984, 1987; Foucault 1989) yet the details at a linguistic level are rarely worked out. Habermas, magpie-like, centres his core theory of communication, for example, via the abstract idealised model of Chomsky, at the same time establishing his programme of communicative reasoning on more 'pragmatic' (in the technical linguistic sense) issues, based for example on the work of the speech act theorists such as Austin (1962). Yet those working within linguistics/sociolinguistics are well aware of the basic incompatibility between the idealised world of core linguistics and the action-centred basis of pragmatics. So here, in one sense, the question is different. Here it is what has sociolinguistics got to offer social theory?, and in my view, quite a substantial amount.

Milroy gives us several examples where individuals become stigmatised and dominated because of specific dialect or accent choices (see also the discussion in Jaworski, Chapter 5). As a result access to forms of education, work, and other forms of lifestyle, become 'off limits'. In this context particular sounds and sound formations, along with specific syntactic choices and formations, become markers of social difference. These formations do not in themselves signal anything other than specific possibilities. It is social groups that impose social meanings on these possibilities: meanings that become utilised for the purposes of domination and segregation. Equally, however, according to Bourdieu, those dominated will adopt a lifestyle habitus which maintains their own values.

The interesting issue is how these very dominated styles can themselves become dominant in certain cultural fields. For example, while Milroy notes that in the United States African American Vernacular speech is highly stigmatised, yet at the same time within the field of popular culture, specifically pop music, rapping styles (based on African American Vernacular English) have had a central role in the music charts. This music/lyrical form, on some levels, permeates the class divide within younger age groupings and may challenge linguistic domination, at least within limited fields. Once more, while social theory clearly links to sociolinguistics through issues of standardisation and dialect, we need to look — as Bourdieu tells us — at the interaction of different levels, otherwise we are in danger, at this micro level, of adopting (to borrow Watts's phrase) a 'static view'. Equally, in this case (and all others I would suggest), we must look both ways before crossing the road, i.e. from sociolinguistics to social theory but also from social theory to sociolinguistics (or is this the same?).

Perhaps looking in only one direction (or looking longer in one direction) Milroy may be in danger of the 'static' view. Interestingly while she applauds 'Rampton's insistence on a flexible view of ethnicity' as correct, in that '. . . like class boundaries ethnic boundaries are non-essentialist and permeable', she then goes on to suggest that:

> . . . Rampton's criticisms of much sociolinguistic work that employs the concept of ethnicity are surely wide of the mark. The problem seems to be not that boundaries are viewed as hard, as it is hard to see how they are viewed; but social variables generally, including ethnicity, are usually untheorised or undertheorised and used in whatever way is most conveni- ent for the linguistic analytic purpose at hand. (Section 1)

Wait a minute! This is the point, is it not? Utilising what is at hand has been, in some views, a convenient 'let out clause' for sociolinguistics. This is what Cameron (1990; see also Cameron *et al.* 1992) criticised in variationist analysis, where social variables were exactly that, socially undertheorised and taken as givens for the task at hand. This was one of the very issues which led some sociolinguists to social theory in the first place; in the search, that is, for specific social theorisations. This is also exactly why in Rampton's chapter he takes great care to indicate which analytic tools he draws on and the reason for particular adopted ontologies. Not simply — I assume — so that we can know what he has used for the task in hand, but so that what is used may be criticised and expanded (developed) with the intention of moving understanding forward (as he himself has attempted via his critique of the normativity found in Gumperz). This volume is meant to be about sociolinguistics and social theory, and social theory very much theorises ethnicity and class, and much else besides. And not only in the grand theory of Bourdieu but in terms of how individual stories become narratives (see papers in Calhoun 1994 for example), or in the reclamation of power and voice within the social sphere (May 1996).

It is to individual stories implicitly revealed in codeswitching that Rampton draws our attention, and in doing so links to the interactional flexibility of a system–actor perspective (Bourdieu/Giddens). The way in which young Asian boys manipulate linguistic choices within and outside Asian/Indian English allows them to explicitly and implicitly carry out several tasks other than simple identifications with particular cultural formations. Indeed, Rampton shows how the manipulation can reverse expectations where Asian English is not a positive reflection of historical roots, but a comment on Anglo-Asian domination: a form of self and other linguistic parody that implies a dominant and colonial past, and projects this to the present sites of available stereotyping which maintain in some contexts the very same domination.

This work challenges standard (static? — that word again) in-group and out-group assumptions and replaces these with an open system of multi-directional shifts negotiated within talk and which align speakers in a number of directions, rather than all heading the same way at the same time. This is an important point, and one echoed in post-modernist rejections of forms of certainty (see Lyotard 1984; Baudrillard 1993). This is something Rampton is aware of, and centres in his work. At times however I lost the plot slightly. He refers at one point to the impact on his informants of being involved in speech to adults. But that is a unitary concept — what is an adult? let alone an adult white male middle-class researcher? When shifts occur, as they clearly do in his data, which aspect is driving the shift: adulthood; maleness; social position and so on, or a combination of the same? This is, of course, a difficult yet interesting question, and one Rampton is well aware of. I am not criticising Rampton for not directly attending to it (I think his very claims do so), but rather extending the strength of his point on the fluidity of linguistic and social interaction (a point taken up in Coupland's Chapter 7; see also below).

What is being suggested is that roles such as adult white male, etc., can be articulated differently depending on a range of social perspectives. Further, these perspectives may be multiply combined for greater understanding (and this is what Rampton is attempting himself). This type of approach seems to fall within the call for 'ecological validity' in discourse research. Here the argument draws our attention '. . . to relevant outside organisational experiences or interactions that are "directly relevant to the way that local exchanges are likely to occur"' (Cicourel 1980). This claim intersects with the case made by Linell (Chapter 4), although for perhaps different reasons. Linell suggests we can escape the stultifying constraints of a linguistic analysis based only on written materials, looking at actual events as they happen. How one can do this is less clear; but it certainly would include more than written representations.

Combined with the call for ecological validity Linell's work suggests that the study of everyday interaction should somehow capture not only what is taking place in all its systemic glory, but also include within this a macro element of consideration wherein social and organisational constraints are also seen as operative and at play. Once again I think this must be right. On the other hand, where do we stop? Other recent research in cognitive science has also followed a call for ecological validity. Developing from original claims by Gibson (1979), emerging areas such as embodied/extended cognition (see Hutchins 1995; Clark 1997) argue for an interactive worldview of the human 'mind'. The mind, or at least, some of it, is not in the head, but rather it is an achievement born of the interaction of brain/body/world resources.

Clark (1997) challenges us to consider the following cases. First a person in front of a computer screen which displays a range of two-dimensional objects. Their task is to fit these objects into appropriate sockets. The assessment of any fit requires the person to mentally rotate the shapes to align them with the sockets. Now consider the same task, but in this case rather than mentally rotating the shapes the person has a button that allows them to rotate the shapes on screen. The interesting question here, according to Clark, is that we cannot explain any difference by simply pointing to the '... skin/skull boundary as justification since the legitimacy of that boundary is precisely what is at issue', at least when one is considering such issues as mind/body. There is an argument to be made that perhaps the mind is not all in the head. The outcome of this approach has been a revaluation of a host of issues regarding mind/brain; nativism; serial Vs connectionist processing; robotics; and even revisionism of evolutionary aspects of brain development.

There are two core suggestions here of interest to us. The first is that the world provides tools for cognition, and these interact with and shape and reshape cognitive processes (some argue actual brain structures: Dennett 1995). For example, while simple multiplication (2×2) may be done in the head, we are assisted in more complex problems (23456×76543) by such things as pen and paper. These are tools which not only aid cognition, they are part of the cognitive process itself. Now if we view the role of language in a similar way, language structures utilised within interaction play a cognitive role in solving problems of living within a social world. The fact that sound patterns are structured in specific ways to represent a range of social identities forms the basis of social cohesion, recognition and rejection, and this is a process learned from the earliest age (see Wilson and Henry 1999). So linguistic clues to class, ethnicity, age, etc., are external tools for shaping our cognitive processing of others. The relevance of this point here is that if one is going to have a truly ecological view of discourse then one must also consider the way in which social forces interact with cognitive processes in creating interactionally based world views.

Now what has this got to do with social theory, or indeed sociolinguistics? First, ecological validity means an explanation that reflects real-world processes. Social organisation constraints, if they do impact on micro level choices, must do so at some level of cognition. Here, Meyerhoff (Chapter 2) meets Foucault, in that discourse formations impact on intentionality and internal representations to modify external assessments and therefore linguistic outcomes. But there is a problem here. There is a clear difference between theoretical calls for the interactive understanding of macro social issues and their relation to micro linguistic issues, and the process of actually doing so. If sociolinguistics can be criticised for not paying enough attention to the detail of social variables and social processes, we must be careful not to go too far in the other direction, that is trying to pay attention to everything. Science has never progressed by such an effort. Progress is replete with the study of the small-scale, the abstracted, and the isolated issues. Only once the smaller steps are taken are we ready to make the larger leaps.

When one combines the concerns of sociolinguistics with social theory the micro and macro may become diffused and confused.

3   Whose theory is it anyway?

There is yet a further issue in comparing sociolinguistics and social theory. Social theories applied to actual samples of language already prefigure that language by the theory itself. This is an issue tackled directly by Potter and Edwards (Chapter 3). As advocates of discursive psychology they spend their lives contrasting the pre-formulated hypotheses and claims of standard psychology with the real-life everyday accounts of people involved in negotiating their way around the world. They challenge the taken for granted language of the analyst, the assumption for example that discourse encounters must, of necessity, contain the micro and the macro. It is not that, for example, Foucauldian discourse formations do or do not limit the freedom of what is said, rather that it is the participants themselves who are central in what they describe in and through the constituting nature of their actions. There is a core issue here of relevance to the interface of sociolinguistics and social theory.

The constitutive nature of discourse is a shared assumption of many of the analysts in this book. It is on the nature of the working out of such an assumption that the authors may differ, and this may only be for reasons of their own (including mine) ideologised training. But sounds are symbols of class and ethnicity, as Milroy suggests. So are clothing and skin colour, and TV preferences, as Bourdieu loudly articulates. Equally, so are large-scale organisational and historical manipulations, as Watts and Heller suggest, and which Foucault reminds us not to forget. But if all this is so then in Heller's terms not only is sociolinguistics a form of social theory, but so is discursive psychology, which is involved in the very process of constituting itself out of the discursive constructions of others.

The main point here is one clearly articulated by Coupland (Chapter 7) in his consideration of the sociolinguistics of ageing. Social theory is set alongside sociolinguistics with age as the problem. Coupland works through the 'time line' perspective of sociolinguistics and contrasts this with core social information on the role of old age in modern and late modern societies. The difference in perspective from the 'time line' analysis is striking. In late modern societies he argues that the institutionalisation of old age through retirement may be becoming deinstitutionalised and deconstructed through older people negotiating their own position and life course within society. Quite correctly Coupland argues that if this is the case then this process should be sociolinguistically marked, and that no one is better placed to study this than sociolinguists themselves.

What his study does is challenge criticism that there is a lack of social validity for linguistic variables within sociolinguistics. Coupland turns such criticism to his advantage by at once showing how a lack of social consideration, or social theorising, does limit sociolinguistic horizons. He indicates how by interrogating social life within the general study of social theory, the different perspective which emerges offers a way forward for sociolinguistics. This is Erickson's point writ large (Chapter 6: also below); here we see how social theory helps free up the limits of sociolinguistic thought on ageing, while at the same time offering social theory the tools to begin to articulate more clearly what it might mean to negotiate different life courses within the ageing process. Here social theory is both tool and backdrop. We understand the reasons for the turn to social theory from the positive outcomes for sociolinguistics — the benefits for social theory are also there (but being selfish — me, not Coupland — that is not the issue). Here we clearly see a counter to my criticism above, that some of the Chapters in this volume might be seen as sociolinguistics only. Only through the consideration of ageing within a concept of late modern society is there the basis for challenging the simple time line analysis previously advocated within sociolinguistics.

4   Using Social Theory

Erickson (Chapter 6) makes a direct attempt to link social theory to sociolinguistics and sociolinguistics back again to social theory, and he does this specifically at the level of discourse. It is at this level, argues Erickson, that there has been 'Movement . . . to connect processes of oral and written discourse with general social processes at the level of political economy and history'. He goes on to say that there is within this movement a tendency to '. . . focus on the influence upon local social action of general social and cultural processes'. Certainly there is much evidence for this in the present volume, but as we have seen, and will see further below, the issue is how far this focus is implicit and contrived as opposed to explicit, necessary and essential.

Erickson's main goal is to suggest that 'grand' theories such as the 'habitus' of Bourdieu suggest a nihilistic context of social struggle. One in which the patterns of behaviour, or action, reinforce and create the structures of dominance which lead to these very patterns in the first place. This is a point echoed in Giddens (1984; 1991) and one that arises in a number of the papers in this volume (for example, among others, Linell; Jaworski). Erickson wants to argue, however, and repeating Garfinkel (1967), that actors are not 'cultural dopes'. As Giddens (1984) says, if one cannot perform actions one is not an actor. By drawing on a number of transcripts of educational counselling Erickson reveals how at particular moments in time the complex range of available social positions, understandings, and identities can interact to challenge the prevailing direction of interaction. In one case the discourse of the failing student becomes reformulated in terms of the counsellor's connection with one student in terms of sport. The claim is that the implicit determinism of Bourdieu's grand theory cannot do justice to the 'on-line' range of flexible positions and options which social interaction provides (a point echoed in Rampton: see above).

I think to read Bourdieu as deterministic is only partly correct. Certainly it is true that habitus presents us with a world in which actors become habituated into particular forms and styles of existence reflecting very closely class orientations. It is not that one cannot escape these, however. As Bourdieu himself points out (Bourdieu and Wacquant 1992: 133):

> Habitus is not the fate that some people read into it. Being the product of history, it is an open system of dispositions that is constantly subjected to experiences, and therefore constantly affected by them in a way that either reinforces or modifies its structures. It is durable but not eternal! Having said this . . . most people are statistically bound to encounter circumstances that tend to agree with those that originally fashioned their habitus.

Shifts within interaction are directly available via this claim. But it is only the recurrent marking of positions as constantly becoming (Heidegger 1962) that creates a change in the habitus. Otherwise they become what the conversation analysts call 'side sequences' (see Ten Have 1999): components taken out of the core interaction for reflection or resolution, but not necessarily redefining interaction itself.

The relationship between both the maintenance and potential flexibility of habitus is implicitly marked in Meyerhoff's chapter. There she explicitly tackles the concept of accommodation theory from within the social psychology of language. Looking directly at interindividual and intergroup variation she argues that 'language variation emerges simply as a function of meaningful social patterns'. I don't think anyone would, or could, disagree. These patterns are generally maintained by the linguistic marking of contexts in habituated ways, which in turn assist in maintaining specific social positions. The question is, is this the same issue as Erickson has highlighted? Do these meaningful social patterns reduce to habitus, or fields of discourse (Foucault 1992)? Not necessarily. While the point is made again that identity reinforces and (re)creates itself through interaction, in this paper issues of intentionality (not always explicitly) enter through concepts such as (un)certainty and individual 'epistemological state(s)'. Meyerhoff argues that a speaker's perception of themselves and others needs to be taken into account in considering variation. But isn't this exactly Erickson's point? In the counselling context the counsellor's perception of the student shifts intentionally within the framework of a shared sports interest. And isn't this all in line with both the durability, and at the same time the potential, of habitus as opposed to its limiting and constraining nature?

In some ways it is unfair to set Meyerhoff alongside Erickson. She is, after all, not working directly within the discourse movement referred to by Erickson, but rather within a variationist tradition in sociolinguistics. This is not a problem; it merely reflects a different focus. As one would expect in a variationist frame, Meyerhoff focusses on shifts in a range of specified linguistic variables. Erickson, on the other hand, and as one expects in a more sociological frame, is more theoretically driven, with data being utilised at a more gross level of interpretation. The core difference is that the social theoretic implications of their work are, to me, radically different.

Erickson is explicitly tackling grand theories within a complex micro interactional framework and suggesting both social theoretic and sociolinguistic pay-offs. While there are certainly issues of power, access, and control in Meyerhoff, they are articulated as weighted options interactionally carved out of task- and talk-oriented uncertainty. These weights become used in the probabilistically produced outcome of speakers as reflected in the operation of salient sociolinguistic variables. At the macro level we saw above how some of the very same issues emerge. The inevitability of social positioning highlighted in habitus becomes in another context the maintenance of ideologies. After all, what are ideologies but relatively stable sets of ideas and beliefs?

In a similar and broader sense to Erickson, Sarangi directly sets out to position both sociolinguistics and social theory as articulatory counterparts in understanding the role of structure/action in constructing the human condition — or probably more simply human discourse. This is an ambitious effort, and the opening sections cover much theoretical and historical ground in social theory, and locate structure/action questions as an appropriate meeting point for social theory and sociolinguistics. Drawing on data from therapeutic interactions he shows, convincingly and correctly, that all aspects of 'worlding' (my term, not Sarangi's), or being and understanding in the world (Heidegger 1962) are language centred. Take an example such as 'pain'. In the medical tradition this would be something objective and measurable. Sarangi argues, however, that this is a discourse notion as much as anything else and it is to be understood as the site of discourse construction and negotiation, rather than being treated as a given. However, as in other cases the will to theorise — or socially theorise — leads to circles and eddies we may glide by while still enjoying the vistas of the data analysis. This may be seen particularly in the Habermas section where Sarangi makes a fair and valiant effort to integrate the concerns of Habermas with examples from real discourse. The trouble with ideal speech situations, like ideal speaker/listeners, is that they don't exist. Sarangi's patients do, however, and it is more heartening to think of the positive real and human outcomes of his analysis than to debate whether Habermas's philosophical motivations may have been achieved.

5   Conclusion: Where to from here?

So as the music dies down, what are we to make of all this? I think Coupland most clearly articulates the way in which social theoretic issues can impinge on sociolinguistics with the force of developing and extending (in some cases replacing) older, less viable theories. But perhaps this is only a more explicit case of what all the papers reveal in their own way. Specifically, that by using social theory as a type of sociolinguistic heuristic they have been able to highlight new, interesting, and important issues in the use of language in society. I think this is true, but at the same time has this not always been the case? While one might criticise early variationist sociolinguistics for undertheorising the social, it is not the case that it wasn't theorised at all. Analysts should use whatever is required to help formulate their problems and solutions as appropriate, but I'm not sure this should be determined beforehand. Or that it is always possible. Consider, for example, the recent work of Eckert and McConnell-Ginet (1992) on what they refer to as a 'community of practice'. This is defined in terms of the way actors utilise behaviours and practices to constitute group membership and degrees of group assimilation. Defined in their terms (1999: 186) a community of practice is '. . . an aggregate of people who, united by a common enterprise, develop shared ways of doing things, ways of talking, beliefs and values'. This community of practice concept is then considered in terms of its sociolinguistic outcomes.

In a number of ways I can see links here between the principle of a community of practice and Bourdieu's concept of habitus, along with the process of distributing symbolic capital to maintain class and group boundaries. There might also be a link to Foucault's account of the role of 'discourse formations', where linguistic choices within a community of practice may be constrained by the positioning of the group or members within the group in relation to each other and other groups. Eckert and McConnell-Ginet do not discuss either possibility — does this make a difference, however? I'm not sure that it does, other than reflecting a link between a similarity of disciplinary concerns. It would be easy for me to criticise Eckert and McConnell-Ginet for not indicating a potential awareness of the links to social theory. Or to suggest that a community of practice, independent of higher-level macro issues, is incomplete, but this shouldn't be enough. There should also be a requirement to say what is wrong with particular claims, and how they become improved, developed or better fitted to the question at hand. Sociolinguistics will benefit from an interface with social theory, and from the interface with many other areas, but it should do so as required and therefore remain sociolinguistics, as I believe the papers in this volume are, social theory or not.

References

Austin, J. (1962) *How to Do Things with Words*. Oxford: Oxford University Press.

Bakhtin, M.M. (1981) *The Dialogical Imagination*. Edited by M. Holquist, translated by C. Emerson and M. Holquist. Austin: University of Texas Press.

Barthes, R. (1996) Inaugural lecture at the Collège de France (1977). Reprinted in R. Kearney and M. Rainwater *The Continental Philosophy Reader*. London: Routledge.

Baudrillard, J. (1983) *Simulations*. New York: Semiotext.

Baudrillard, J. (1993) *Symbolic Exchange and Death*. London: Sage.

Bourdieu, P. (1977) *Outline of a Theory of Practice*, translated by R. Nice. Cambridge: Cambridge University Press.

Bourdieu, P. (1992) *Language and Symbolic Power*. Cambridge: Polity Press.

Bourdieu, P. and Wacquant, L.J. (1992) *An Invitation to Reflexive Sociology*. Cambridge: Polity Press.

Calhoun, C. (1994) *Social Theory and the Politics of Identity*. Oxford: Blackwell.

Callinicos, A. (1999) *Social Theory. A Historical Introduction*. Cambridge: Polity Press.

Cameron, D. (1990) Demystifying sociolinguistics: or, why language does not reflect society. In J. Joseph and T. Taylor *Ideologies of Language*. London: Routledge.

Cameron, D. (1994) *Verbal Hygiene*. London: Routledge.

Cameron, D., Frazer, E., Harvey, P., Rampton, M.B.H., and Richardson, K. (1992) *Researching Language: Issues of Power and Method*. London: Routledge.

Cicourel, A. (1980) Three models of discourse analysis: the role of social structure. *Discourse Processes* 3: 101–132.

Clark, A. (1997) *Being There*. Cambridge, MA: MIT Press.

Dennett, D. (1995) *Darwin's Dangerous Idea*. Harmondsworth: Penguin.

Eckert, P. and McConnell-Ginet, S. (1992) Think practically and look locally: language and gender as community based practice. *Annual Review of Anthropology* 21: 461–490.

Eckert, P. and McConnell-Ginet, S. (1999) New generalisations and explanations in language and gender research. *Language and Society* 28: 185–201.

Fairclough, N. (1984) *Discourse and Social Change*. Oxford: Blackwell.

Foucault, M. (1989) *The Archaeology of Knowledge*. London: Routledge.

Foucault, M. (1992) *The Order of Things*. London: Routledge.

Foucault, M. (1996) The Discourse on Language. Lecture at the Collège de France (1970). Reprinted in R. Kearney and M. Rainwater *The Continental Philosophy Reader*. London: Routledge.

Garfinkel, H. (1967) *Studies in Ethnomethodology*. New Jersey: Prentice Hall.

Geertz, G. (1993) *The Interpretation of Culture*. London: Fontana.

Gibson, J.J. (1979) *The Ecological Approach to Visual Perception*. Boston: Houghton Mifflin.

Giddens, A. (1984) *The Constitution of Society: Outline of a Theory of Structuration*. Cambridge: Polity Press.

Giddens, A. (1991) *Modernity and Self Identity*. Cambridge: Polity Press.

Habermas, J. (1984) *A Theory of Communicative Action. Vol. 1: Reason and the Rationalisation of Society*. London: Heinemann.

Habermas, J. (1987) *A Theory of Communicative Action. Vol. 2: Lifeworld and System: A Critique of Functionalist Reason*. Cambridge: Polity Press.

Heidegger, M. (1962) *Being and Time*. New York: Harper & Row.

Honey, J. (1998*) Language and Power: the Story of Standard English and its Enemies*. London: Faber and Faber.

Hutchins, F. (1995) *Cognition in the Wild*. Oxford: Blackwell.

Lyotard, J.F. (1984) *The Postmodern Condition: A Report on Knowledge*. Manchester: Manchester University Press.

May, T. (1996) *Situating Social Theory*. Buckingham: Open University Press.

Milroy, J. and Milroy, L. (1998) *Authority in Language*, 3rd edn. London: Routledge.

Nietzsche, F. (1966) *Beyond Good and Evil*. New York: Random House.

Pullum, G. (1997) Language that dare not speak its name. *Nature* 386, March 1997: 321–322.

Shotter, J. (1993) *Cultural Politics of Everyday Life*. Buckingham: Open University Press.

Ten Have, P. (1999) *Doing Conversational Analysis*. London: Sage.

Wilson, J. (1987) The sociolinguistic paradox: data as a methodological product. *Language and Communication* 7: 161–179.

Wilson, J. (1997) Review of J. Milroy and L. Milroy (1992) Authority in Language. *European Journal of Communication Disorders*.

Wilson, J. (2000) Communication communication everywhere, doesn't it make you think? *Semiotica* 129 1/4: 91–111.

Wilson, J. and Henry, A. (1999) Parameter setting within a socially realistic linguistics. *Language and Society* 27(1): 1–23.

Wodak, R. (1996) *Disorders of Discourse*. London: Longman.

'Motivational relevancies': Some methodological reflections on social theoretical and sociolinguistic practice
Srikant Sarangi and Christopher N. Candlin

1 Introduction

In this final chapter we raise methodological issues concerning social theory and sociolinguistics — as a complement to the introductory chapter where Coupland offers an exhaustive account of what sociolinguistic theory 'is' vis-à-vis social theory, arguing against the general perception that sociolinguistics is a theory-deficit discipline. In support of this response, all the contributors to this book engage with the writings of social theorists of various persuasions to suggest that social theory continues to inform sociolinguistic analysis and findings. However, while both social theorists and sociolinguists may share the domain of social life as their object of study, the ways in which they go about studying social phenomena can be characteristically different.[1] Wilson and Roberts, in particular, as commentators on the chapters in this volume, take this opinion further by adopting a reflexive position on the theoretical and practical usefulness of social theory for our understanding of sociolinguistic practice. For instance, Roberts singles out reproduction theory as offering some presuppositions, as does postmodern theory, on issues of ethnicity and identity, but it is in the local context of production, and in the history of particular interaction orders, she suggests, that social explanation lies. In a similar way, Wilson urges us to consider how social forces interact with cognitive processes in creating interactionally-based worldviews. Many of the contributors to this volume (for example Erickson, Heller, Potter/Edwards, Rampton, Sarangi) show that the determinism of grand theory cannot do justice to the range of flexible on-line positions and options which the study of social interaction provides.

Given the engagement of these contributors, we will not revisit these issues here, but instead focus on some of the methodological debates surrounding social theoretical research which sociolinguists, both in this volume and elsewhere, implicitly or explicitly draw upon. This may sound as if theory and method can be discussed in isolation of each other. On the contrary, Coupland, along with many others, draws our attention to the way theoretical stances can influence what constitutes data, and also can direct what analytic frameworks are thought to be appropriate to be applied to data analysis. In support of this position, our argument here is to show how theory and method are intricately intertwined, that is, how conceptualisations of the object of research have an overriding impact on how to study such phenomena.

This notwithstanding, we may still say that many social theorists have kept their theorising separate from systematic observation of data. In his foreword to Weber (1949 [1904]), Shils remarks:

> But it does seem that in the present state of social science in which theory and observation have tended to run apart from one another, and in which there has been a scatter of attention over a large number of unconnected particular problems, some serious consideration of the criteria of problem-selection would be fruitful. (Shils 1949: viii)

With the exception of Bourdieu (see below), this position still holds true of social theory in general. It is against this background that Durkheim issued his call for what constitute 'social facts' to be worthy of sociological (as opposed to psychological or biological) attention, while at the same time maintaining that not everything and anything can be studied by sociologists, if they were to aspire to the rigour of scientificity. According to Durkheim (1964: 34):

> Every scientific investigation is directed toward a limited class of phenomena, included in the same definition. The first step of the sociologist, then, ought to be to define the things he treats, in order that his subject matter may be known. This is the first and most indispensable condition of all proofs and verifications.

In the Durkheimian tradition, the 'limited class of phenomena' which qualify for sociological analysis include suicide, punishment, family kinship, etc. In saying so, however, Durkheim excluded everyday ordinary practices as being outside the sociological remit, and, as we know, the ethnomethodological revolution in sociology was partly instituted to counter such a stance, as Garfinkel (1967: 11) makes clear:

> I use the term ethnomethodology to refer to the investigation of the rational properties of indexical expressions and other practical actions as contingent, ongoing accomplishments of organized artful practices of everyday life.

Likewise Goffman (1974) distances himself from the core matters of sociology — social organisation and social structure — as he outlines a programme for the study of the 'organisation of experience as something that an individual actor can take into his mind, and not the organisation of society' (p. 13). Sacks (1984: 22) extends this programme to argue against 'an overriding interest in what are in the first instance known to be "big issues", and not those which are terribly mundane, occasional, local, and the like'. This theoretical orientation has later come to mean recording of natural data in everyday settings, (i.e., what is 'stably describable'), and the adoption of participants' perspectives in the analysis of the interaction order.

From a sociolinguistic and empirical perspective, one might argue the case that social theory not only deals with grand issues, but also appears to be lacking in methodology. From this perspective, and by extension, there might be very little for sociolinguistic methodology to look for in social theoretical writings. This might still be so despite regular reference by some social theorists, for example Bourdieu, to the contribution made to social theory by sociolinguists like Labov, especially through the evidential data they provide in support of social theoretical positions. At the same time, we need also to recognise that insofar as sociolinguistics is seen by some social theorists like Bourdieu as inheriting the structures and codes of linguistics, remaining in consequence closely empirical and still essentially Saussurean, such an endorsement by Bourdieu might mean much less than it appeared to say.

The question we are concerned with in this chapter is not so much what constitutes *the* sociolinguistic method, but rather how sociolinguists (including the contributors to this volume) relate to methodological issues, and what might be their motivations about matching certain data types with certain theoretical and analytic frameworks. The notion of methodology as we use it here involves more than merely the collection and interpretation of empirical data. Indeed, the reduction of methodology to certain types of data and certain types of analysis already assumes a specific theoretical stance (see McHugh's (1968: 59) characterisation of method as 'theories of data'). There are broader epistemological and ontological issues in play which underline methodological debates, as can be seen in the classic texts of Durkheim's *The Rules of Sociological Method* and Weber's *The Methodologies of the Social Sciences*. One of our tasks in this chapter is to foreground these sociological debates and, where possible, to connect them to sociolinguistic practices.[2]

We begin with an historical perspective, focussing in particular on past 'grand masters' of sociological thinking, especially Durkheim and Weber. We will suggest that while much sociolinguistics can be situated against this thinking, perhaps more obvious points of contact are to be discovered in the works of Bourdieu and Foucault. Bourdieu, for instance, at different times and places, appears to underpin the sociolinguistic enterprise, as the following extract from *Language and Symbolic Power* (1991: 54) makes clear:

a structural sociology of language, inspired by Saussure but constructed in opposition to the abstraction he imposes, must take as its object the relationship between the structured systems of sociologically pertinent linguistic differences and the equally structured systems of social differences.

Bourdieu is, however, careful to make the point that linguists (including sociolinguists) are still 'trapped in the logic of a (structuralist) theoretical model which (by appeal to "context" and "situation") they were rightly trying to supersede' (Bourdieu 1977: 26). Such a statement might well have served as a social theoretical preamble to Labov's (1972c) New York City project, and it certainly resonates with Hymes's (1972) call for sociolinguistics to provide a strong linkage between social and linguistic practices.

Foucault (1972), though focussing on discursive relations and discursive practices rather than on (socio)linguistic forms, in his *Archaeology of Knowledge* nonetheless evidences clear links to the sociolinguistics of Hymes in setting out a methodological programme for what he terms the 'formation of enunciative modalities'. This programme requires the identification by the researcher of qualified (ratified) speakers, institutional sites, subject positions in relation to other group and domain members, and varied roles of participants. Indeed in relation to the latter, his position comes close to the social underpinnings of Sarangi and Roberts's (1999) concept of hybridity:

> . . . a whole group of relations are involved (for the doctor in clinical discourse) . . . relations between the field of immediate observations and the domain of acquired information; relations between the doctor's therapeutic role, his pedagogic role, his role as an intermediary in the diffusion of medical knowledge, and his role as a responsible representative of public health in social space. (Foucault 1972: 53)

Building on an historical overview, we concentrate on the methodological stances adopted by Hymes, Labov and Gumperz — that is, how their thinking about what to study and how to study it resonates with social theoretical thinking (such as Bourdieu and Foucault) and at the same time responds to linguistic methodology (such as Chomsky and Halliday).

In the final section of the chapter we identify a set of key methodological issues: the status of observation, distinctions to be drawn between descriptive and explanatory goals of research, objectivism versus subjectivism, and differences to be acknowledged between the perspectives of participants and analysts. We review how the microsocial analysis characteristic of Garfinkel (1967) and Goffman (1974), despite their individual differences and despite their lack of focus on the close analysis of linguistic data, has nonetheless become a point of methodological anchorage for sociolinguistic practice. Where necessary, we revisit some of the methodological issues raised by the contributors to this volume. Finally, in order to contextualise our discussion further, we focus on the analysis of professional discourse, with its demands on researchers to take note of and account for Goffman's backstage and frontstage competencies in relation to different audiences, as an illustrative site for sociolinguistic methodological practice. In referring here to the analysis of professional discourse, we identify this less in terms of discourse data gathered from professional sites than as issues involved in the 'ecologically valid' *interpreting* of professional discourse data (Cicourel 1992). In this professional discourse analysis, or what we have chosen to call *communication in public life*, the issue of participant versus analyst descriptions takes on a new perspective.

2   Sociolinguistics, social science and natural science

The problem faced by sociolinguistics is not confined to making itself accountable to linguistics, but also to social science and natural science. This implies taking a stance about its methods of activity. The difficulty for sociolinguists in addressing this double accountability is exacerbated by the position taken by some linguists that linguistics is properly a science, and by the position of sociolinguists, quite generally, and by Labov in particular, that the pursuit of empirical knowledge, central to natural science enquiry, is equally fundamental to sociolinguistic theory construction.

Much of the debate about sociolinguistic methodology centres around the relationship between social science and natural science, in particular, whether social sciences have their roots in the principles of natural scientific procedures and whether methods of observation and explanation can be transferable across research paradigms.[3] One consequence of this is that differences within paradigms may be overlooked or reduced. Although one can discover different theoretical and methodological tropes between, say, biology, chemistry and anatomy, for many, the scientific method is summarised as follows by Cohen ([1931] 1964: 76): 'In the first positive stage it simply collects facts; in the second, it classifies them; then it lets the facts themselves suggest a working hypothesis to explain them'. He goes on to stress (op. cit.: 82) that

> In thus emphasising the role of reason in scientific method we do not minimise the appeal to experiment and observation, but make the latter more significant. The appeal to experience is thus involved throughout: first as the matrix in which inquiry arises (as that which suggests questions), and then as that on which all theories must be tested.

When it comes to the relationship between natural science and social science, two opposing stances emerge. At one pole lies the classical empiricist position which argues that there is no difference in principle between the study of natural phenomena and social phenomena. This position is enshrined in the work of J.S. Mill, especially his (1875) book *A System of Logic*, which foregrounds the value of causal, inductively-established explanation of all phenomena. Winch (1958), however, in his critique of Mill, argues strongly why social science should not adopt the logic of science. For him, the notion of human society is logically incompatible with scientific explanation. Thus, at the other pole lies the hermeneutic position, which regards social phenomena as having the dimension of 'meaningfulness', involving constructs of purpose and intention, and requiring in consequence a distinct investigative stance (see Bleicher 1982). In short, while natural science deals with facts, social science has to deal with facts *and* value. This is the stance of Weber, among others, but this does not mean that social inquiry should be subjective, intuitive and non-empirical.

3   Methodology in social sciences: Weber and Durkheim

It is interesting to note here that Weber (1949) warns precisely against too close a relationship between social science and natural science. For him, the issue is clear: arriving at general laws and explaining concrete phenomena through deductive reasoning based on general laws is appropriate for natural science, but not for social science, which, in fact, he prefers to call *cultural sciences*. As he puts it (1949: 80), 'in the cultural sciences, the knowledge of the universal or general is never valuable in itself'. General theory should act as an instrument when analysing actual observations, rather than as the source of rules from which to make deductions. Weber argues strongly how scientific objectivity is not only impossible to achieve, but that it should not be a goal in cultural sciences. The indefiniteness of social and cultural life makes 'one-sided' and motivated analysis a necessity. The task for social and cultural analysis is therefore to strive for an 'analytical ordering of empirical social reality'. According to Weber (1949: 68):

> It is now no accident that the term: 'social' which seems to have a quite general meaning, turns out to have, as soon as one carefully examines its application, a particularly colored though often indefinite meaning. Its 'generality' rests on nothing but its ambiguity. It provides, when taken in its 'general' meaning, no specific point of view, from which the significance of given elements of culture can be analyzed.

For Weber, then, empirical knowledge is to be kept separate from motivated analysis in real-life settings geared towards understanding, or 'recovery of meaning' in the hermeneutic sense. Different interpretations of social life, although this sounds relativistic, do not necessarily amount to a lack of objectivity: 'by juxtaposing the various points of view, each perspective may be recognised as such and thereby a new level of objectivity attained' (Kaufmann 1958: 186). Here an evaluative point of view — a *motivational relevance* — acts both as a constraint, and, in the context of the central debate on the relationship between social science and natural science, as a means of differentiation. Social and natural sciences differ not only in terms of methods but also in their objectives. A natural scientific position reduces complex social action to stimulus-led behaviour, atomised so that these can be measured using statistical procedures. In reducing action to such measurable behaviour, the researcher is positioned as an outsider who does not, and should not, affect the object of study. The researcher is barred from bringing unwarranted sentiments to the procedures of data gathering and analysis, and is secured against this by the presumed possibility of objectification of the object of study and by a process of socialisation into the practices of scientific research.

Weber emphasises the notion of the 'value concept' in cultural sciences which makes it distinct from natural science. For him, the significance of cultural events is grounded in one's prior experience of concrete events:

> We cannot discover, however, what is meaningful to us by means of a 'presuppositionless' investigation of empirical data. Rather perception of its meaningfulness to us is the presupposition of its becoming an object of investigation. (1949: 76)

Even in the socio-economic sphere, he points out, a motivated reading of empirical data is unavoidable:

> . . . the degree of significance which we are to attribute to economic factors is decided by the class of causes to which we are to impute those specific elements of the phenomenon in question to which we attach significance in given cases and in which we are interested. (1949: 71)

Such a stance excludes 'meaning' as a central category in the study of social phenomena. A non-natural-scientific view is, in contrast, interpretive and hermeneutic, but this still does not remove the struggle between subjectivist and objectivist readings of meaningful social phenomena.

Notwithstanding his formulation of the 'the principle of subjectivity', Weber still argues that subjectivity has to be understood against some 'ideal type'.

> The ideal type is formed by the one-sided accentuation of one or more points of view, and by the synthesis of a great many diffuse, discrete more or less present and occasionally absent concrete individual phenomena which are arranged according to those one-sidedly emphasised viewpoints

into a unified analytical construct. In its conceptual purity, this mental construct cannot be found anywhere in reality. It is a utopia. (1949: 90)

This suggests that the 'ideal' is an analytic construct unavailable to participants, but which can nonetheless serve as a basis for a descriptive methodology:

> When we adopt the kind of scientific procedure which involves the construction of types, we can investigate and make fully comprehensible all those irrational, affectively determined, patterns of meaning which influence action, by representing them as 'deviations' from a pure type of action as it would be if it proceeded in a rationally purposive way. (Weber 1978: 9)

In postulating the 'ideal type' as an abstract construct against which to set 'irrational patterns of meaning', it may be that Weber is less distant from Durkheim than might at first appear. Like Weber, Durkheim argues that social science should be distinct from natural science in its object of study, but still insists on maintaining a methodological connection to the natural science method. This is what he calls a 'scientific mentality' in the study of social facts as 'things' rather than as 'ideas'. His definition of what constitutes a 'social fact' stresses this methodological point:

> A social fact is every way of acting, fixed or not, capable of exercising on the individual an external constraint; or again, every way of acting which is general throughout a given society, while at the same time existing in its own right independent of its individual manifestations. (Durkheim 1964: 13)

This, then, forms the basis for not doing a kind of social science which 'proceeds from ideas to things, not from things to ideas' (op. cit.: 15). In contrast, Durkheim stresses the need for the study of 'thing-like' social facts 'directly, objectively, "from outside", by systematic observation; precisely as one studies the rest of the things "out there"' (Bauman 1990: 221).

Weber's measuring of patterns against the ideal may thus come close to Durkheim's position. In his conceptualisation, Durkheim emphasises the normative aspect of behaviour — what one might call 'ideal types' — as a means of accounting for deviations — 'it is logically implied in the social type'. Action in relation to a body of rules always allows for the possible violation of them, and this, for Durkheim, is not just in the imagination of the analyst. It is not difficult to make the link here between this methodological position and that of the classic variationist sociolinguistics of Labov. 'Variables', in Labov's classic remark, are there to be 'sniffed out', not as realities but as abstract *emic* constructs arising from carefully calculated observation of linguistic phenomena, and against which constructs the *etic* variation of empirical facts can be set and accounted for by 'rule'. This is of course a classic descriptive linguistic position going back to Bloomfield and earlier, with the important and crucial development by Labov and his followers of a statistically enabled probabilistic analysis. Such empirical facts (*things*) are not accessible to introspection; not for Durkheim, nor for Weber, nor for Labov. As in J.S. Mill's (1875) favouring of natural science as a model for social science, and his concept of 'methodological individualism', objectivity of statements about physical objects can only become meaningful through 'tests of experience', or the 'logic of experience', that is, by using inductive methods.[4]

4   Sociological mentality: Bourdieu and Foucault

In ways similar to Durkheimian definitions of social facts and what should be the object of study, but without the 'scientific mentality', Bourdieu identifies 'field' in his Algerian research (marriage strategies, honour) as his object of investigation, and not *groups* as such in the traditional anthropological sense. One notices here a connection between his theoretical framework about *field* and *habitus*, which also translates into methodological practice. Not, however, into a methodological practice which takes a participant perspective. As he (1977: 81) writes:

> when we speak of class habitus, we are insisting, against all forms of the occasionist illusion which consists of directly relating practices to properties inscribed in the situation, that 'interpersonal' relations are never, except in appearance, individual-to-individual relationships, and that the truth of the interaction is never entirely contained within the interaction.

Bourdieu's move from a structuralist model of rule and exception to one in which individuals' strategic choices are governed by their habitus, but still remain open to exploitation and transformation of that governing habitus, is characteristically reflexive in principle.[5]

Notwithstanding this stance, Bourdieu's ethnography still remains more in the structuralist tradition than it does in, say, the interpretive tradition of Geertz (1973). In distancing himself from structuralism, Bourdieu continues to operate within an objectivist paradigm, perhaps positioning himself uncomfortably between objectivism and subjectivism, between the participant's perspective and that of the analyst. This struggle of perspective is clearly present in his concept of habitus as an 'immanent law', 'laid down in each agent by his earliest upbringing'. For Bourdieu, habitus is a locus of a dialectic between 'objective structures' and the 'cognitive and motivating structures which they produce and which tend to reproduce them', and a construct whose 'mediating' function is to make individual practices 'sensible' and 'reasonable' to others. He writes (1991: 64):

... the interactionist approach which fails to go beyond the actions and reactions apprehended in their daily visible immediacy, is unable to discover that the different agents' linguistic strategies are strictly dependent on their positions in the structure of distribution of linguistic capital, which can be shown to depend, via the structure of chances of access to the educational system on the structure of class relations.

In acknowledging Bourdieu's position *contra* structuralism, it is worth drawing a distinction between Bourdieu's views about ethnography and the ethnographic status of his fieldwork data. It seems from his fieldwork with the Kabyle as if this reflexivity is not that which is associated with reflexivity in practice, as found in ethnographic texts (Clifford and Marcus 1986, Marcus and Fischer 1986). There is no discussion there, for example, of the 'point of view' or of the 'motivated relevance' of the subjective bias in 'ways of seeing'. Much of his data about the Kabyle, after all, were collected through survey questionnaires, and are less than recognisably ethnographic. Bourdieu's book, *Distinction*, for example, is replete with the graphs, charts, survey interviews of a more structuralist account. Still, he is committed to providing an analysis of the middle ground 'which differs from the blind insight of the participants without becoming the sovereign gaze of the impartial observer' (1984: 511).

Although, unlike Bourdieu, Foucault did not carry out extensive fieldwork, he nonetheless held strong views about ethnography as a method of investigation. He sets out his position as a researcher:

I actually attempt to place myself outside the culture, to which we belong in order to analyse its formal conditions for the purpose of, so to speak, achieving its critique; not, however, in order to devalue its accomplishments, but rather to see how they actually arose. By analysing the conditions of our rationality, I also call into question our language, my language, whose origins I am analysing. (Cited in Honneth, 1991: 108)

This method is what he labels ethnology, which, like psychoanalysis, allows one to question the conditions of 'possible knowledge about man in general'. Foucault compares ethnology to linguistics as a way of escaping from anthropology, and characterises linguistics, alongside ethnology and psychoanalysis, as a counter-science in order to undermine anthropology, which, in his view, can deal systematically with what is not so apparent:

Like the two other counter-sciences, it [linguistics] would make visible, in a discursive mode, the frontier forms of human sciences; like them, it would situate its experience in those enlightened and dangerous regions where the knowledge of man acts out, in the form of the unconscious and of historicity, its relation with what renders them possible. (1970: 381)

It is worth noting in this regard (see Kritzman 1988)[6] that Foucault is happy to associate himself with Lévi-Strauss as a human anthropologist, an empiricist with a strong commitment to history. *Discipline and Punish* (Foucault 1977) is a classic example of the Foucauldian method of drawing on documentation — the archive — to make concrete statements about the nature of specific social institutions and at the same time draw more general conclusions about the social order, in particular the pervasiveness of power. Of interest here also is his commitment in that book to make his writing more generally accessible to the interested public. In this we may detect an application of anthropological methodology to the critical explanation of issues of social concern, which comes close to the charter of critical discourse analysis (Fairclough 1989, 1992). However, in *The Archaeology of Knowledge*, Foucault (1972: 48) resists linking linguistic analysis to his analysis of discourse:

> . . . to suppress the stage of "the things themselves" is not necessarily to return to the linguistic analysis of meaning. When one describes the formation of objects of a discourse, one tries to locate the relations that characterise a discursive practice, one determined neither by the lexical organization nor the scansions of the semantic field.

He nonetheless provides, as we noted earlier, a rather explicit methodology for the explanatory analysis of a domain of discourse and the roles of its participants (specifically, doctors and patients in the clinic). (op. cit.: 50)

Foucault characterises his methodological stance as one of 'thinking from outside', and this coincides with his critique of the concept of the subject in the philosophy of reflection. In concrete terms, he questions the myth of the knowing subject, especially in research interviews, and in this way challenges the central status of social scientific data. In the same way he argues that language does not represent, but rather constitutes categories; the order of things cannot be reduced to an order of linguistic categories. Something of this caveat is taken up in this volume in Rampton's chapter, when he writes that there is a 'danger of overgeneralising linguistic models, of assuming syntax-like standards of precision in the study of society and of shuttling up too fast to grand theory from theories of data' (p. 262). Rampton points out that opposing the (dis)orderliness of polyphony, intertextuality and hybridity to some presumed stability and coherence must imply a distinctive methodology, one of 'flow' rather than one of 'stasis and structure'. In a similar way, Erickson (this volume) argues for a methodology of *bricolage*, one which can accommodate indeterminism, constant and local. Using a somewhat similar metaphor, we may say that Foucault's preference for archaeology over history can be summed up as follows: while history is about tradition, continuity, influences and causes, archaeology is about ruptures, discontinuities and disjunctions. The 'document' thus gives way to the 'monument'.

5 Sociolinguistic practice: Hymes, Labov and Gumperz

In beginning this section with the contributions to methodological concerns and practices by Hymes, Labov and Gumperz, it is worth noting that these three scholars, at the forefront of sociolinguistic research, all contributed to the first issue of the journal *Language in Society* in 1972, which has since remained a mainstream sociolinguistic journal. We take this as a critical moment to explore the points of departure for sociolinguistics as an emergent discipline vis-à-vis linguistics and social theory. Indeed, in his editorial introduction to *Language in Society*, Hymes (1972: 1) identified two types of problems:

> One is the patent need for research pertinent to the many ways in which language, especially diversity of language, poses questions of policy and choice. The other is the need, gradually recognised, for control of social factors in linguistic research, and of linguistic factors in social research.

Hymes's first point relates to the practical applications of sociolinguistics, and parallels Durkheim's call for the selection of social facts which are worthy of scientific investigation. Hymes's second concern has centrally to do with sociolinguistic methodology. He elaborates this further (1972: 9):

> The greatest challenge for sociolinguistic research is to develop the methods, concepts and findings that will enable one ultimately to approach language, from the linguistic side, not only as grammar, but also as language organised in use; from the social side, to approach social structure, cultural pattern, values, and the like, in terms of their realisations in verbal and symbolic action.

In so saying, Hymes underscores the point that there is no one-to-one correspondence between language form and function. But in echoing (though not drawing on) Bourdieu, he also acknowledges the variable capacities and resources people have, and draw upon, to communicate meanings in an intersubjective way. Hymes's view, thus, corresponds with the Hallidayan (1973) framework of 'meaning potential'.

Hymes also draws explicitly on Marx's notion of social relationships as the basic unit of analysis. For Marx, as Smith (1990: 94) puts it, 'The basis of analysis is not the act, the action, or the actor. It is the social relation coordinating individual activity and giving people's activities form and determination'. Marx's method of 'substructing' stresses the fact that categories are part of lived practice, and social relations are not sociologically-abstracted norms, but coordinated activities of actual people. In this sense, one might even say that Marx was a proto-ethnomethodologist. This relational focus is also highlighted by Parsons (1951: 23) when he argues that the individual is no longer the centre of analysis:

> the social system is composed of relationships of individual actors and only of such relationships . . . For most analytical purposes, the most significant unit of social structure is not the person but the role.

For Hymes, the basic unit of sociolinguistic analysis is 'the means of speech in human communities, and their meanings to those who use them' — what he regularly referred to as 'ways of speaking'. With this hermeneutic stance, he parts company with Chomsky for whom the units of syntax serve as the units of language analysis. He still remains however within a structuralist and synchronic linguistic methodology of establishing differences, rather than, say, aligning with Foucault's emphasis on acknowledging the historicity and the social and personal conditions which give rise to utterances (discourses), including those potential but not yet attested. Hymes's commitment to an ethnography of speaking (Saville-Troike 1982) is clear from the following quotation, in which, in talking about means of speech and meanings, he comes close to philosophical speech act analysis (Searle 1969) but goes beyond it:

> The means by which a social meaning, say, intimacy vs. distance, is expressed, may range from choice of pronouns to choice of dialect or language, through choice of voice timbre, of norms as to turn-taking, permissible length of pause, and the like. Again, understanding of individual cases, and a theory, must start from the standpoint of means of speech and the meanings they serve. (Hymes 1972: 7)

Here we note not only the salience of the ethnography of speaking model with its emphasis on the various levels of context analysis, but also a clear, although not mutually acknowledged, link to Bourdieu's partial characterisation of an individual's communicative capacity.

What Hymes's stance implies methodologically is a reliance 'primarily upon methods of observation and analysis developed in the social science' (1972: 9). At first, it may appear as if Hymes is endorsing the Durkheimian 'scientific mentality' for the study of 'the objective reality of social facts' (see above). But, Hymes's call for a sociolinguistic methodology based upon observation keeps clear of any positivistic stance directed at the uncovering of some Durkheimian 'permanently existing rules'. In fact, in his work on Native American languages, Hymes documents the significance of socio-historical/cultural experience as a basis for studying communicative competence.

In the same introductory issue of the *Language in Society* journal is Labov's paper entitled 'Some principles of linguistic methodology'.[7] In this paper Labov offers a comprehensive overview of various modes of data collection for sociolinguistic inquiry. What we read is that in response to the debate about the incompatibility of scientific and social science paradigms, Labov adopts a thoroughly natural scientific stance. He positions himself against the nineteenth-century tradition of historical linguistics as he focusses on 'language in use within the speech community, aiming at a linguistic theory adequate to account for these data' (1972a: 183). For him, empirical evidence, as opposed to intuitive data, is crucial to support patterns of language change and evolution. As he puts it,

> it is difficult to avoid the common-sense conclusion that the object of linguistics must ultimately be the instrument of communication used by the speech community; and if we are not talking about that language, there is something trivial in our proceeding. (1972a: 187)

It would be a mistake, however, to view Labov's call for a new methodology to focus on acts of speaking and methods of observing them, as constituting in practice a methodological revolution. Broader questions such as the nature of sociolinguistic investigation, and/or what constitutes sociolinguistic knowledge, are not addressed by Labov. In fact, his call remains deeply traditional, in keeping with his position that sociolinguistics is, above all, a linguistic, rather than any form of sociological enterprise, in terms of its goals.

This is not to say that in linguistic terms his call was not innovative. Clearly, his emphasis on the careful and thorough study of performance, exemplified notably in his New York City studies, was a reaction against both the Saussurean *and* the Chomskyan paradigms. Against Saussure ([1916] 1966), in terms of his structuralist paradigm, but more significantly against Chomsky's (1957, 1965) essentially cognitive theorising of the universal nature of language, even if that meant describing smaller and smaller segments of language. Chomsky stressed, after Saussure, that linguistics is the study of native speaker competence in the abstract, homogeneous speech community, and in the same vein the Saussurean model insists that 'explanations of linguistic facts be drawn from other linguistic facts, not from any "external" data on social behaviour' (Labov 1972a: 185). Labov formulates this as the Saussurean Paradox: 'the social aspect of language is studied by observing any one individual, but the individual aspect only by observing language in its social context' (1972a: 186). This leads Labov to respond to Chomsky in two senses: firstly, that performance is not defective, and there *is* a logic to nonstandard English, and secondly, that linguistic theorising has to be done on the basis of empirical data instead of relying on intuition and introspection.[8] Relevant here is Coupland's (this volume) overview of sociolinguistic research on age and ageing — especially his critique of how Chambers (1995) actively repositions variationist sociolinguistic research within the broader aims of Chomsky's paradigm. As Coupland observes, this is mainly done through an endorsement of the Labovian position that one should study language in its social context in order to obtain better data, which, in turn, will feed into better theories about the nature of language and linguistic change.

Against this backdrop, Labov (1972b: 225) offers a rationale and a procedure for the study of the vernacular as follows:

> The form of black English vernacular used by lames will be compared with that used by members of the dominant social groups of the vernacular culture. The findings will be of considerable sociological interest, since it appears that the consistency of certain grammatical rules is a fine-grained index of membership in the street culture. The data should also be of interest to theoretical linguistics, since it appears that patterns of social interaction may influence grammar in subtle and unsuspected ways. Finally, we will consider the serious methodological problem which these findings pose for linguists in general. It is in fact the same methodological problem with which this study begins: locating the most consistent and reliable data for describing the grammar of the speech community.

In the light of the above, two comments are in order. Firstly, Labov's correlational studies remained, from a social theoretical perspective, essentially Parsonian, that is, that one borrowed in, as it were, a social account of the populations in question as a stable construct against which to make one's (socio)linguistic correlations.[9] And, secondly, his emphasis on the careful collection of empirical data was as much directed against the methodology of some structuralist descriptive linguists as it was against Chomsky's theoretical position, as he makes clear in the conclusion to his chapter, *The linguistic consequences of being a lame*:

> When we now hear linguists speaking at every hand about 'my dialect' and 'dialect variation' we are bound to wonder what basis they have for their claims. The only data usually provided is that some other linguist has disagreed with their intuitive judgements on certain sentences, and it is therefore decided that the critic is speaking a different dialect... It is difficult for us, caught up in current linguistic practice, to evaluate the overwhelming reliance of our field on the theorist's own intuitions as data. Scholars of the future who must eventually review and explain our behaviour may find it hard to understand our casual acceptance of confused and questionable data, the proliferation of ad hoc dialects, and the abandonment of the search for intersubjective agreement... our current trend is supported by a more than local ideology; a theoretical stance can become a congenial way of life... The student of his own intuitions, producing both data and theory, in a language abstracted from every social context, is the ultimate lame. (Labov 1972b: 292)

Such a statement is, of course, of its time (though it does have a continuing and current relevance), and was directed, as we note, at a Chomskyan linguistics using introspection as a method, with a focus on formalism. In this tradition, introspective, abstract data is produced by the analyst as a means for the confirmation of theory. Labov's position offers as a counterpoint the interest of sociolinguists not just in naturalistic data — *parole* and performance — *per se*, but also in deviance and difference. Such a position, characteristic since Labov of sociolinguistics more generally, is not however without its challenges within sociology, as when Bourdieu (1977: 26) writes:

> But the linguists and anthropologists who appeal to 'context' or 'situation' in order, as it were to 'correct' what strikes them as unreal and abstract in the structuralist model, are in fact still trapped in the logic of the theoretical model which they are rightly trying to supersede. The method of 'situational analysis' which consists of 'observing people in a variety of social situations' in order to determine 'the way in which individuals are able to exercise choices within the limits of a specified social structure' remains locked within the framework of the rule and the exception.

Such a caveat is worth remembering, when Labov, in dismissing Chomsky's method of theory construction based on intuitive data and the notion of an idealised speaker (even an ideal hearer is absent from Chomsky's theorising),[10] argues in favour of an alternative methodology. In Labov's framework different types of data — texts, elicitations, intuitions and observations — and their differential status are linked to particular types of context, as they classically are in his reliance on the targeted elicitation of presumed clearly boundaried speech styles. Note also that once elicited and 'captured', such data are presented in a highly objectivised and quantified manner within the terms of the typical variationist sociolinguistic model (Sankoff 1978). Labov is quite aware of the issues surrounding this scenario:

> The problem we as linguists face in dealing directly with the data of language is not peculiar to our discipline. This is a general problem for all the social sciences. Garfinckel [sic] (1967) has demonstrated that there exists in every field of research an inevitable gap between the raw data as it occurs and the protocols in which the data are recorded as input to the theoretical pursuit ... There are many acts of perceiving, remembering, selecting, interpreting, and translating that lie between the data and the linguist's report ... As Garfinckel [sic] has pointed out, every coding and reporting procedure that transforms the data will show an ineradicable residue of common-sense operation which cannot be reduced to rule. To come to grips with language, we must look as closely and directly at the data of everyday speech as possible, and characterise its relationship to our

> grammatical theories as accurately as we can, amending and adjusting the theory so that it fits the object in view. We can then turn again and re-examine the methods we have used, an inquiry which will greatly increase our understanding of the object we are studying. (Labov (1972a: 201)

Labov's principal concern has always been with the quality of the data which can, and which should, form a sound basis for constructing linguistic theory, especially theories of linguistic change. Although reference to contexts of use is implicit in the methodology of his early and classic work (as in his New York and his Martha's Vineyard studies) there is always in that methodology a lack of analysis of the interactional, microsocial context. This lack is evident even within his very influential and explicitly institutionally contextualised work with Fanshel (Labov and Fanshel 1977) on psychotherapeutic discourse. Here, in terms of the analysis of professional discourse, there is little reflection on the therapeutic context, something which is hard to grasp when one notes that Labov's collaborator was a psychotherapist. This is in contrast to the work of Foucault, and also to more recent work on the discourse of psychotherapy. The main underpinning of the study still appears to be linguistic, even if its theory is derived more from speech act analysis (Searle 1969) than it is from formalist linguistic analysis. Its functional orientation remains less central than its attempt to provide rule-governed accounts of the basis for strategic linguistic choices. Such a stance presupposes the contingent argument (Ryan 1970) that the social facts are out there to be gathered and explained in a non-ideological way.

Opposing a generative paradigm does not escape the Saussurean (Durkheimian) commitment to objectivism, as Bourdieu (1977) notes. Nor is it obviated by the use of methodological devices (cf. 'danger of death questions') as a means of controlling for 'the observer's paradox' (Labov 1972a). However 'accessible' to the researcher such devices may make the 'uncontaminated' vernacular, and however important it is for his sociolinguistics that subjects lose their conscious attentiveness to their modes of speaking, Labov's main concern remains for the data–theory relation, rather than for the role relations between the researcher as observer and the participants, and what that means for interpreting the raw data. Even for those, like one of the present authors, trained by Labov to minimise such contamination, the focus was *always* on the data, *not* interaction.

Gumperz's (1972) contribution to that introductory journal issue is classified as a report on 'research in progress'. If Hymes stipulates the broad goals of sociolinguistic research, with Labov setting out some methodological principles, it is Gumperz who offers some concrete evidence of sociolinguistic methodology in action, in the context of his fieldwork in the rural settings of India and Austria. Gumperz draws on this field research to make some important observations about the limitations of the notion of 'linguistically uniform speech communities'. In this, he provides the precursive argument which underpins both Rampton's and Erickson's chapters in this volume. Gumperz's choice of a bilingual site to study code alternation (codeswitching) motivates however more than merely a challenge to a prevailing Chomskyan orthodoxy. Gumperz's innovation in sociolinguistics is his argument that on the evidence from communities where linguistic diversity is commonplace, code choice is to be explained less by appeal to some speakers' unitary grammatical competence than it is by postulating a series of contextually determined, and co-implicational, choices deriving from speakers' broad communicative repertoires. Note that this position is not merely driven by the facts of linguistic diversity in the interlingual sense; it is, for Gumperz, a general linguistic principle applying as much intralingually within a language as it does across languages.

Two further implications for sociolinguistics arise from Gumperz's work. The first is the introduction of the construct of *situational context* as a conditioning factor on code choice; the second, and even more far-reaching methodologically, is the implicit assumption that, given the indeterminate, dynamic and adaptable nature of situated language data, its description and analysis must require a sociolinguistic methodology which can accommodate and can capture this variability and adaptability. Here again Gumperz heralds a number of chapters in this volume, those by Rampton, Erickson and Heller in particular. Not that Gumperz would go so far as the conversational analysts in this regard, but adopting this contextual and dynamic position does lead him to argue that the construct of a linguistic or communicative repertoire, rather than one resting on an inferred grammatical competence drawn from intuitive data from a single language, is a better starting point for analysis. We may say that in one sense his position is deeply traditional, asserting as it does that in (socio)linguistic description one should not rely on *a priori* assumptions about what constitutes normal speech. As we note, Erickson's chapter in this book in particular highlights the consequences of this Gumperzian position, without, however, attributing to him the later shift to a sociolinguistics of action, or any necessary engagement of such micro analysis with the influence of large-scale social forces. As we saw in our discussion of Hymes above, it is interesting to note how Bourdieu reflects Gumperz's concern for describing the micro-linguistic phenomena at the heart of interaction (Gumperz's 'contextualisation cues') when he writes:

> ...hence communication is only possible when accompanied by a practical spotting of cues, which, in enabling speakers to situate others in hierarchies of age, wealth, power, or culture, guides them unwittingly towards the type of exchange best suited in form and content to the objective situation between the interacting individuals. (Bourdieu 1977: 26)

It may also be not too far-fetched to draw a connection between Gumperz's position on what is required of such a methodology with Foucault's explicitly methodological remarks in *The Archaeology of Knowledge* in the section on 'the formation of strategies'. Foucault (1972: 65–66) writes (albeit in relation to 'discourses' rather than to linguistic forms in Gumperz's sense):

> Determine the possible 'points of diffraction' of a discourse. These are first characterized as points of incompatibility (i.e. within the same discursive formation but not in the same series of statements (enonces) . . . they are then characterised as points of equivalence . . . lastly characterized as link points of systematization. Then describe the specific authorities that guided the choices that were made from all those that could have been made. For this one must study the economy of the discursive constellation to which the discourse being studied belongs.

Foucault here goes beyond Gumperz's concerns, but it is not a dissimilar set of methodological injunctions to those Gumperz at least implies. Although Foucault moves beyond the empirical and strictly Labovian sociolinguistics with his call for a speculative engagement with *what might have been uttered* as a means of understanding *what was uttered*, such a position is basically at one with Gumperz's constructs of repertoire, capacity and motivated choice.

The links between Gumperz and Labov may perhaps be best made in relation to their parallel claims about the relevance of sociolinguistic fieldwork and sociolinguistic data to the understanding of the mechanisms and processes of language change. Both locate linguistic change in a combination of externally- and socially-motivated forces occasioning what then become internally conditioned, and not necessarily separately socially-motivated, consequent changes and adjustments to the language system. They share a commitment to the notion of language as action even though the direction of their projects is distinctive: Labov towards linguistics and language, and Gumperz towards ethnography and society. Both, however, see the researcher as essentially external to the (inter)action (see Figueroa's (1994) detailed review of the theoretical bases of Labov, Hymes and Gumperz).

6   Points of view and microsocial investigation

The foregoing provides some insights into our choice of the term *motivational relevancies* in the title of this methodological chapter. Goffman borrows the term from Schutz (1962) to make the point that social scientists study social phenomena in line with their own preferred motivations. In arguing that much of scientific categorisation is value-laden, Weber (1949) is making a similar claim, as is Bourdieu in his use of the term 'points of view' (see Bourdieu *et al.* 2000) to underscore how the point or source of any 'view' is inseparable from what is viewed, and how the reporting of interview data cannot be seen as detached glosses. Weber adopts a related but more general stance as far as motivation is concerned:

> ... in social sciences the stimulus to the posing of scientific problems is in actuality always given by practical 'questions'. Hence the very recognition of the existence of a scientific problem coincides, personally, with the possession of specifically oriented motives and values. (1949: 61)

Two examples of this motivation are clear from the works of Hymes, Labov and Gumperz referred to earlier: their interest in real-life settings, especially the lifeworld of the underprivileged. Recall here Labov's dedication to his 1972 paper on 'lames':

> To the Jets, the Cobras, and the Thunderbirds
> who took on all odds and were dealt all low cards

The Chomskyan 'ideal speaker' is thus denied his/her pride of place within Labovian sociolinguistics.

A second but related reading of the term *motivational relevancies* has to do with a notion of *context*. The canonical question 'what is it that's going on here?' can be 'described in terms of a focus that includes a wide swath or a narrow one and — as a related but not identical matter — in terms of a focus that is close-up or distant' (Goffman 1974: 8). Embedded in this question are a range of methodological concerns such as 'where to look', how much retrospection to allow, how many layers of context to deal with, and how to balance the perspectives of participants and those of the analysts.[11] We shall return later to the fundamental issues that these methodological concerns raise, for example that of the interrelationship between data and theory; subjective and objective accounts of reality; internal and external contexts of interpretation; the juxtaposition between scientific and commonsense interpretations. At the descriptive and at the evaluative level we may say that *motivational relevancy* involves engagement with at least, firstly, focus and ground relations as set out in Duranti and Goodwin (1992); secondly, layering of context to take into account social and ideological dimensions of language use as in critical discourse analysis (Fairclough 1992); and, thirdly, Cicourel's (1992) concern for the 'ecological validity' of research into context.

A third perspective on *motivational relevancy* has to do with mode and field. The preoccupation and prime concern of sociolinguists with talk or, more generally, with language-in-use, undoubtedly motivates where we look for data. As Halliday (1978) sets out in his study of language as social semiotic, mode is ineluctably bound up with the choice of field and topic. Hak's (1999) example from the medical domain is apposite here. As he writes, because our interest is in talk, it is likely that we will select the consultation as an object of study. Again, if, like West (1984), our interest lies in gendered ways of speaking, it is plausible that our focus of analysis will fall on patterns of interruption in doctor–patient interaction. The issue here thus becomes one of search versus discovery, in particular our ability and our preparedness to notice and identify what we want to describe and account for. According to Winch (1958: 85):

> For to notice something is to identify relevant characteristics which means that the noticer must have some concept of such characteristics; this is possible only if he is able to use some symbol according to a rule which makes it refer to those characteristics.

To continue this example, we need to realise however that talk *alone* does not constitute professional practice, and in the same sense, a medical consultation may not *necessarily* be a site for participants to behave in gendered ways. Bourdieu (1977: 78) makes a similar point in discussing the relationship between 'ordinary practices' and the acquisition and transformation of the *habitus*:

> ... these practices cannot be directly deduced either from the objective conditions ... or from the conditions which produced the durable principle of their production.

However, once we acknowledge a 'point of view' and the *motivational relevancies* that we bring to bear upon our object of study, this issue of search versus discovery becomes less of a problem. In our search we retain the capacity to discover. In any case, as Weber (1949) cautions, as analysts we should not be claiming practical relevance for our searched-for discoveries. That is a matter for practitioners to acknowledge and decide (Sarangi and Roberts 2000).

7 Methodological underpinnings of microsocial analysis

Discussion so far on early sociolinguistic studies has highlighted some commonalities, as well as differences, between the methodologies of social science and natural science. Sociolinguistics in the post-1972 era is highly compartmentalised, and is marked by a microsocial turn as is clearly evident from the range of contributions to the recently founded *Journal of Sociolinguistics*. Microsocial analysis, which is particularly characteristic of the works of Garfinkel and Goffman, is not without its tensions and problems when we deal with sociolinguistic data. So, in what follows, we revisit the central tenets of a microsocial methodology: that of the status of observational method in general, and, in particular, distinctions between description and explanation, and between objectivism and subjectivism — all of which bear upon the contrast to be made between participants' and analysts' perspectives.

7.1 Observational method

In making the point that 'observation, from the seventeenth century onwards, is a perceptible knowledge furnished with a series of systematically negative conditions', Foucault (1970: 132–3) draws attention to the notions of certainty, proof and generality, which are crucial to all scientific investigation. Across different research paradigms, however, we may expect that observational tools will differ and become more sophisticated. Although 'sight' for Foucault retains 'an exclusive privilege' (over other senses), different 'expert' ways of seeing become the basis for claiming professional credibility.

> To attempt to improve one's power of observation by looking through a lens, one must renounce the attempt to achieve knowledge by means of the other senses or hearsay. A change of scale in the visual sphere must have more value than the correlations between the various kinds of evidence that may be provided by one's impressions, one's reading, or learned compilations. (Foucault 1970: 133)

In a similar way, as we note earlier, Durkheim accords perceptual data scientific status, and thus claims for it objectivity, a position which allows him to maintain a methodological link with natural science while still pursuing the study of 'social facts'. In this sense his sociology becomes a 'science of observation'. As Goffman (1974: 9) notes: 'To speak of something happening before the eyes of observers is to be on firmer ground than in the usual social sciences; but the ground is still shaky, and the crucial question of how a seeming agreement was reached concerning the identity of the "something" and the inclusiveness of "before the eyes" still remains'.

This tradition is maintained in ethnographic sociological and sociolinguistic studies, with (participant) observation as its key activity. Such observation, however, is not uniform in practice; for example, it takes on a distinctive mode in the study of talk-in-interaction, as Erickson makes plain in his chapter in this volume. Studies of interaction involve the recording and transcribing of natural conversation, which can then be subjected to detailed analysis and verification (see Moerman 1988 for the interface between ethnography and conversation analysis). The nature and sourcing of talk data are, however, not without controversy. Sacks (1984), for example, refers to Weinreich's call for the study of language 'under conditions of its full fledged utilisation' and the need to avoid samples of casual, ceremonial or 'desemanticised' speech. Such an argument from linguistics has the effect of de-privileging certain kinds of data, setting out a programme of what is *not* to be observed and consequently not studied. In response, Sacks (1984: 24) adopts the ethnomethodological position when he announces: 'It is possible that detailed study of small phenomena may give an enormous understanding of the way humans do things and the kinds of objects they use to construct and order their affairs'. Both conventional sociological survey research and anthropological inquiry discover orderliness . . . 'they could be seen as a consequence of the fact that, given the possibility that there is overwhelming order, it would be extremely hard not to find it, no matter how or where we looked' (op. cit.: 23). Nonetheless, it is important also to note the caveat introduced by Haberland and Mey (1977) in their inaugural Editorial to the *Journal of Pragmatics*, that researchers into naturally occurring language data should avoid the collecting of unconnected 'objets trouvés' of indiscriminate text, a position taken up strongly by critical discourse analysts (Fairclough 1989, 1992).

Although much of Goffman's and Garfinkel's research is based on the close observation of everyday life, unlike studies in conversational analysis it is not grounded in the recording or analysis of real-life talk data. It retains a theoretical orientation, especially in the case of Garfinkel's ethnomethodological programme with its focus on 'practical actions as contingent ongoing accomplishments of organized artful practices of everyday life' (Garfinkel 1967: 11). In saying this, Garfinkel owes a debt to Durkheim's 'objective reality of social facts as sociology's fundamental principle' and, indeed, to the Parsonian concept of society as practical achievement. It was largely left to Sacks (1984), as Garfinkel's student, to put Garfinkel's ethnomethodological programme into practice, and to realise the claim for 'observation as a basis for theorising' (p. 25) and to achieve the aim 'to get into a position to transform, in an almost literal, physical sense, our view of "what happened," from a matter of particular interaction done by particular people, to a matter of interactions as products of a machinery' (p. 26). In this way, not only is transcription a theoretical practice, but observation itself is deeply theory-laden (Ochs 1979).

Observation has always been central to sociolinguistic practice, as we have noted, both within the Labovian sociolinguistic tradition and the Hymesian ethnography of speaking. As a defining practice, however, it provides no guarantee of objectivity, *pace* Foucault and Durkheim. Not only is observation subject to theory, it is in itself problematic in terms of the validity of its procedures and its evidence. 'Talk' is clearly not enough; the conditions of its sourcing and gathering need critical review. Labov in particular draws attention to this when he writes:

> We are then left with the Observer's Paradox: the aim of linguistic research in the community must be to find out how people talk when they are not being systematically observed; yet we can only obtain these data by systematic observation . . . One way of overcoming the paradox is to break

through the constraints of the interview situation by various devices which divert attention away from speech, and allow the vernacular to emerge . . . cf. 'danger of death' questions, 'Have you ever been in a situation where you were in serious danger of being killed?' (Labov 1972a: 209)

One possible reading of what Labov calls 'attention away from speech' may suggest that the 'danger of death' questions enable informants to articulate their experience in a language of description which is potentially devoid of a metalanguage of reflection and explanation.

7.2   Description vs explanation

Although observation remains a unifying tool across various sciences, natural and social, such problematic issues as those above with the sourcing, and thus the status, of observational data, are matched by parallel concerns with what researchers do with observational data once gathered. Conventionally in the natural sciences, the observed object is held to be describable in a detached way, whereas in the social sciences it is possible to conflate what is being observed with the person(s) doing the observing. The methodology of participant observation in anthropological fieldwork is a case in point where the reporting of an observed event is most likely to reveal as much about the object of inquiry as about the perspective the participant-observer adopts. In short, the latter context of research produces motivational readings, offering only one of potentially many perspectives on the object under study. Nor are multiple perspectives the only issue, since the degree and extent of the description can also vary considerably, and are themselves subject to principled positions on the disciplinary nature of the research inquiry. For example, the so-called 'thick' description in Geertz's (1973) sense is not just a matter of expanding the context of the data; its procedures derive from a particular principled position on what constitutes ethnography, and the relationship he seeks to draw between 'describing' social facts and 'explaining' them.

Smith (1990: 104) equates description with 'factual accounts' which allow us in our readings to 'pass through the text to an actuality "on the other side".'[12] For Smith, description is a language game in the sense that it relies heavily on the 'referencing method of meaning, taking the terms to intend something out there, object or action, beyond the text' (Smith 1990: 104). By a similar token, explanation would constitute a different language game, where analytic constructs are used to make sense of what is observed.

We should also note that explanation is not only directed at the observable object, but can focus on what lies, so to speak, beneath or behind the object, as Foucault would have it. Lévi-Strauss, for example, unlike many anthropologists, was not especially interested in explaining the organisation of particular societies, but in discovering the fundamental structures of the human mind. For him, 'ethnographic analysis tries to arrive at invariants beyond the empirical diversity of human societies' (1966: 247). Moreover, even in those projects which appear premissed upon the immediacy of members' methods, like ethnomethodology, there is a recognition of the need to take account of what lies beneath and behind what can be empirically observed. Garfinkel (1967: 4) makes this point in relation to Husserl:

> Husserl spoke of expressions whose sense cannot be decided by an auditor without his necessarily knowing or assuming something about the biography and the purposes of the user of the expression, the circumstances of the utterance, the previous course of the conversation or the particular relationship of actual or potential interaction that exists between the expression and the auditor.

Further, the continuing influence of the concept of scientific detachment can also be seen in ethnomethodology's notion of 'ethnomethodological indifference', directed at the task of describing the formal structures of everyday life by restricting oneself to the task of describing members' accounts. Note here how for Sacks, 'sociology can be a natural observational science [which] seeks to describe methods persons use in doing social life' (1984: 21). What is less apparent from this detached stance is his view on the status of the analyst. Indeed, we might conclude that the alignment of the analyst with the participant suggests that no difference is held to exist between layperson and scientist. The layperson is given the status of an expert, very much in the manner suggested by Garfinkel (1967: 10) of his Suicide Prevention Centre staff and others:

> ... for Suicide Prevention Centre staff, for coders, for jurors, the rational properties of their practical actions *somehow* consist in the concerted work of making evidence from fragments — from 'codified' but essentially vague catalogues of experience and the like how a person died in society, or by what criteria patients were selected for psychiatric treatment ... *Somehow* is the problematic crux of the matter.

Interestingly enough in the light of what Garfinkel writes — especially given Labov's firm placing of sociolinguistics within linguistics — Sacks offers linguistics as a role-model for this work in the description of everyday interaction:

> We would want to name those objects and see how they work, as we know how verbs and adjectives and sentences work. Thereby we can come to see how an activity is assembled, as we see a sentence assembled with a verb, a predicate, and so on. Ideally, of course, we would have a formally describable method, as the assembling of a sentence is formally describable. The description not only would handle sentences in general, but particular

sentences. What we would be doing, then, is developing another grammar. And grammar, of course, is the model of routinely observable, closely ordered social activities. (1984: 24–25)

The core issues still remain, however, whether one can actually keep description separate from explanation, and what kinds of observational data and descriptive accounts are necessary conditions for any social explanation to be valid. Consider Winch's example (1958: 73–4) of 'the cat writhes':

Suppose I describe his complex movements in purely mechanical terms, using a set of space–time co-ordinates. This is, in a sense, a description of what is going on as much as is the statement that the cat is writhing in pain. But the one statement could not be substituted for the other. The statement which includes the concept of writhing says something which no statement of the other sort, however detailed, could approximate to.

Here 'writhing', with its evaluative tone, takes on an explanatory character. It tells us as much about 'the observed' as about the observer's viewpoint. Note that this notion of explanation is different from the notion of explanation in historical-structuralist terms. As in critical discourse analysis, and in Heller's contribution to this volume, explanation constitutes a linkage between discursive and social practices and the historical provenance of such practices. At the same time it evokes a question about the basic relationship between sociolinguistic description and explanation. In brief, it is one thing to attempt a detailed description of language use, and quite another to explain what people do with language (as, for example, in language attitude studies). Indeed, for Geach (1967), those ascriptivists concerned with agency are not engaged in the same world of explanation as are natural scientists. For him social explanation deviates from scientific, and descriptive, explanation.

Ascriptivists hold that to say an action x was voluntary on the part of an agent A is not to describe the act as caused in a certain way, but to ascribe it to A, to hold A responsible for it . . . descriptive language is in quite a different logical realm from ascriptive language. (1967: 224)

According to Lévi-Strauss, for example (1977: ix), 'structuralism uncovers a unity and coherence within things which could not be revealed by simple description of the facts somehow scattered and disorganised before the eyes of knowledge'. It seems that what is at heart here is the need to impose some methodological order on disorder as a necessary precursor to the explanatory revelation of order. In a similar way, Durkheim and Foucault emphasise the need for an ordered comparativist approach so that description takes on an explanatory dimension. For Foucault,

> It is possible, a priori, to state that these techniques [of comparison] are of two types. Either that of making total comparisons, but only within empirically constituted groups in which the number of resemblances is manifestly so high that the enumeration of the differences will not take long to complete; and in this way, step by step, the establishment of all identities and distinctions can be guaranteed. Or that of selecting a finite and relatively limited group of characteristics, whose variations and constants may be studied in any individual entity that presents itself. This last procedure was termed the System, the first the method. (1970: 139)

While for Durkheim, the comparative method goes beyond mere ideological analysis, and towards objectivity:

> We shall begin by classifying societies according to the degree of organisation they present. Taking as a basis the perfectly simple society or the society of one segment. Within these types we shall distinguish different varieties according to whether a complete coalescence of the initial segments does or does not appear. (1964: 86)

His (1970) treatise on suicide, for instance, adopts a comparative perspective, spread across demographic and temporal lines. For Durkheim (1964: 139), in reaction to the historical method and to psychological explanation, such a comparative method — seen as 'indirect experiment' — is central to sociological analysis. 'Comparative sociology is not a particular branch of sociology; it is sociology itself, in so far as it ceases to be purely descriptive and aspires to account for facts'. Where a comparative method is absent, the data are often used for illustrative purposes rather than for demonstration; itself a useful distinction that he draws our attention to.

The comparative method is by definition motivationally oriented. It presumes some imposed order on the methodology and suggests a particular analytical stance on the part of the researcher. In professional discourse studies, for instance, one may want to juxtapose in a study the communicative practices of patients with doctors and nurses (Fisher 1991) or examine in one study various forms of client–practitioner relations across a range of professional settings. The issue is whether such *motivatedness* is necessary to the discovery of social facts. Sacks for one would argue against it. For him, unmotivated observation is crucial, and in this sense not only is any data adequately suitable for the uncovering of the interaction order, but also no particular motivation is required of the analyst in addressing such data. The issue then becomes, on the one hand, rather like Labov's chance encounters with variables, whether one can ever warrant such naïve and unmotivated approaches in practice, and on the other, as in Wittgenstein's remark, 'what if observation does not enable us to see any clear rule, and the question brings none to light?'. Meanwhile, for Sacks,

Treating some actual conversation in an unmotivated way, that is, giving some consideration to whatever can be found in any particular conversation we happen to have our hands on, subjecting it to investigation in any direction that can be produced from it, can have strong payoffs. Recurrently, what stands as a solution to some problem emerges from unmotivated examination of some piece of data, where, had we started out with a specific interest in the problem, it would not have been supposed in the first instance that this piece of data was a resource with which to consider, and come up with a solution for, that particular problem. (1984: 27)

This stance is, as we have noted earlier, the opposite of Durkheim's. In a sense, the striking difference between Sacks and Durkheim makes the tension between description and explanation all the more salient. Unlike Sacks's unmotivated description of what 'we happen to have our hands on', Durkheim not only insists on motivated looking, he even urges (1964: 90) that social explanation has to go beyond a functional approach: 'To show how a fact is useful is not to explain how it originated or why it is what it is'. For him, facts exist independently of their functions:

Consequently, to explain a social fact it is not enough to show the cause on which it depends; we must also, at least in most cases, show its function in the establishment of social order. (1964: 97)

Accordingly, instead of psychological explanations, 'we must, then, seek the explanation of social life in the nature of society itself' (p. 102).[13] This is how he went about explaining the cause of suicide. 'The determining cause of a social fact should be sought among the social facts preceding it and not among the states of the individual consciousness' (p. 110). At issue here is the question of admissible evidence, where to look, and what to use, and what not to use as data. If Durkheim argues that to reveal the causes of suicide in a given population one should rather use official statistics than use survey questionnaires from representatives of that population, then what is at issue is not only the role of history in the study of contemporary events, but also the weight that can be accorded to objective over subjective data in the drawing of (social) scientific conclusions. For Durkheim, the subjective view, that is, 'the point of view of the person thought as acting', is to be preferred over the objective 'point of view of the outside observer'.

7.3   Objectivism vs subjectivism

As we note earlier in our references to Saussure and to Lévi-Strauss, the call for objectivism in social science has its root in structuralism and the methodology of natural science. Objectivism, in its classic interpretation, implies that phenomena exist independently of that which we, as participants or analysts, as it were, bring with us, and the characteristics of such phenomena can be described without personal prejudice. In extreme terms, this would imply in (socio)linguistics that words carry with them fixed meanings and can accordingly be precisely categorised. To continue the analogy, subjectivism, on the contrary, would presumably imply that words derived their value entirely from their use, and that variation in such use would, accordingly, impact on the range of potential meaning value of the words in question.

As Lakoff and Johnson (1980) point out in their influential work on metaphor, neither extreme is a tenable one for the interpretation of linguistic phenomena. They would presumably concur with Schutz (1962: 64), who points out that '. . . all scientific explanations of the social world can, and for certain purposes must, refer to the subjective meaning of the actions of human beings from which social reality originates'. In part, the issue for Schutz is one of perspective. He refines Weber's 'principle of subjectivity' by distinguishing between the meaning of an action as perceived by the agent and by the observer and proposes an integration of what he terms 'objective meaning-contexts of subjective meaning-contexts' (Schutz and Lukann 1974: 241). As Meyerhoff (this volume) illustrates in the case of explaining language variation, theoretical articulation of goals might translate into methods that combine objective, quantitative analyses of data from a speech community, with the subjective analysis of individual discourses.

Symbolic interactionism reaffirms the principle of subjectivity. As Blumer notes (1969: 2, 73–4),

> Since action is forged by the actor out of what he perceives, interprets, and judges, one would have to see the operating situation as the actor sees it, perceive objects as the actor perceives them, ascertain their meaning in terms of the meaning they have for the actor, and follow the actor's line of conduct as the actor organises it — in short, we have to take the role of the actor and see the world from his standpoint.

Blumer thus questions (p. 74) the position of the detached outside observer: 'the objective approach holds the danger of the observer substituting his view of the field of action for the view held by the actor'. In this, we note a position not dissimilar to that generally held by conversational analysis, and one akin to that adopted by Potter and Edwards (this volume: 94) in their discussion of discursive psychology, where they remark: 'We do not need to know about such entities or processes to find important phenomena, to study them and to identify their implications. The analytical preference of discursive psychology is to study the use of descriptions in natural discourse, where their involvement with particular actions is more easily identified'. The privileging of the participant's perspective, and the concentration on discourse as a locally managed co-constructed resource does not imply any necessary departure from Blumer's position that in social science 'methodological principles have to meet the fundamental requirements of empirical science'. Indeed, their methodology would underscore it.

8   Participants' and analysts' perspectives: Alignment or transformation?

In this concluding section we revisit the main methodological problematic that pervades both social theoretical and sociolinguistic studies of social life. This has to do with striking a relationship between participants' and analysts' perspectives on social data. Two positions can be discerned. First, we could say that participants and analysts bring different perspectives to data, very much in the objectivist, scientific mode of inquiry. Such an assumption of difference leads to the analyst imposing or transforming the 'observed' into a form of order.[14] A second position would maintain that participants and analysts view the world in the same way, through the same lens, using the same coding devices — very much in the hermeneutic, ethnomethodological mode of inquiry. Here the assumption is one of similarity demanding that both perspectives need to be aligned in any study of social events.

What the privileging of the participant's perspective must imply, however, beyond the general adoption of the requirements of empirical science, is some considerable mutuality of experience between researcher and researched. Accessing Schutz's 'commonsense knowledge' in relation to how people carry out their social lives presupposes not only that anthropologists or socio-linguists studying these social processes should not be imposing their views on the interpretation of these processes, but that they are equipped to recognise their views in the first place. Schutz (1976: 16) suggests that social scientists must create what he terms 'constructs of the second degree', that is that their typifications should align with typifications employed by those under study in everyday lives:

> ... that each term in such a scientific model of human action must be constructed in such a way that a human act performed within the real world by an individual actor as indicated by the typical construct would be understandable to the actor himself as well as to his fellow men in terms of commonsense interpretation of everyday life.

This position begs the questions of (a) what is knowable from various positions and through various metalanguages, and (b) who makes the assessment of 'good recognition' and 'sameness of judgement' (Coupland, personal communication). This is surely precisely what Goffman (1974: 9) has in mind when he legitimises motivational relevancy as one which limits the analyst's point of view 'to one that participants would easily recognise to be valid'. Goffman cites Carnap:

> The sentences, definitions, and rules of the syntax of a language are concerned with the forms of that language. But, now, how are these sentences, definitions, and rules themselves to be correctly expressed? Is a kind of super-language necessary for the purpose? And, again, a third language to explain the syntax of this superlanguage, and so on to infinity? Or is it possible to formulate the syntax of a language within that language itself? (Carnap 1937: 3)

Needless to say, Carnap favours the latter option. A similar point is raised by Giddens (1976: 15) as he points to the theoretical shift towards studying social life as a process: 'the production of society is a skilled performance, sustained and "made to happen" by human beings'. On this basis, he argues (1976: 16) that,

> Such resources [i.e., people's knowledge and theories] as such are not corrigible in the light of the theories of social scientists, but are routinely drawn upon by them in the course of any researches they may prosecute. That is to say, a grasp of the resources used by members of society to generate social interaction is a condition of the social scientist's understanding of their conduct in just the same way as it is for those members themselves.

On the surface, this suggests that analysts should not only draw upon their experience when they approach their object of study, they should also use the language of everyday life in their explanation of social phenomena. Indeed many sociologists follow this line (see Marx's use of everyday categories such as values, wages, profit, etc.). As Smith (1990: 103) points out, it is one thing to make a case for aligning participants' and analysts' perspectives, but it is quite another to accomplish 'descriptions relevant to the relation between the language of the setting and the language of the description'. She writes:

> . . . our problem in part arises out of a confounding of the practices of one language-game with those of another, and that as we understand how they are related, so too we can begin to see, first how we have attributed to the actuality intended by the description properties of the relation in which the description arises, and second, how we might proceed with an alternative descriptive strategy making use of everyday life as its point d'appui. (Smith 1990: 86–87)

In the same way, and following the Sapir–Whorf position, Cicourel warns (1964: 1):

My basic assumption is that the clarification of sociological language is important because linguistic structure and use affects the way people interpret and describe their world. Since sociologists have evolved their own theoretical terminologies and frequently discuss, on the one hand, in these varying terms the language and substance of each other's theories and on the other hand the language of persons in everyday life whose behaviour they are interested in explaining and predicting, it is quite likely that the syntax and meaning of these languages will become entangled.

Cicourel's own critique of objectivist sociology is based on the fact that 'any and all information imputed or extracted from members' descriptive accounts requires the utilisation and assumes the existence of "background expectancies" or tacit knowledge' (1964: 6). Analysts do have a pre-understanding of what they are describing and do not come naïve to data. This is true even for grand theorising, pointing out its reliance on everyday subjective understanding (Douglas 1971). In this light, practical methodologies of constructing questionnaires or conducting research interviews always presuppose the reality of some shared agreement between researcher and informants.

As we note earlier, Garfinkel's 'ethnomethodological indifference' becomes quite revealing in his study of jury deliberations, which to date remains a critical methodological moment. Garfinkel (1967: 105) argues that there cannot be a distinction between participants' and analysts' methods of sense-making, although jurors may modify slightly the rules used in daily life when they decide between 'what actually happened and what "merely appeared" to happen'. When analysing jurors' deliberation practices, Garfinkel concurs, both jurors and analysts do have recourse to similar interpretive procedures, that is, the documentary method of interpretation.

The issue of interpretation becomes more complicated once we take into account the identity and the positioning of the analyst in the research setting and the requirement to produce an account which is in alignment with members' methods. Garfinkel's breaching experiments offer a good example. These were chiefly designed to support Garfinkel's thesis about what is taken for granted in everyday life, and not framed as *scientific* experiments. The experiments required his students to take up the roles of strangers in familiar settings, and Garfinkel himself admits that this was not easily accomplished. Unsurprisingly, the student-analysts found it hard to offer objective accounts of their research experience based on criteria such as clarity, accuracy, distinctiveness, and the difficulties they experienced must raise questions about conflating participant and analyst perspectives. Such questions are not merely a matter of the difficulty of seeking objectivity through achieving some mutuality of subjective impression. They touch also on the relationship between researchers' analysis and participants' records of 'commonsense'. Schegloff's (1996) devotion, for example, to a distinction between the two becomes suspect, if the distinction only rests on the manner of formulation of accounts. To argue, as he does, that the representations of conversational analysis are demotic and thus more nearly achieve a participants' perspective, as opposed to the more distinctively analytical perspective in a more obviously distanced technical (socio)linguistic analysis, is merely to ignore the extreme artfulness and codified practices of conversational analysis. A preference for an apparently 'natural' representation does nothing to bring analysts' and participants' perspectives into line, it merely wilfully avoids an available and more precise mode of representation.

The issue is more than one of modes of representation and codification, of course. It has to do with mutuality of perspective and with membership. Smith (1990) is sympathetic to the ethnomethodological critique of macrosocial description, but at the same time she questions the very device 'members' method' which serves to objectify what we already know as insiders. For her,

> The issue is to transform 'members' practices' into our practices as members, or rather to discover how to take up methods of inquiry in which the method itself is explicated as an integral aspect of the inquiry. (1990: 91)

The whole question of what constitutes 'membership' is open to critique, since analysts may break their membership criteria once they turn to academically sanctioned genres of interpretation (Coupland, personal communication). An ethnomethodological position constrains what can be studied by implying that analysts need to be full participants of the group under study. In this sense, one can only interpret what one shares as background knowledge. This may be a reason why we find few ethnomethodological studies within multicultural and intercultural settings, in that it is hard for analysts to claim membership, mutuality, and shared competence in two cultures. As Churchill (1971: 182) perceptively comments:

> Ethnomethodologists in sociology rarely study primitive peoples; they study present-day Americans. This difference is more than a matter of taste. In their theorising, ethnomethodologists rely heavily on their knowledge of American culture learned by being members of the culture.

If this perception holds, then it gives little purchase to the position that ethnomethodology offers a descriptive methodology which is characteristically participant-centred, and where analyst's and participant's perspectives can, and indeed, from its manifesto (Garfinkel 1967), *must* confidently merge.

This difficulty is not merely a local one concerning *culture* in Churchill's sense. It is in fact a quite general problem, and nowhere more true, in our experience, than when studying professional sites. Here, analysts routinely find it very difficult to adopt a participant perspective. But, as Sarangi (this volume) shows in his analysis of psychotherapeutic talk, it is possible to map participants' perspectives on to a variety of social theoretical accounts of language–action relationship. The question, however, remains as to whether a social theoretical transformation of participants' worldview, notwithstanding the different worldviews of therapists and clients, facilitates our understanding of what goes on in a given psychotherapeutic encounter.

In the context of communication in public and professional life, discourse analysts are bound to remain outsiders while seeking to make sense of the practices of the professional group, in a very similar way to the workings of Lave and Wenger's (1991) concept of 'legitimate peripheral participation'. Considerable time and effort, and considerable negotiation, is needed in order to immerse oneself in the research site so as to enable access to necessary tacit knowledge. Equally, a lack of methodological fit, as for example entering a site of professional and public communication without any *motivational relevancies*, as is the case with so-called open-ended discourse analytic studies, has to be viewed with considerable suspicion (Clarke 2000). Against this backdrop, reflexivity and collaborative interdisciplinary research become a necessity. Nor is this merely a matter of 'professional' sites. The issue of shared perspectives of analyst and participant is, quite clearly and routinely, an issue of access to mutuality.

In our view, sociolinguistics in the post-1972 era has taken a reflexive turn, as can be seen from the contributions to this volume and elsewhere. This aligns with similar shifts in anthropology and sociology. In other words, by looking elsewhere, and in producing observational accounts of various social phenomena, one can critically reflect on one's own practices, without necessarily getting distracted to a meta-level of substituting one's descriptive practice with the practices of inquiry. To conclude, the more sociolinguistics aspires to become a 'people's science', the greater is the need for such a reflexive alignment of our accounting practices. This would help us to understand social life from the inside, while striving to make sociolinguistic description and explanation socially relevant. This kind of reflexivity, in the context of this volume's focus on the interrelationship between social theory and sociolinguistics, would mean that sociolinguistics must adopt a critical, but open, theoretical and methodological stance. Such a caveat aligns with Coupland's caution against sociolinguists pursuing an implicit theoretical agenda. To put this in Popper's (1970: 56) words:

> . . . at any moment we are prisoners caught in the framework of our theories; our expectations; our past experiences; our language. But we are prisoners in a Pickwickian sense; if we try, we can break out of our framework at any time. Admittedly, we shall find ourselves again in a framework, but it will be a better and roomier one; and we can at any moment break out of it again.

Notes

1. Although disciplinary boundaries are often drawn in terms of each discipline defining a slice of social life as its territory, it may be that methodology remains the defining feature of disciplines as themes and topics cut across disciplinary boundaries. In other words, method is rather stable and discipline-specific. In a recent forum involving a group of philosophers, theologians and social scientists (including one of the present authors — SS), there was discussion about a joint research project in the area of genetic knowledge and its impact on society. At the end of the first session, there seemed to be broad agreements about topics of study, but when the attention shifted to methodology, differences between the groups emerged. Especially when some social scientists suggested the possibility of using focus groups to understand whether people's religious beliefs are changing because of new genetic knowledge, the theologians and the philosophers saw such a methodology as trivialising the object of inquiry. In their terms, it was constructing social scientific knowledge rather than investigating what is out there.

2. Throughout this chapter, at the cost of some length, we have deliberately chosen to cite the voices of those we reference, so that readers can come to their own views, rather than relying on the bias of our paraphrase.

3. Feyerabend (1977) goes to the extent of challenging the very authority of the scientific method, and argues in favour of anarchism replacing rationalism in the theory of knowledge.

4. The doctrine of methodological individualism emphasises that social phenomena can only be understood through the actions and experience of individuals. See Lukes (1977) for a critical summary.

5. Here one can see a parallel to Halliday's (1978) methodological concern for accounting for choices within a model of communication, unlike Chomskyan obsession with grammatical rules.

6. Kritzman (1988: 109) offers evidence of this in his interview with Foucault on the issue of the popularity of the human sciences after 1960.

7. Note that Labov's main concern is about linguistic theory construction based on authentic data. Hence in the title we have 'linguistic methodology', not 'sociolinguistic methodology', although Labov goes on to discuss the complexities involved in collecting data for the study of language in context, and, as we note later in this chapter, the status of such data as evidence needs to be problematised.

8. Note that there are two senses in which we may interpret 'intuition': firstly, what a native speaker would say, as in the Chomskyan tradition; and, secondly, what participants would report post-hoc following an interactional encounter, as Gumperz would suggest for purposes of data triangulation.

9. This was Labov's position at least in 1966 (personal communication: CNC) in an inaugural lecture series on Sociolinguistics at the LSA Summer Institute.

10. The ideal speaker has played a significant role in the theorisation of applied linguistics, (socio)linguistics and pragmatics. Within pragmatics, for instance, the ideal rational person is central to Sperber and Wilson's (1986) theory of relevance, Brown and Levinson's (1987) principles of politeness, and Grice's (1975) maxims of cooperation.

11. Note that a full descriptive account of 'what is going on here' may not necessarily be compatible with participants' perspective. Like participants, analysts can also revert to disattending various tracks of the activity in question.

12. Smith (1978, 1990), however, illustrates how textual organisation, or accounting practices in general, can stand for discovery of knowledge, thus making pure description of 'what is out there' almost impossible. This holds for much of scientific fact construction (Bazerman 1988).

13. In contrast, a formalist model such as Chomsky's would look for system-internal explanations for data at hand: language data need to be explained in relation to the language system rather than external factors.

14. Participant vs observer dualism has also been an issue within text linguistics (Harweg 1968, de Beaugrande 2000). When linguists seek informants' intuition about the grammaticalness or otherwise of a sentence, they are primarily asking informants to formulate consciously their unconscious knowledge about language. See also Firth's (1968) distinction between 'language under description' and 'language of description'.

References

Bauman, Z. (1990) *Thinking Sociologically*. Oxford: Blackwell.

Bazerman, C. (1988) *Shaping Written Knowledge: The Genre and Activity of the Experimental Article in Science*. Madison: University of Wisconsin Press.

Bleicher, J. (1982) *The Hermeneutic Imagination: Outline of a Positive Critique of Scientism and Sociology*. London: Routledge & Kegan Paul.

Blumer, H. (1969) *Symbolic Interaction*. Englewood Cliffs, NJ: Prentice-Hall.

Bourdieu, P. (1977) *Outline of a Theory of Practice*. Cambridge: Cambridge University Press.

Bourdieu, P. (1984) *Distinction: A Social Critique of the Judgement of Taste*. London: Routledge.

Bourdieu, P. (1991) *Language and Symbolic Power*. Ed. J.B. Thompson; translated by G. Raymond and M. Adamson. Cambridge: Polity Press.

Bourdieu, P. *et al.* (2000) *The Weight of the World: Social Suffering in Contemporary Society*. Cambridge: Polity Press.

Brown, P. and Levinson, S. ([1978] 1987) *Politeness: Some Universals in Language Usage*. Cambridge: Cambridge University Press.

Carnap, R. (1937) *Logical Syntax of Language*. London: Kegan Paul, Trench, Trubner.

Chambers, J.K. (1995) *Sociolinguistic Theory: Linguistic Variation and its Social Significance*. Oxford: Blackwell.

Chomsky, N. (1957) *Syntactic Structures*. The Hague: Mouton.

Chomsky, N. (1965) *Aspects of the Theory of Syntax*. Cambridge, MA: MIT Press.

Churchill, A. (1971) Ethnomethodology and measurement. *Social Forces* 50, December.

Cicourel, A.V. (1964) *Method and Measurement in Sociology*. New York: Free Press.

Cicourel, A.V. (1992) The interpenetration of communicative contexts: examples from medical encounters. In A. Duranti and C. Goodwin (eds) *Rethinking Context: Language as an Interactive Phenomenon*. Cambridge: Cambridge University Press, 291–310.

Clarke, A. (2000) On being a subject of discourse research. Paper presented at the *International Conference on Text and Talk at Work*. Ghent, 16–19 August.

Clifford, J. and Marcus, G.E. (eds) (1986) *Writing Culture: The Poetics and Politics of Ethnography*. Berkeley: University of California Press.

Cohen, M.R. ([1931] 1964) *Reason and Nature: The Meaning of Scientific Method*. Glencoe: Free Press.

de Beaugrande, R. (2000) Text linguistics at the millennium: corpus data and missing links. *Text* 20, 2.

Douglas, J.D. (ed.) (1971) *Understanding Everyday Life: Toward the Reconstruction of Sociological Knowledge*. London: Routledge & Kegan Paul.

Duranti, A. and Goodwin, C. (eds) (1992) *Rethinking Context: Language as an Interactive Phenomenon*. Cambridge: Cambridge University Press.

Durkheim, E. (1964) *The Rules of Sociological Method*. New York: Free Press.

Durkheim, E. (1970) *Suicide: A Study in Sociology*. London: Routledge & Kegan Paul.

Fairclough, N. (1989) *Language and Power*. London: Longman.

Fairclough, N. (1992) *Discourse and Social Change*. Cambridge: Polity Press.

Feyerabend, M. (1977) *Against Method*. London: Verso.

Figueroa, E. (1994) *Sociolinguistic Metatheory*. Oxford: Perganon.

Firth, J.R. (1968) *Selected Papers of J.R. Firth*. Ed. R. Palmer, London: Longman.

Fisher, S. (1991) A discourse of the social: medical talk/power/power talk/oppositional talk? *Discourse and Society* 2, 2, 157–182.

Foucault, M. (1970) *The Order of Things: An Archaeology of the Human Sciences*. London: Tavistock.

Foucault, M. (1972) *The Archaeology of Knowledge*. London: Tavistock.

Foucault, M. (1977) *Discipline and Punish: The Birth of the Prison*. London: Allen Lane.

Garfinkel, H. (1967) *Studies in Ethnomethodology*. Englewood Cliffs, NJ: Prentice Hall.

Geach, G.T. (1967) Ascriptivism. In R. Rorty (ed.) *Linguistic Turn: Recent Essays in Philosophical Method*. Chicago: University of Chicago Press, 224–231.

Geertz, C. (1973) *The Interpretation of Cultures*. New York: Basic Books.

Giddens, A. (1976) *New Rules of Sociological Method*. London: Hutchinson.

Goffman, E. (1974) *Frame Analysis*. Harvard: Harvard University Press.

Grice, H.P. (1975) Logic and conversation. In P. Cole and J.L. Morgan (eds) *Syntax and Semantics, vol. III: Speech Acts*. New York: Academic Press, 41–58.

Gumperz, J.J. (1972) The communicative competence of bilinguals: some hypotheses and suggestions for research. *Language in Society* 1, 143–154.

Haberland, H. and Mey, J. (1977) Editorial: Linguistics and pragmatics. *Journal of Pragmatics* 1, 1–12.

Hak, T. (1999) 'Text' and 'con-text': talk bias in studies of health care work. In S. Sarangi and C. Roberts (eds) *Talk, Work and Institutional Order: Discourse in Medical, Mediation and Management Settings.* Berlin: Mouton de Gruyter, 427–451.

Halliday, M.A.K. (1973) *Explorations in the Functions of Language.* London: Longman.

Halliday, M.A.K. (1978) *Language as Social Semiotic.* London: Edward Arnold.

Harweg, R. (1968) *Pronomina und Textkonstitution.* Munich: Fink.

Honneth, A. (1991) *The Critique of Power: Reflective Stages in a Critical Social Theory.* Translated by K. Baynes. Cambridge, MA: MIT Press.

Hymes, D. (1972) Editorial introduction to *Language in Society. Language in Society* 1, 1–14.

Kaufmann, F. (1958) *Methodologies of the Social Sciences.* London: Thames & Hudson.

Kritzman, L.D. (1988) Introduction: Foucault and the politics of experience. In L.D. Kritzman (ed.) *Politics, Philosophy, Culture: Interviews and Other Writings: M. Foucault.* Translated by A. Sheridan. New York: Routledge.

Labov, W. (1972a) *Sociolinguistic Patterns.* Philadelphia: Pennsylvania University Press.

Labov, W. (1972b) *Language in the Inner City: Studies in the Black English Vernacular.* Oxford: Basil Blackwell.

Labov, W. (1972c) Some principles of linguistic methodology. *Language in Society* 1, 97–120.

Labov, W. and Fanshel, D. (1977) *Therapeutic Discourse: Psychotherapy as Conversation.* New York: Academic Press.

Lakoff, G. and Johnson, M. (1980) *Metaphors We Live By.* Chicago: University of Chicago Press.

Latour, B. and Woolgar, S. (1979) *Laboratory Life: The Social Construction of Scientific Facts.* Beverly Hills: Sage.

Lave, J. and Wenger, E. (1991) *Situated Learning: Legitimate Peripheral Participation.* Cambridge: Cambridge University Press.

Lévi-Strauss (1966) *The Savage Mind.* Chicago: Chicago University Press.

Lévi-Strauss (1977) *Structural Anthropology, vol. II.* Harmondsworth: Penguin.

Lukes, S. (1977) *Essays in Social Theory.* London: Macmillan.

Lynch, M. (1993) *Scientific Practice and Ordinary Action: Ethnomethodology and Social Studies of Science.* Cambridge: Cambridge University Press.

Marcus, G.E. and Fischer, M.M.J. (1986) *Anthropology as Cultural Critique.* Chicago: Chicago University Press.

McHugh, P. (1968) *Defining the Situation: The Organisation of Meaning in Social Interaction.* Indianapolis: Bobbs–Merrill.

Mill, J.S. (1875) *A System of Logic.* London: Longman, Green & Co.

Moerman, M. (1988) *Talking Culture: Ethnography and Conversation Analysis.* Philadelphia: Pennsylvania University Press.

Mulkay, M.J. (1979) *Science and the Sociology of Knowledge.* London: Allen & Unwin.

Ochs, E. (1979) Transcription as theory. In E. Ochs and B. Schieffelin (eds) *Developmental Pragmatics.* San Francisco: Academic Press, 43–72.

Parsons, T. (1951) *The Social System.* London: Routledge.

Popper, K. (1970) Normal science and its dangers. In I. Lakatos and A. Musgrave (eds) *Criticism of the Growth of Knowledge.* Cambridge: Cambridge University Press.

Ryan, A. (1970) *The Philosophy of the Social Sciences.* London: Macmillan.

Sacks, H. (1984) Notes on methodology. In J.M. Atkinson and J. Heritage (eds) *Structures in Social Action: Studies in Conversation Analysis*. Cambridge: Cambridge University Press, 21–27.

Sankoff, D. (ed.) (1978) *Linguistic Variation: Models and Methods*. New York: Academic Press.

Sarangi, S. and Roberts, C. (eds) (1999) *Talk, Work and Institutional Order: Discourse in Medical, Mediation and Management Settings*. Berlin: Mouton de Gruyter.

Sarangi, S. and Roberts, C. (2000) Uptake of discourse research in interprofessional settings. Paper presented at the *International Conference on Text and Talk at Work*. Ghent, 16–19 August.

Saussure, F. ([1916] 1966) *Course in General Linguistics*. Translated by W. Baskin. New York: McGraw Hill.

Saville-Troike, M. (1982) *The Ethnography of Communication*. Oxford: Basil Blackwell.

Schegloff, E.A. (1966) Turn organisation: one intersection of grammar and interaction. In E. Ochs, E.A. Schegloff and S.A. Thompson (eds) *Interaction and Grammar*. Cambridge: Cambridge University Press, 52–133.

Schutz, A. (1962) *Collected Papers I: The Problem of Social Reality*. Ed. M. Natanson. The Hague: Martinus Nijhoff.

Schutz, A. (1976) *Collected Papers II: Studies in Social Theory*. Ed. A. Brodersen. The Hague: Martinus Nijhoff.

Schutz, A. and Lukann, T. (1974) *The Structures of the Life-World*. Translated by R. Zaner and H.T. Engelhardt. London: Heinemann.

Searle, J.R. (1969) *Speech Acts: An Essay in the Philosophy of Language*. Cambridge: Cambridge University Press.

Smith, D. (1978) K is mentally ill. *Sociology* 12, 23–53.

Smith, D. (1990) *Texts, Facts and Femininity: Exploring Relations of Ruling*. London: Routledge.

Sperber, D. and Wilson, D. (1986) *Relevance: Communication and Cognition*. Oxford: Blackwell.

Weber, M. (1949 [1904]) *The Methodology of the Social Sciences*. Chicago: Free Press.

Weber, M. (1978) *Selections in Translation*. Translated by E. Matthews, ed. W.G. Runciman. Cambridge: Cambridge University Press.

West, C. (1984) *Routine Complications: Troubles in Talk between Doctors and Patients*. Bloomington: Indiana University Press.

Winch, P. (1958) *The Idea of a Social Science*. London: Routledge & Kegan Paul.

Index